CRIMINAL MACABRE™

a cal mcdonald mystery™

To my loving wife, Nikki.
— Steve

To caffeine, for all that company
on those long nights.
— Ben

CRIMINAL MACABRE ™

a cal mcdonald mystery™

Story by **Steve Niles**

Art by **Ben Templesmith**

Letters by **Pat Brosseau for Blambot™**

Dark Horse Books™

Editor **Scott Allie**

Associate Editor **Shawna Ervin-Gore**

Collection Designer **Lani Schreibstein**

Art Directors **Lia Ribacchi & Mark Cox**

Publisher **Mike Richardson**

Special thanks to Dan Jackson

This book collects the five-issue series *Criminal Macabre — A Cal McDonald Mystery*, as well as a short story from *Drawing on Your Nightmares*, published by Dark Horse Comics.

Published by Dark Horse Books,
A division of Dark Horse Comics, Inc.
10956 SE Main Street
Milwaukie, OR 97222

April 2004
First edition
ISBN: 1-56971-935-7

1 3 5 7 9 10 8 6 4 2

Printed in China

INTRODUCTION

Rob Zombie

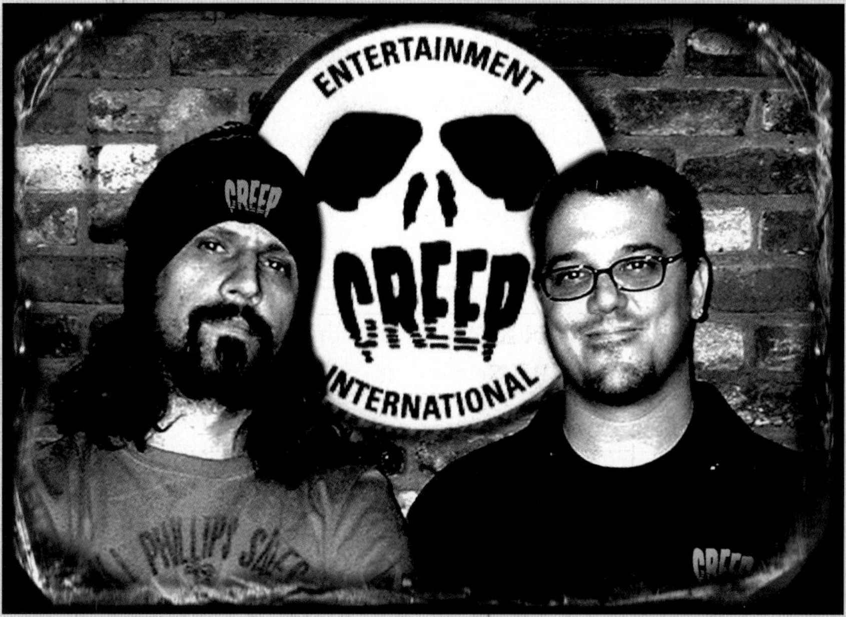
ENTERTAINMENT
CREEP
INTERNATIONAL

Being asked to write an intro is a heavy weight to bear. I mean, really — the nerve of some people to request such a thing. What am I, friggin' Hemingway? Come on, how can you really sum up a bizarre individual like Steve Niles and his world of funny books in a few short paragraphs? It can't be done. It shouldn't be done! Why would you even try?

But screw it, I'll give it a go. I mean the guy paid me twenty bucks in advance, so what the hell? Where should I begin? Maybe I should start by mentioning that Mr. Niles is an ex-punk rocker with a snotty attitude, a fake British accent, and a homemade anarchy tattoo hidden under that insanely dense head of hair? Seriously, the world ain't seen hair that thick since Michael Landon turned into a werewolf or Jack Lord patrolled the beaches of the Big Kahuna. Anyway, I digress.

I wonder, would it be wrong of me to mention that he is, without a doubt, the freak spawn of a strange scientific experiment gone berserk in some two-bit chop shop laboratory? One can only assume that thirty-some-odd years ago the DNA of Richard Matheson and Raymond Chandler were forced to cross breed and grow like some diseased alien spore into the creature we now refer to as Niles. I mean, how else would you explain the dark, monster-filled, film-noir world spewing from his oversized brainiac mind? This Niles kid has created one bad-ass world for his lovable stable of characters to run wild in ... and run wild they do! This ain't your mamma's world of Metropolis, populated by the likes of Jimmy Olsen, Lois Lane, and that dork with the glasses and the goofy red cape and underwear combo. This is the real deal, Holyfield!

Let's discuss Mr. Niles's main man standing dead center in this, dank, seedy underworld. This guy lives to kick the shit out of the underbelly of the beast. He is the ultimate anti-hero bastard, known to funny-book readers around the globe as Cal McDonald. Let's break it down for the new kids on the block — Mr. McDonald is an ass-kicking combination of Sam Spade, Steve McQueen, and Charles Bukowski all rolled into one doped-up, broken-nosed, hung-over, "I don't give a shit, fuck you" package. Talk about hardcore dudes, this cat makes your normal, run-of-the-mill funny-book tough guys like mutant poster-boy Wolverine look like one of the friggin' PowerPuff Girls.

In closing, I would just like to say that you fanboys should get off the couch, drop the fruit roll-ups, and get right down on your chubby, fat, scabby knees to thank whatever God you pray to that this kid called Niles has come along and made funny-books cool again. What? What did you say? That's right, chump — there ain't nothing funny about these books. Read on before Cal kicks your ass.

Rob Zombie
Dec. 10, 2003
Hollywood, CA

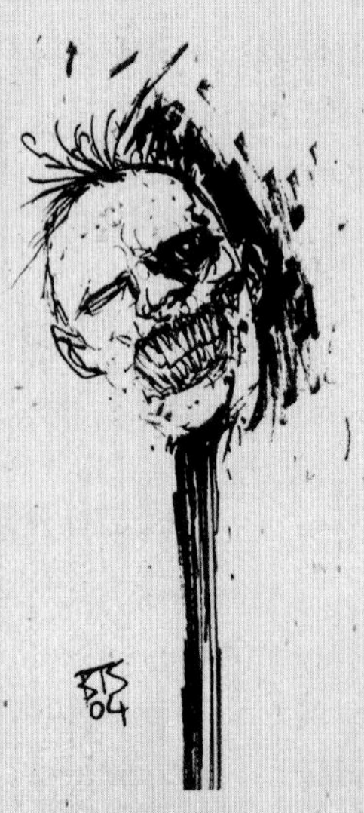

BTS
04

CHAPTER ONE
Strange Gatherings

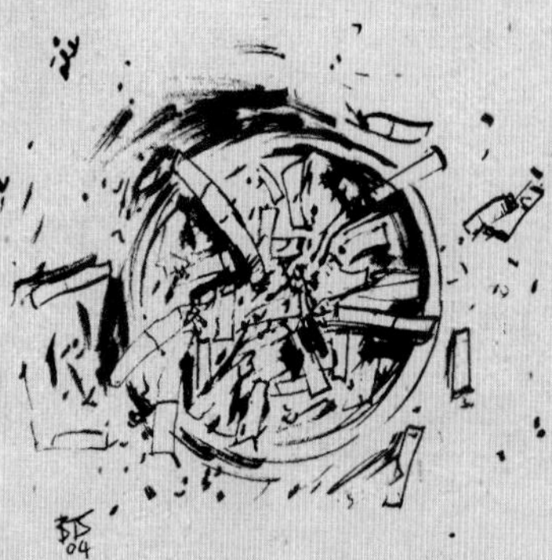

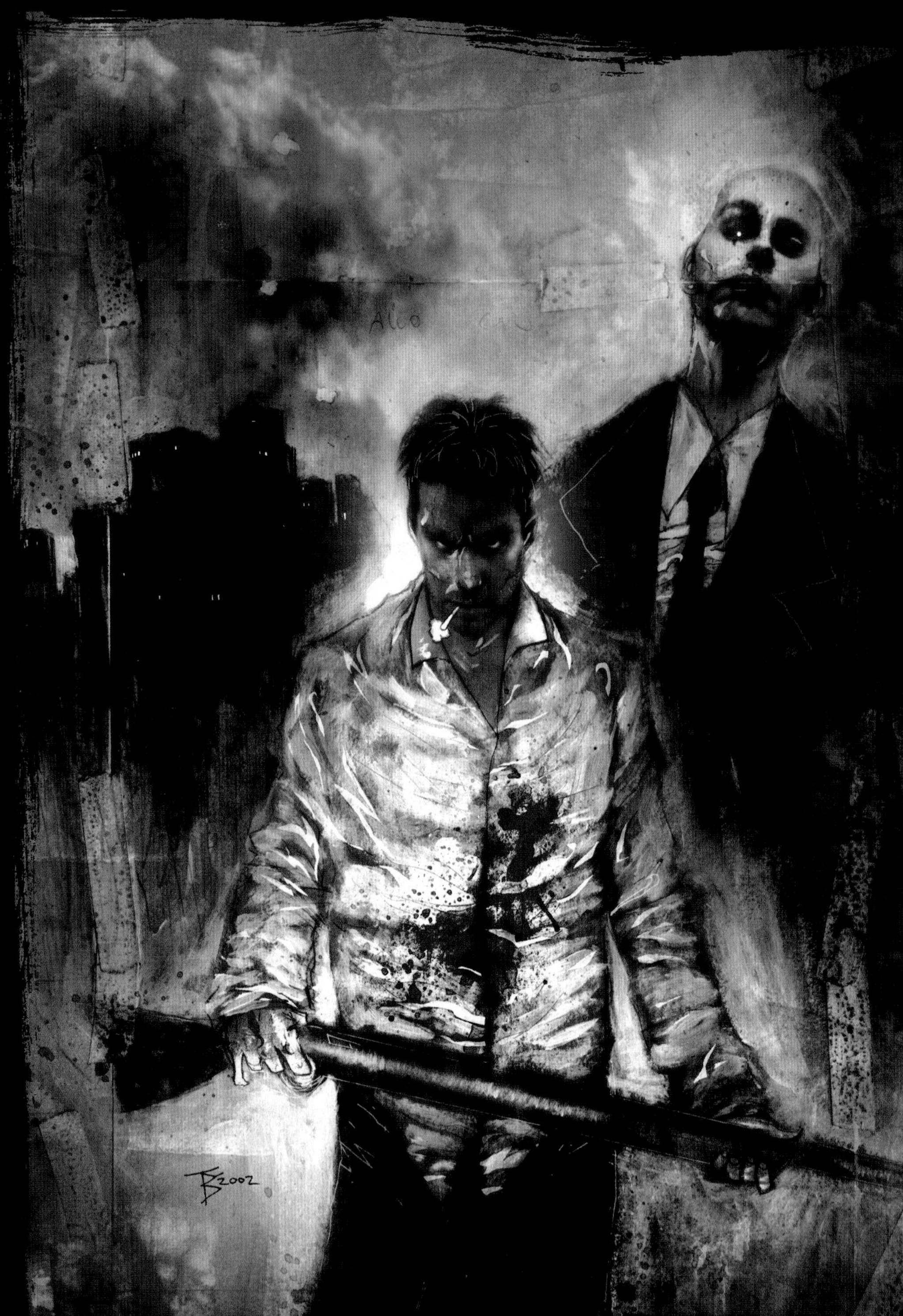

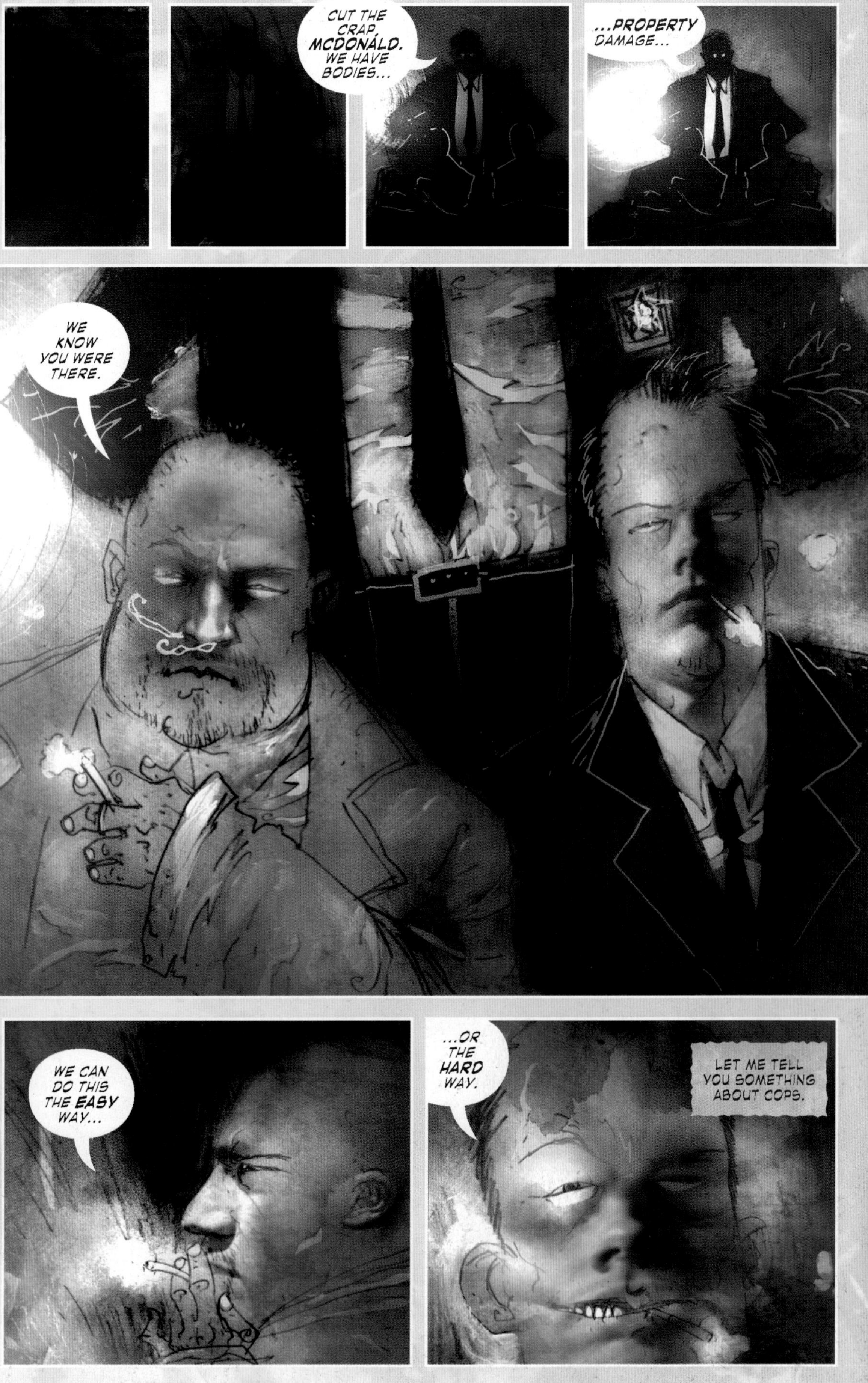

CUT THE CRAP, MCDONALD. WE HAVE BODIES...
...PROPERTY DAMAGE...
WE KNOW YOU WERE THERE.
WE CAN DO THIS THE EASY WAY...
...OR THE HARD WAY.
LET ME TELL YOU SOMETHING ABOUT COPS.

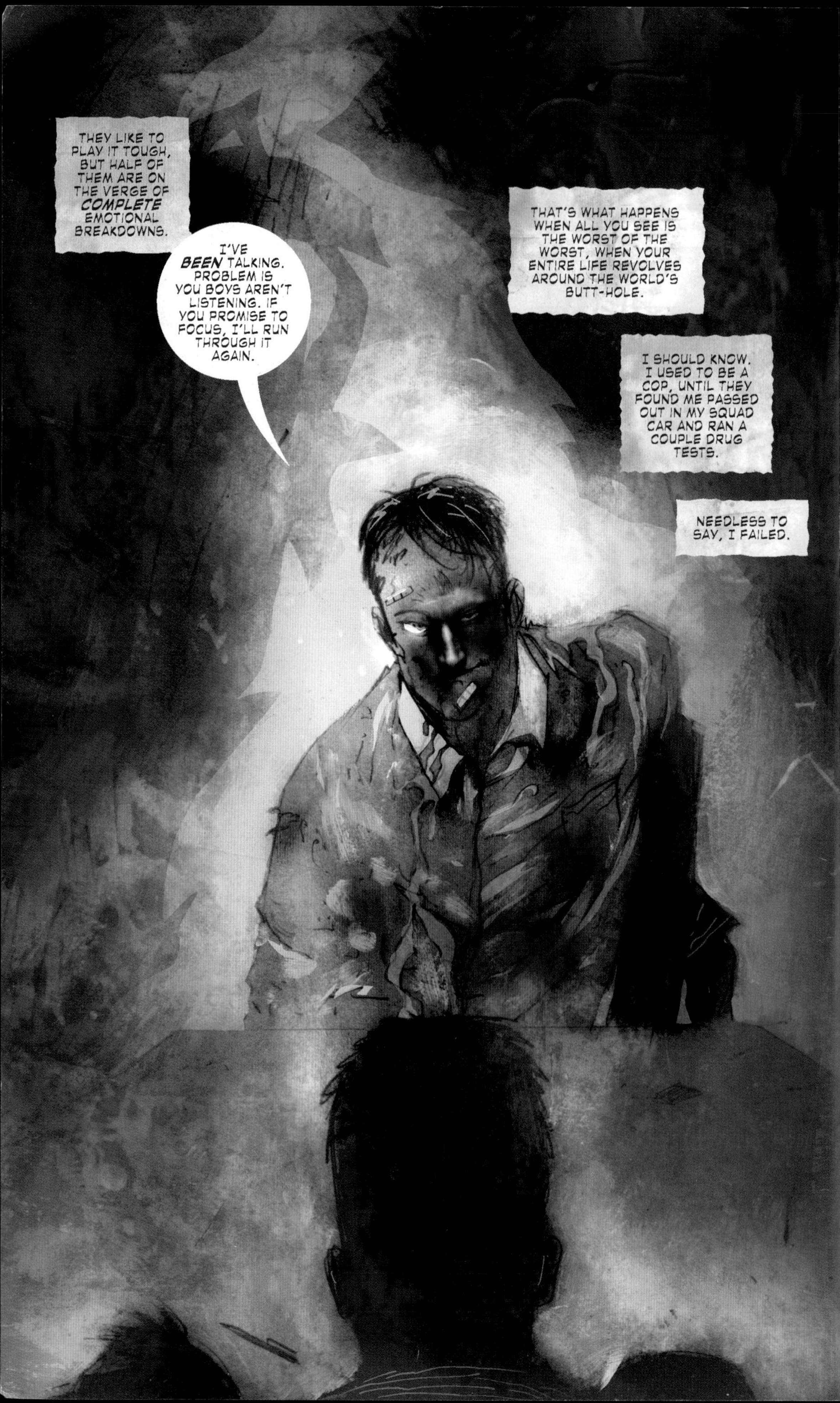
THEY LIKE TO PLAY IT TOUGH, BUT HALF OF THEM ARE ON THE VERGE OF COMPLETE EMOTIONAL BREAKDOWNS.
I'VE BEEN TALKING. PROBLEM IS YOU BOYS AREN'T LISTENING. IF YOU PROMISE TO FOCUS, I'LL RUN THROUGH IT AGAIN.
THAT'S WHAT HAPPENS WHEN ALL YOU SEE IS THE WORST OF THE WORST, WHEN YOUR ENTIRE LIFE REVOLVES AROUND THE WORLD'S BUTT-HOLE.
I SHOULD KNOW. I USED TO BE A COP, UNTIL THEY FOUND ME PASSED OUT IN MY SQUAD CAR AND RAN A COUPLE DRUG TESTS.
NEEDLESS TO SAY, I FAILED.

BUT I FIND THEY GET REALLY TESTY WHEN ALL YOU TALK ABOUT ARE *MONSTERS.*

OKAY... ONE MORE TIME, AND TRY TO INSERT A LITTLE *REALITY* INTO THIS ONE.

GOT A BUTT?

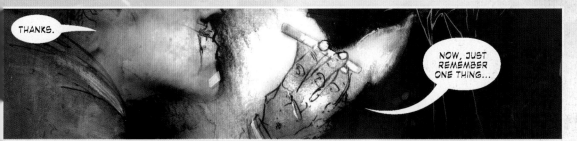

THANKS.

NOW, JUST REMEMBER ONE THING...

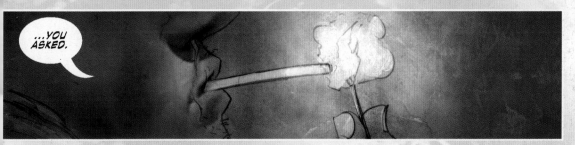

...YOU *ASKED.*

LIKE I SAID BEFORE...

...IT ALL STARTED AS A QUICK, OPEN-AND-SHUT CASE OF *VAMPIRISM.*

NOTHING MORE, NOTHING LESS...

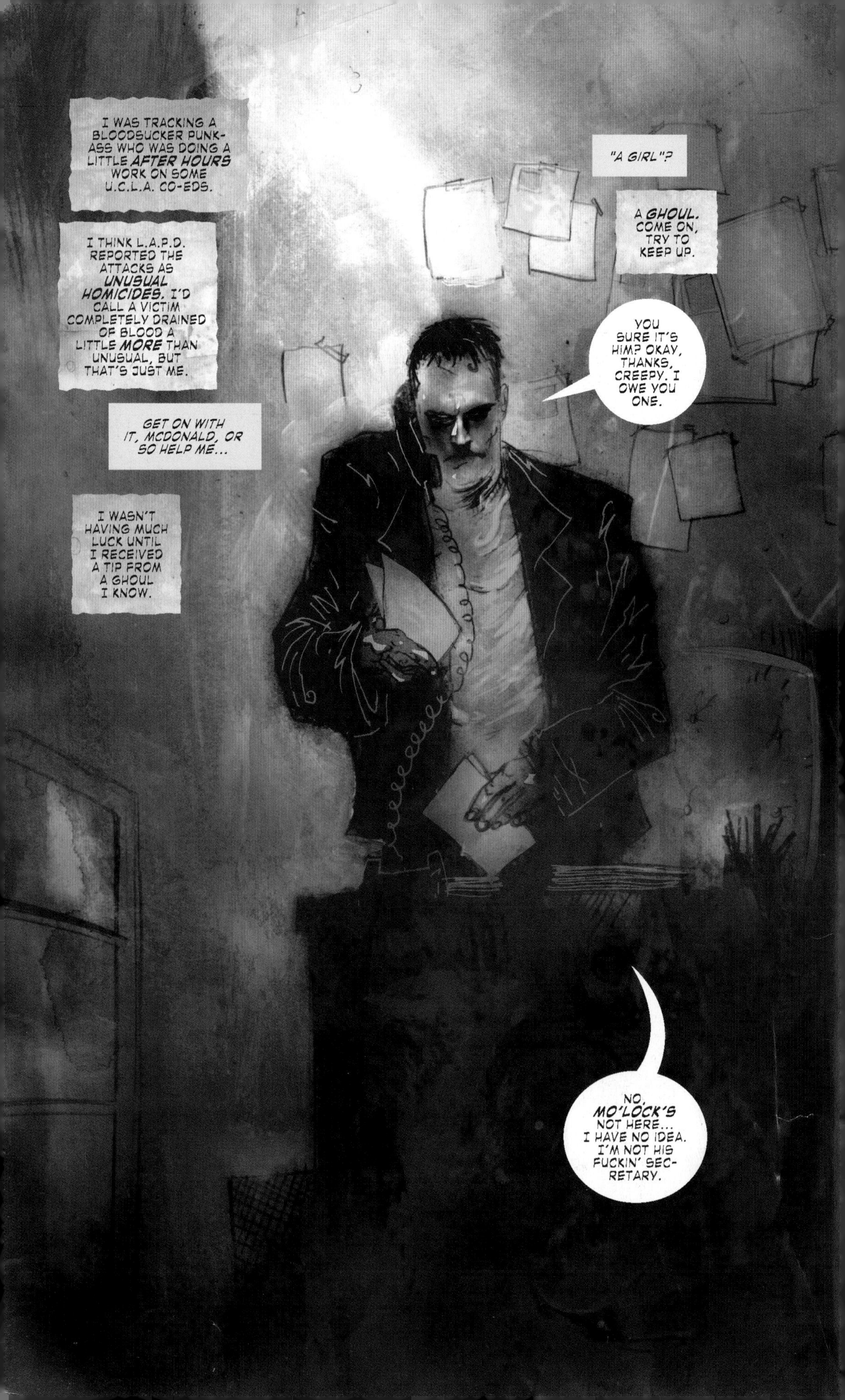

I WAS TRACKING A BLOODSUCKER PUNK-ASS WHO WAS DOING A LITTLE *AFTER HOURS* WORK ON SOME U.C.L.A. CO-EDS.
I THINK L.A.P.D. REPORTED THE ATTACKS AS *UNUSUAL HOMICIDES.* I'D CALL A VICTIM COMPLETELY DRAINED OF BLOOD A LITTLE *MORE* THAN UNUSUAL, BUT THAT'S JUST ME.
GET ON WITH IT, MCDONALD, OR SO HELP ME...
I WASN'T HAVING MUCH LUCK UNTIL I RECEIVED A TIP FROM A GHOUL I KNOW.
"A GIRL"?
A *GHOUL.* COME ON, TRY TO KEEP UP.
YOU SURE IT'S HIM? OKAY, THANKS, CREEPY. I OWE YOU ONE.
NO, *MO'LOCK'S* NOT HERE... I HAVE NO IDEA. I'M NOT HIS FUCKIN' SEC-RETARY.

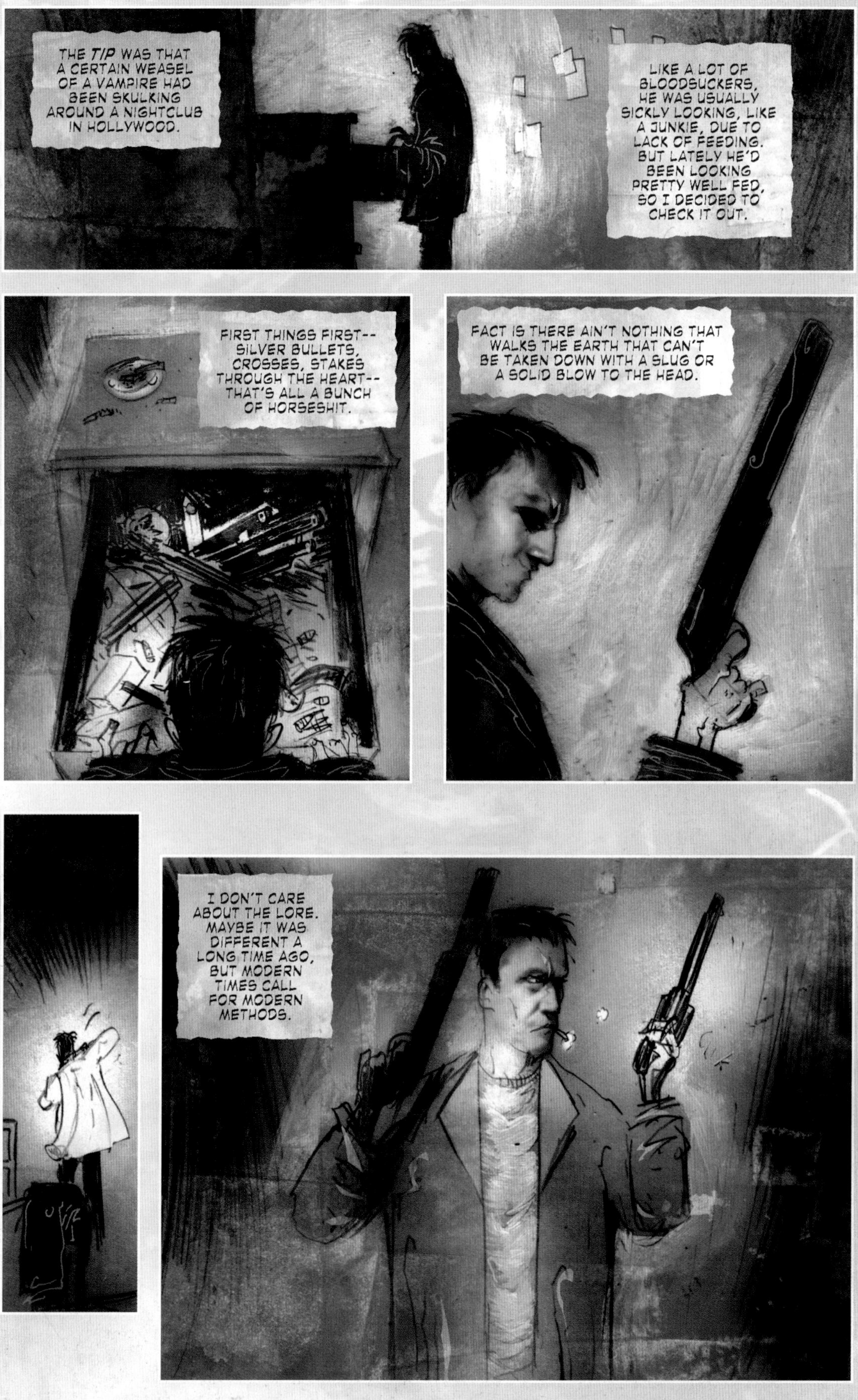

THE TIP WAS THAT A CERTAIN WEASEL OF A VAMPIRE HAD BEEN SKULKING AROUND A NIGHTCLUB IN HOLLYWOOD.
LIKE A LOT OF BLOODSUCKERS, HE WAS USUALLY SICKLY LOOKING, LIKE A JUNKIE, DUE TO LACK OF FEEDING. BUT LATELY HE'D BEEN LOOKING PRETTY WELL FED, SO I DECIDED TO CHECK IT OUT.
FIRST THINGS FIRST-- SILVER BULLETS, CROSSES, STAKES THROUGH THE HEART-- THAT'S ALL A BUNCH OF HORSESHIT.
FACT IS THERE AIN'T NOTHING THAT WALKS THE EARTH THAT CAN'T BE TAKEN DOWN WITH A SLUG OR A SOLID BLOW TO THE HEAD.
I DON'T CARE ABOUT THE LORE. MAYBE IT WAS DIFFERENT A LONG TIME AGO, BUT MODERN TIMES CALL FOR MODERN METHODS.

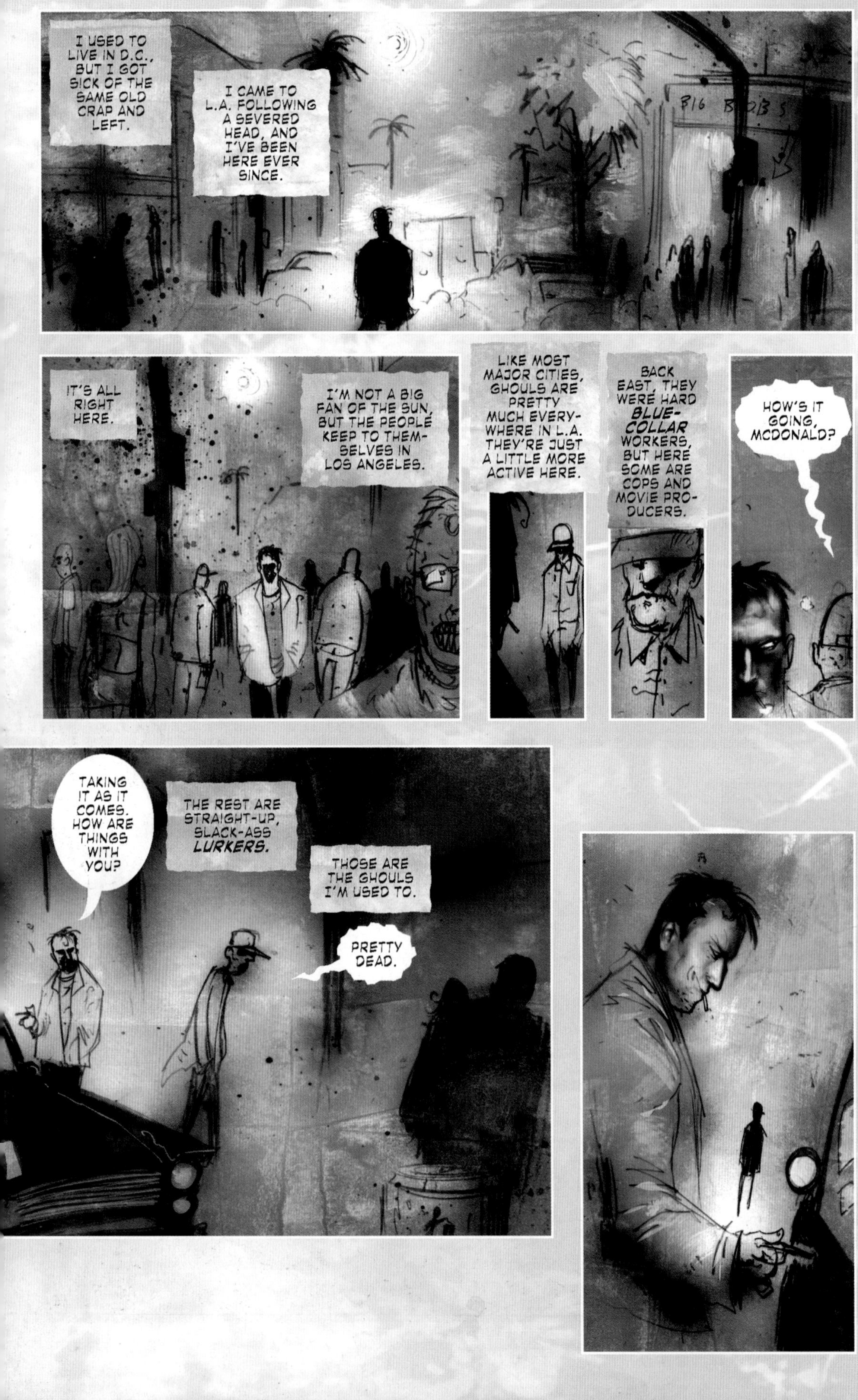

I USED TO LIVE IN D.C., BUT I GOT SICK OF THE SAME OLD CRAP AND LEFT.
I CAME TO L.A. FOLLOWING A SEVERED HEAD, AND I'VE BEEN HERE EVER SINCE.
BIG BOBS
IT'S ALL RIGHT HERE.
I'M NOT A BIG FAN OF THE SUN, BUT THE PEOPLE KEEP TO THEMSELVES IN LOS ANGELES.
LIKE MOST MAJOR CITIES, GHOULS ARE PRETTY MUCH EVERYWHERE IN L.A. THEY'RE JUST A LITTLE MORE ACTIVE HERE.
BACK EAST, THEY WERE HARD *BLUE-COLLAR* WORKERS, BUT HERE SOME ARE COPS AND MOVIE PRODUCERS.
HOW'S IT GOING, MCDONALD?
TAKING IT AS IT COMES. HOW ARE THINGS WITH YOU?
THE REST ARE STRAIGHT-UP, SLACK-ASS *LURKERS.*
THOSE ARE THE GHOULS I'M USED TO.
PRETTY DEAD.

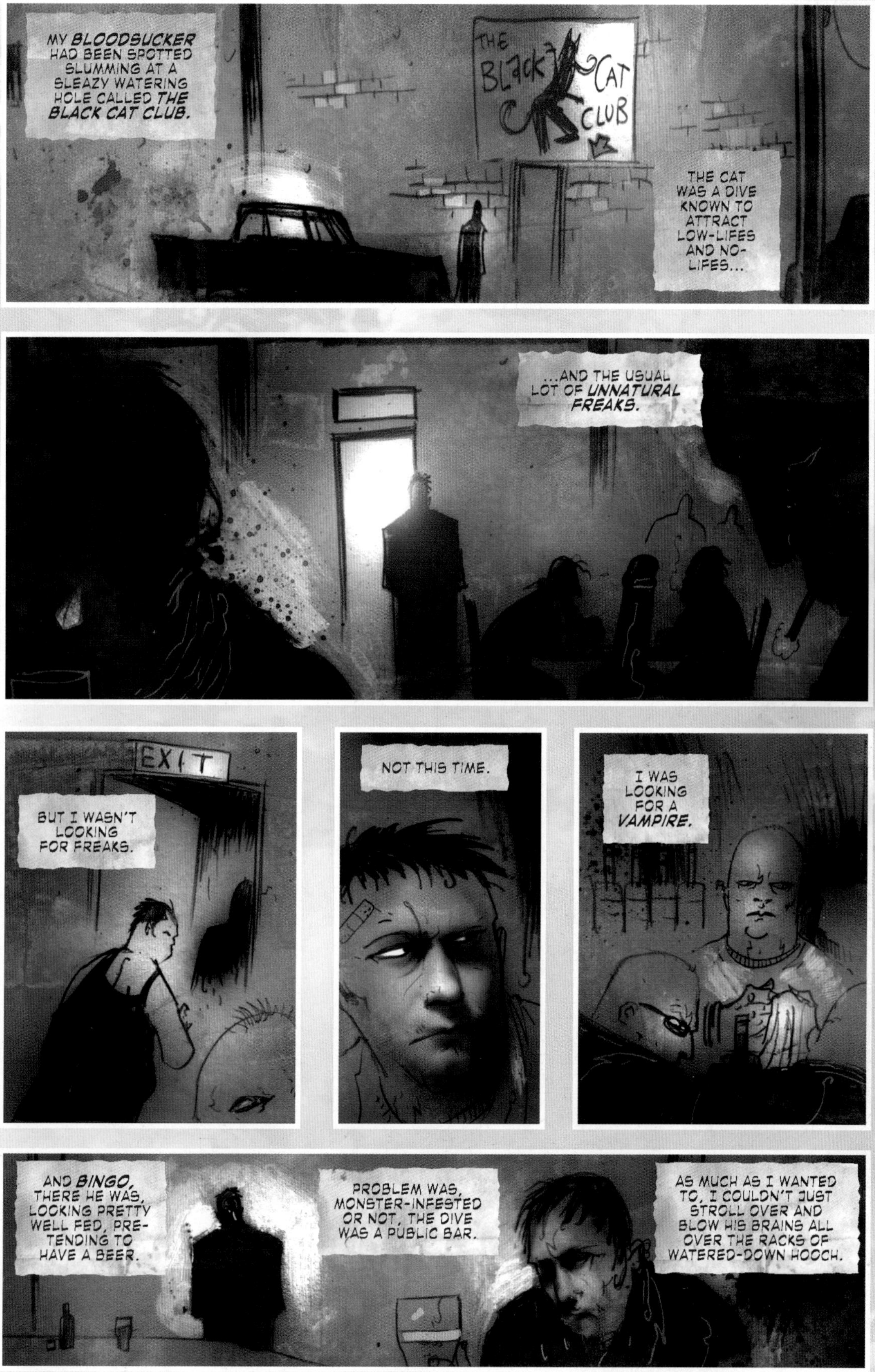
MY BLOODSUCKER HAD BEEN SPOTTED SLUMMING AT A SLEAZY WATERING HOLE CALLED THE BLACK CAT CLUB.
THE BLACK CAT CLUB
THE CAT WAS A DIVE KNOWN TO ATTRACT LOW-LIFES AND NO-LIFES...
...AND THE USUAL LOT OF UNNATURAL FREAKS.
EXIT
BUT I WASN'T LOOKING FOR FREAKS.
NOT THIS TIME.
I WAS LOOKING FOR A VAMPIRE.
AND BINGO, THERE HE WAS, LOOKING PRETTY WELL FED, PRETENDING TO HAVE A BEER.
PROBLEM WAS, MONSTER-INFESTED OR NOT, THE DIVE WAS A PUBLIC BAR.
AS MUCH AS I WANTED TO, I COULDN'T JUST STROLL OVER AND BLOW HIS BRAINS ALL OVER THE RACKS OF WATERED-DOWN HOOCH.

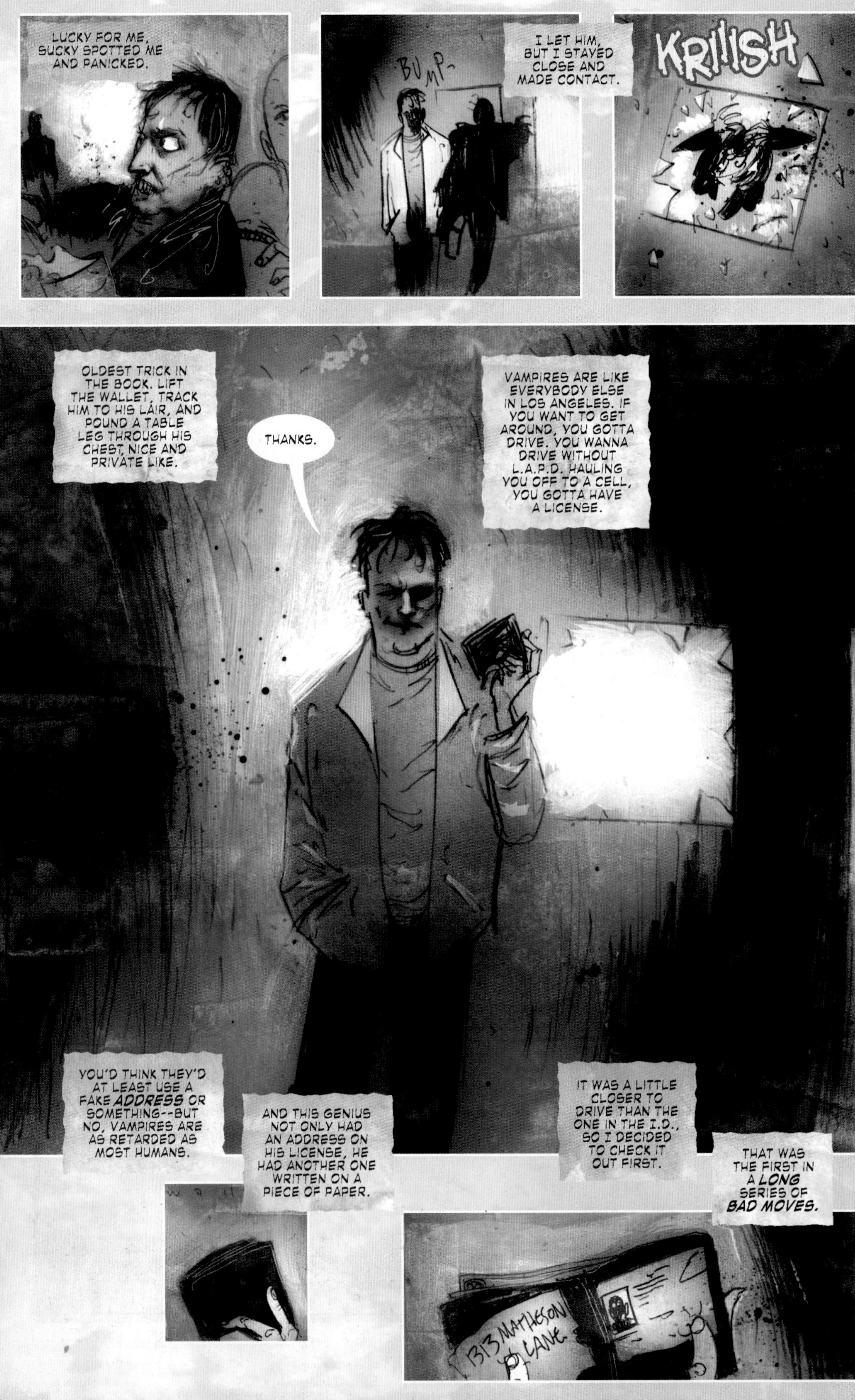

LUCKY FOR ME, SUCKY SPOTTED ME AND PANICKED.
BUMP
I LET HIM, BUT I STAYED CLOSE AND MADE CONTACT.
KRIIISH
OLDEST TRICK IN THE BOOK. LIFT THE WALLET, TRACK HIM TO HIS LAIR, AND POUND A TABLE LEG THROUGH HIS CHEST, NICE AND PRIVATE LIKE.
THANKS.
VAMPIRES ARE LIKE EVERYBODY ELSE IN LOS ANGELES. IF YOU WANT TO GET AROUND, YOU GOTTA DRIVE. YOU WANNA DRIVE WITHOUT L.A.P.D. HAULING YOU OFF TO A CELL, YOU GOTTA HAVE A LICENSE.
YOU'D THINK THEY'D AT LEAST USE A FAKE *ADDRESS* OR SOMETHING--BUT NO, VAMPIRES ARE AS RETARDED AS MOST HUMANS.
AND THIS GENIUS NOT ONLY HAD AN ADDRESS ON HIS LICENSE, HE HAD ANOTHER ONE WRITTEN ON A PIECE OF PAPER.
IT WAS A LITTLE CLOSER TO DRIVE THAN THE ONE IN THE I.D., SO I DECIDED TO CHECK IT OUT FIRST.
THAT WAS THE FIRST IN A *LONG* SERIES OF *BAD MOVES.*
1313 MATHESON LANE

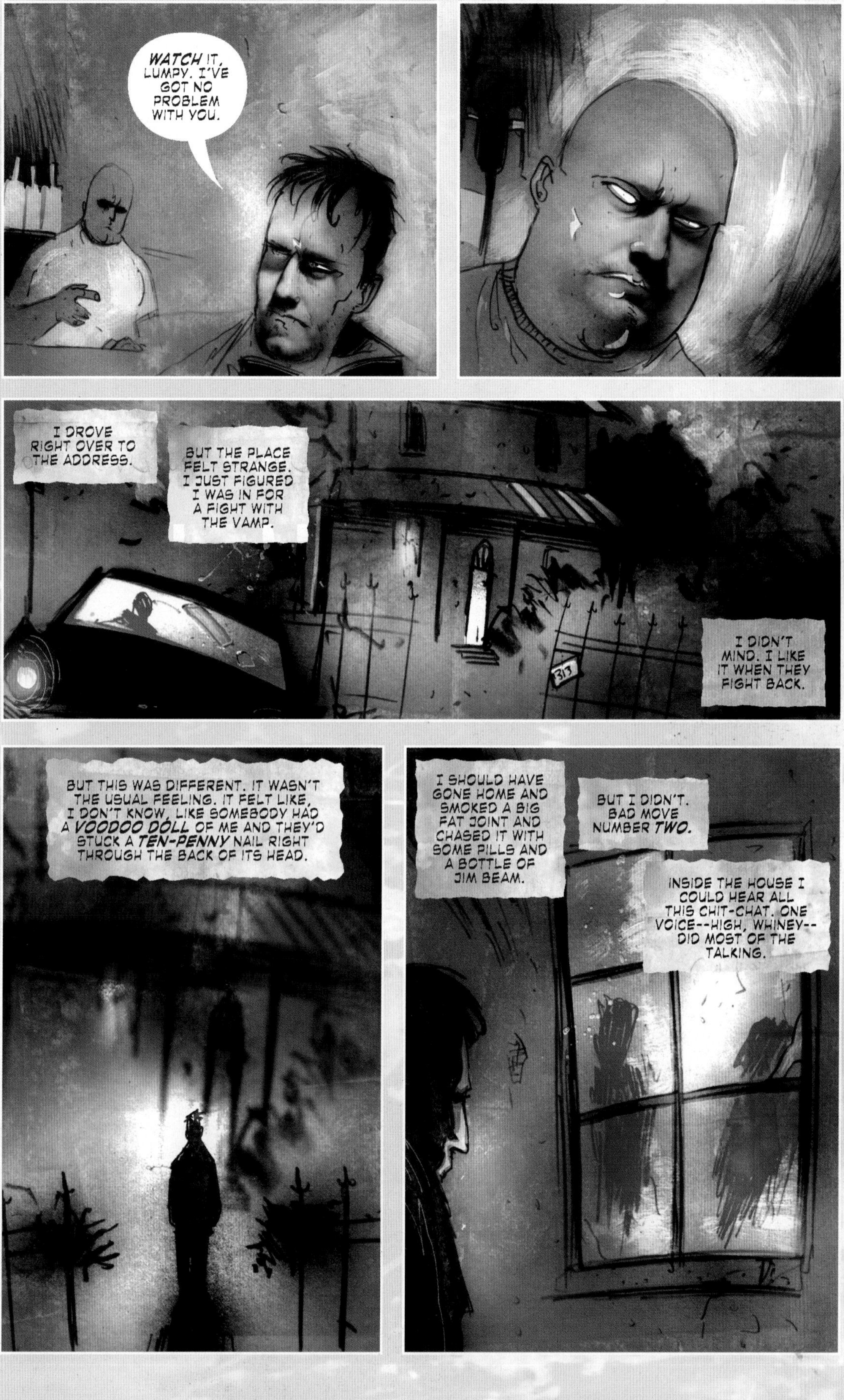
WATCH IT, LUMPY. I'VE GOT NO PROBLEM WITH YOU.
I DROVE RIGHT OVER TO THE ADDRESS.
BUT THE PLACE FELT STRANGE. I JUST FIGURED I WAS IN FOR A FIGHT WITH THE VAMP.
313
I DIDN'T MIND. I LIKE IT WHEN THEY FIGHT BACK.
BUT THIS WAS DIFFERENT. IT WASN'T THE USUAL FEELING. IT FELT LIKE, I DON'T KNOW, LIKE SOMEBODY HAD A VOODOO DOLL OF ME AND THEY'D STUCK A TEN-PENNY NAIL RIGHT THROUGH THE BACK OF ITS HEAD.
I SHOULD HAVE GONE HOME AND SMOKED A BIG FAT JOINT AND CHASED IT WITH SOME PILLS AND A BOTTLE OF JIM BEAM.
BUT I DIDN'T. BAD MOVE NUMBER TWO.
INSIDE THE HOUSE I COULD HEAR ALL THIS CHIT-CHAT. ONE VOICE--HIGH, WHINEY--DID MOST OF THE TALKING.

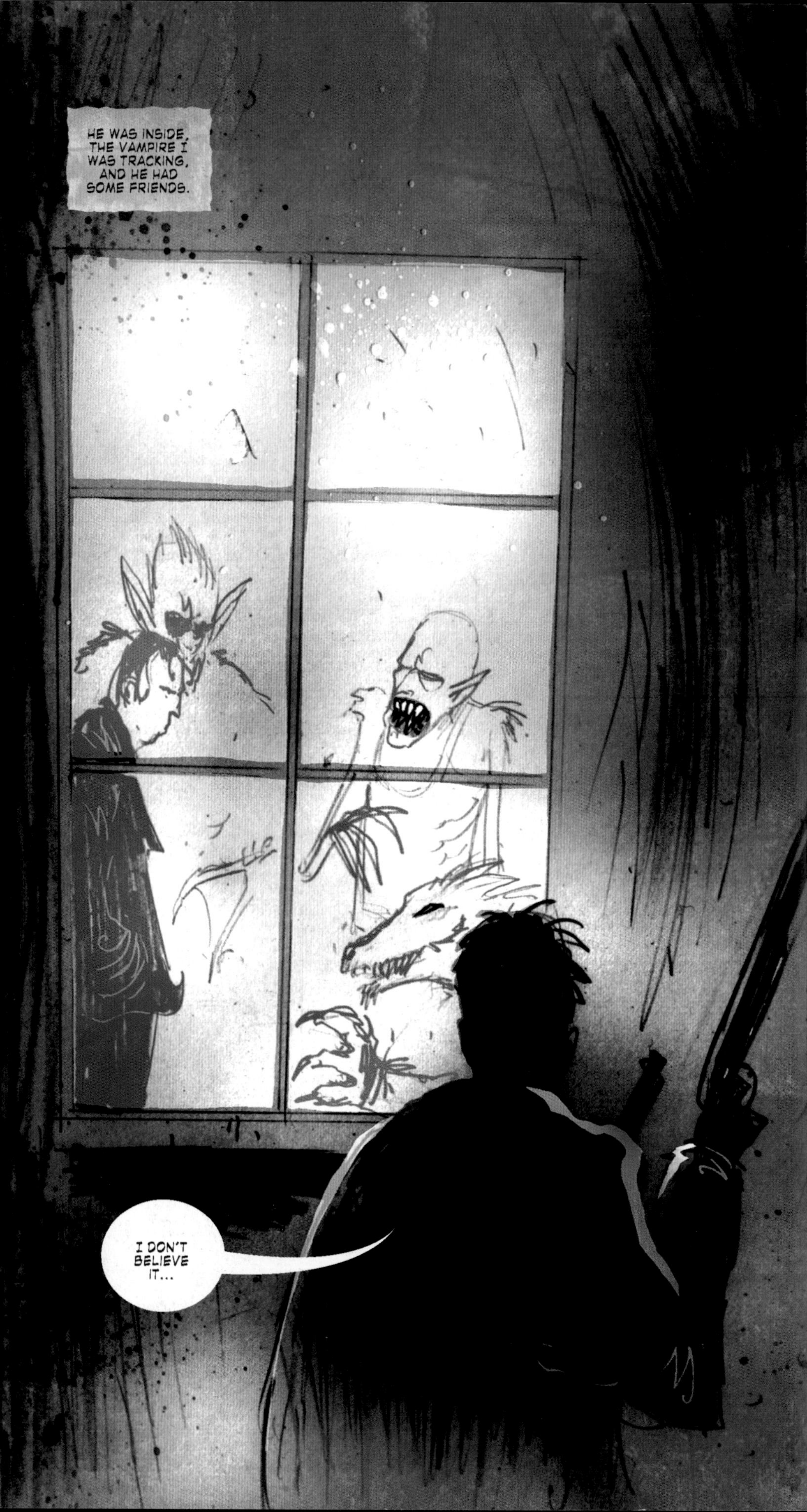
HE WAS INSIDE, THE VAMPIRE I WAS TRACKING, AND HE HAD SOME FRIENDS.
I DON'T BELIEVE IT...

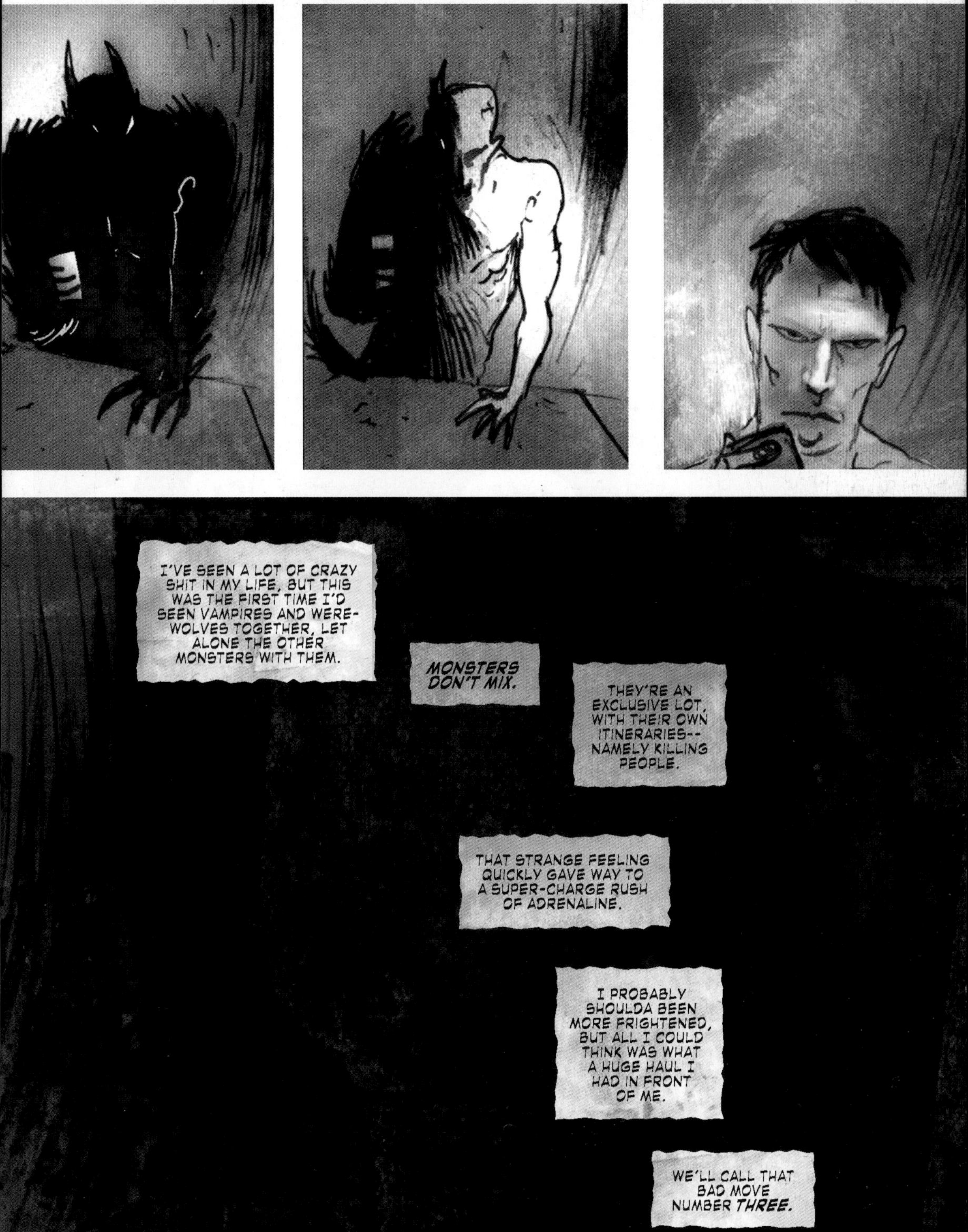
I'VE SEEN A LOT OF CRAZY SHIT IN MY LIFE, BUT THIS WAS THE FIRST TIME I'D SEEN VAMPIRES AND WERE-WOLVES TOGETHER, LET ALONE THE OTHER MONSTERS WITH THEM.
MONSTERS DON'T MIX.
THEY'RE AN EXCLUSIVE LOT, WITH THEIR OWN ITINERARIES-- NAMELY KILLING PEOPLE.
THAT STRANGE FEELING QUICKLY GAVE WAY TO A SUPER-CHARGE RUSH OF ADRENALINE.
I PROBABLY SHOULDA BEEN MORE FRIGHTENED, BUT ALL I COULD THINK WAS WHAT A HUGE HAUL I HAD IN FRONT OF ME.
WE'LL CALL THAT BAD MOVE NUMBER *THREE.*

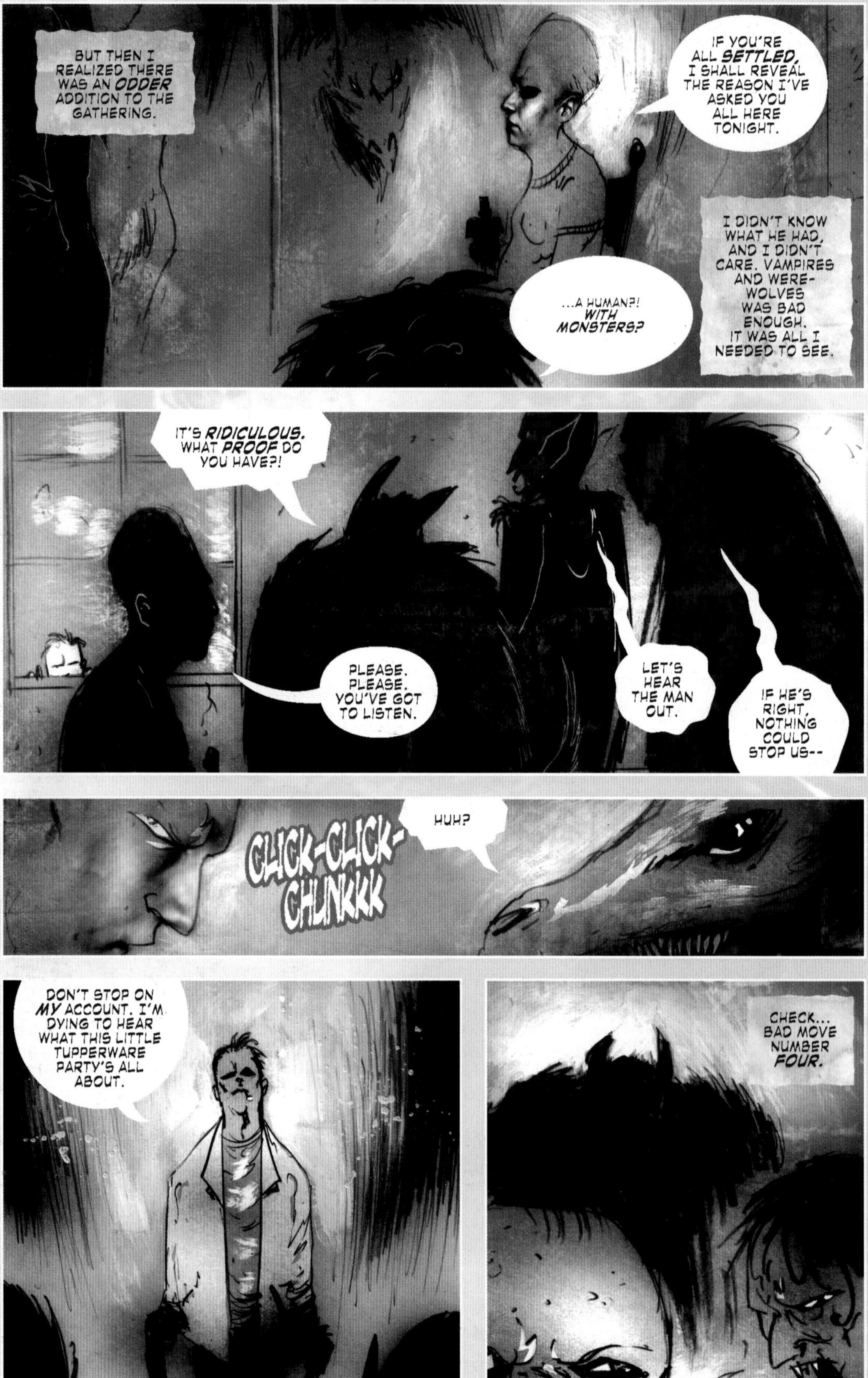
BUT THEN I REALIZED THERE WAS AN ODDER ADDITION TO THE GATHERING.
IF YOU'RE ALL SETTLED, I SHALL REVEAL THE REASON I'VE ASKED YOU ALL HERE TONIGHT.
...A HUMAN?! WITH MONSTERS?
I DIDN'T KNOW WHAT HE HAD, AND I DIDN'T CARE. VAMPIRES AND WERE-WOLVES WAS BAD ENOUGH. IT WAS ALL I NEEDED TO SEE.
IT'S RIDICULOUS. WHAT PROOF DO YOU HAVE?!
PLEASE. PLEASE. YOU'VE GOT TO LISTEN.
LET'S HEAR THE MAN OUT.
IF HE'S RIGHT, NOTHING COULD STOP US--
CLICK-CLICK-CHUNKKK
HUH?
DON'T STOP ON MY ACCOUNT. I'M DYING TO HEAR WHAT THIS LITTLE TUPPERWARE PARTY'S ALL ABOUT.
CHECK... BAD MOVE NUMBER FOUR.

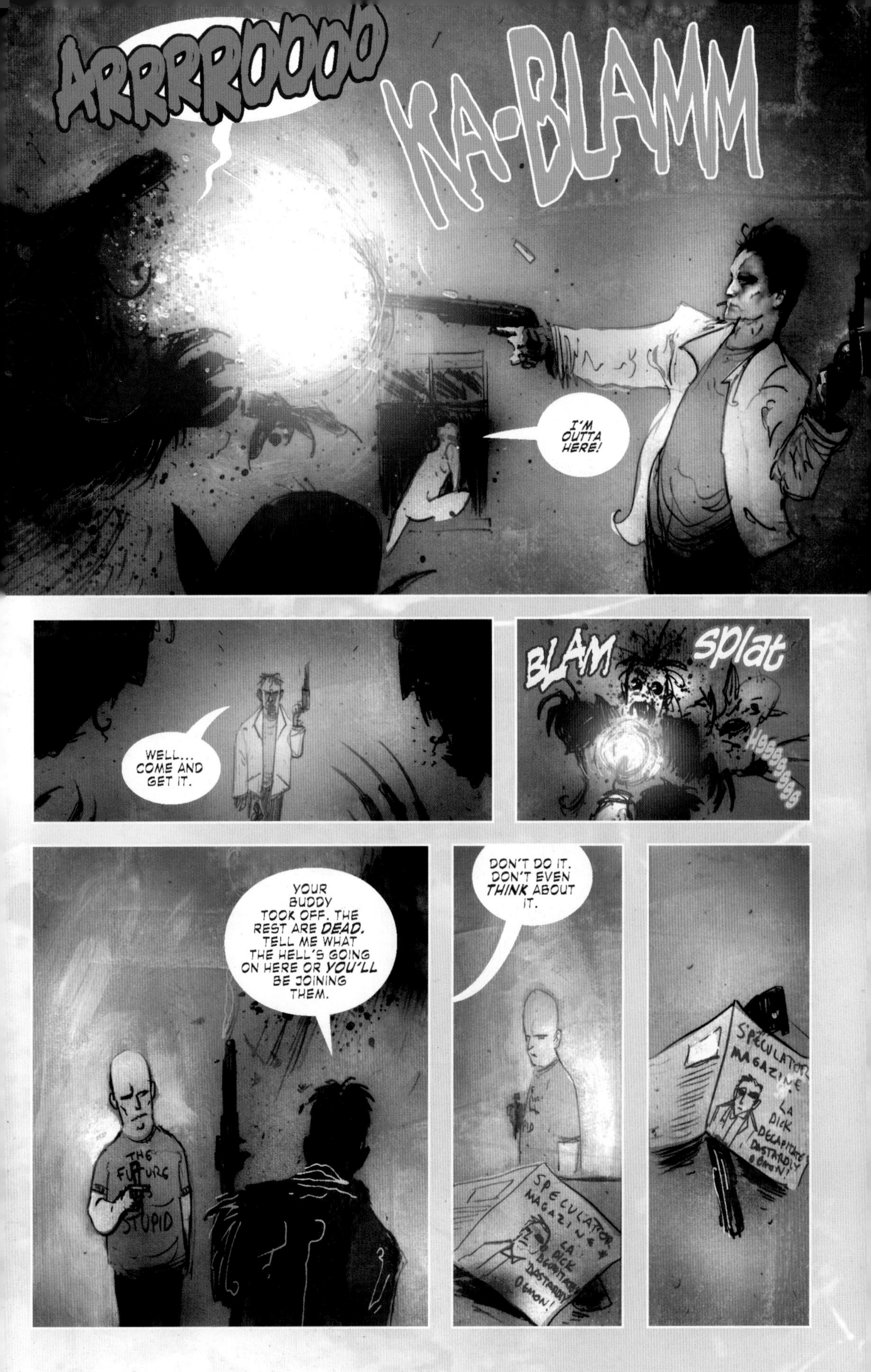
ARRRROOOO
KA-BLAMM
I'M OUTTA HERE!
WELL... COME AND GET IT.
BLAM
splat
YOUR BUDDY TOOK OFF. THE REST ARE *DEAD.* TELL ME WHAT THE HELL'S GOING ON HERE OR *YOU'LL* BE JOINING THEM.
DON'T DO IT. DON'T EVEN *THINK* ABOUT IT.
SPECULATOR MAGAZINE
LA DICK
SPECULATOR MAGAZINE
LA DICK

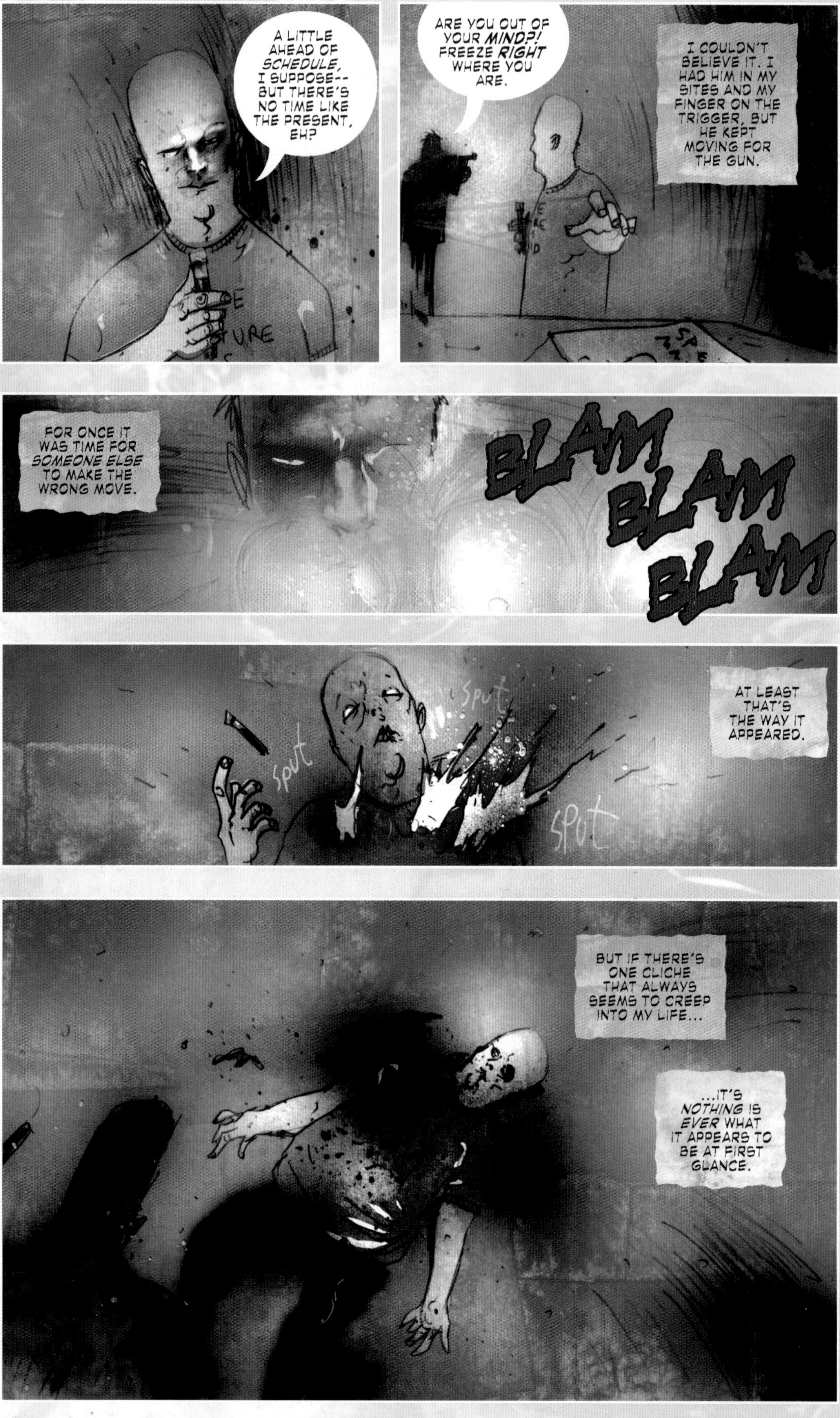
A LITTLE AHEAD OF SCHEDULE, I SUPPOSE-- BUT THERE'S NO TIME LIKE THE PRESENT, EH?
ARE YOU OUT OF YOUR MIND?! FREEZE RIGHT WHERE YOU ARE.
I COULDN'T BELIEVE IT. I HAD HIM IN MY SITES AND MY FINGER ON THE TRIGGER, BUT HE KEPT MOVING FOR THE GUN.
FOR ONCE IT WAS TIME FOR SOMEONE ELSE TO MAKE THE WRONG MOVE.
BLAM BLAM BLAM
SPUT
SPUT
SPUT
AT LEAST THAT'S THE WAY IT APPEARED.
BUT IF THERE'S ONE CLICHE THAT ALWAYS SEEMS TO CREEP INTO MY LIFE...
...IT'S NOTHING IS EVER WHAT IT APPEARS TO BE AT FIRST GLANCE.

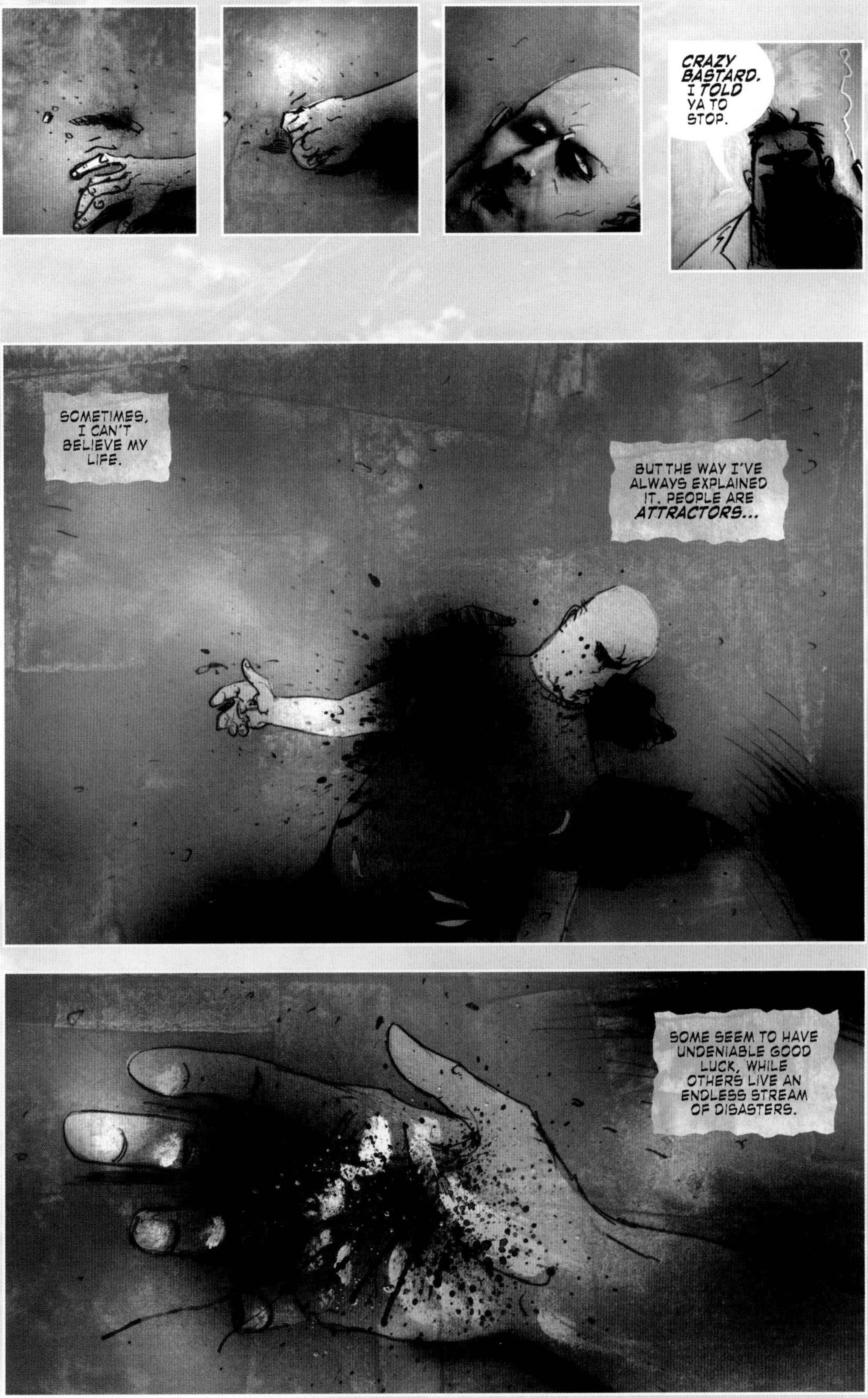
CRAZY BASTARD. I TOLD YA TO STOP.
SOMETIMES, I CAN'T BELIEVE MY LIFE.
BUT THE WAY I'VE ALWAYS EXPLAINED IT. PEOPLE ARE ATTRACTORS...
SOME SEEM TO HAVE UNDENIABLE GOOD LUCK, WHILE OTHERS LIVE AN ENDLESS STREAM OF DISASTERS.

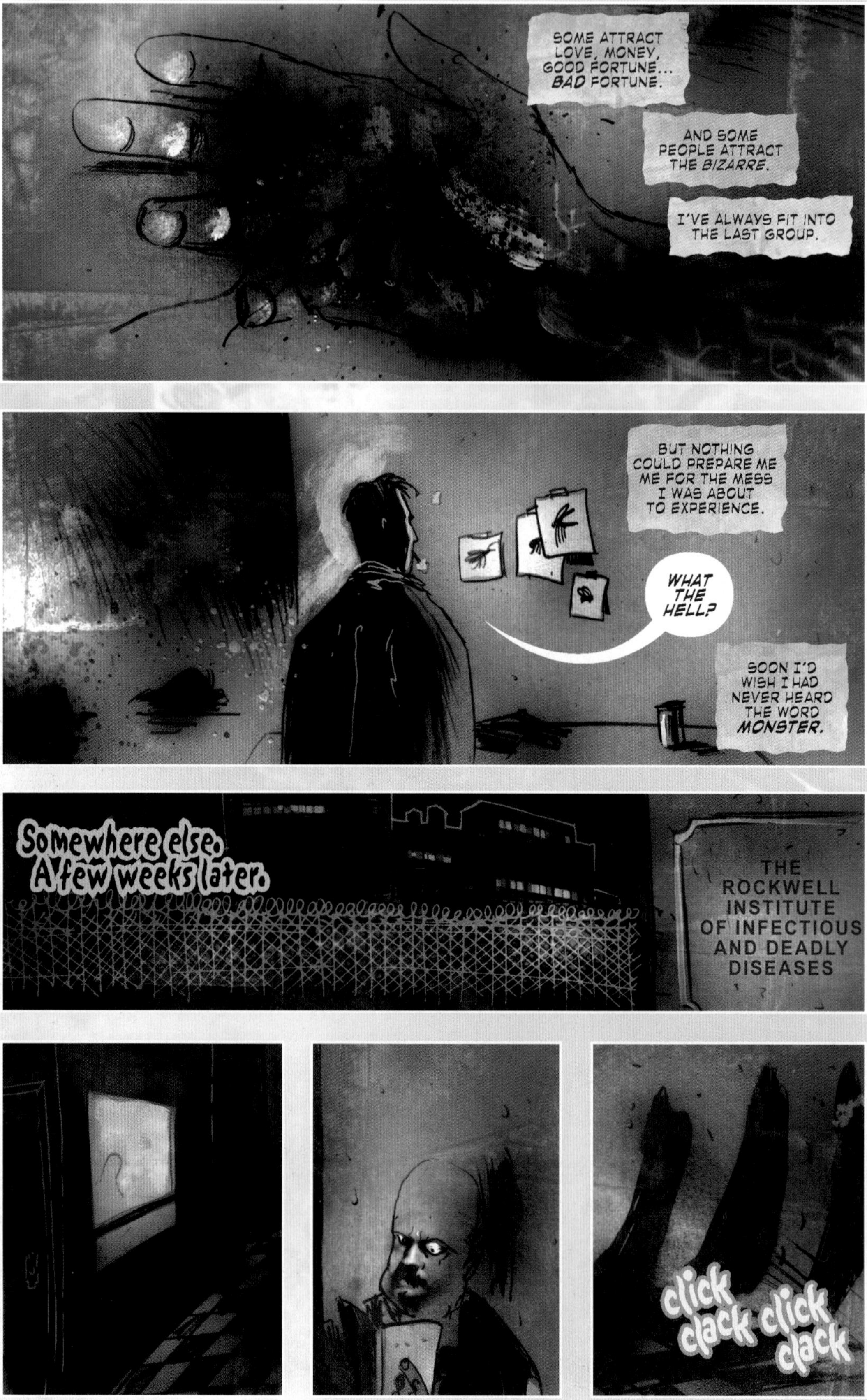
SOME ATTRACT LOVE, MONEY, GOOD FORTUNE... *BAD* FORTUNE.
AND SOME PEOPLE ATTRACT THE *BIZARRE*.
I'VE ALWAYS FIT INTO THE LAST GROUP.
BUT NOTHING COULD PREPARE ME ME FOR THE MESS I WAS ABOUT TO EXPERIENCE.
WHAT THE HELL?
SOON I'D WISH I HAD NEVER HEARD THE WORD *MONSTER*.
Somewhere else. A few weeks later.
THE ROCKWELL INSTITUTE OF INFECTIOUS AND DEADLY DISEASES
click clack click clack

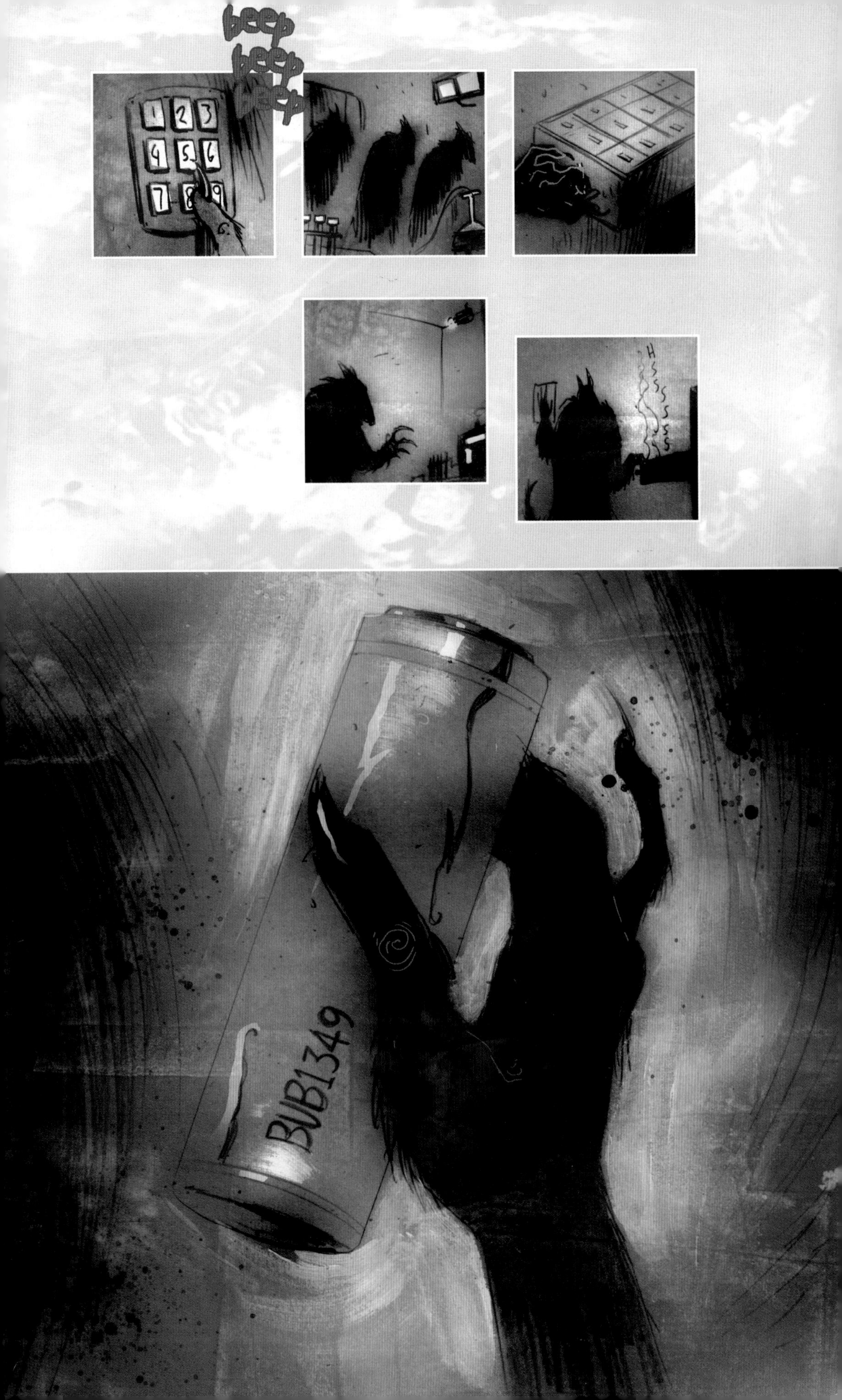

beep
beep
beep
1 2 3
4 5 6
7 8 9
HSSSSSS
BUB1349

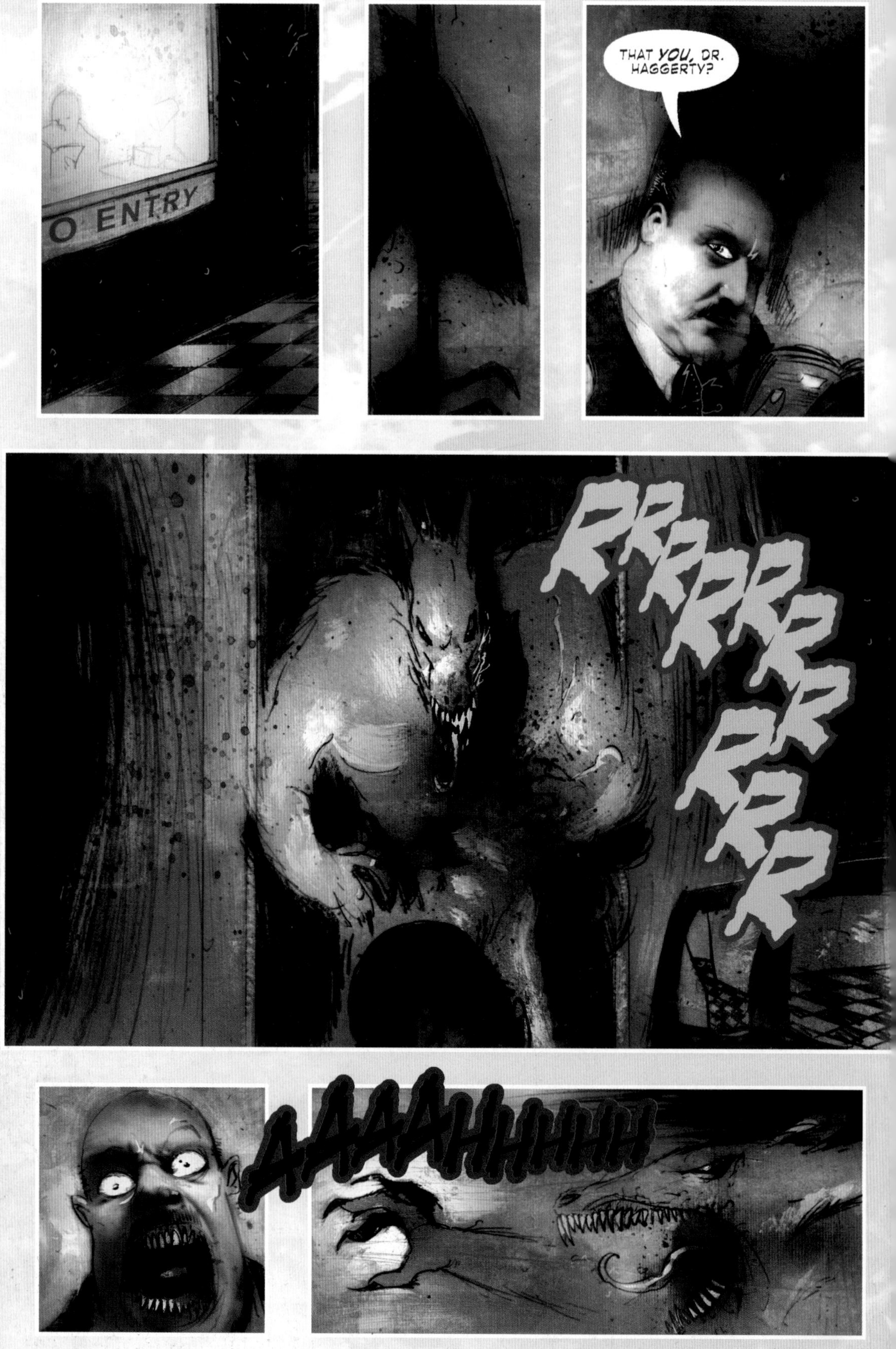
O ENTRY
THAT YOU, DR. HAGGERTY?
RRRRRRRRRRR
AAAAHHHHH

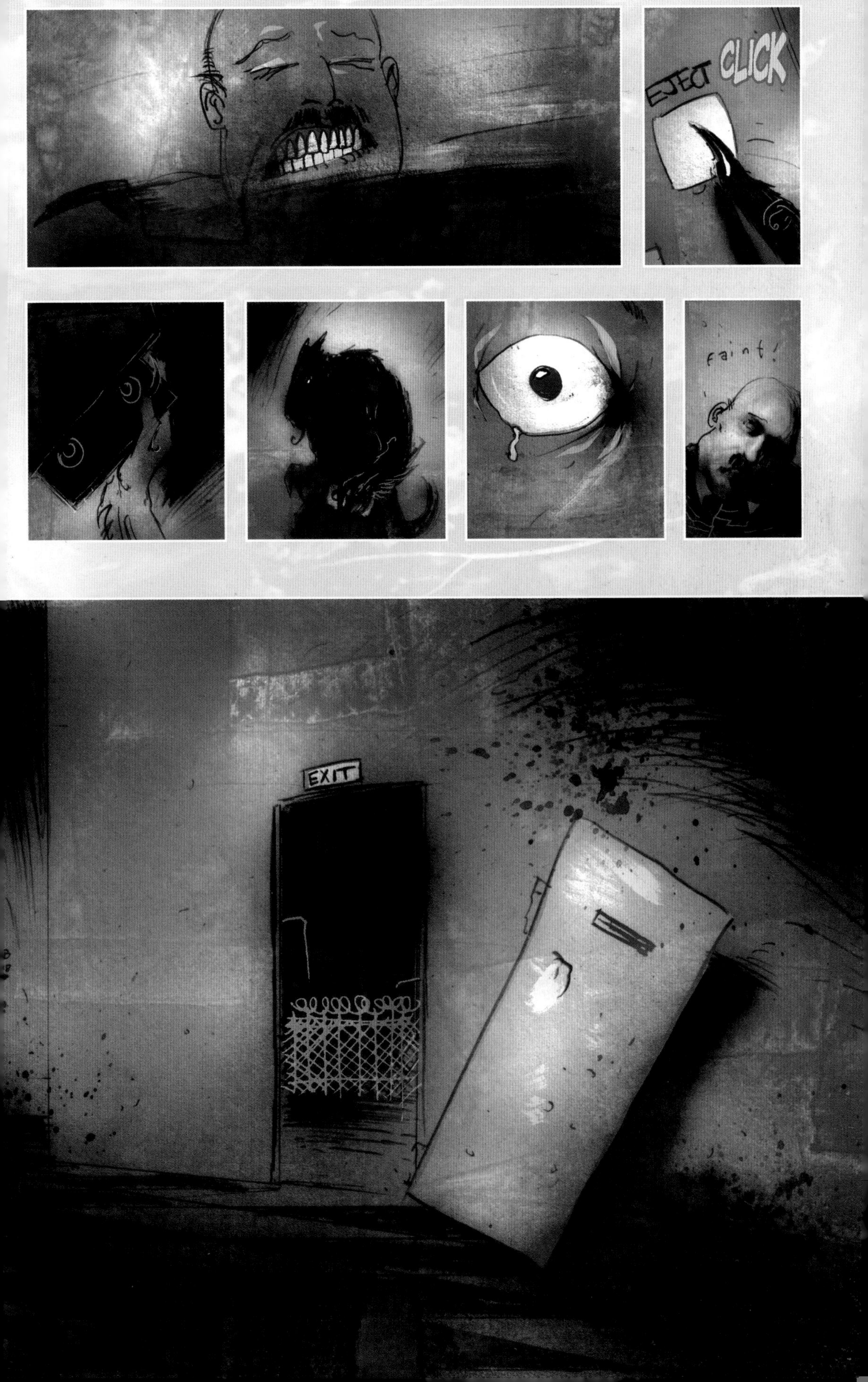
EJECT
CLICK
faint!
EXIT

THE ROCKWELL INSTITUTE

POLICE LINE DO NOT CROSS POLICE LINE DO NOT CROSS POLICE LINE DO NOT CROSS POLI

--AND ITS *HAIR* COVERED EVERY-WHERE. ITS TEETH WERE LIKE--

GRAAAA!

HERE'S THE LIST YOU ASKED FOR, MISS BRUEGER.

THAT'S *DETECTIVE LIEUTENANT* BRUEGER. THAT'S ALL THAT WAS TAKEN?

YES--NEAR AS I CAN TELL, EVERYTHING *ELSE* IS WHERE I LEFT IT.

WHAT'S *BUB1349?*

IT'S A RARE STRAIN OF BUBONIC PLAGUE THAT--

PLAGUE!?

IT'S A RARE STRAIN THAT HAS *NEVER* BEEN ATTRIBUTED TO ANY RECORDED DEATHS SINCE IT INITIALLY BROKE OUT IN--

A SMALL EUROPEAN VILLAGE BE-TWEEN 1337 AND 1350 WHEN THE *BLACK DEATH* MAXED OUT.

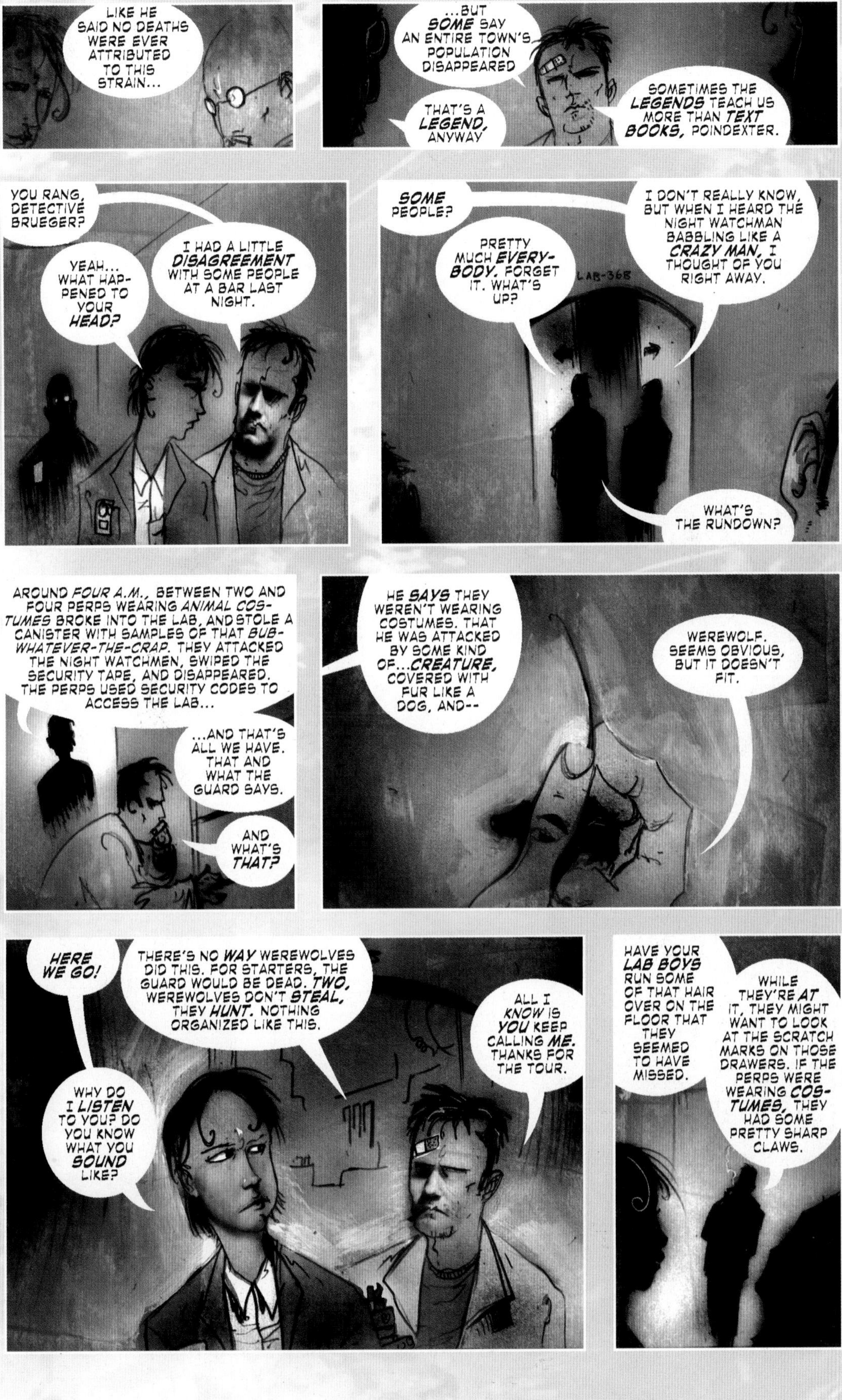

LIKE HE SAID NO DEATHS WERE EVER ATTRIBUTED TO THIS STRAIN...
...BUT SOME SAY AN ENTIRE TOWN'S POPULATION DISAPPEARED
THAT'S A LEGEND, ANYWAY
SOMETIMES THE LEGENDS TEACH US MORE THAN TEXT BOOKS, POINDEXTER.
YOU RANG, DETECTIVE BRUEGER?
YEAH... WHAT HAP-PENED TO YOUR HEAD?
I HAD A LITTLE DISAGREEMENT WITH SOME PEOPLE AT A BAR LAST NIGHT.
SOME PEOPLE?
PRETTY MUCH EVERY-BODY. FORGET IT. WHAT'S UP?
I DON'T REALLY KNOW, BUT WHEN I HEARD THE NIGHT WATCHMAN BABBLING LIKE A CRAZY MAN, I THOUGHT OF YOU RIGHT AWAY.
LAB-368
WHAT'S THE RUNDOWN?
AROUND FOUR A.M., BETWEEN TWO AND FOUR PERPS WEARING ANIMAL COS-TUMES BROKE INTO THE LAB, AND STOLE A CANISTER WITH SAMPLES OF THAT BUB-WHATEVER-THE-CRAP. THEY ATTACKED THE NIGHT WATCHMEN, SWIPED THE SECURITY TAPE, AND DISAPPEARED. THE PERPS USED SECURITY CODES TO ACCESS THE LAB...
...AND THAT'S ALL WE HAVE. THAT AND WHAT THE GUARD SAYS.
AND WHAT'S THAT?
HE SAYS THEY WEREN'T WEARING COSTUMES. THAT HE WAS ATTACKED BY SOME KIND OF...CREATURE, COVERED WITH FUR LIKE A DOG, AND--
WEREWOLF. SEEMS OBVIOUS, BUT IT DOESN'T FIT.
HERE WE GO!
THERE'S NO WAY WEREWOLVES DID THIS. FOR STARTERS, THE GUARD WOULD BE DEAD. TWO, WEREWOLVES DON'T STEAL, THEY HUNT. NOTHING ORGANIZED LIKE THIS.
WHY DO I LISTEN TO YOU? DO YOU KNOW WHAT YOU SOUND LIKE?
ALL I KNOW IS YOU KEEP CALLING ME. THANKS FOR THE TOUR.
HAVE YOUR LAB BOYS RUN SOME OF THAT HAIR OVER ON THE FLOOR THAT THEY SEEMED TO HAVE MISSED.
WHILE THEY'RE AT IT, THEY MIGHT WANT TO LOOK AT THE SCRATCH MARKS ON THOSE DRAWERS. IF THE PERPS WERE WEARING COS-TUMES, THEY HAD SOME PRETTY SHARP CLAWS.

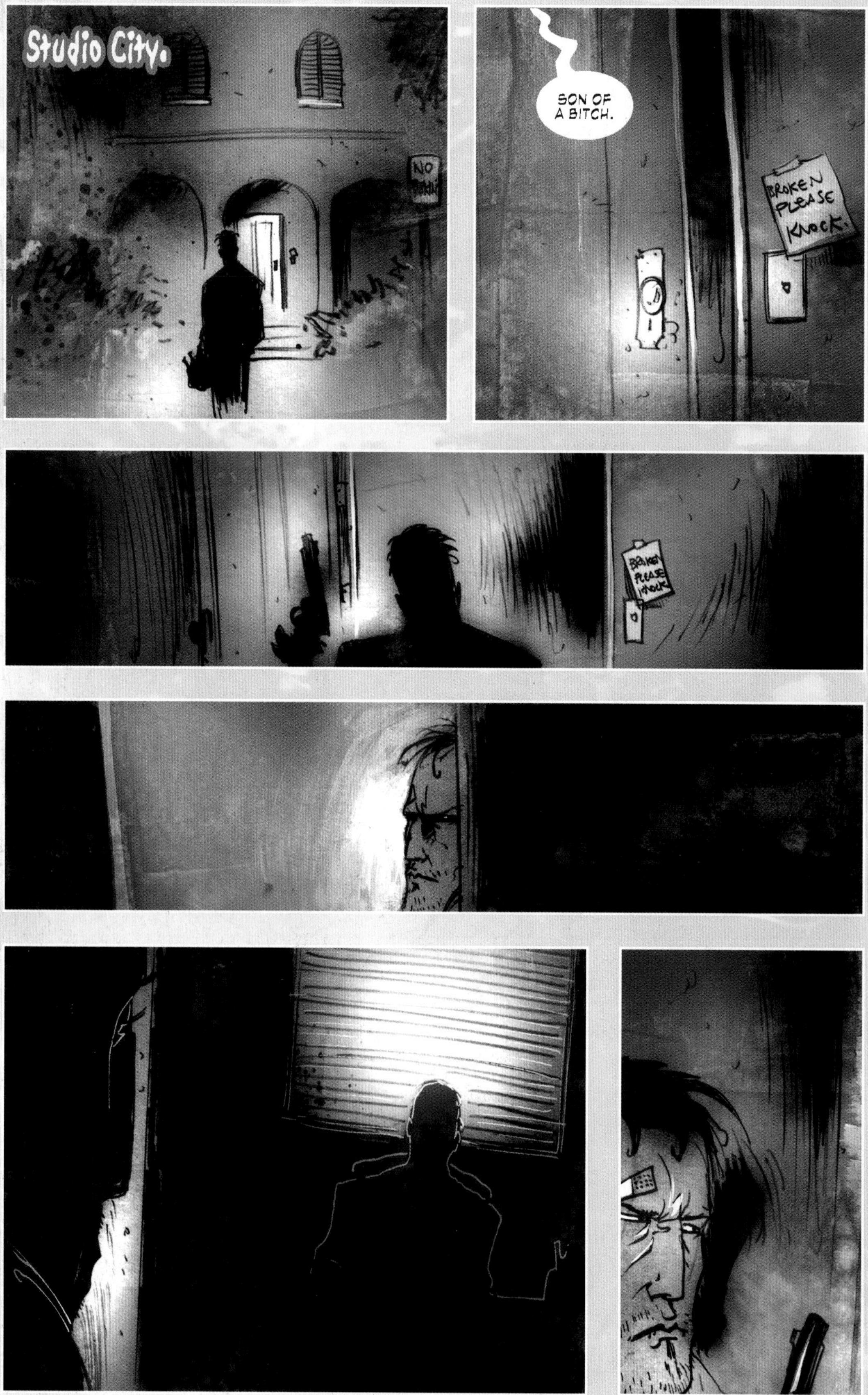
Studio City.
SON OF A BITCH.
BROKEN PLEASE KNOCK.
BROKEN PLEASE KNOCK

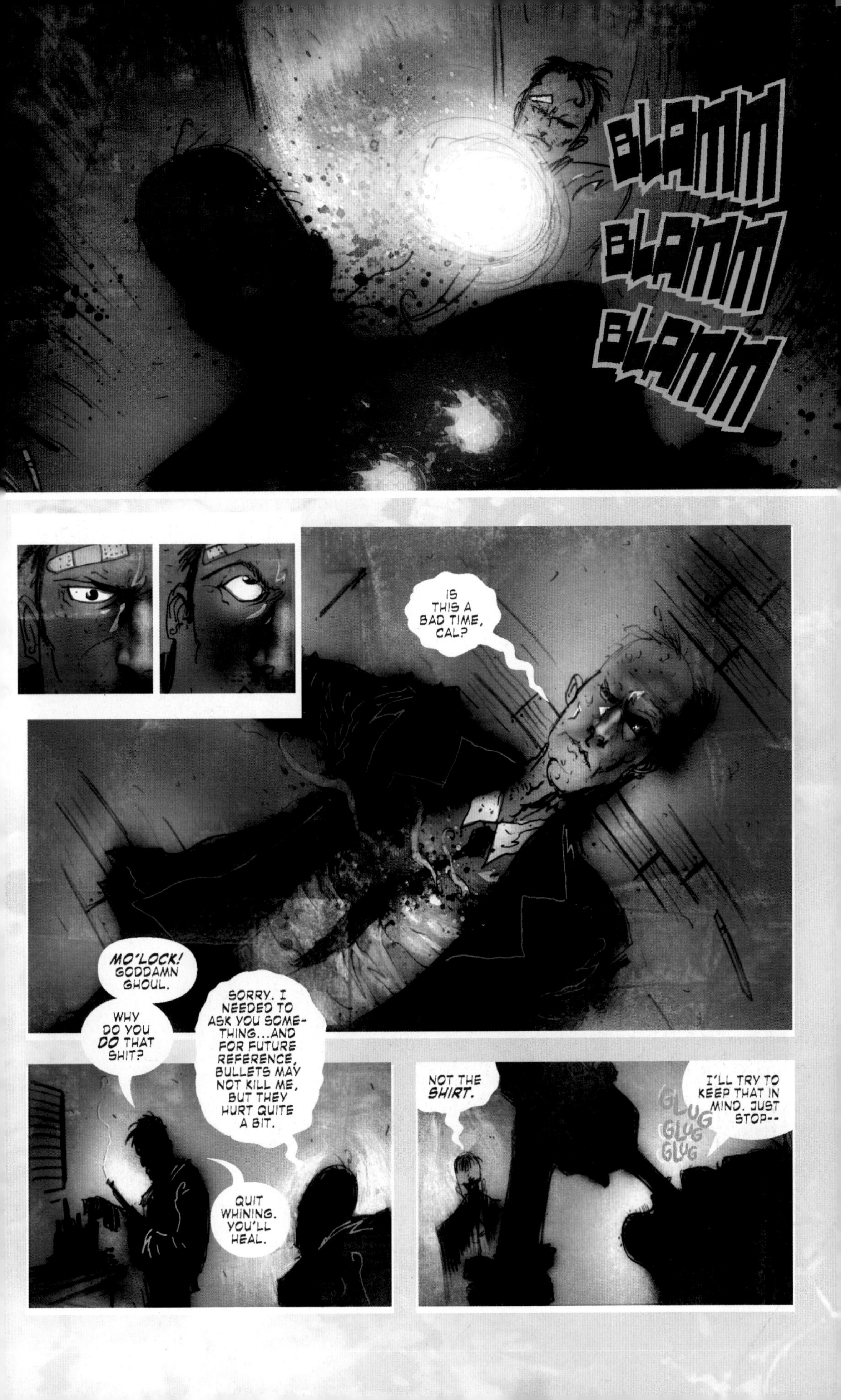
BLAMM
BLAMM
BLAMM
IS THIS A BAD TIME, CAL?
MO'LOCK! GODDAMN GHOUL.
WHY DO YOU DO THAT SHIT?
SORRY. I NEEDED TO ASK YOU SOME-THING...AND FOR FUTURE REFERENCE, BULLETS MAY NOT KILL ME, BUT THEY HURT QUITE A BIT.
QUIT WHINING. YOU'LL HEAL.
NOT THE SHIRT.
GLUG GLUG GLUG
I'LL TRY TO KEEP THAT IN MIND. JUST STOP--

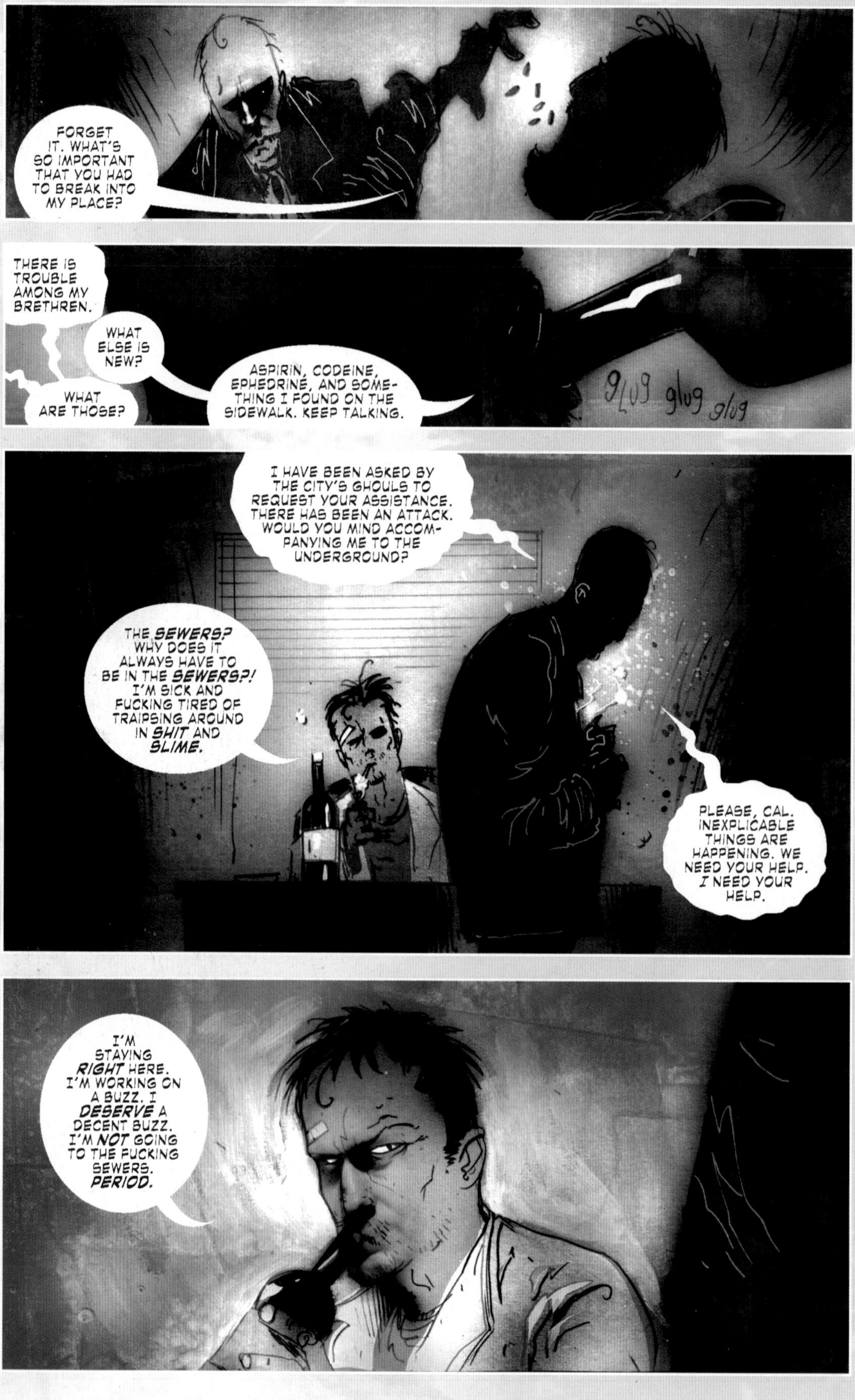
FORGET IT. WHAT'S SO IMPORTANT THAT YOU HAD TO BREAK INTO MY PLACE?
THERE IS TROUBLE AMONG MY BRETHREN.
WHAT ELSE IS NEW?
WHAT ARE THOSE?
ASPIRIN, CODEINE, EPHEDRINE, AND SOMETHING I FOUND ON THE SIDEWALK. KEEP TALKING.
glug glug glug
I HAVE BEEN ASKED BY THE CITY'S GHOULS TO REQUEST YOUR ASSISTANCE. THERE HAS BEEN AN ATTACK. WOULD YOU MIND ACCOMPANYING ME TO THE UNDERGROUND?
THE SEWERS? WHY DOES IT ALWAYS HAVE TO BE IN THE SEWERS?! I'M SICK AND FUCKING TIRED OF TRAIPSING AROUND IN SHIT AND SLIME.
PLEASE, CAL. INEXPLICABLE THINGS ARE HAPPENING. WE NEED YOUR HELP. I NEED YOUR HELP.
I'M STAYING RIGHT HERE. I'M WORKING ON A BUZZ. I DESERVE A DECENT BUZZ. I'M NOT GOING TO THE FUCKING SEWERS. PERIOD.

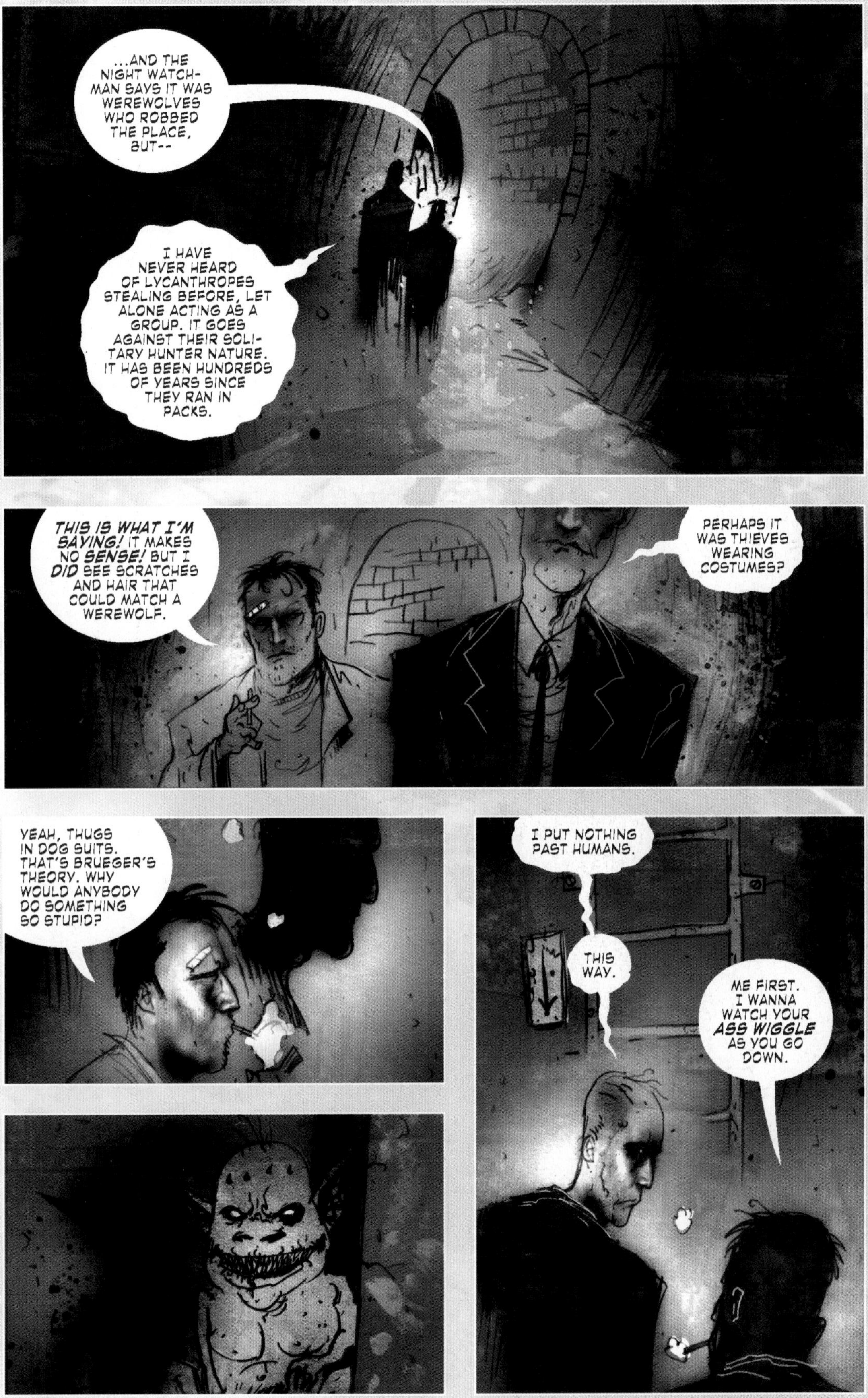

...AND THE NIGHT WATCH-MAN SAYS IT WAS WEREWOLVES WHO ROBBED THE PLACE, BUT--
I HAVE NEVER HEARD OF LYCANTHROPES STEALING BEFORE, LET ALONE ACTING AS A GROUP. IT GOES AGAINST THEIR SOLI-TARY HUNTER NATURE. IT HAS BEEN HUNDREDS OF YEARS SINCE THEY RAN IN PACKS.
THIS IS WHAT I'M SAYING! IT MAKES NO SENSE! BUT I DID SEE SCRATCHES AND HAIR THAT COULD MATCH A WEREWOLF.
PERHAPS IT WAS THIEVES WEARING COSTUMES?
YEAH, THUGS IN DOG SUITS. THAT'S BRUEGER'S THEORY. WHY WOULD ANYBODY DO SOMETHING SO STUPID?
I PUT NOTHING PAST HUMANS.
THIS WAY.
ME FIRST. I WANNA WATCH YOUR ASS WIGGLE AS YOU GO DOWN.

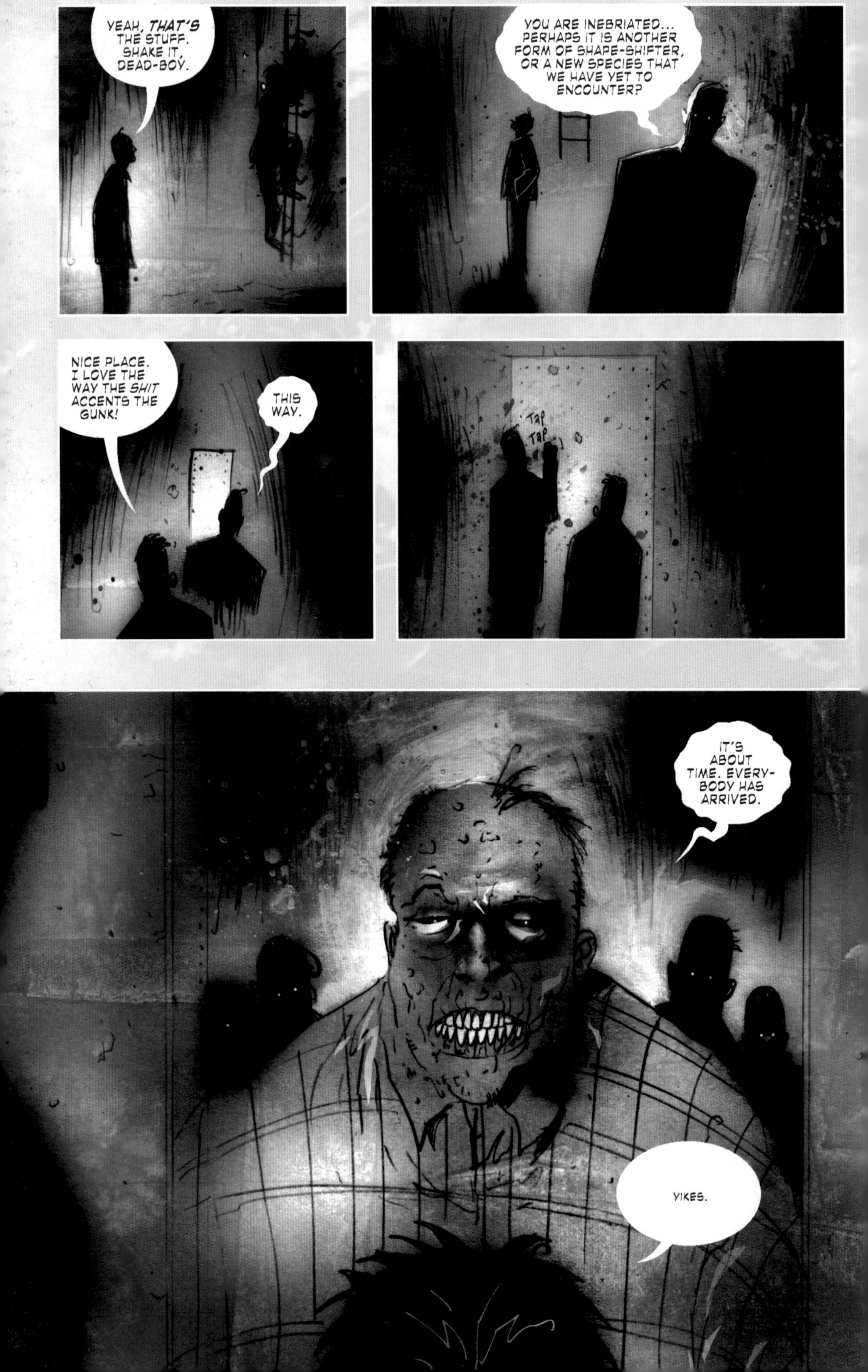
YEAH, *THAT'S* THE STUFF. SHAKE IT, DEAD-BOY.
YOU ARE INEBRIATED... PERHAPS IT IS ANOTHER FORM OF SHAPE-SHIFTER, OR A NEW SPECIES THAT WE HAVE YET TO ENCOUNTER?
NICE PLACE. I LOVE THE WAY THE *SHIT* ACCENTS THE GUNK!
THIS WAY.
Tap Tap
IT'S ABOUT TIME. EVERY-BODY HAS ARRIVED.
YIKES.

CHAPTER TWO
What's a Ghoul to Do?

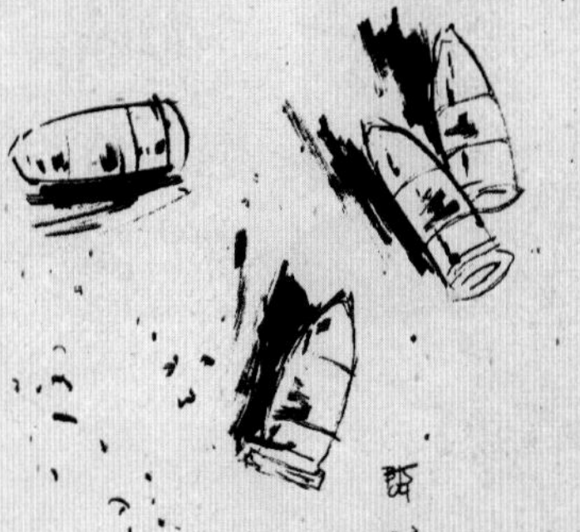

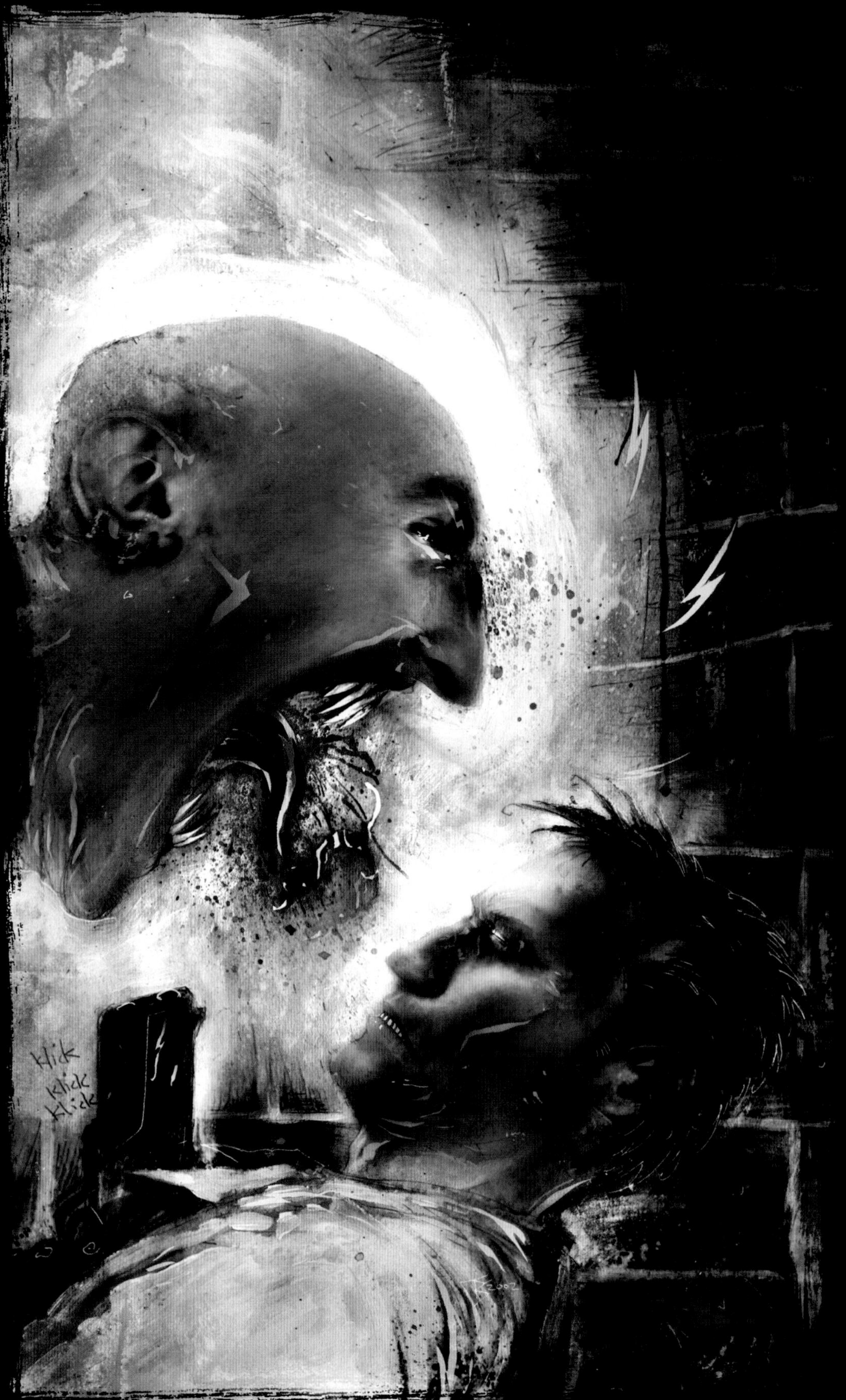
klick
klick
klick

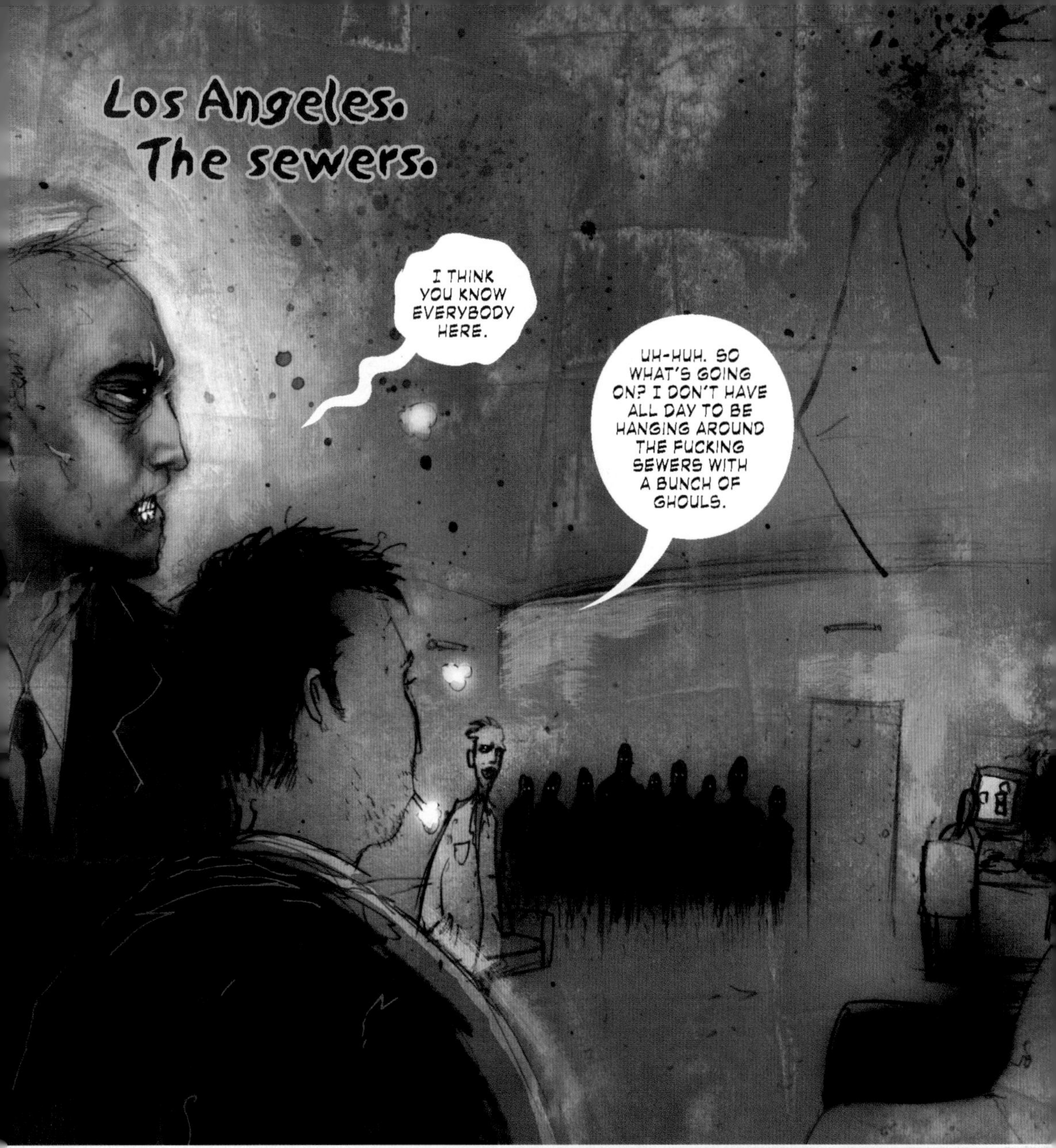
Los Angeles.
The sewers.
I THINK YOU KNOW EVERYBODY HERE.
UH-HUH. SO WHAT'S GOING ON? I DON'T HAVE ALL DAY TO BE HANGING AROUND THE FUCKING SEWERS WITH A BUNCH OF GHOULS.

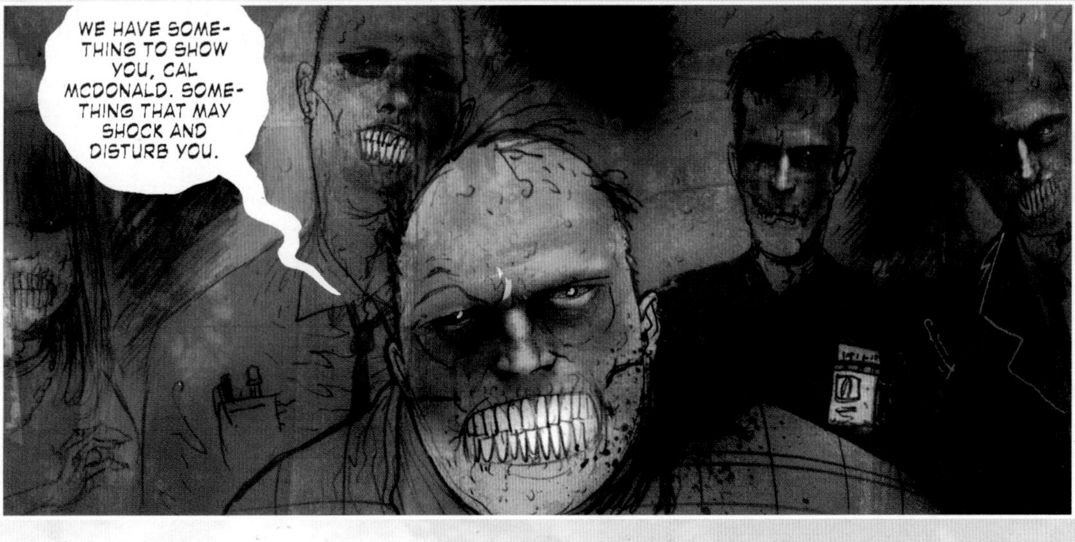
WE HAVE SOMETHING TO SHOW YOU, CAL MCDONALD. SOMETHING THAT MAY SHOCK AND DISTURB YOU.

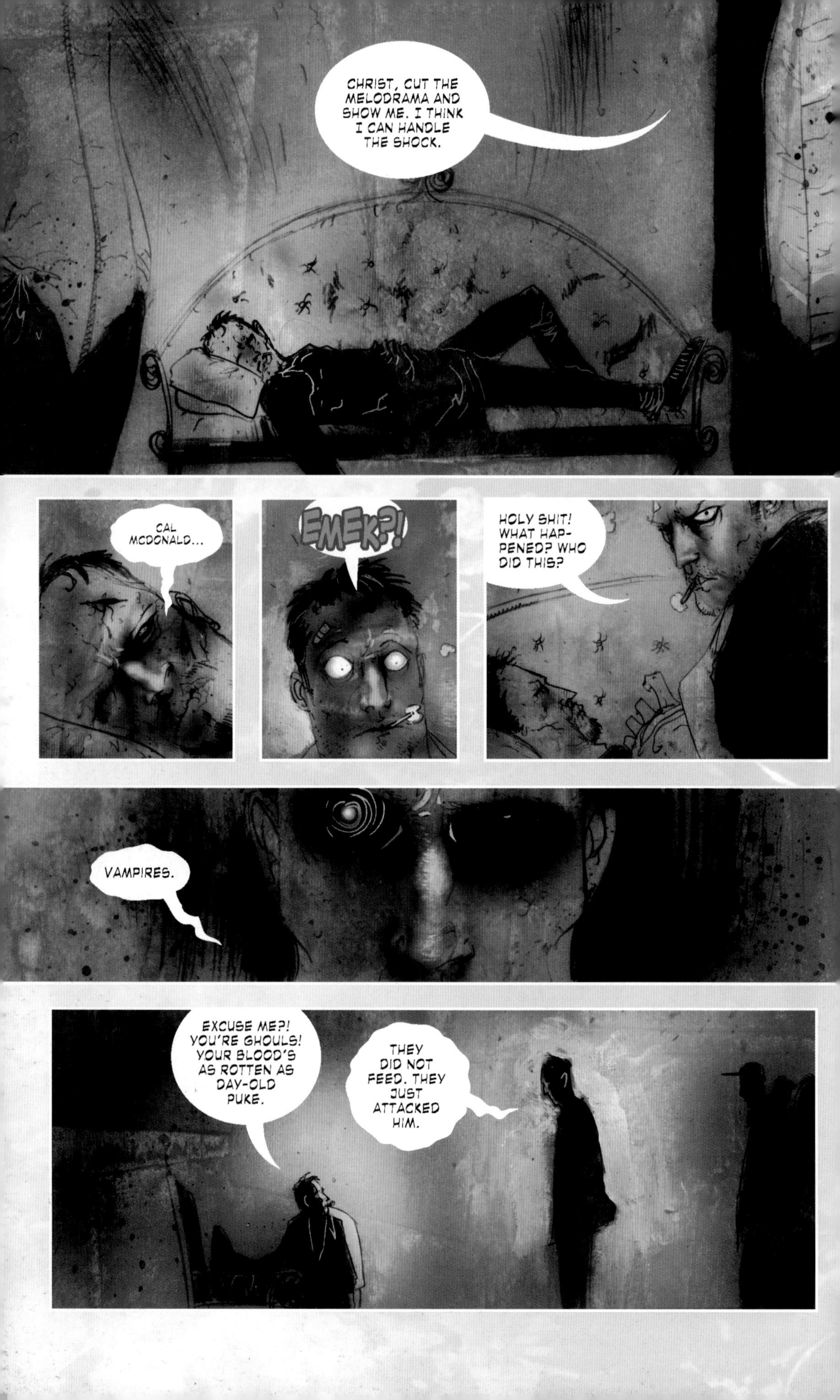
CHRIST, CUT THE MELODRAMA AND SHOW ME. I THINK I CAN HANDLE THE SHOCK.
CAL MCDONALD...
EMEK?!
HOLY SHIT! WHAT HAP-PENED? WHO DID THIS?
VAMPIRES.
EXCUSE ME?! YOU'RE GHOULS! YOUR BLOOD'S AS ROTTEN AS DAY-OLD PUKE.
THEY DID NOT FEED. THEY JUST ATTACKED HIM.

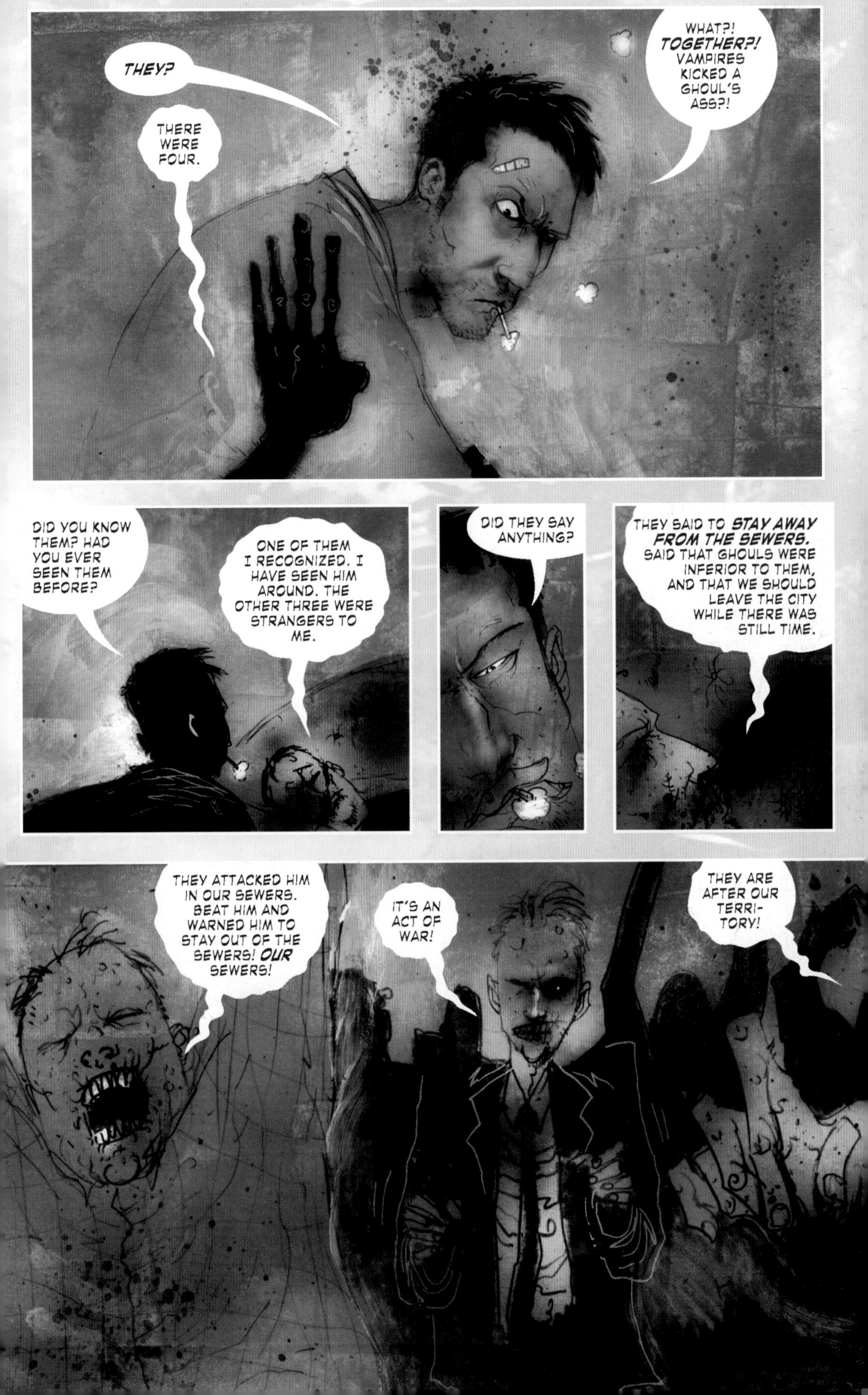
THEY?
THERE WERE FOUR.
WHAT?! TOGETHER?! VAMPIRES KICKED A GHOUL'S ASS?!
DID YOU KNOW THEM? HAD YOU EVER SEEN THEM BEFORE?
ONE OF THEM I RECOGNIZED. I HAVE SEEN HIM AROUND. THE OTHER THREE WERE STRANGERS TO ME.
DID THEY SAY ANYTHING?
THEY SAID TO STAY AWAY FROM THE SEWERS. SAID THAT GHOULS WERE INFERIOR TO THEM, AND THAT WE SHOULD LEAVE THE CITY WHILE THERE WAS STILL TIME.
THEY ATTACKED HIM IN OUR SEWERS. BEAT HIM AND WARNED HIM TO STAY OUT OF THE SEWERS! OUR SEWERS!
IT'S AN ACT OF WAR!
THEY ARE AFTER OUR TERRI-TORY!

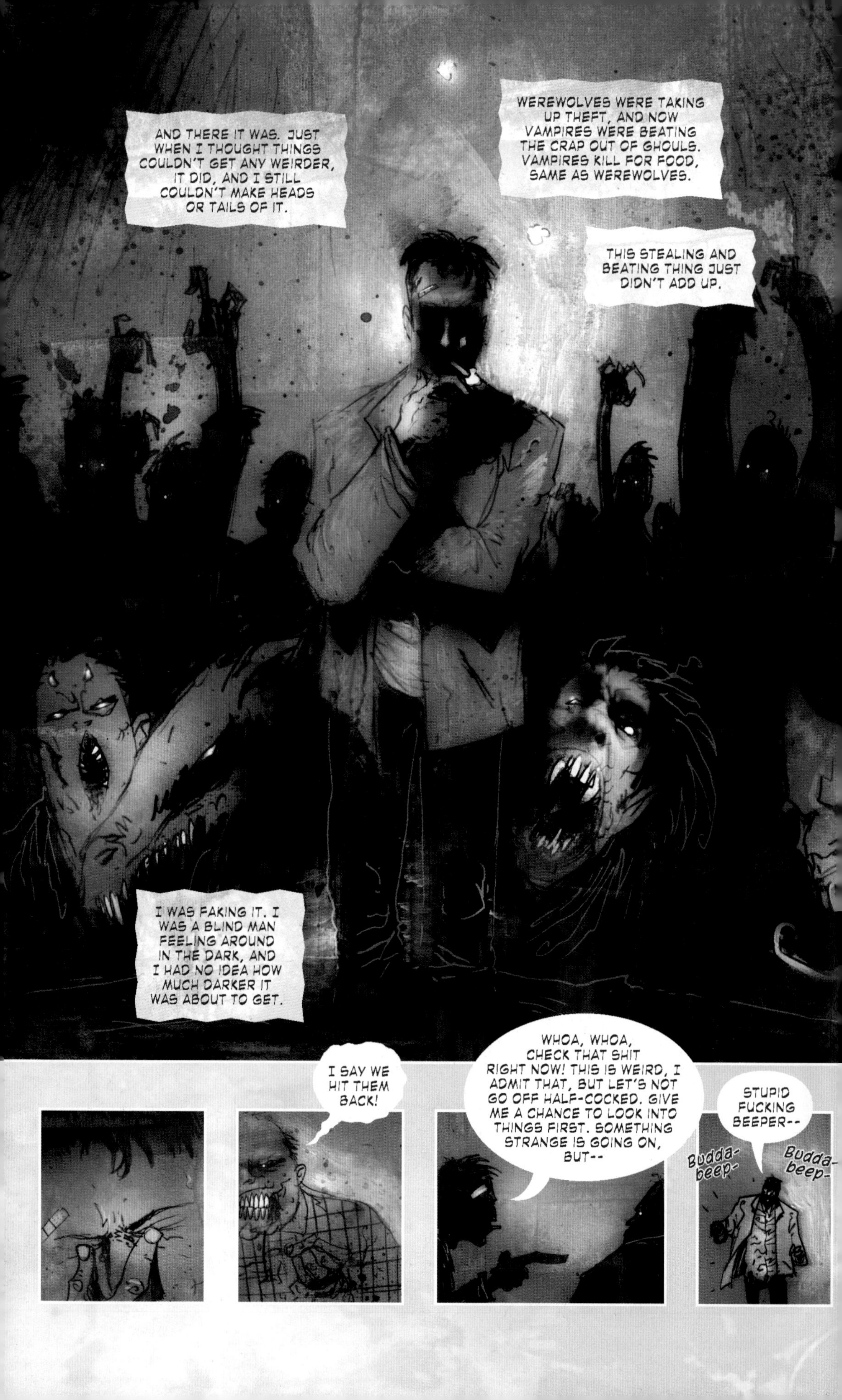
AND THERE IT WAS. JUST WHEN I THOUGHT THINGS COULDN'T GET ANY WEIRDER, IT DID, AND I STILL COULDN'T MAKE HEADS OR TAILS OF IT.
WEREWOLVES WERE TAKING UP THEFT, AND NOW VAMPIRES WERE BEATING THE CRAP OUT OF GHOULS. VAMPIRES KILL FOR FOOD, SAME AS WEREWOLVES.
THIS STEALING AND BEATING THING JUST DIDN'T ADD UP.
I WAS FAKING IT. I WAS A BLIND MAN FEELING AROUND IN THE DARK, AND I HAD NO IDEA HOW MUCH DARKER IT WAS ABOUT TO GET.
I SAY WE HIT THEM BACK!
WHOA, WHOA, CHECK THAT SHIT RIGHT NOW! THIS IS WEIRD, I ADMIT THAT, BUT LET'S NOT GO OFF HALF-COCKED. GIVE ME A CHANCE TO LOOK INTO THINGS FIRST. SOMETHING STRANGE IS GOING ON, BUT--
Budda-beep-
STUPID FUCKING BEEPER--
Budda-beep-

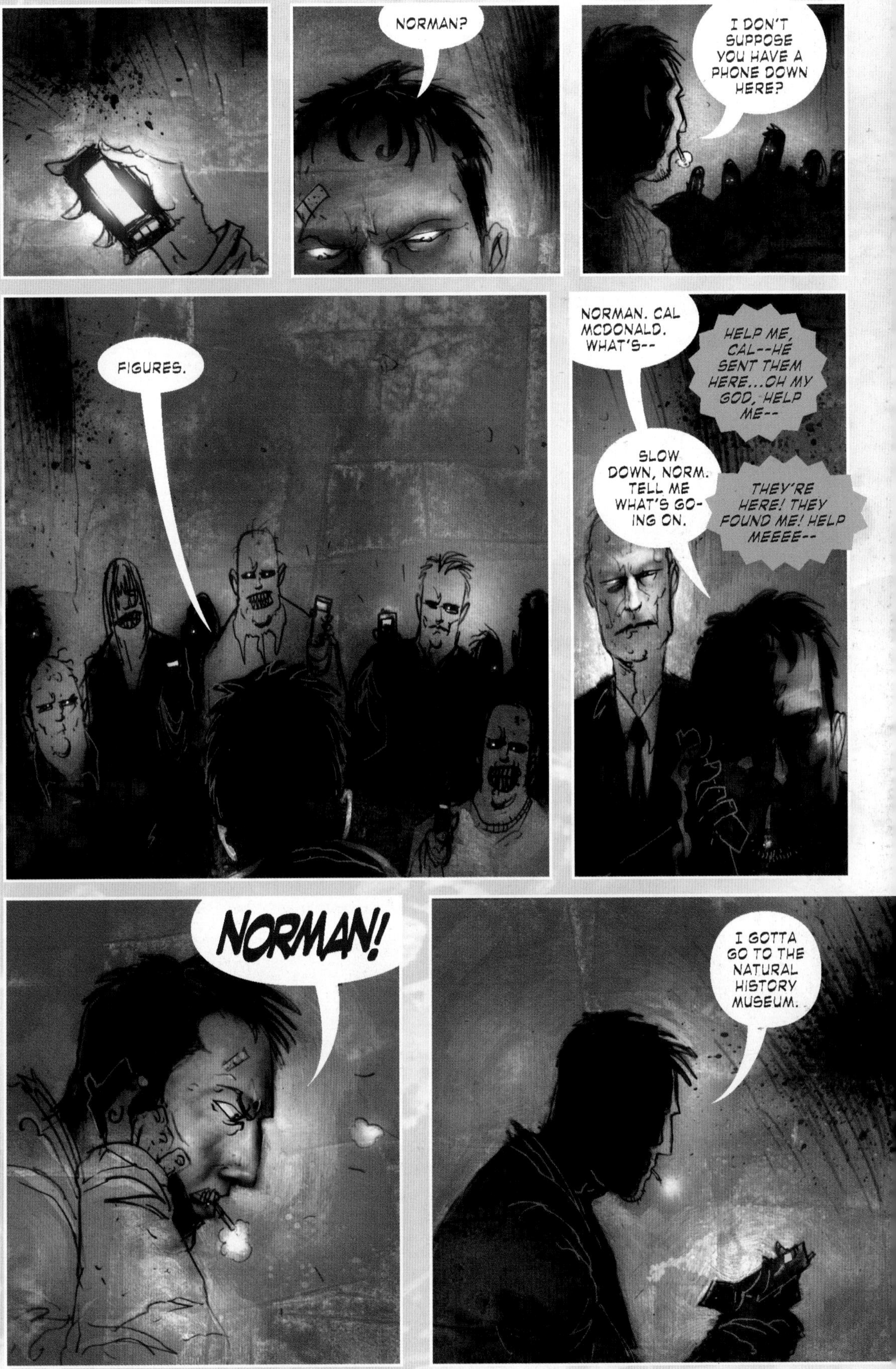
NORMAN?
I DON'T SUPPOSE YOU HAVE A PHONE DOWN HERE?
FIGURES.
NORMAN. CAL MCDONALD. WHAT'S--
HELP ME, CAL--HE SENT THEM HERE...OH MY GOD, HELP ME--
SLOW DOWN, NORM. TELL ME WHAT'S GO-ING ON.
THEY'RE HERE! THEY FOUND ME! HELP MEEEE--
NORMAN!
I GOTTA GO TO THE NATURAL HISTORY MUSEUM.

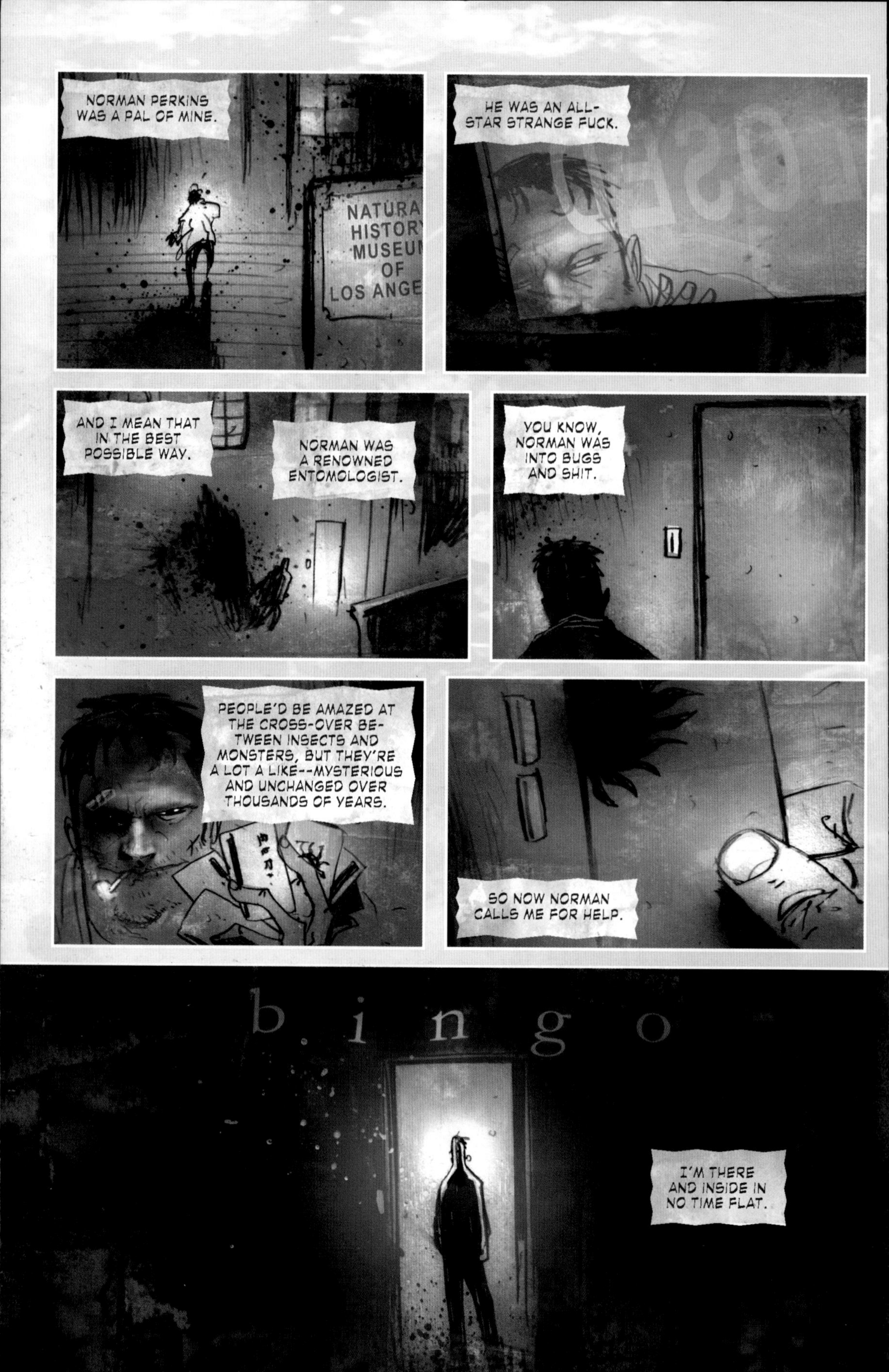
NORMAN PERKINS WAS A PAL OF MINE.
NATURA HISTORY MUSEUM OF LOS ANGE
HE WAS AN ALL-STAR STRANGE FUCK.
AND I MEAN THAT IN THE BEST POSSIBLE WAY.
NORMAN WAS A RENOWNED ENTOMOLOGIST.
YOU KNOW, NORMAN WAS INTO BUGS AND SHIT.
PEOPLE'D BE AMAZED AT THE CROSS-OVER BE-TWEEN INSECTS AND MONSTERS, BUT THEY'RE A LOT A LIKE--MYSTERIOUS AND UNCHANGED OVER THOUSANDS OF YEARS.
SO NOW NORMAN CALLS ME FOR HELP.
b i n g o
I'M THERE AND INSIDE IN NO TIME FLAT.

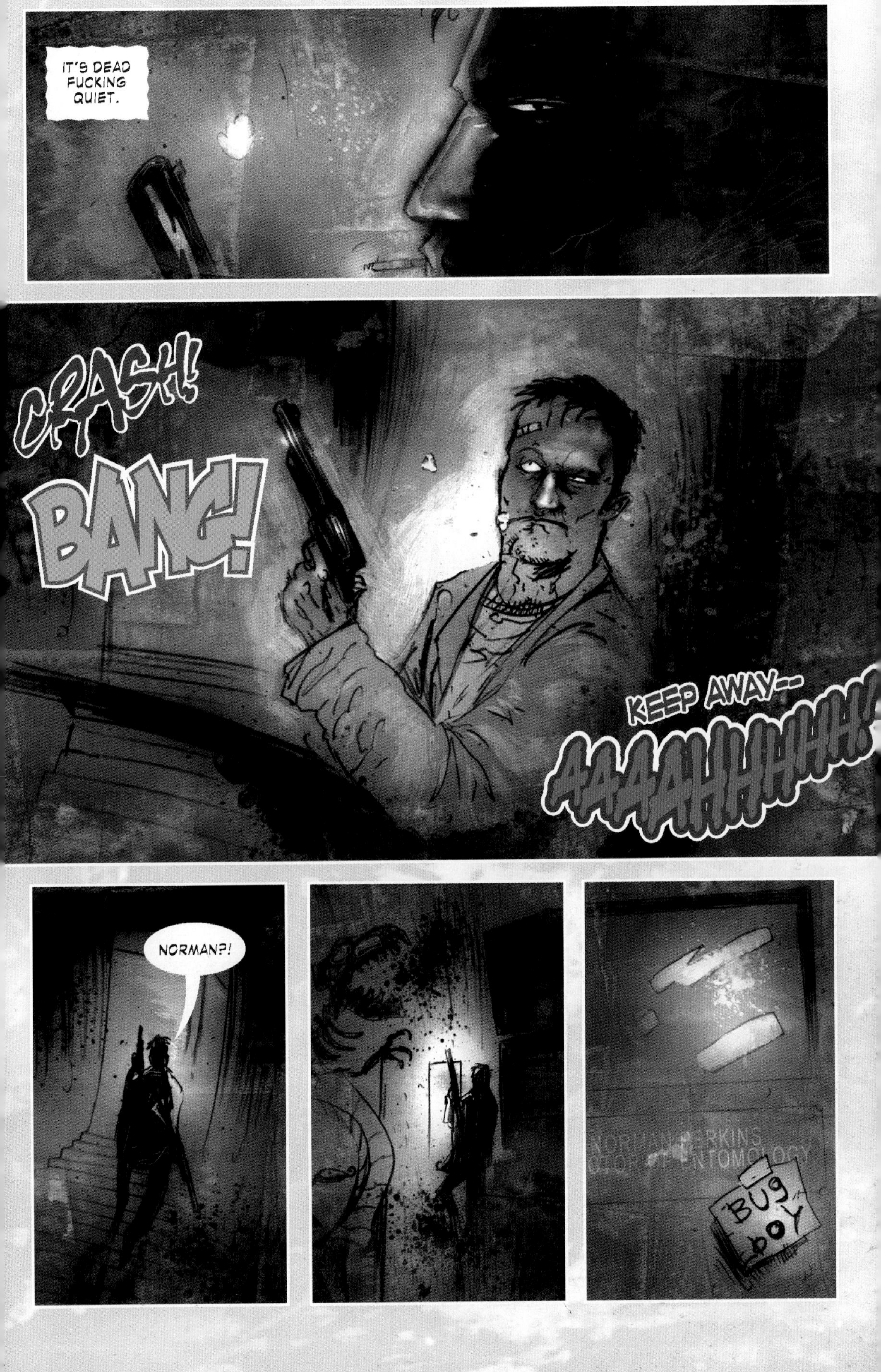
IT'S DEAD FUCKING QUIET.
CRASH!
BANG!
KEEP AWAY--
AAAAHHHHH!
NORMAN?!
NORMAN PERKINS
BUG BOY

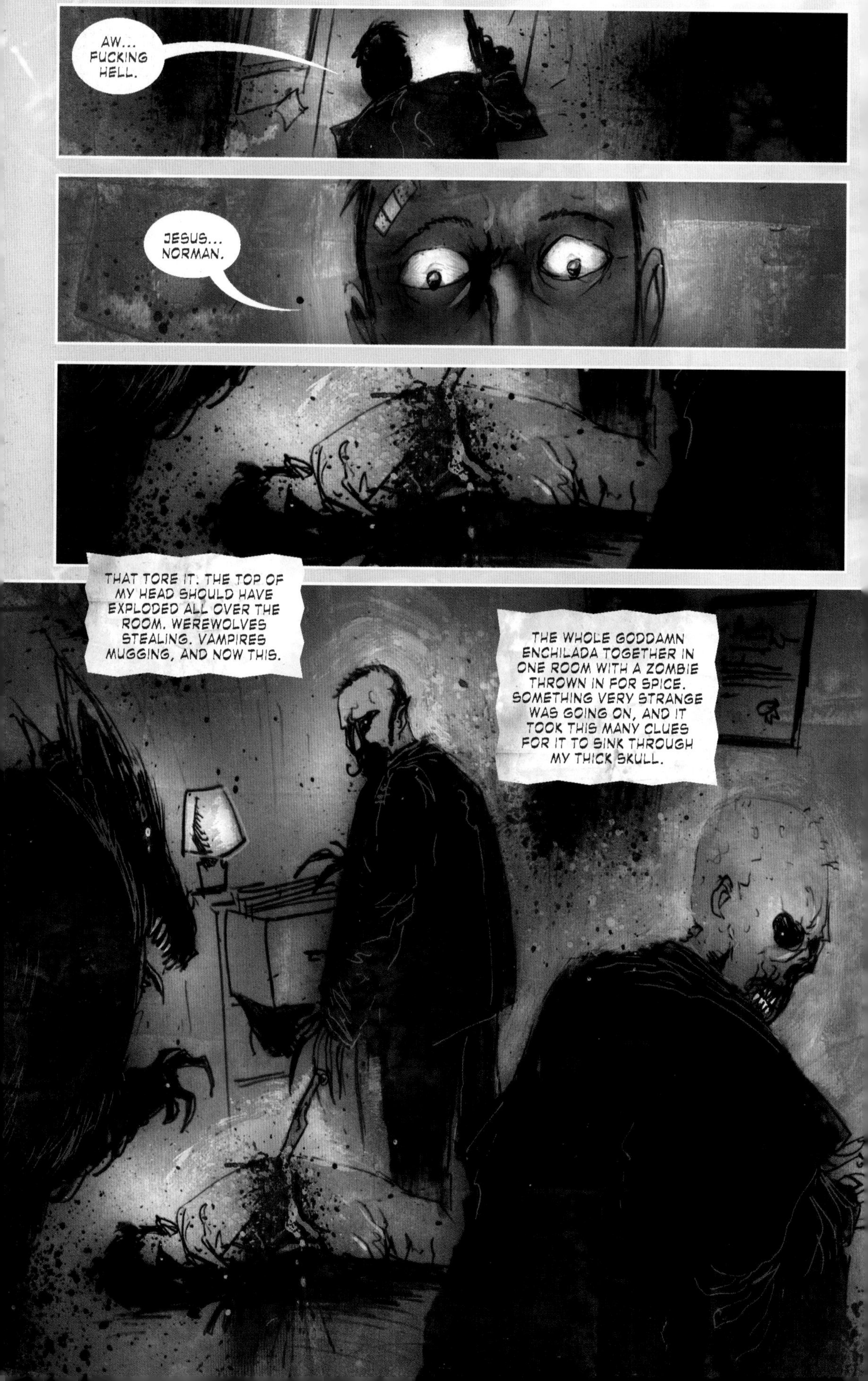
AW... FUCKING HELL.
JESUS... NORMAN.
THAT TORE IT. THE TOP OF MY HEAD SHOULD HAVE EXPLODED ALL OVER THE ROOM. WEREWOLVES STEALING. VAMPIRES MUGGING, AND NOW THIS.
THE WHOLE GODDAMN ENCHILADA TOGETHER IN ONE ROOM WITH A ZOMBIE THROWN IN FOR SPICE. SOMETHING VERY STRANGE WAS GOING ON, AND IT TOOK THIS MANY CLUES FOR IT TO SINK THROUGH MY THICK SKULL.

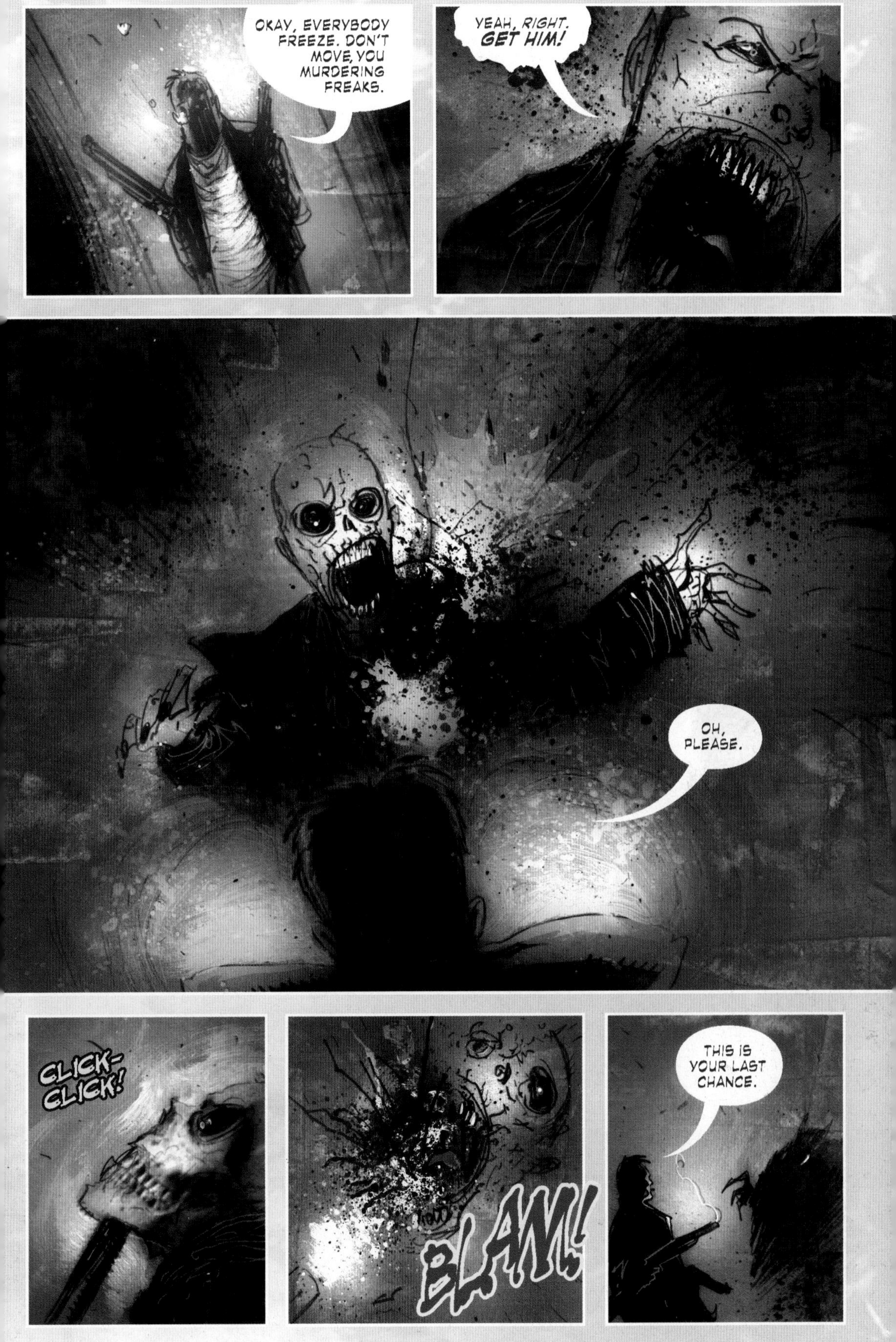
OKAY, EVERYBODY FREEZE. DON'T MOVE, YOU MURDERING FREAKS.
YEAH, RIGHT. GET HIM!
OH, PLEASE.
CLICK-CLICK!
BLAM!
THIS IS YOUR LAST CHANCE.

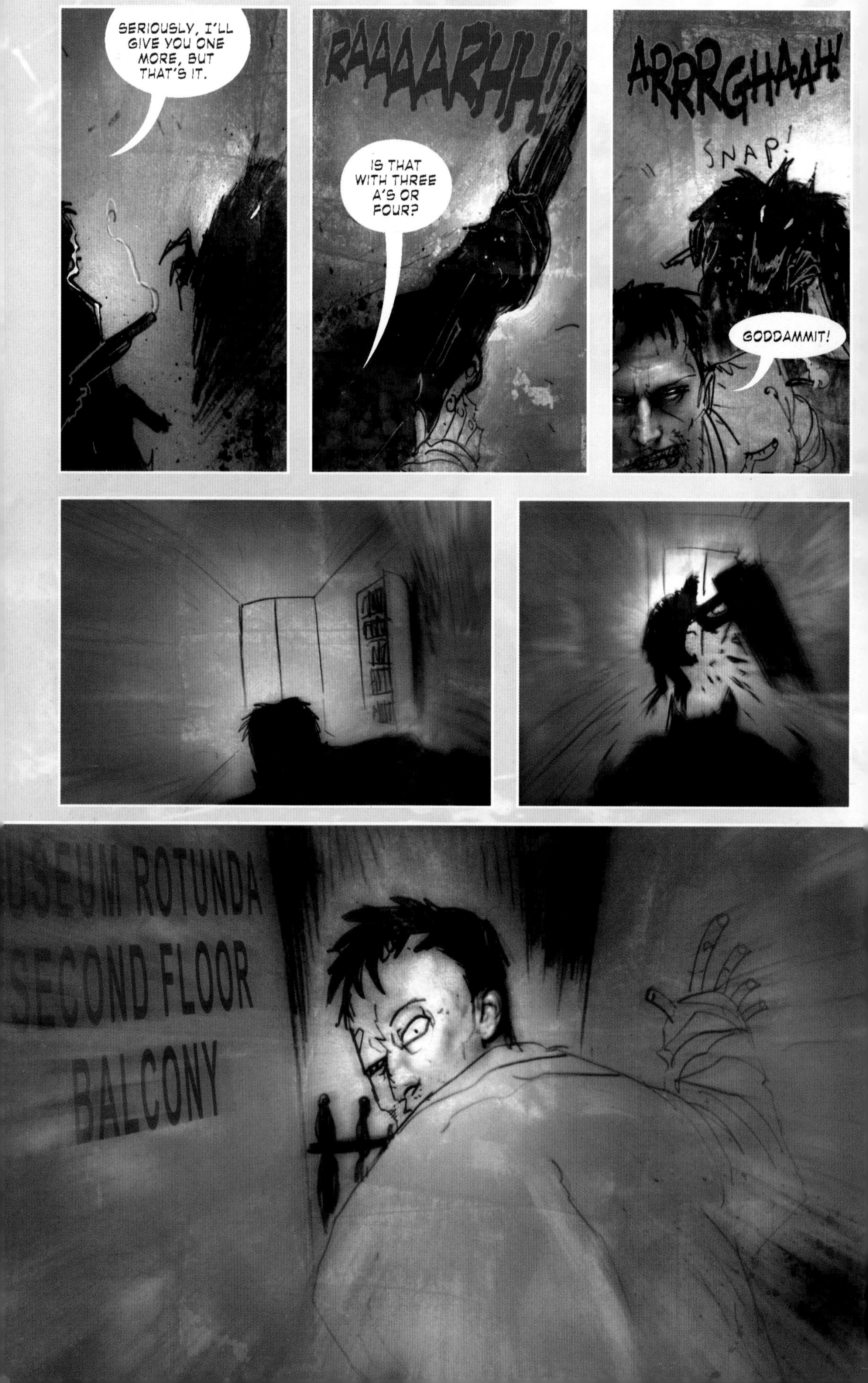
SERIOUSLY, I'LL GIVE YOU ONE MORE, BUT THAT'S IT.
RAAAARHH!!
IS THAT WITH THREE A'S OR FOUR?
ARRRGHAAH!
SNAP!
GODDAMMIT!
USEUM ROTUNDA
SECOND FLOOR
BALCONY

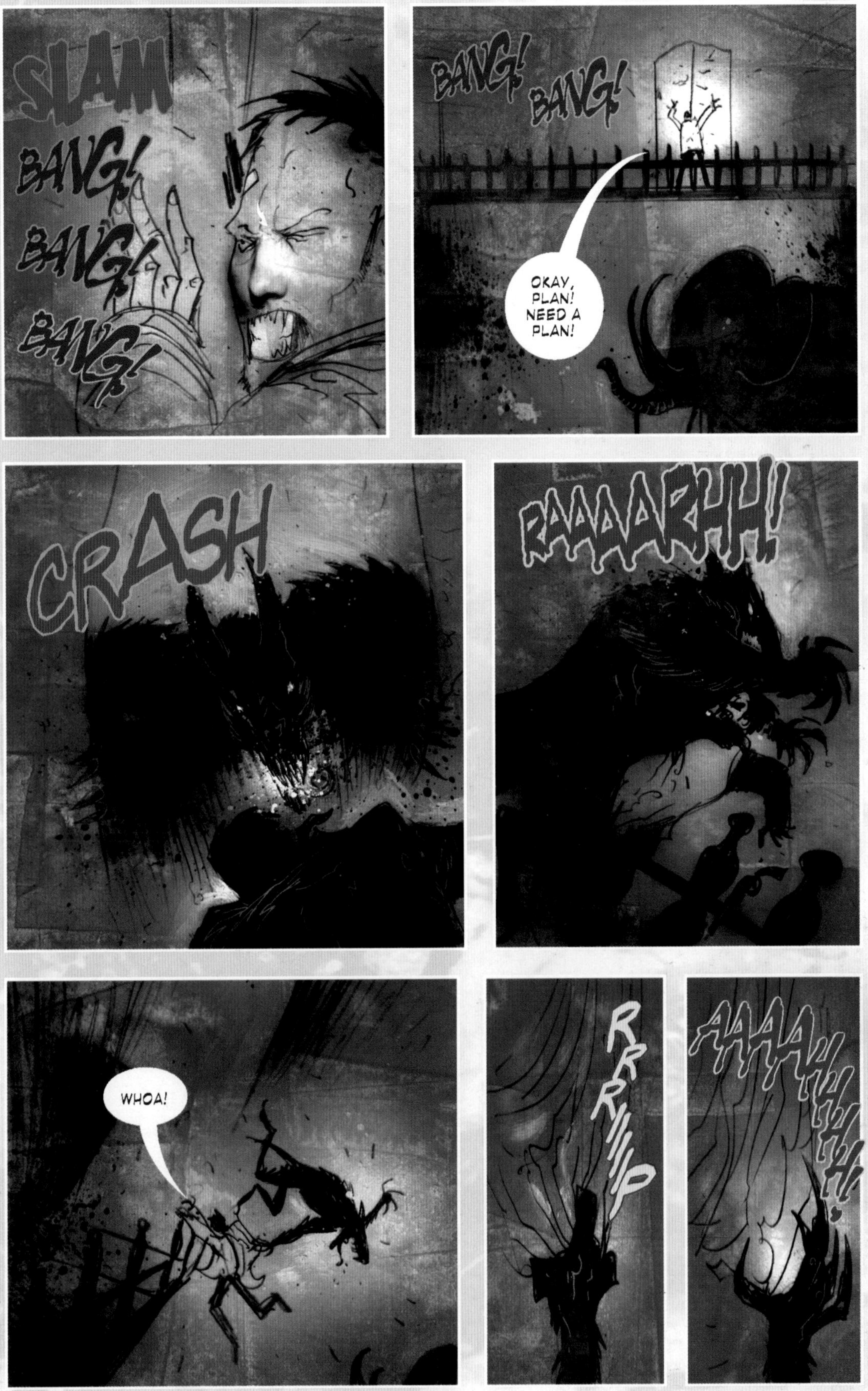

SLAM
BANG!
BANG!
BANG!
BANG!
BANG!
OKAY, PLAN! NEED A PLAN!
CRASH
RAAAARHH!
WHOA!
RRRIIIIP
AAAAHHHH!

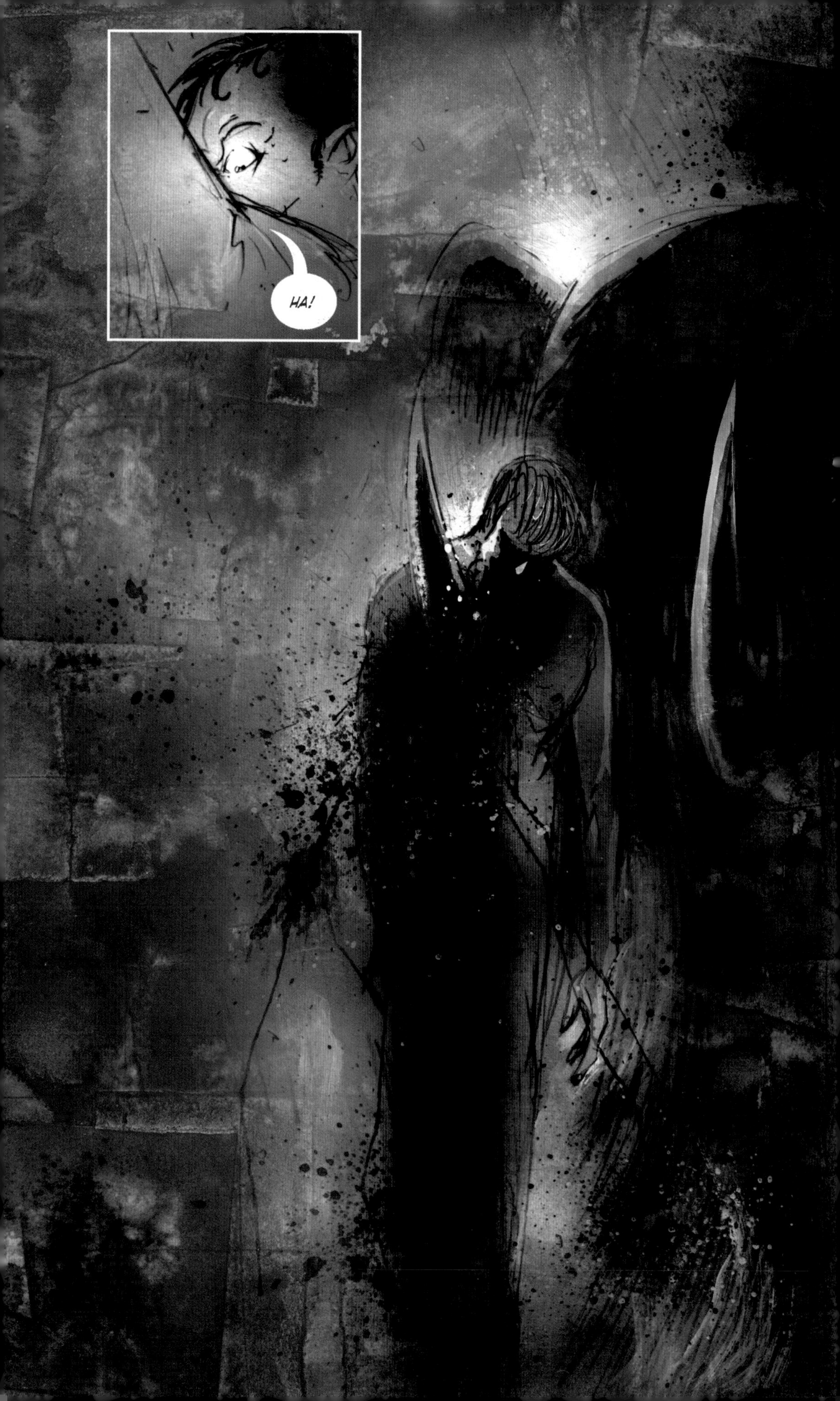
HA!

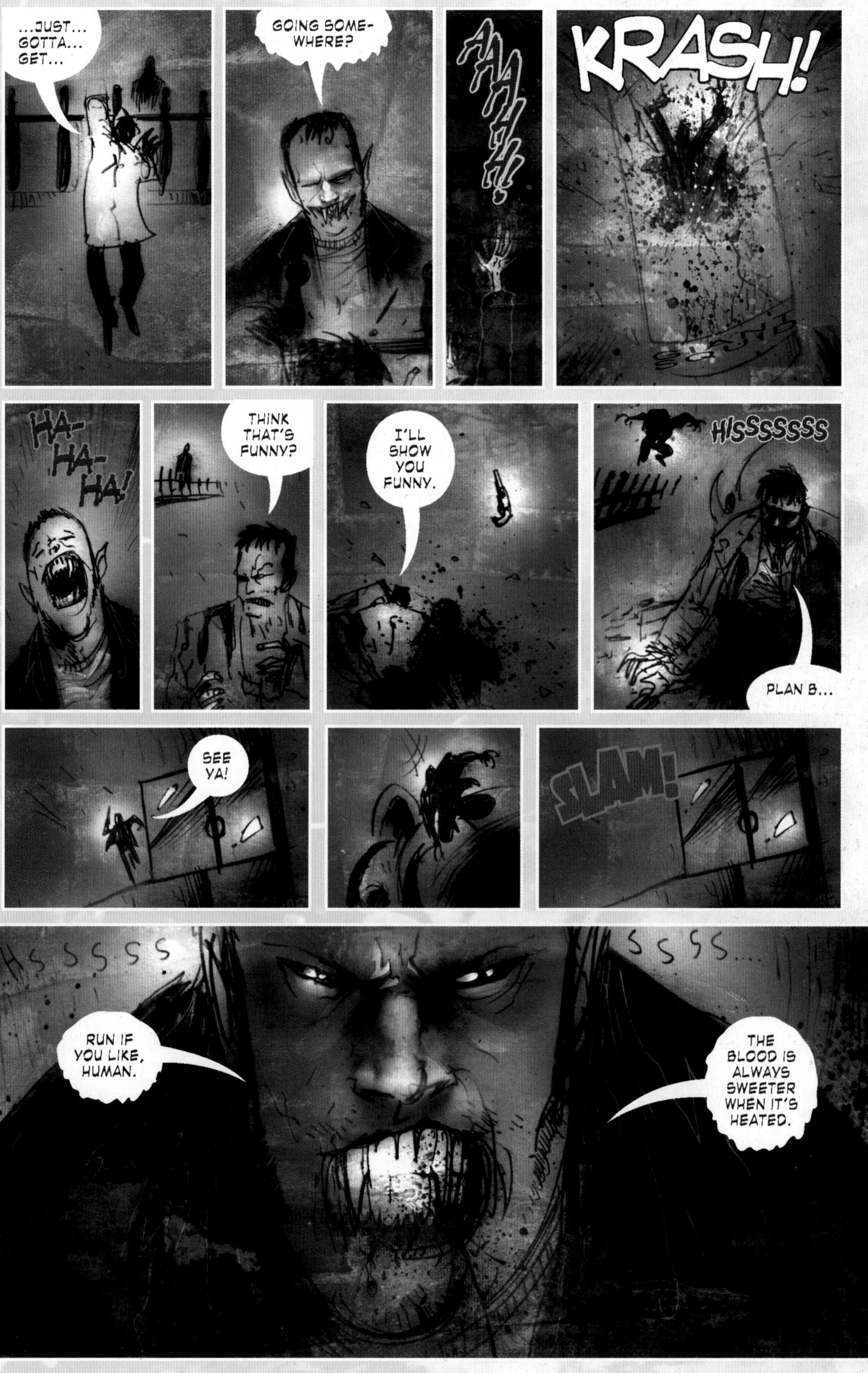
...JUST... GOTTA... GET...
GOING SOME-WHERE?
AAAHHH!!
KRASH!
HA-HA-HA!
THINK THAT'S FUNNY?
I'LL SHOW YOU FUNNY.
HISSSSSSS
PLAN B...
SEE YA!
SLAM!
HSSSSS
SSSS....
RUN IF YOU LIKE, HUMAN.
THE BLOOD IS ALWAYS SWEETER WHEN IT'S HEATED.

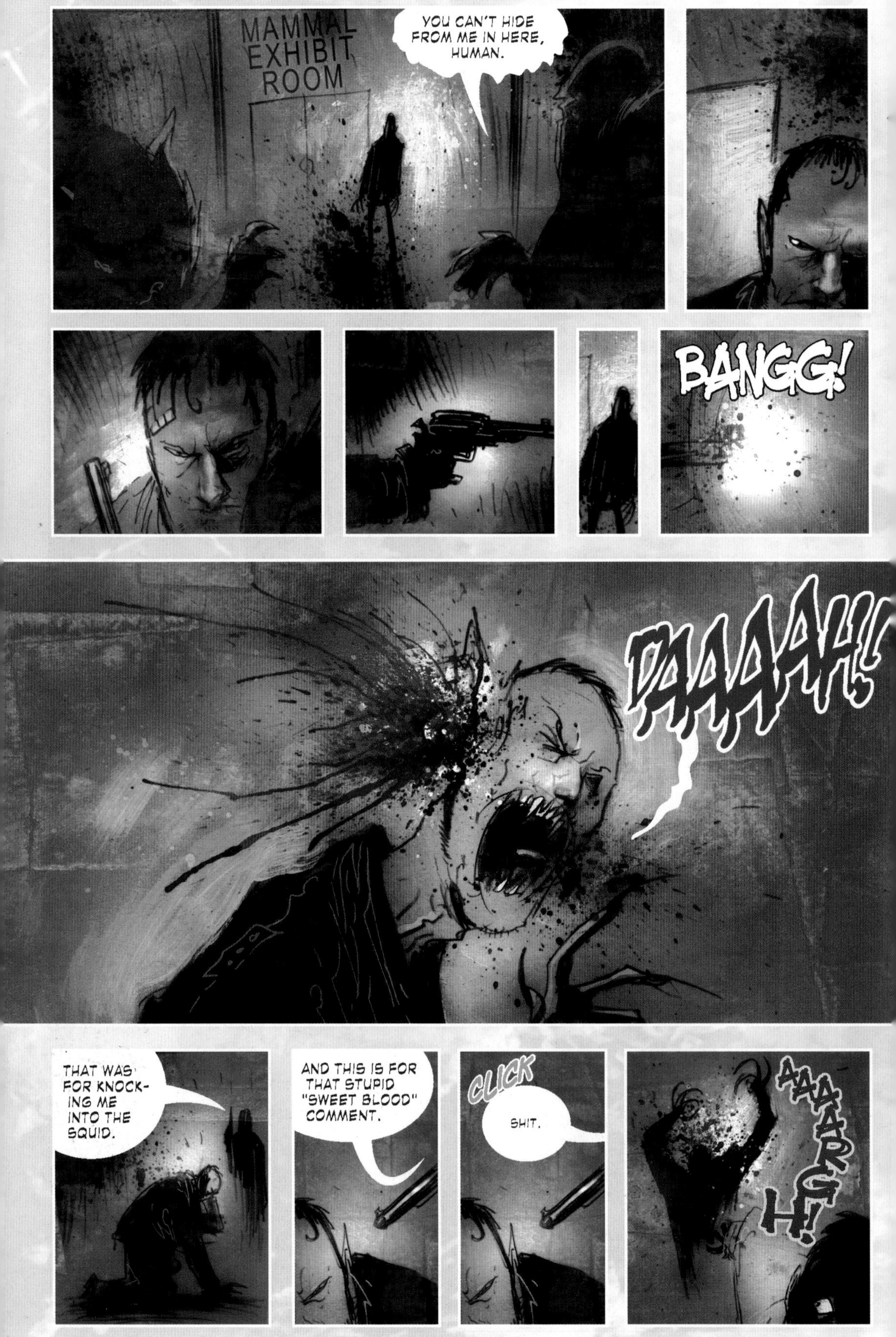
MAMMAL EXHIBIT ROOM
YOU CAN'T HIDE FROM ME IN HERE, HUMAN.
BANGG!
DAAAAH!!
THAT WAS FOR KNOCK-ING ME INTO THE SQUID.
AND THIS IS FOR THAT STUPID "SWEET BLOOD" COMMENT.
CLICK
SHIT.
AAAARGH!

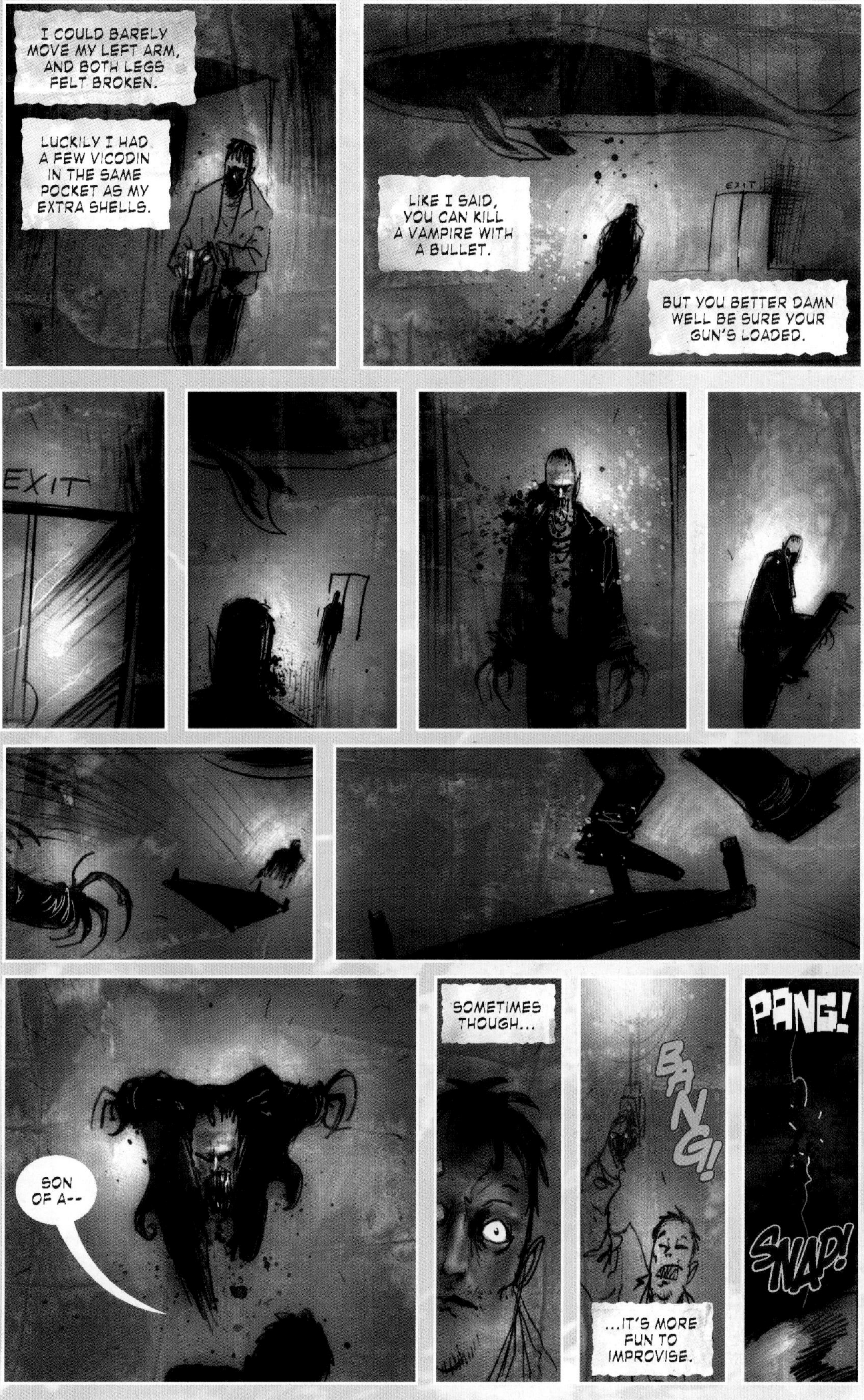
I COULD BARELY MOVE MY LEFT ARM, AND BOTH LEGS FELT BROKEN.
LUCKILY I HAD A FEW VICODIN IN THE SAME POCKET AS MY EXTRA SHELLS.
LIKE I SAID, YOU CAN KILL A VAMPIRE WITH A BULLET.
EXIT
BUT YOU BETTER DAMN WELL BE SURE YOUR GUN'S LOADED.
EXIT
SON OF A--
SOMETIMES THOUGH...
BANG!
...IT'S MORE FUN TO IMPROVISE.
PANG!
SNAP!

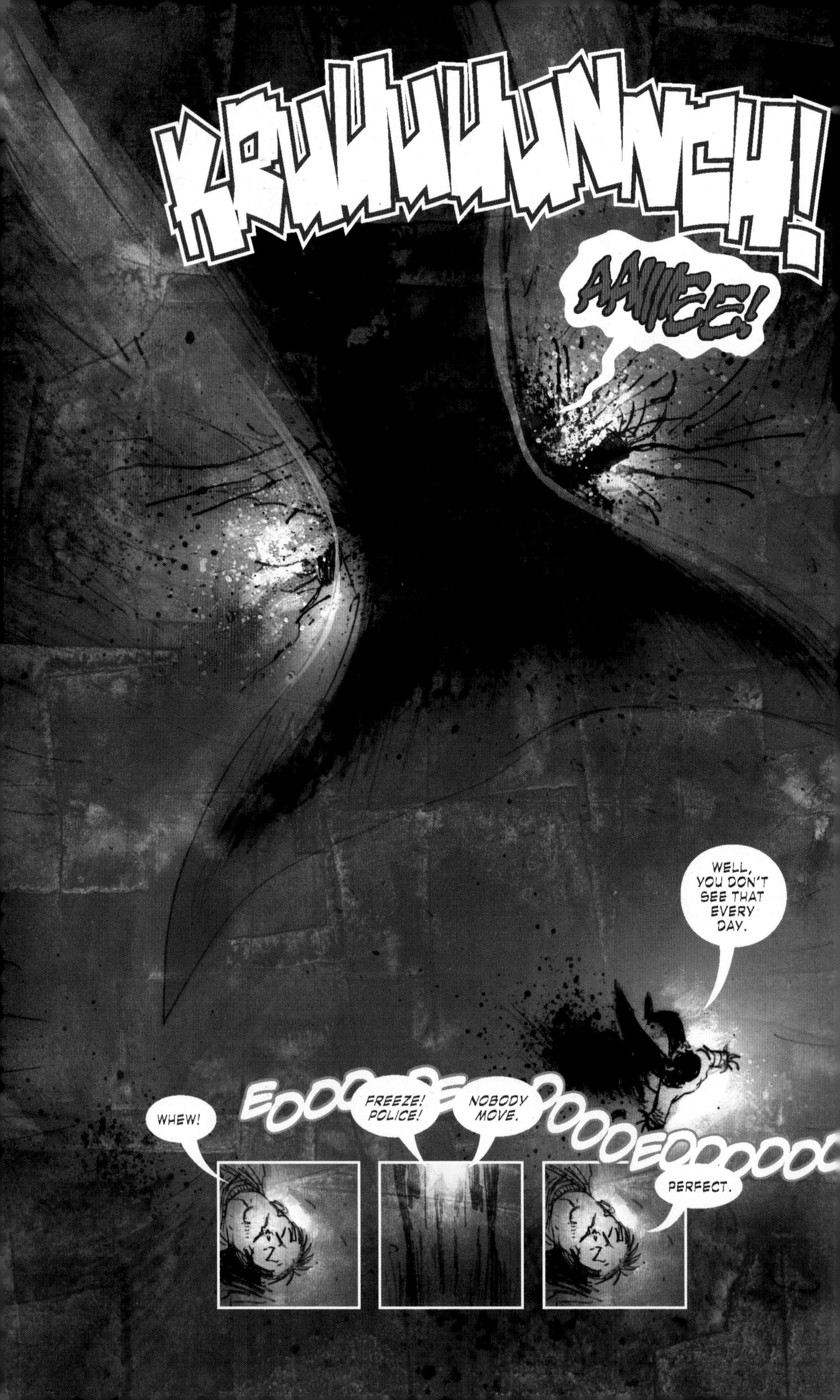
KRUUUUUNNCH!
AAIIIEE!
WELL, YOU DON'T SEE THAT EVERY DAY.
WHEW!
FREEZE! POLICE!
NOBODY MOVE.
PERFECT.

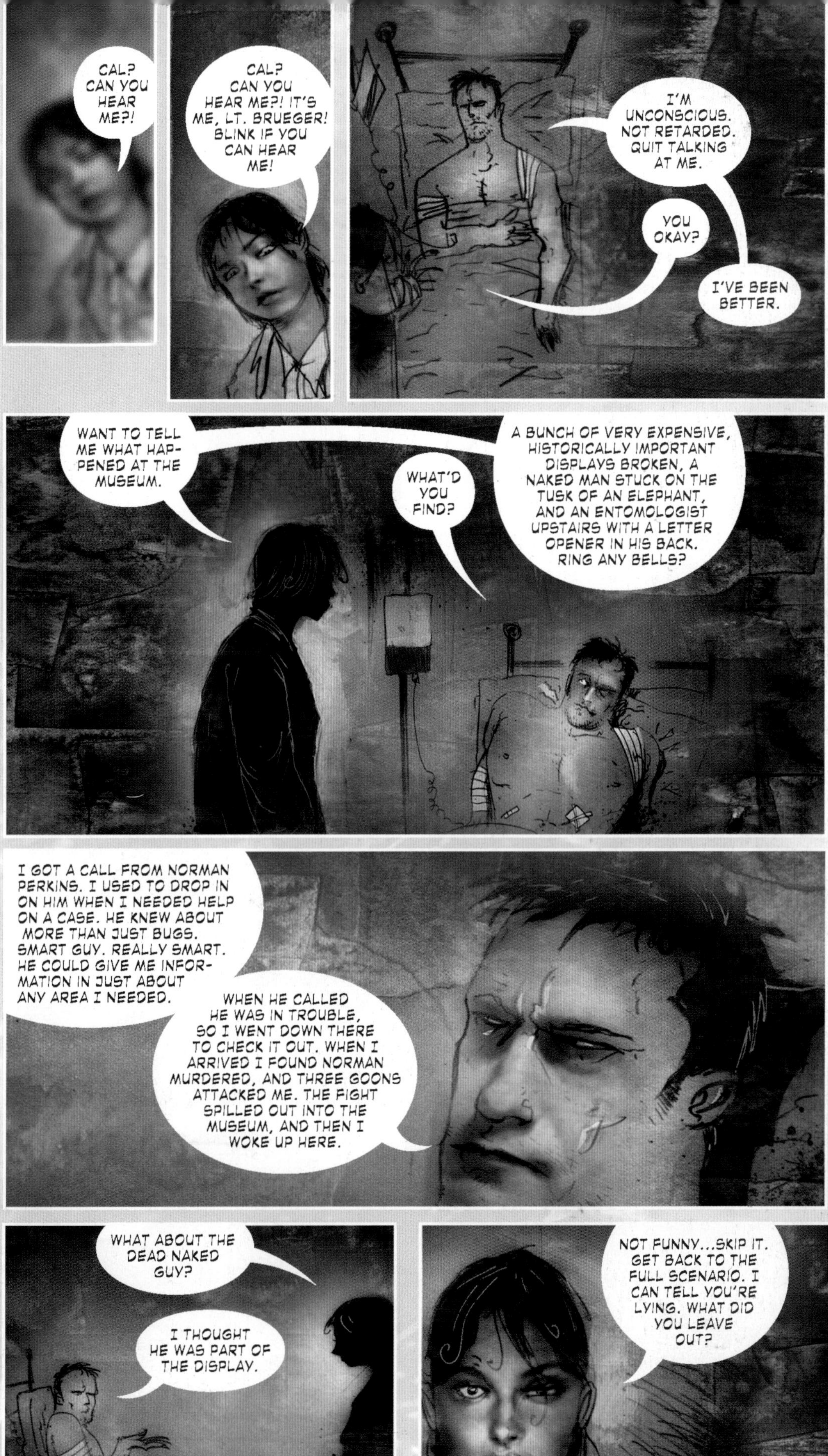
CAL? CAN YOU HEAR ME?!
CAL? CAN YOU HEAR ME?! IT'S ME, LT. BRUEGER! BLINK IF YOU CAN HEAR ME!
I'M UNCONSCIOUS. NOT RETARDED. QUIT TALKING AT ME.
YOU OKAY?
I'VE BEEN BETTER.
WANT TO TELL ME WHAT HAPPENED AT THE MUSEUM.
WHAT'D YOU FIND?
A BUNCH OF VERY EXPENSIVE, HISTORICALLY IMPORTANT DISPLAYS BROKEN, A NAKED MAN STUCK ON THE TUSK OF AN ELEPHANT, AND AN ENTOMOLOGIST UPSTAIRS WITH A LETTER OPENER IN HIS BACK. RING ANY BELLS?
I GOT A CALL FROM NORMAN PERKINS. I USED TO DROP IN ON HIM WHEN I NEEDED HELP ON A CASE. HE KNEW ABOUT MORE THAN JUST BUGS. SMART GUY. REALLY SMART. HE COULD GIVE ME INFORMATION IN JUST ABOUT ANY AREA I NEEDED.
WHEN HE CALLED HE WAS IN TROUBLE, SO I WENT DOWN THERE TO CHECK IT OUT. WHEN I ARRIVED I FOUND NORMAN MURDERED, AND THREE GOONS ATTACKED ME. THE FIGHT SPILLED OUT INTO THE MUSEUM, AND THEN I WOKE UP HERE.
WHAT ABOUT THE DEAD NAKED GUY?
I THOUGHT HE WAS PART OF THE DISPLAY.
NOT FUNNY...SKIP IT. GET BACK TO THE FULL SCENARIO. I CAN TELL YOU'RE LYING. WHAT DID YOU LEAVE OUT?

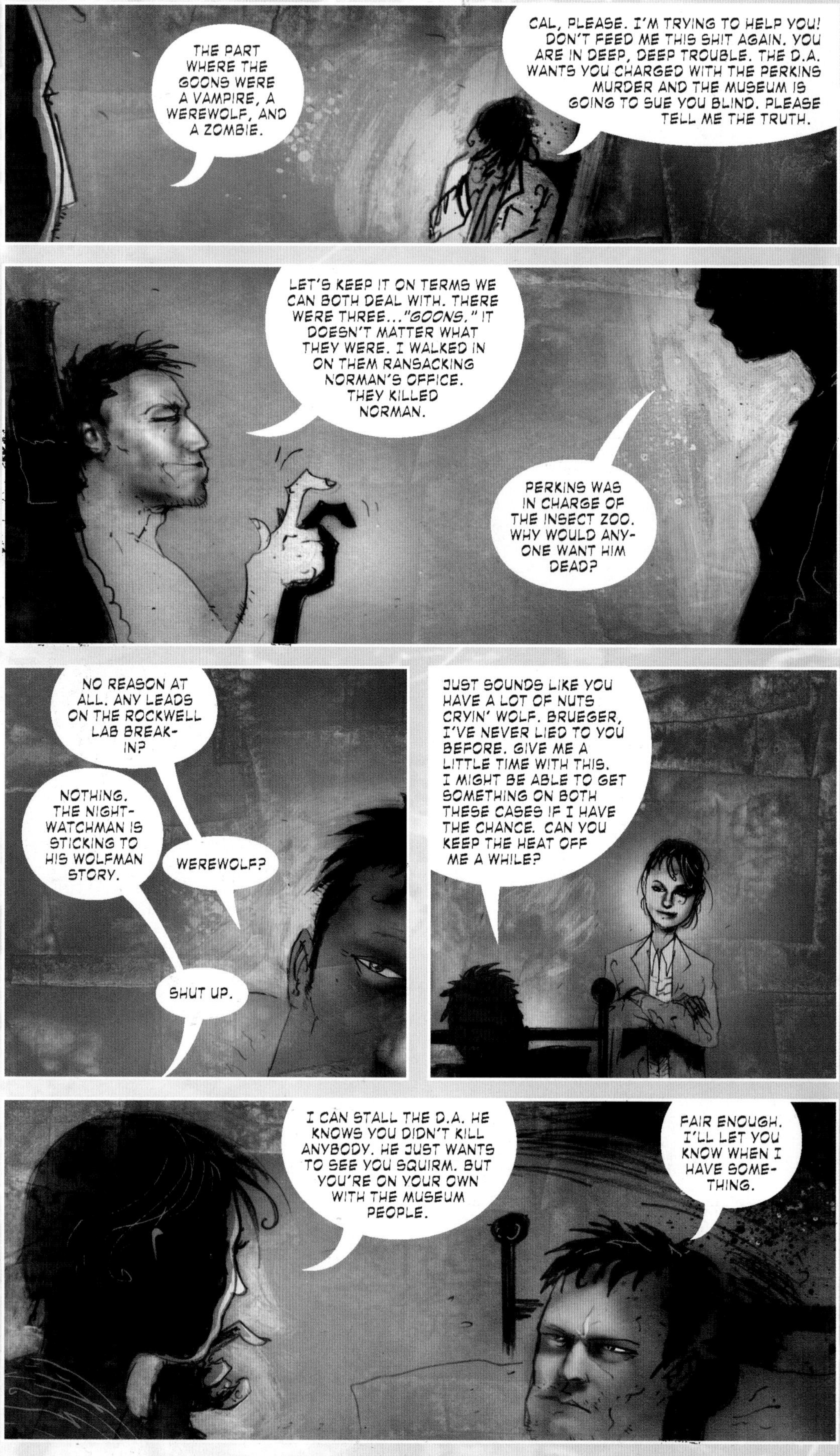
THE PART WHERE THE GOONS WERE A VAMPIRE, A WEREWOLF, AND A ZOMBIE.
CAL, PLEASE. I'M TRYING TO HELP YOU! DON'T FEED ME THIS SHIT AGAIN. YOU ARE IN DEEP, DEEP TROUBLE. THE D.A. WANTS YOU CHARGED WITH THE PERKINS MURDER AND THE MUSEUM IS GOING TO SUE YOU BLIND. PLEASE TELL ME THE TRUTH.
LET'S KEEP IT ON TERMS WE CAN BOTH DEAL WITH. THERE WERE THREE..."GOONS." IT DOESN'T MATTER WHAT THEY WERE. I WALKED IN ON THEM RANSACKING NORMAN'S OFFICE. THEY KILLED NORMAN.
PERKINS WAS IN CHARGE OF THE INSECT ZOO. WHY WOULD ANY-ONE WANT HIM DEAD?
NO REASON AT ALL. ANY LEADS ON THE ROCKWELL LAB BREAK-IN?
NOTHING. THE NIGHT-WATCHMAN IS STICKING TO HIS WOLFMAN STORY.
WEREWOLF?
SHUT UP.
JUST SOUNDS LIKE YOU HAVE A LOT OF NUTS CRYIN' WOLF. BRUEGER, I'VE NEVER LIED TO YOU BEFORE. GIVE ME A LITTLE TIME WITH THIS. I MIGHT BE ABLE TO GET SOMETHING ON BOTH THESE CASES IF I HAVE THE CHANCE. CAN YOU KEEP THE HEAT OFF ME A WHILE?
I CAN STALL THE D.A. HE KNOWS YOU DIDN'T KILL ANYBODY. HE JUST WANTS TO SEE YOU SQUIRM. BUT YOU'RE ON YOUR OWN WITH THE MUSEUM PEOPLE.
FAIR ENOUGH. I'LL LET YOU KNOW WHEN I HAVE SOME-THING.

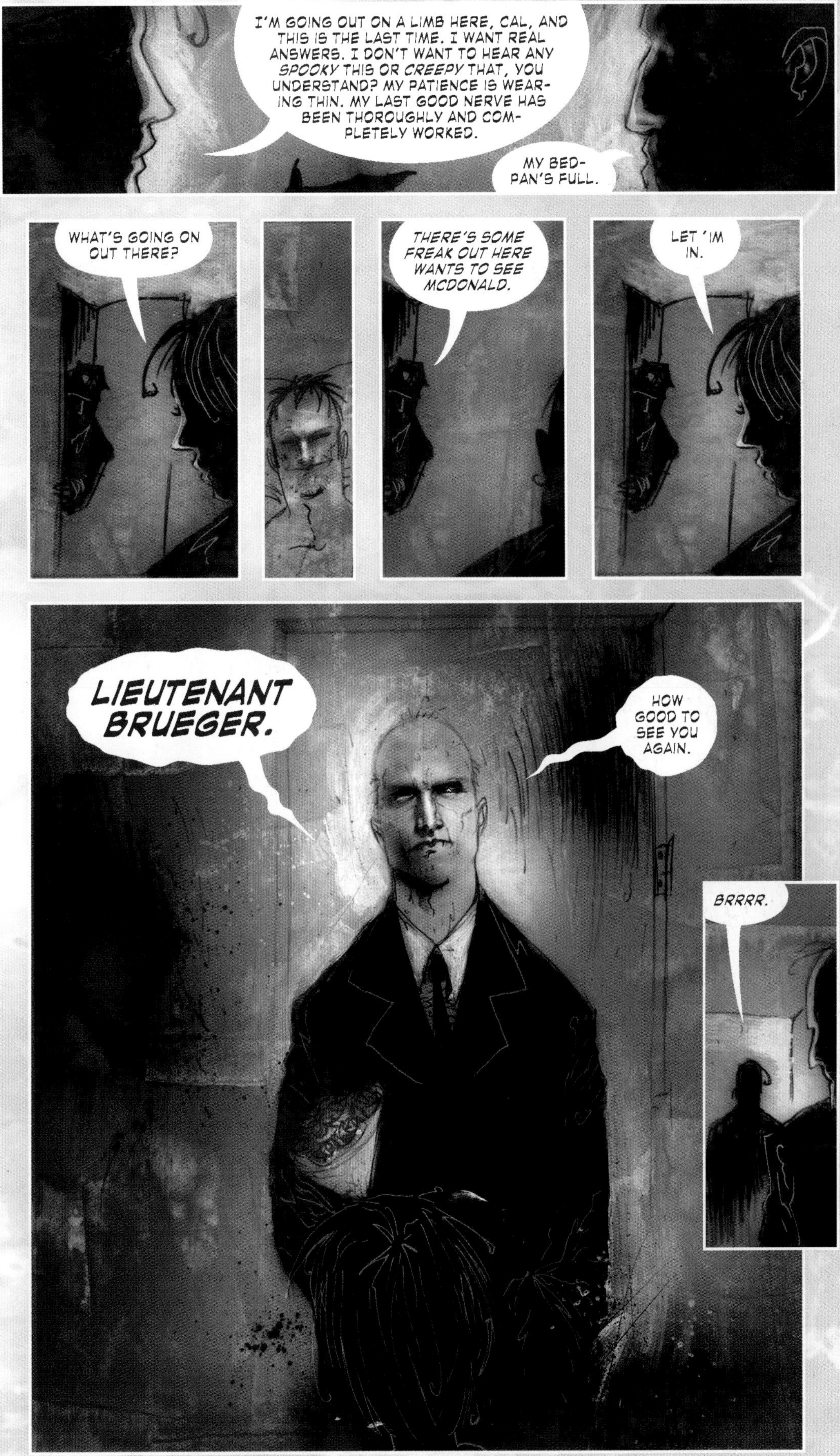

I'M GOING OUT ON A LIMB HERE, CAL, AND THIS IS THE LAST TIME. I WANT REAL ANSWERS. I DON'T WANT TO HEAR ANY *SPOOKY* THIS OR *CREEPY* THAT, YOU UNDERSTAND? MY PATIENCE IS WEAR-ING THIN. MY LAST GOOD NERVE HAS BEEN THOROUGHLY AND COM-PLETELY WORKED.
MY BED-PAN'S FULL.
WHAT'S GOING ON OUT THERE?
THERE'S SOME FREAK OUT HERE WANTS TO SEE MCDONALD.
LET 'IM IN.
LIEUTENANT BRUEGER.
HOW GOOD TO SEE YOU AGAIN.
BRRRR.

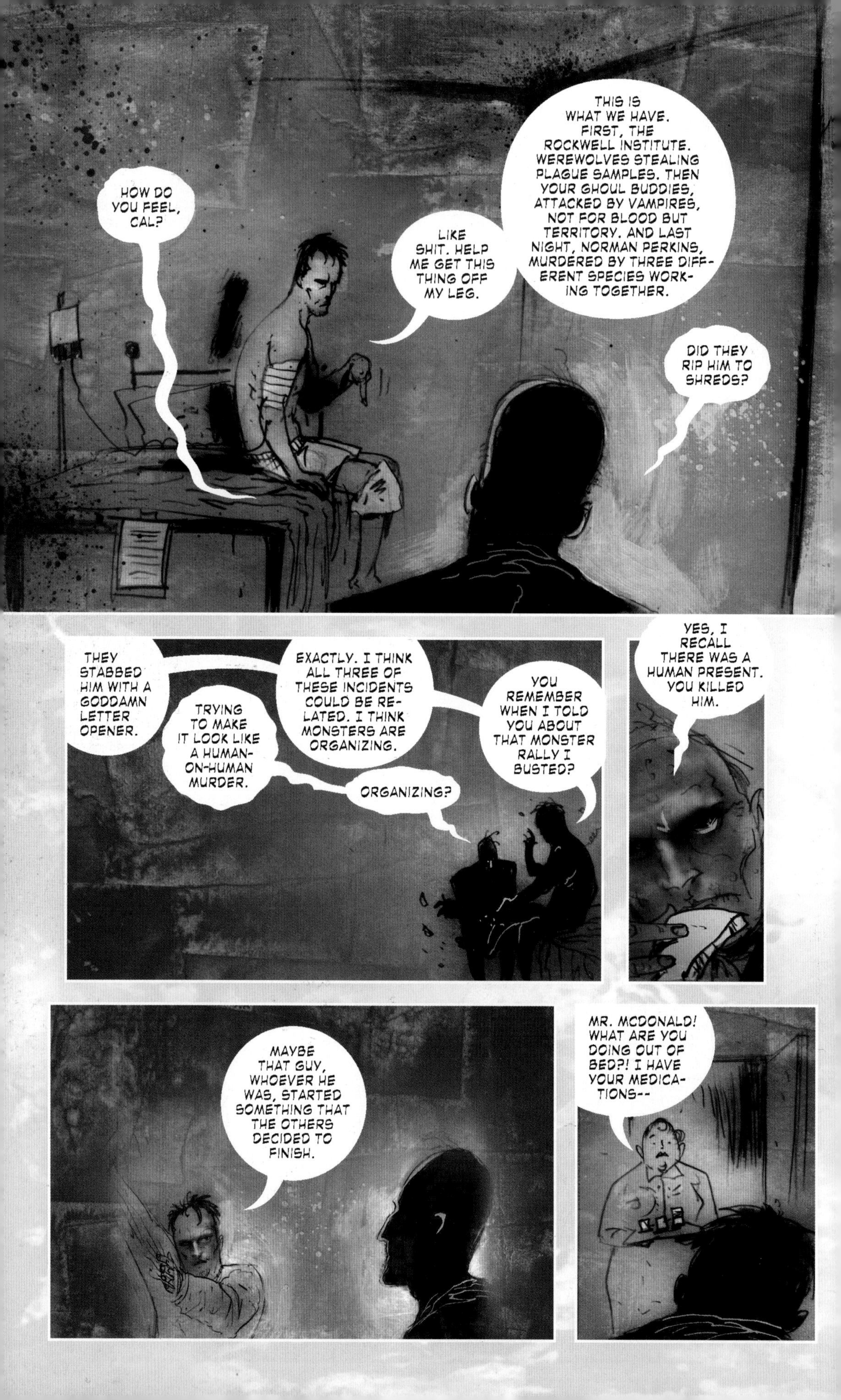
HOW DO YOU FEEL, CAL?
LIKE SHIT. HELP ME GET THIS THING OFF MY LEG.
THIS IS WHAT WE HAVE. FIRST, THE ROCKWELL INSTITUTE. WEREWOLVES STEALING PLAGUE SAMPLES. THEN YOUR GHOUL BUDDIES, ATTACKED BY VAMPIRES, NOT FOR BLOOD BUT TERRITORY. AND LAST NIGHT, NORMAN PERKINS, MURDERED BY THREE DIFF-ERENT SPECIES WORK-ING TOGETHER.
DID THEY RIP HIM TO SHREDS?
THEY STABBED HIM WITH A GODDAMN LETTER OPENER.
TRYING TO MAKE IT LOOK LIKE A HUMAN-ON-HUMAN MURDER.
EXACTLY. I THINK ALL THREE OF THESE INCIDENTS COULD BE RE-LATED. I THINK MONSTERS ARE ORGANIZING.
ORGANIZING?
YOU REMEMBER WHEN I TOLD YOU ABOUT THAT MONSTER RALLY I BUSTED?
YES, I RECALL THERE WAS A HUMAN PRESENT. YOU KILLED HIM.
MAYBE THAT GUY, WHOEVER HE WAS, STARTED SOMETHING THAT THE OTHERS DECIDED TO FINISH.
MR. MCDONALD! WHAT ARE YOU DOING OUT OF BED?! I HAVE YOUR MEDICA-TIONS--

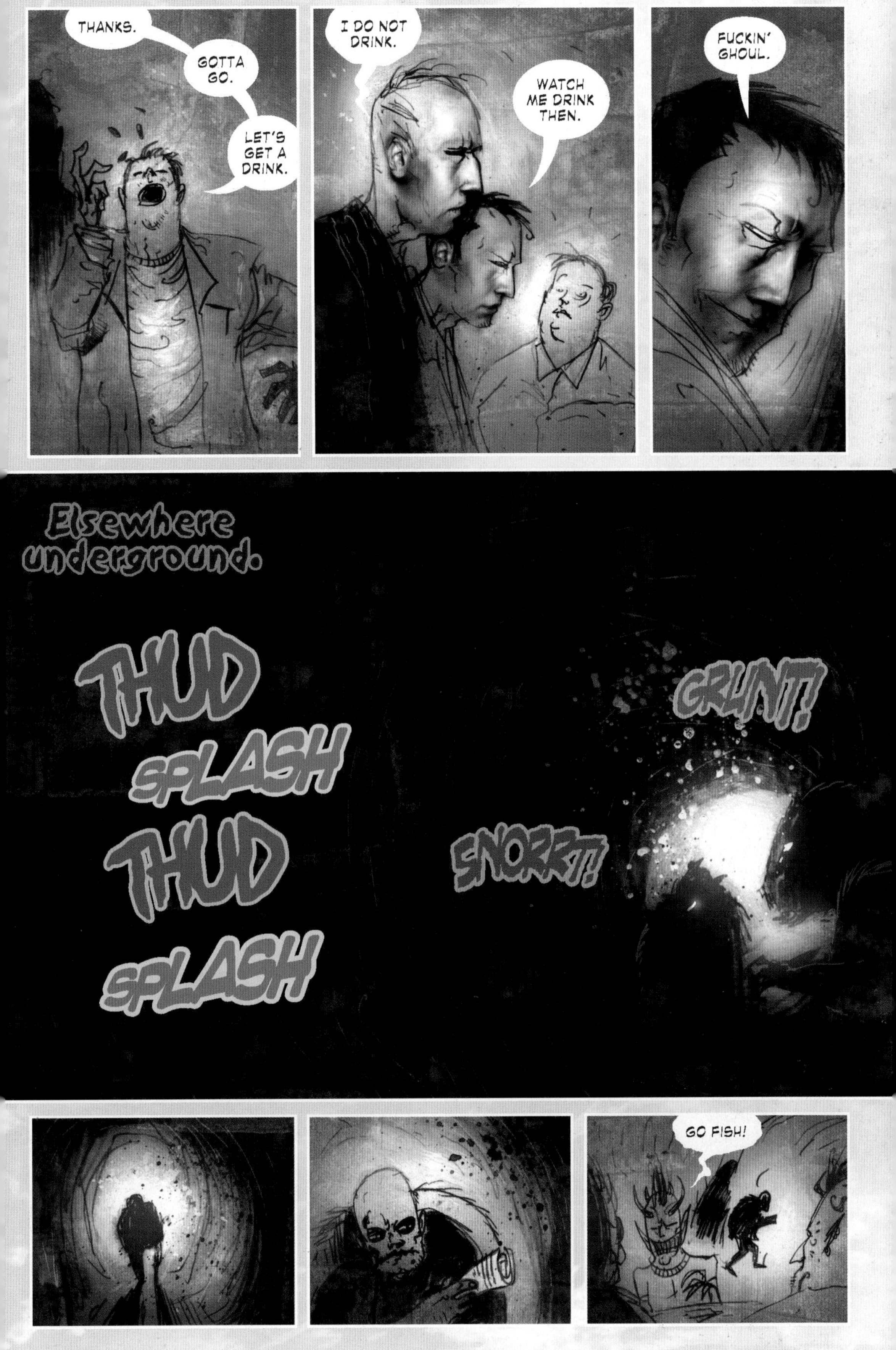
THANKS.
GOTTA GO.
LET'S GET A DRINK.
I DO NOT DRINK.
WATCH ME DRINK THEN.
FUCKIN' GHOUL.
Elsewhere underground.
THUD
SPLASH
THUD
SPLASH
SNORRT!
GRUNT!
GO FISH!

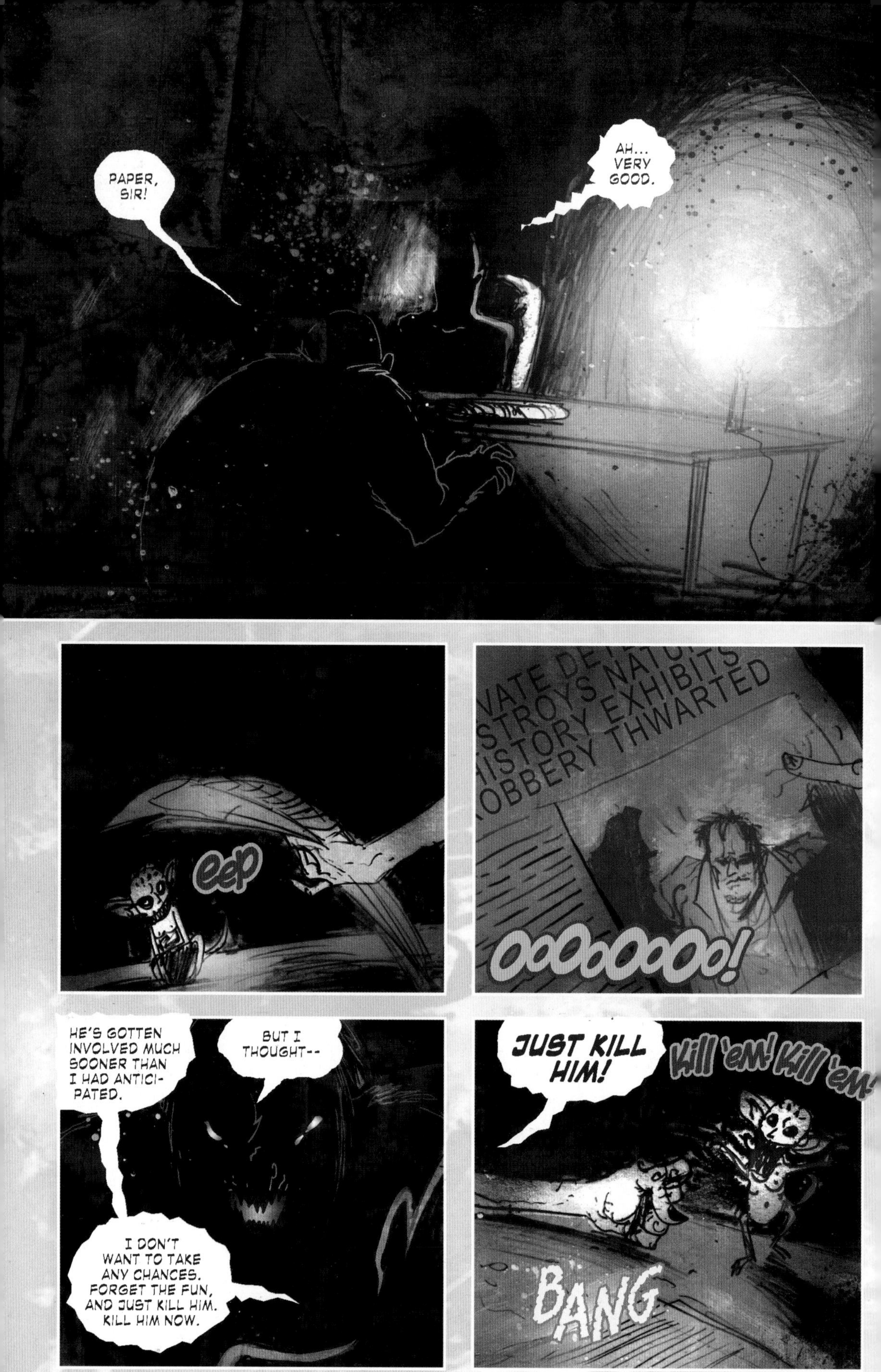
PAPER, SIR!
AH... VERY GOOD.
eep
VATE DE
STROYS NATU
ISTORY EXHIBITS
OBBERY THWARTED
OOOoOOOOo!
HE'S GOTTEN INVOLVED MUCH SOONER THAN I HAD ANTICI-PATED.
BUT I THOUGHT--
I DON'T WANT TO TAKE ANY CHANCES. FORGET THE FUN, AND JUST KILL HIM. KILL HIM NOW.
JUST KILL HIM!
Kill 'em! Kill 'em!
BANG

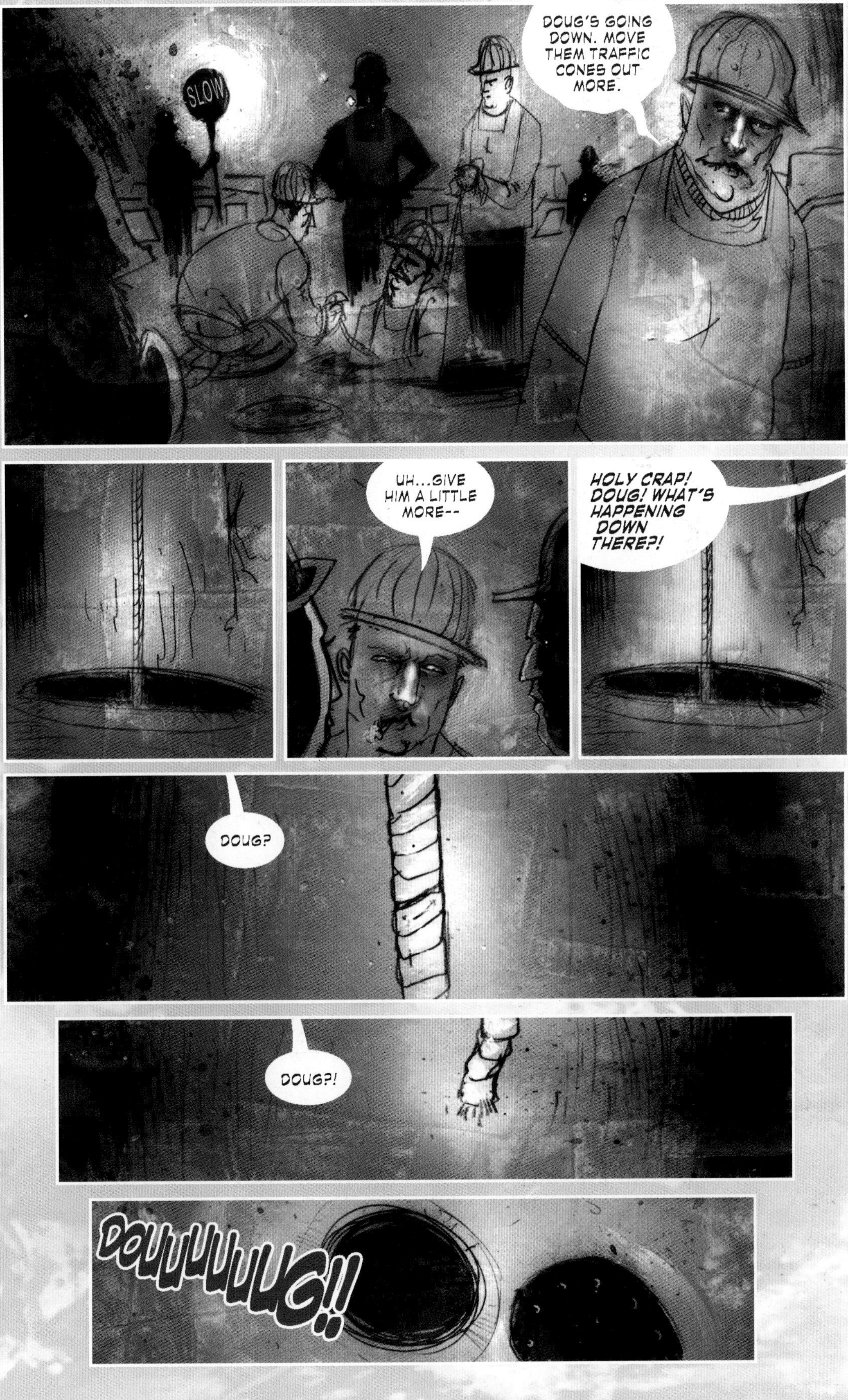
SLOW
DOUG'S GOING DOWN. MOVE THEM TRAFFIC CONES OUT MORE.
UH...GIVE HIM A LITTLE MORE--
HOLY CRAP! DOUG! WHAT'S HAPPENING DOWN THERE?!
DOUG?
DOUG?!
DOUUUUUUG!!

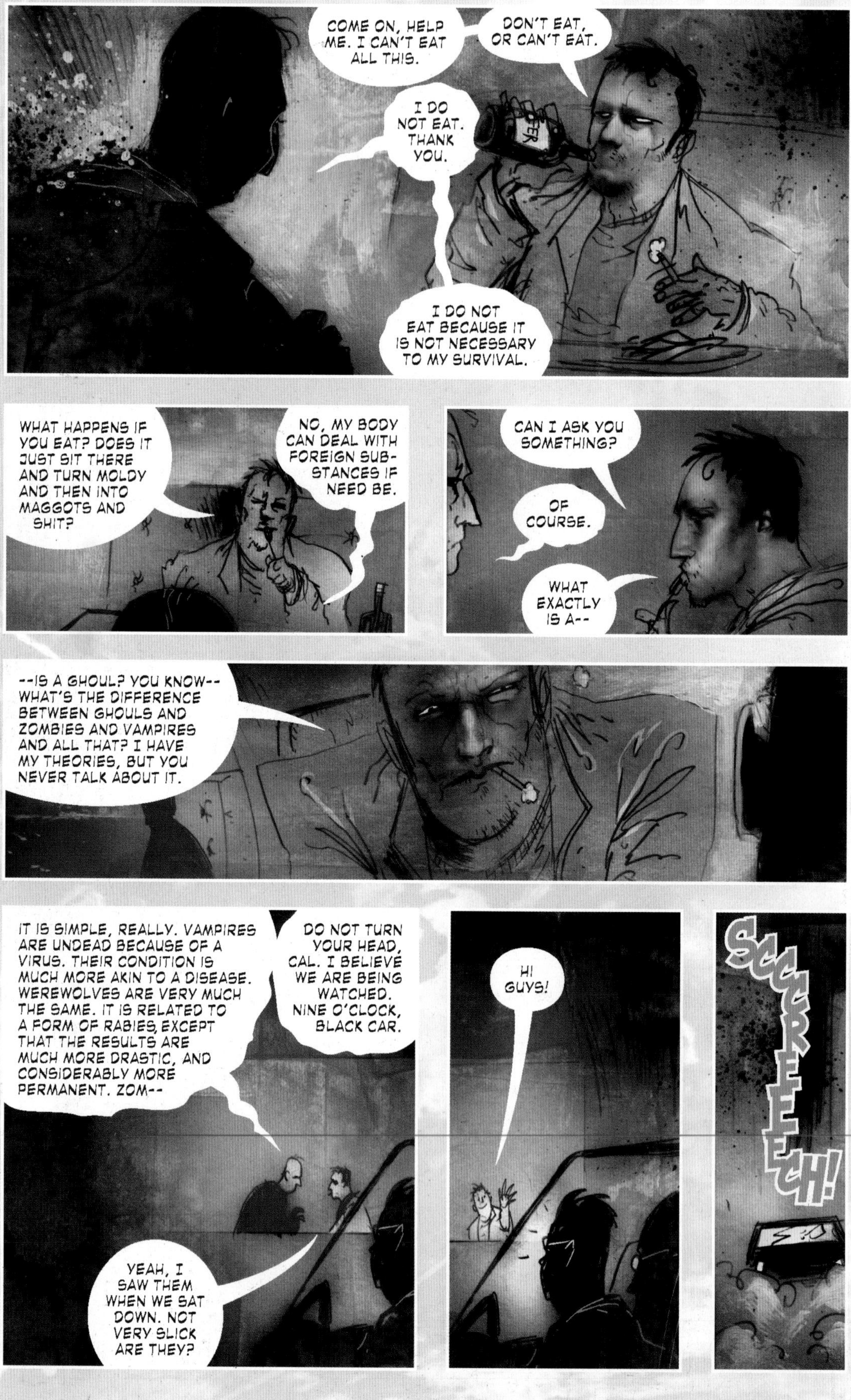
COME ON, HELP ME. I CAN'T EAT ALL THIS.
DON'T EAT, OR CAN'T EAT.
I DO NOT EAT. THANK YOU.
I DO NOT EAT BECAUSE IT IS NOT NECESSARY TO MY SURVIVAL.
WHAT HAPPENS IF YOU EAT? DOES IT JUST SIT THERE AND TURN MOLDY AND THEN INTO MAGGOTS AND SHIT?
NO, MY BODY CAN DEAL WITH FOREIGN SUB-STANCES IF NEED BE.
CAN I ASK YOU SOMETHING?
OF COURSE.
WHAT EXACTLY IS A--
--IS A GHOUL? YOU KNOW-- WHAT'S THE DIFFERENCE BETWEEN GHOULS AND ZOMBIES AND VAMPIRES AND ALL THAT? I HAVE MY THEORIES, BUT YOU NEVER TALK ABOUT IT.
IT IS SIMPLE, REALLY. VAMPIRES ARE UNDEAD BECAUSE OF A VIRUS. THEIR CONDITION IS MUCH MORE AKIN TO A DISEASE. WEREWOLVES ARE VERY MUCH THE SAME. IT IS RELATED TO A FORM OF RABIES, EXCEPT THAT THE RESULTS ARE MUCH MORE DRASTIC, AND CONSIDERABLY MORE PERMANENT. ZOM--
DO NOT TURN YOUR HEAD, CAL. I BELIEVE WE ARE BEING WATCHED. NINE O'CLOCK, BLACK CAR.
YEAH, I SAW THEM WHEN WE SAT DOWN. NOT VERY SLICK ARE THEY?
HI GUYS!
SCCCREEECH!

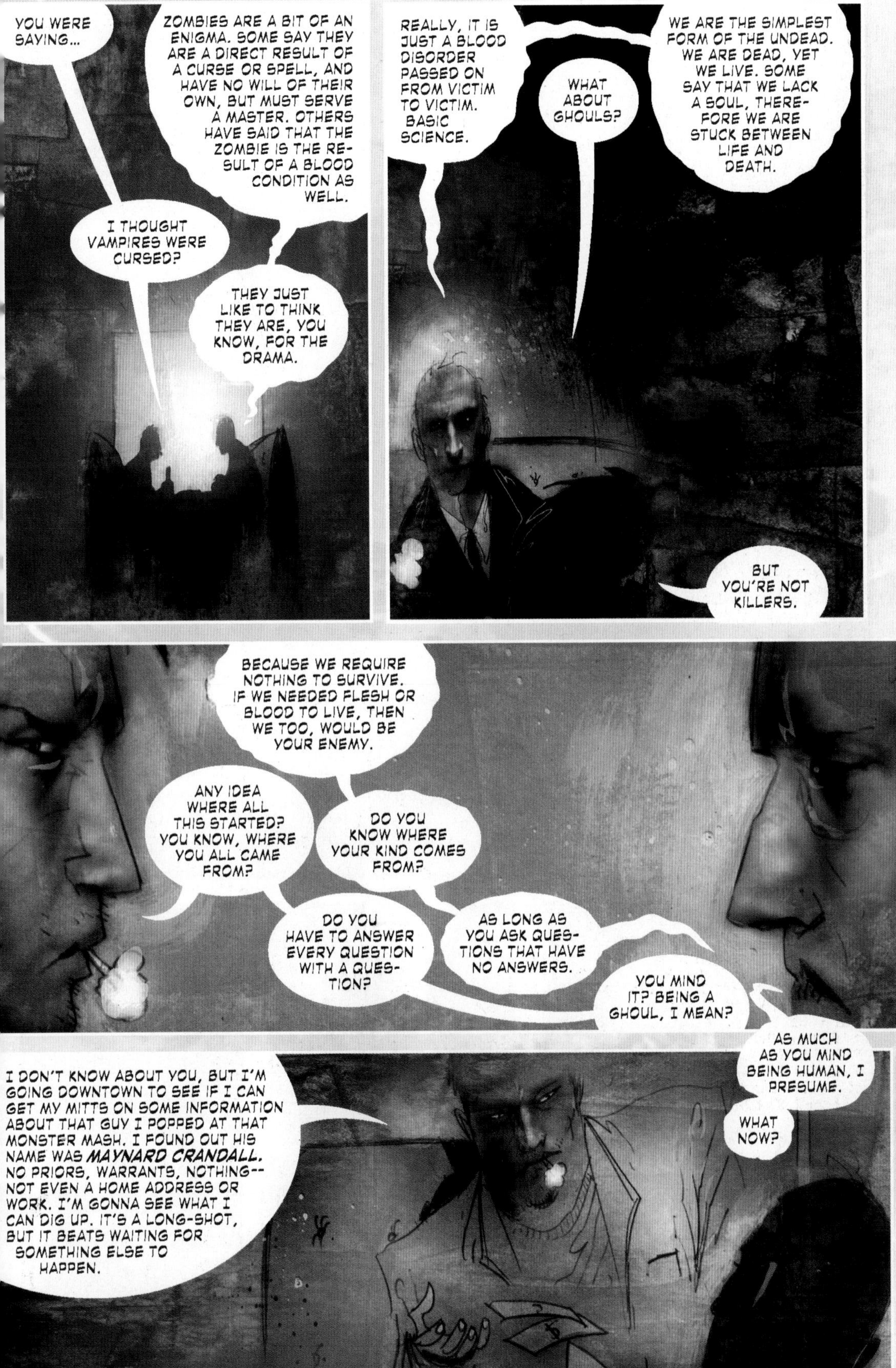

YOU WERE SAYING...
ZOMBIES ARE A BIT OF AN ENIGMA. SOME SAY THEY ARE A DIRECT RESULT OF A CURSE OR SPELL, AND HAVE NO WILL OF THEIR OWN, BUT MUST SERVE A MASTER. OTHERS HAVE SAID THAT THE ZOMBIE IS THE RESULT OF A BLOOD CONDITION AS WELL.
I THOUGHT VAMPIRES WERE CURSED?
THEY JUST LIKE TO THINK THEY ARE, YOU KNOW, FOR THE DRAMA.
REALLY, IT IS JUST A BLOOD DISORDER PASSED ON FROM VICTIM TO VICTIM. BASIC SCIENCE.
WHAT ABOUT GHOULS?
WE ARE THE SIMPLEST FORM OF THE UNDEAD. WE ARE DEAD, YET WE LIVE. SOME SAY THAT WE LACK A SOUL, THEREFORE WE ARE STUCK BETWEEN LIFE AND DEATH.
BUT YOU'RE NOT KILLERS.
BECAUSE WE REQUIRE NOTHING TO SURVIVE. IF WE NEEDED FLESH OR BLOOD TO LIVE, THEN WE TOO, WOULD BE YOUR ENEMY.
ANY IDEA WHERE ALL THIS STARTED? YOU KNOW, WHERE YOU ALL CAME FROM?
DO YOU KNOW WHERE YOUR KIND COMES FROM?
DO YOU HAVE TO ANSWER EVERY QUESTION WITH A QUESTION?
AS LONG AS YOU ASK QUESTIONS THAT HAVE NO ANSWERS.
YOU MIND IT? BEING A GHOUL, I MEAN?
AS MUCH AS YOU MIND BEING HUMAN, I PRESUME.
WHAT NOW?
I DON'T KNOW ABOUT YOU, BUT I'M GOING DOWNTOWN TO SEE IF I CAN GET MY MITTS ON SOME INFORMATION ABOUT THAT GUY I POPPED AT THAT MONSTER MASH. I FOUND OUT HIS NAME WAS MAYNARD CRANDALL. NO PRIORS, WARRANTS, NOTHING-- NOT EVEN A HOME ADDRESS OR WORK. I'M GONNA SEE WHAT I CAN DIG UP. IT'S A LONG-SHOT, BUT IT BEATS WAITING FOR SOMETHING ELSE TO HAPPEN.

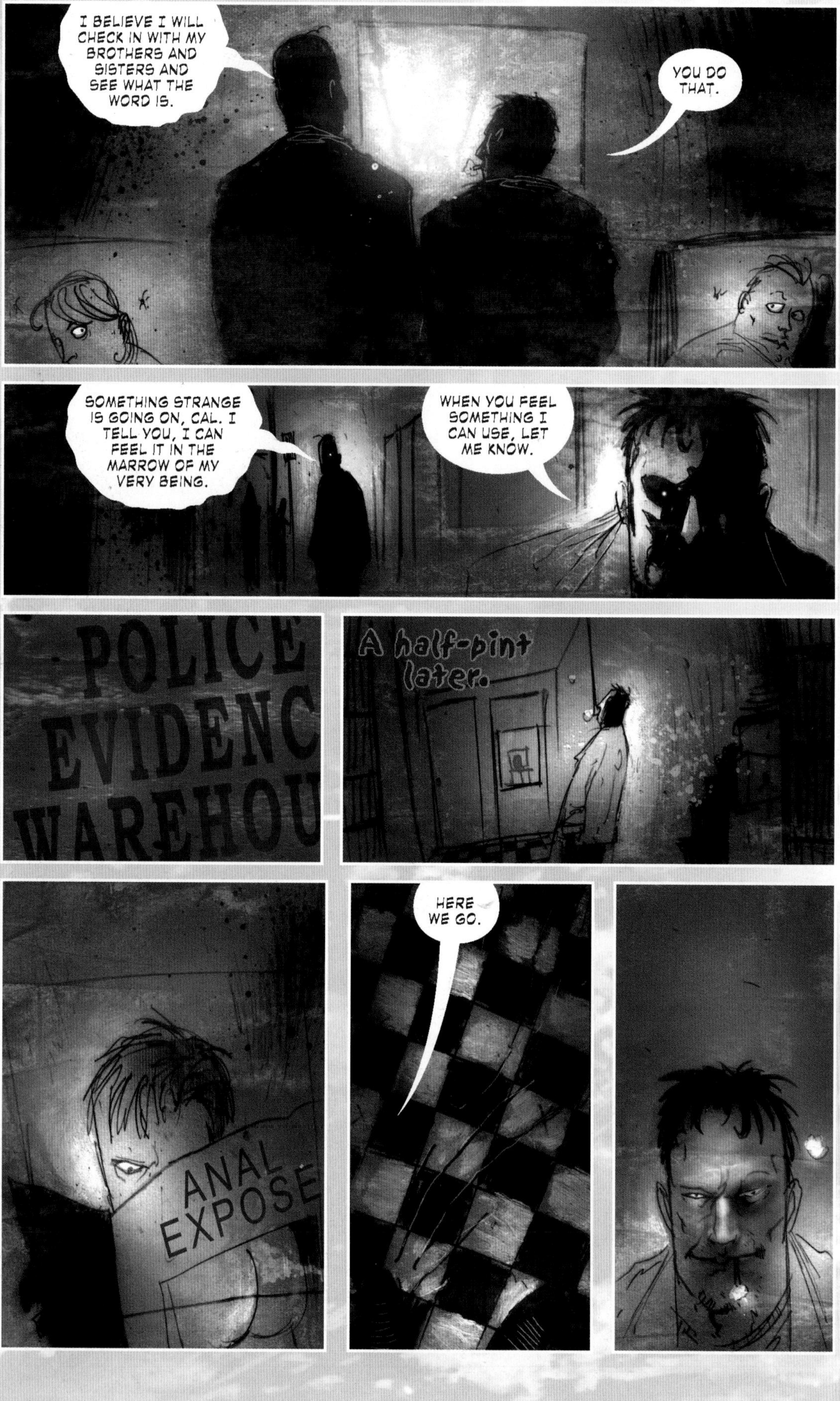
I BELIEVE I WILL CHECK IN WITH MY BROTHERS AND SISTERS AND SEE WHAT THE WORD IS.
YOU DO THAT.
SOMETHING STRANGE IS GOING ON, CAL. I TELL YOU, I CAN FEEL IT IN THE MARROW OF MY VERY BEING.
WHEN YOU FEEL SOMETHING I CAN USE, LET ME KNOW.
POLICE EVIDENC WAREHOU
A half-pint later.
ANAL EXPOSE
HERE WE GO.

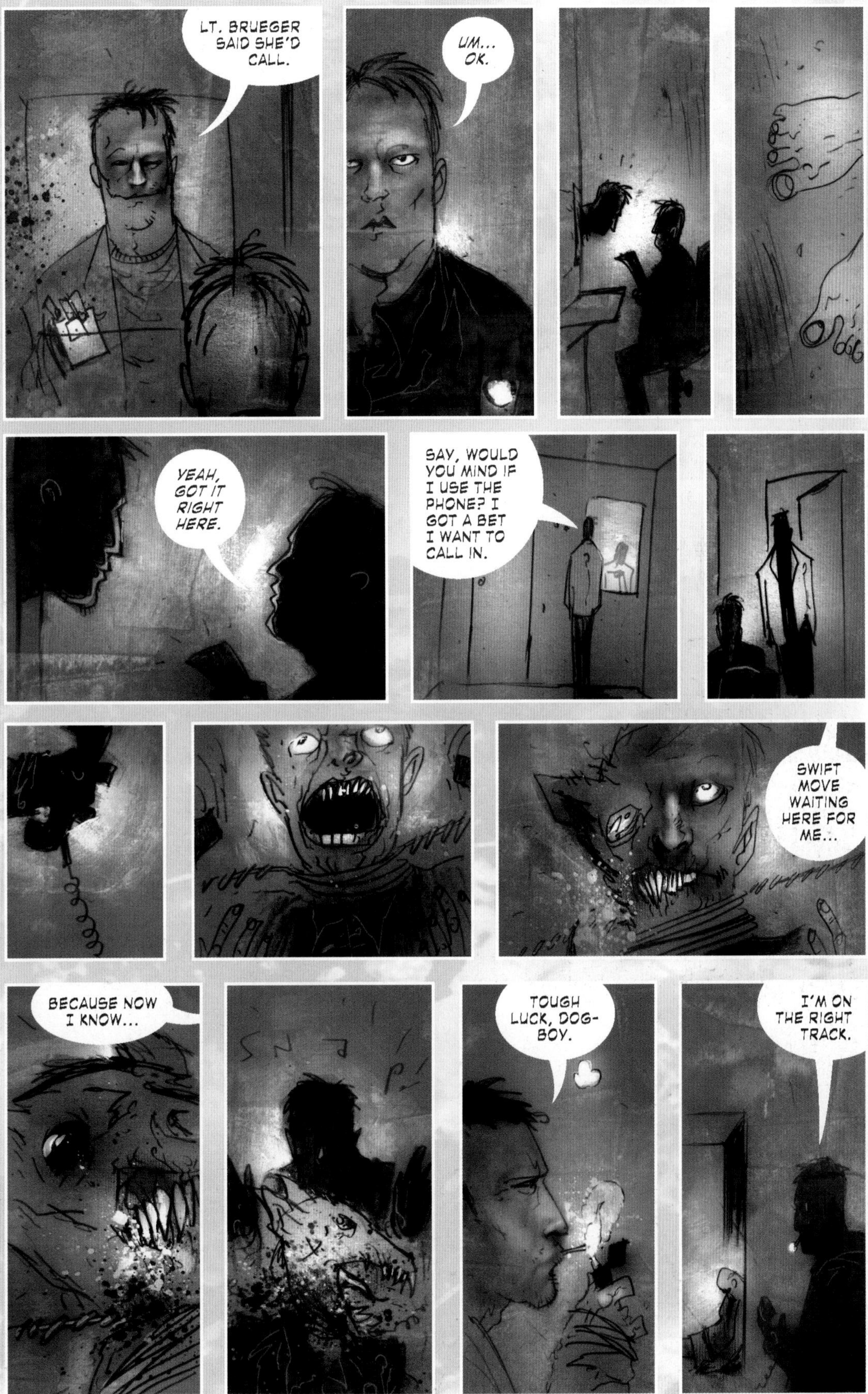
LT. BRUEGER SAID SHE'D CALL.
UM... OK.
YEAH, GOT IT RIGHT HERE.
SAY, WOULD YOU MIND IF I USE THE PHONE? I GOT A BET I WANT TO CALL IN.
SWIFT MOVE WAITING HERE FOR ME...
BECAUSE NOW I KNOW...
TOUGH LUCK, DOG-BOY.
I'M ON THE RIGHT TRACK.

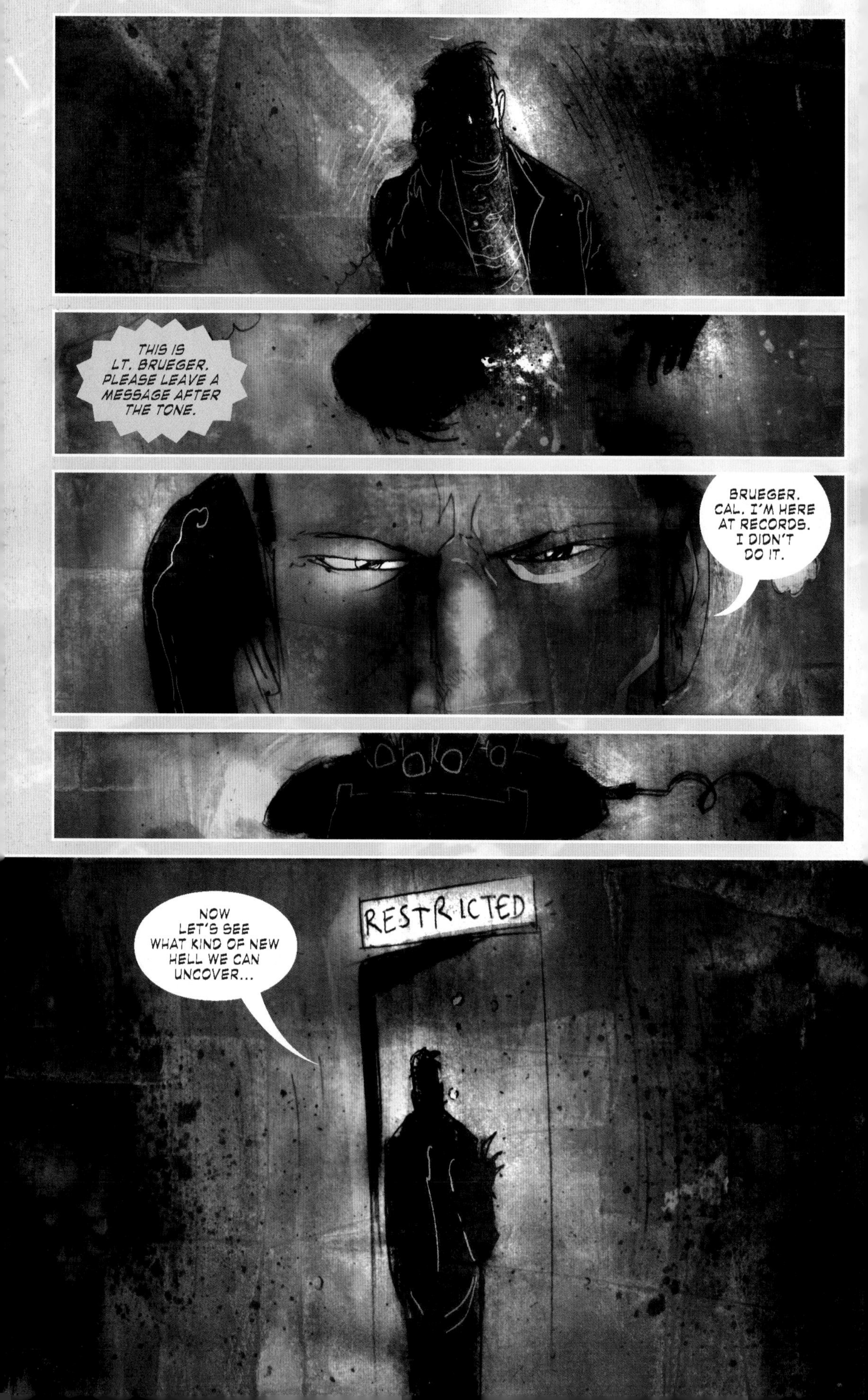
THIS IS LT. BRUEGER. PLEASE LEAVE A MESSAGE AFTER THE TONE.
BRUEGER. CAL. I'M HERE AT RECORDS. I DIDN'T DO IT.
RESTRICTED
NOW LET'S SEE WHAT KIND OF NEW HELL WE CAN UNCOVER...

CHAPTER THREE
Geekenstein

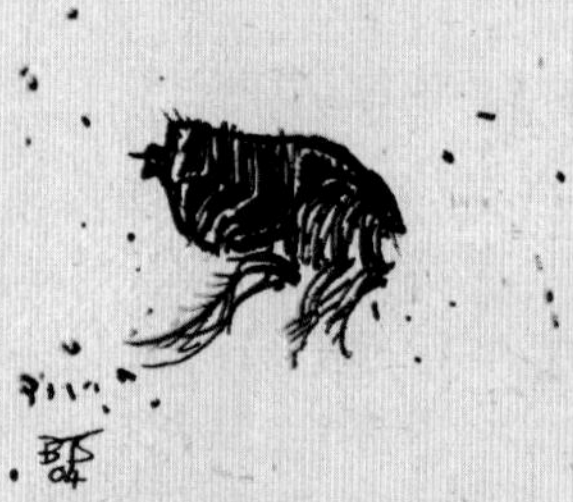

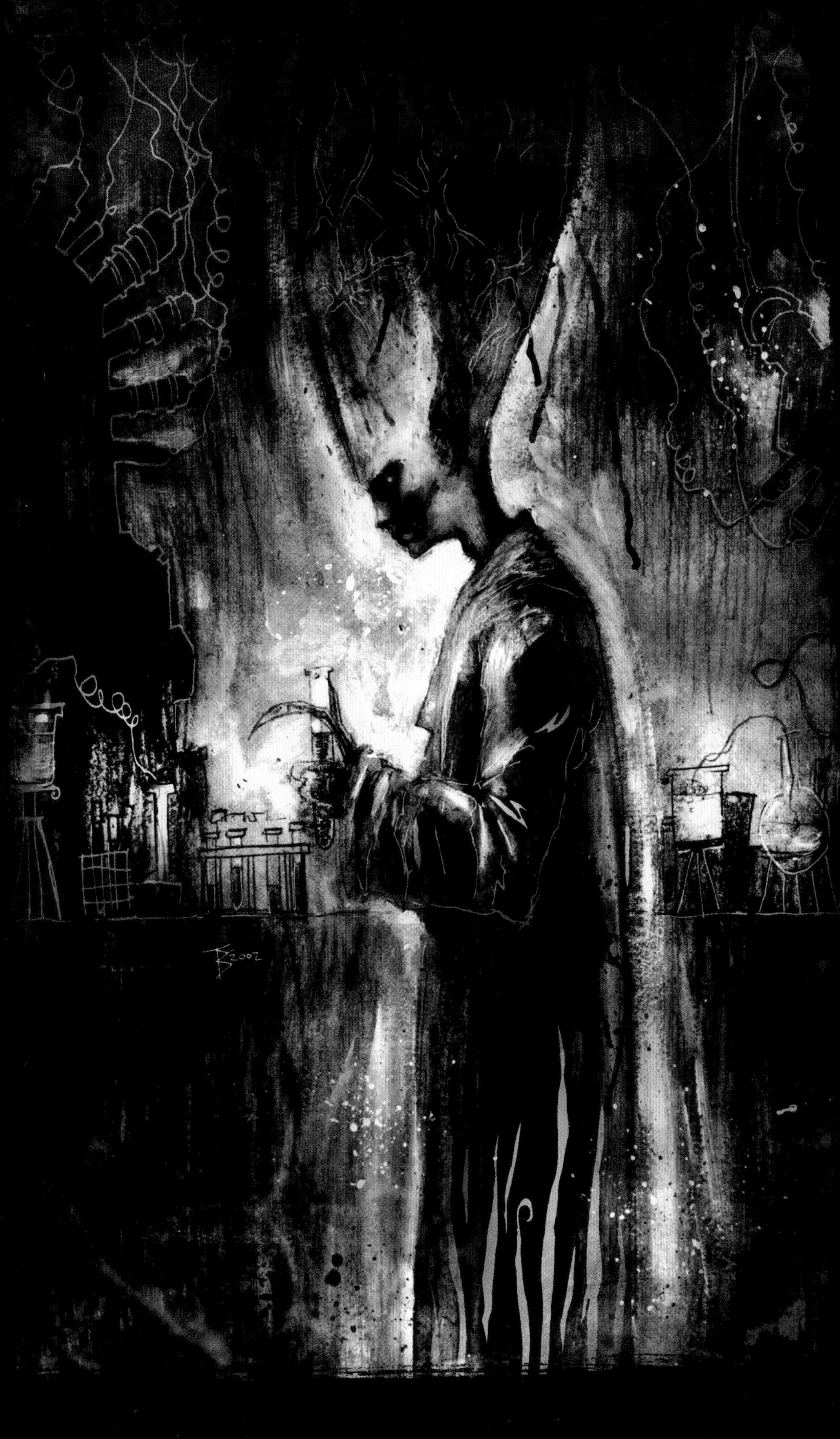

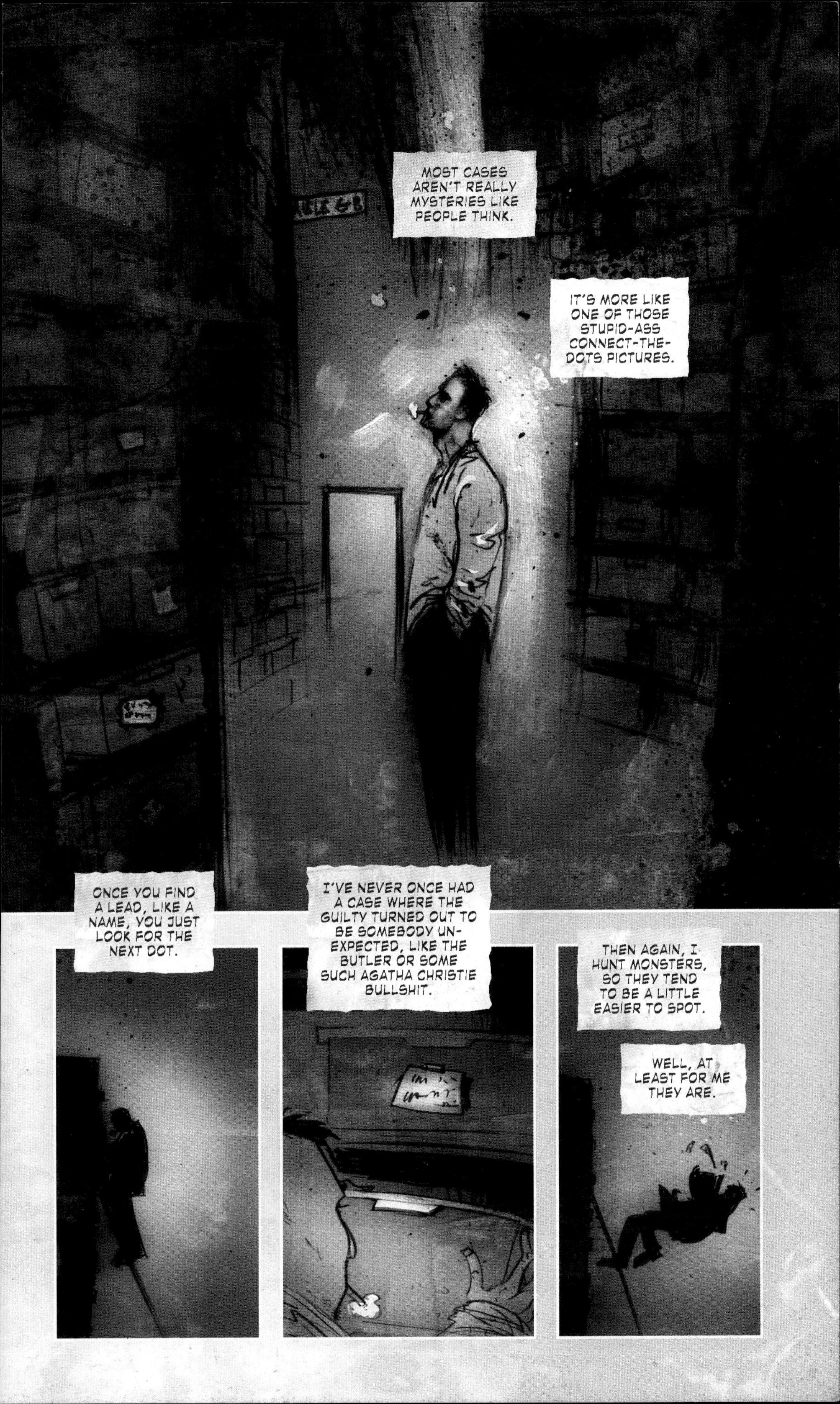
MOST CASES AREN'T REALLY MYSTERIES LIKE PEOPLE THINK.
IT'S MORE LIKE ONE OF THOSE STUPID-ASS CONNECT-THE-DOTS PICTURES.
ONCE YOU FIND A LEAD, LIKE A NAME, YOU JUST LOOK FOR THE NEXT DOT.
I'VE NEVER ONCE HAD A CASE WHERE THE GUILTY TURNED OUT TO BE SOMEBODY UN-EXPECTED, LIKE THE BUTLER OR SOME SUCH AGATHA CHRISTIE BULLSHIT.
THEN AGAIN, I HUNT MONSTERS, SO THEY TEND TO BE A LITTLE EASIER TO SPOT.
WELL, AT LEAST FOR ME THEY ARE.

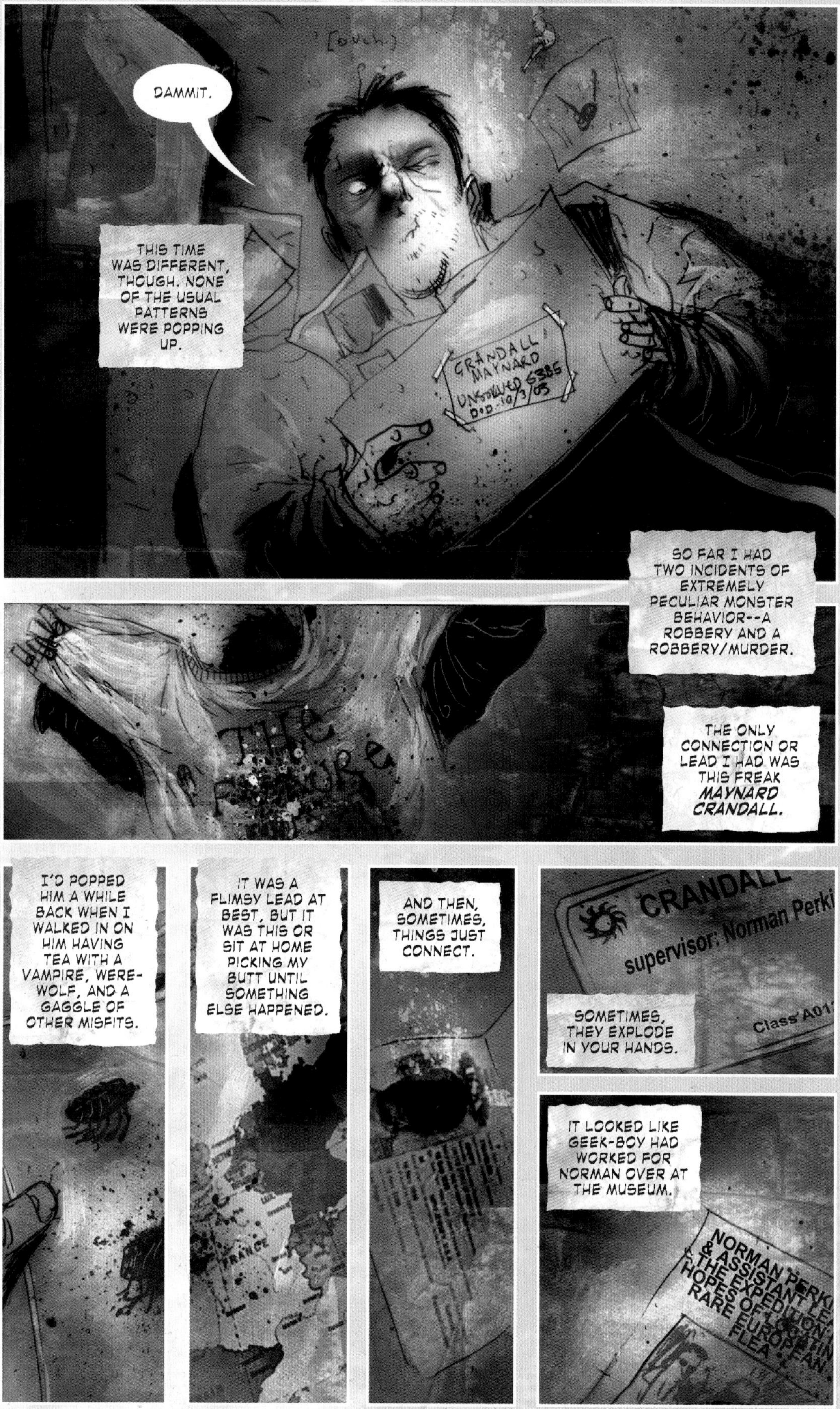

[ouch.]
DAMMIT.
THIS TIME WAS DIFFERENT, THOUGH. NONE OF THE USUAL PATTERNS WERE POPPING UP.
CRANDALL MAYNARD UNSOLVED 6385 D.O.D. 10/3/03
SO FAR I HAD TWO INCIDENTS OF EXTREMELY PECULIAR MONSTER BEHAVIOR--A ROBBERY AND A ROBBERY/MURDER.
THE ONLY CONNECTION OR LEAD I HAD WAS THIS FREAK ***MAYNARD CRANDALL.***
I'D POPPED HIM A WHILE BACK WHEN I WALKED IN ON HIM HAVING TEA WITH A VAMPIRE, WERE-WOLF, AND A GAGGLE OF OTHER MISFITS.
IT WAS A FLIMSY LEAD AT BEST, BUT IT WAS THIS OR SIT AT HOME PICKING MY BUTT UNTIL SOMETHING ELSE HAPPENED.
AND THEN, SOMETIMES, THINGS JUST CONNECT.
CRANDALL
supervisor: Norman Perki
Class' A01
SOMETIMES, THEY EXPLODE IN YOUR HANDS.
IT LOOKED LIKE GEEK-BOY HAD WORKED FOR NORMAN OVER AT THE MUSEUM.
NORMAN PERKI
& ASSISTANT LEA
THE EXPEDITION
HOPES OF LOCATIN
RARE EUROPEAN
FLEA

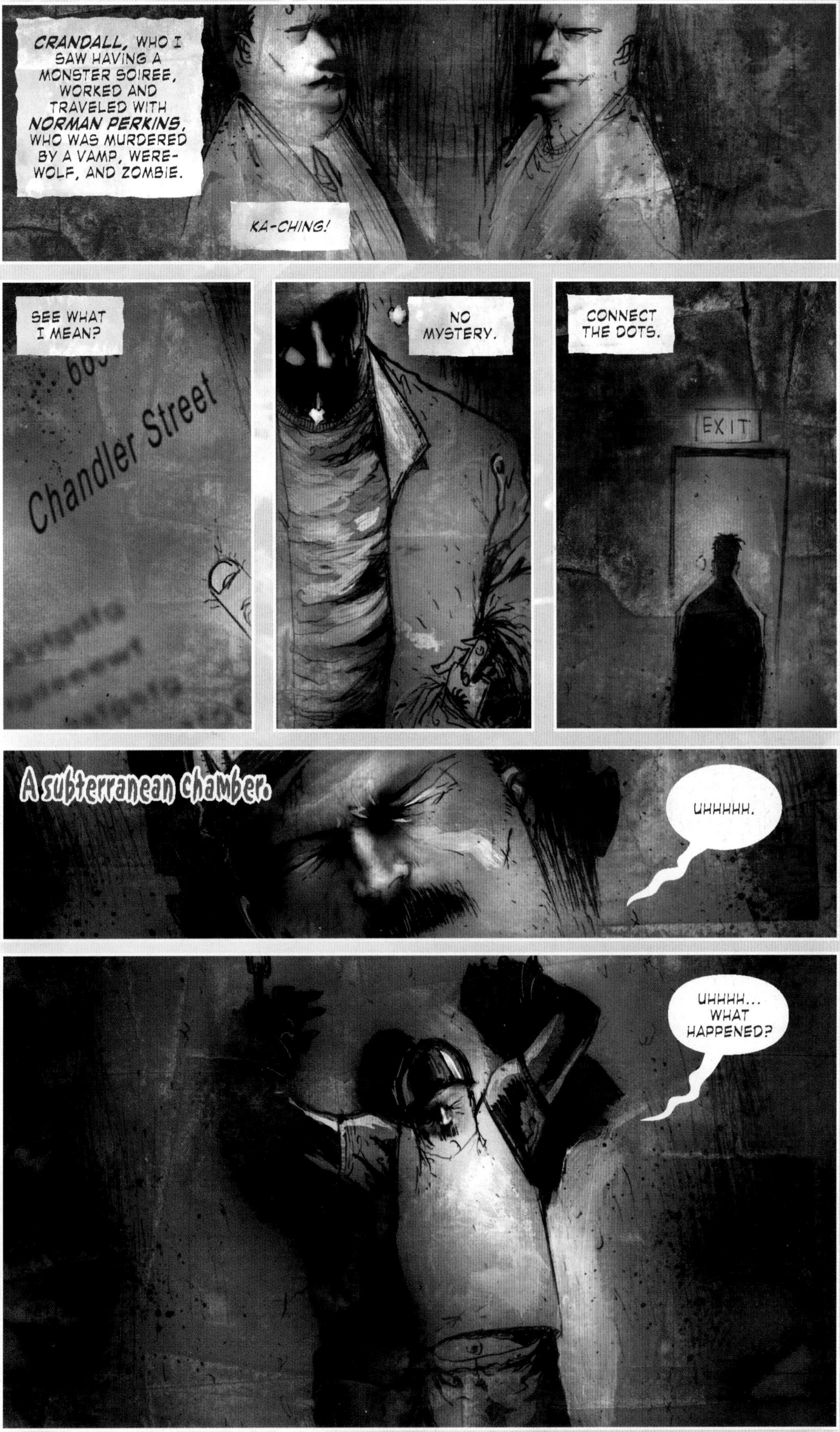

CRANDALL, WHO I SAW HAVING A MONSTER SOIREE, WORKED AND TRAVELED WITH NORMAN PERKINS, WHO WAS MURDERED BY A VAMP, WERE-WOLF, AND ZOMBIE.
KA-CHING!
SEE WHAT I MEAN?
Chandler Street
NO MYSTERY.
CONNECT THE DOTS.
EXIT
A subterranean chamber.
UHHHHH.
UHHHH... WHAT HAPPENED?

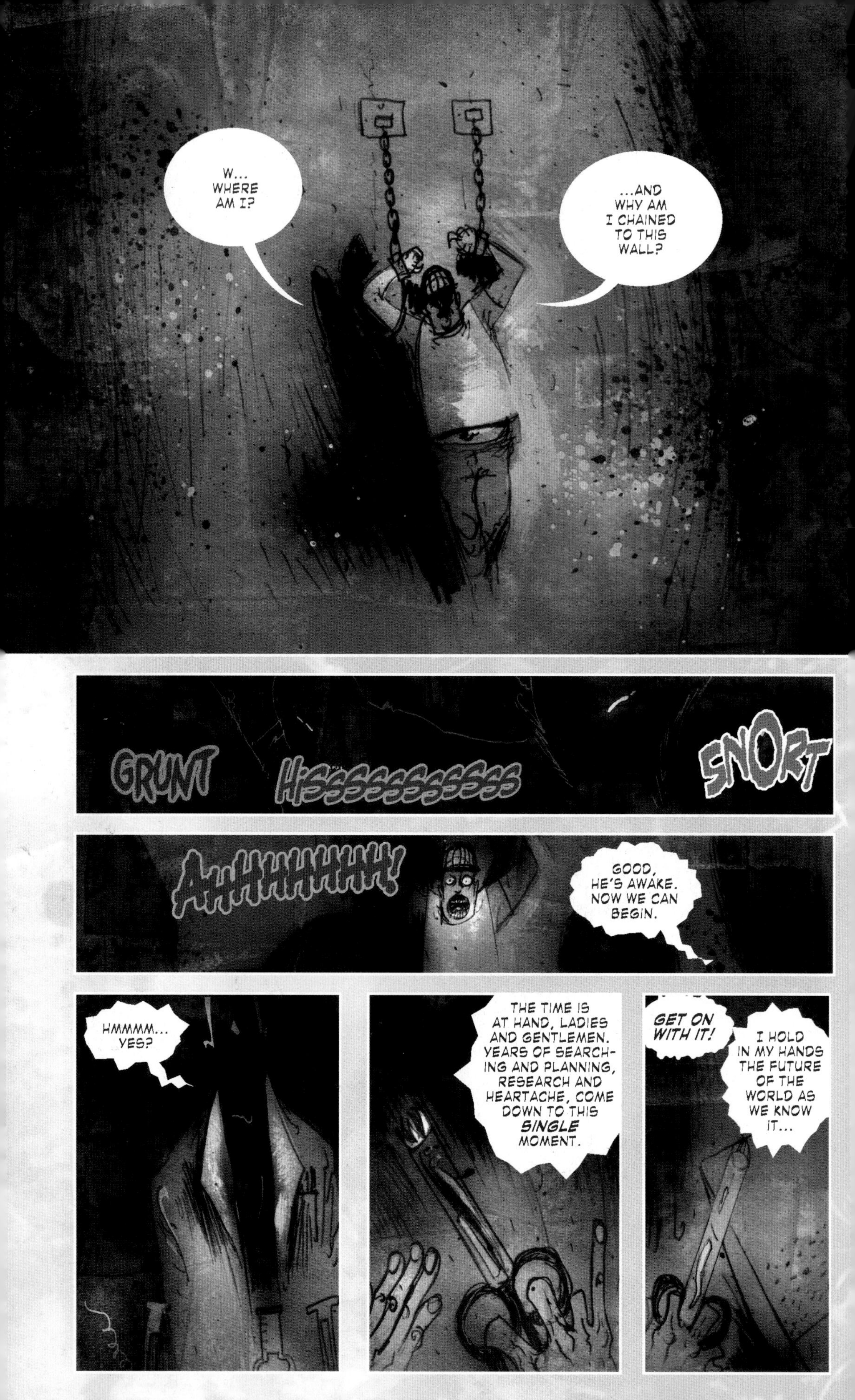
W... WHERE AM I?
...AND WHY AM I CHAINED TO THIS WALL?
GRUNT
HISSSSSSSSSSS
SNORT
AHHHHHHHHH!
GOOD, HE'S AWAKE. NOW WE CAN BEGIN.
HMMMM... YES?
THE TIME IS AT HAND, LADIES AND GENTLEMEN. YEARS OF SEARCHING AND PLANNING, RESEARCH AND HEARTACHE, COME DOWN TO THIS *SINGLE* MOMENT.
GET ON WITH IT!
I HOLD IN MY HANDS THE FUTURE OF THE WORLD AS WE KNOW IT...

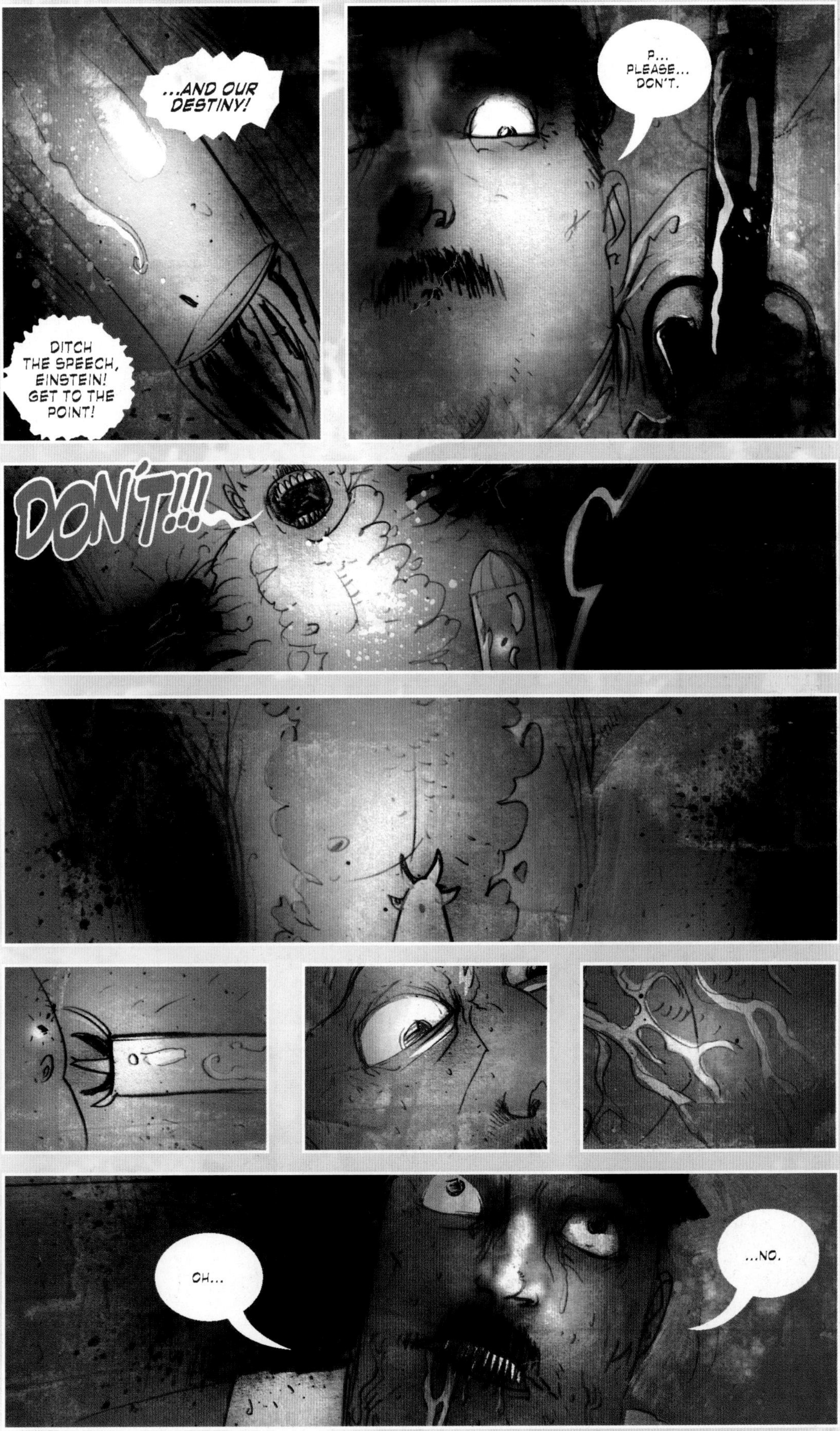
...AND OUR DESTINY!
DITCH THE SPEECH, EINSTEIN! GET TO THE POINT!
P... PLEASE... DON'T.
DON'T!!!
OH...
...NO.

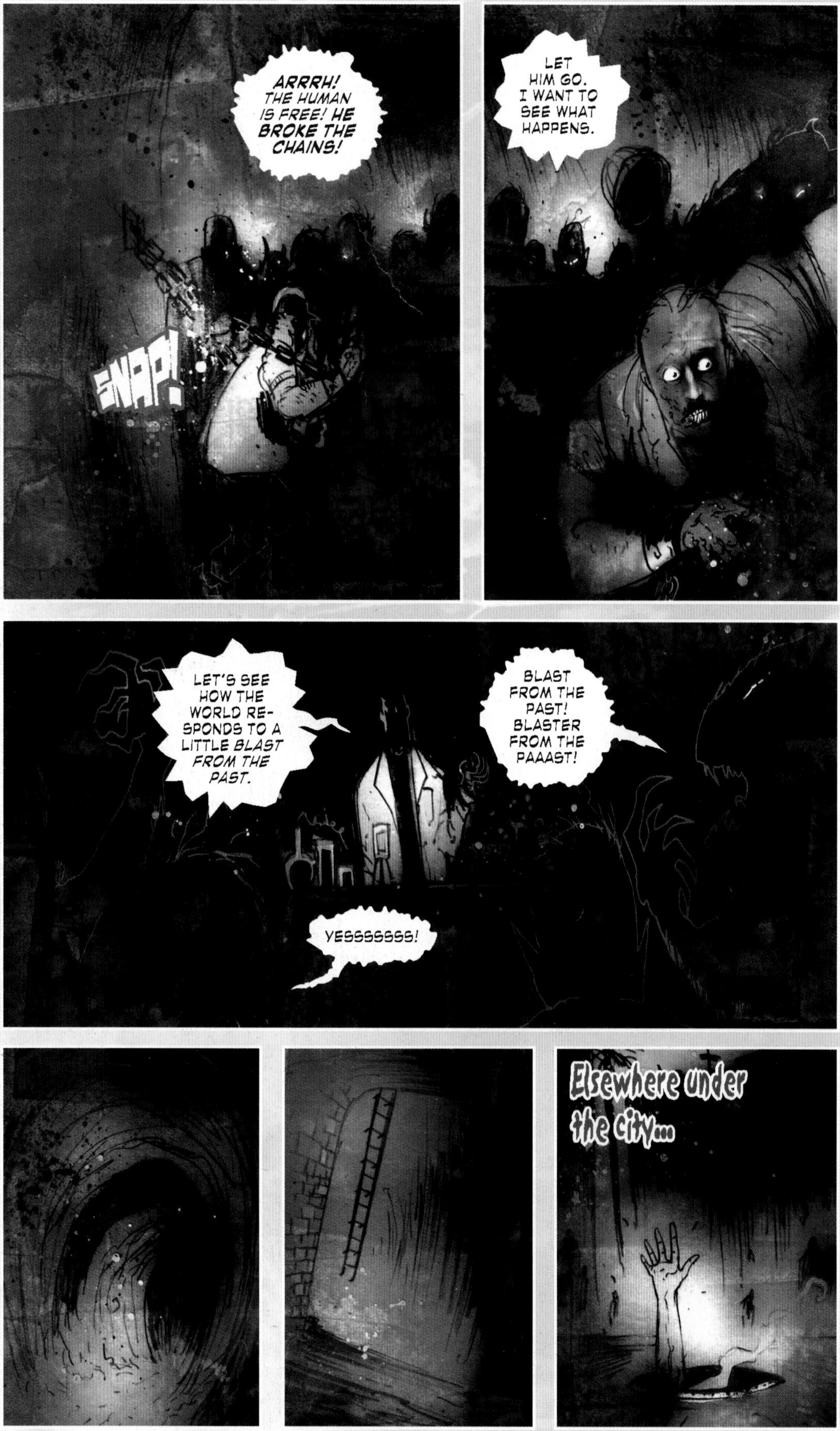
ARRRH! THE HUMAN IS FREE! HE BROKE THE CHAINS!
SNAP!
LET HIM GO. I WANT TO SEE WHAT HAPPENS.
LET'S SEE HOW THE WORLD RE-SPONDS TO A LITTLE BLAST FROM THE PAST.
BLAST FROM THE PAST! BLASTER FROM THE PAAAST!
YESSSSSSS!
Elsewhere under the city...

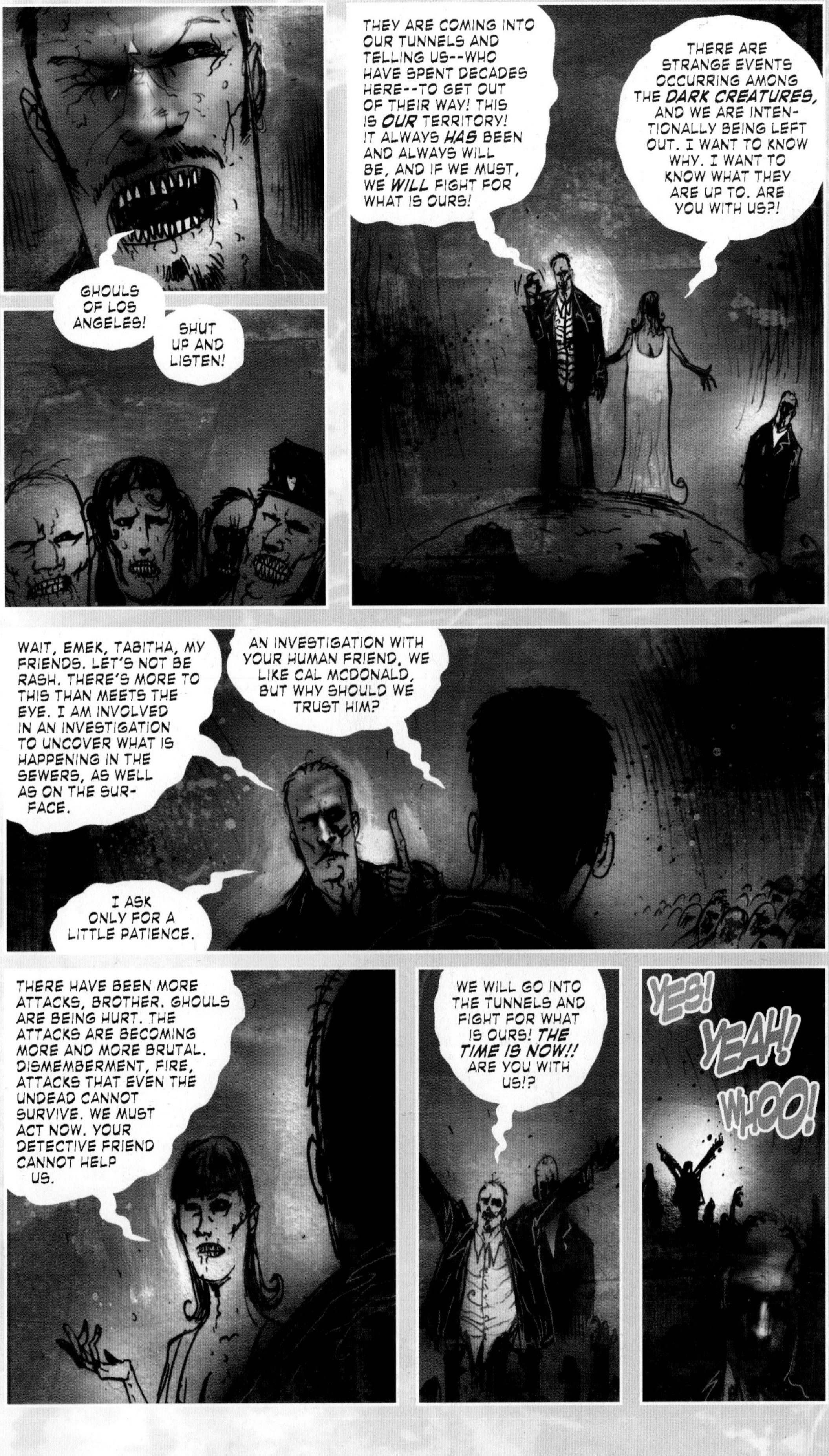
GHOULS OF LOS ANGELES!
SHUT UP AND LISTEN!
THEY ARE COMING INTO OUR TUNNELS AND TELLING US--WHO HAVE SPENT DECADES HERE--TO GET OUT OF THEIR WAY! THIS IS OUR TERRITORY! IT ALWAYS HAS BEEN AND ALWAYS WILL BE, AND IF WE MUST, WE WILL FIGHT FOR WHAT IS OURS!
THERE ARE STRANGE EVENTS OCCURRING AMONG THE DARK CREATURES, AND WE ARE INTENTIONALLY BEING LEFT OUT. I WANT TO KNOW WHY. I WANT TO KNOW WHAT THEY ARE UP TO. ARE YOU WITH US?!
WAIT, EMEK, TABITHA, MY FRIENDS. LET'S NOT BE RASH. THERE'S MORE TO THIS THAN MEETS THE EYE. I AM INVOLVED IN AN INVESTIGATION TO UNCOVER WHAT IS HAPPENING IN THE SEWERS, AS WELL AS ON THE SURFACE.
AN INVESTIGATION WITH YOUR HUMAN FRIEND. WE LIKE CAL MCDONALD, BUT WHY SHOULD WE TRUST HIM?
I ASK ONLY FOR A LITTLE PATIENCE.
THERE HAVE BEEN MORE ATTACKS, BROTHER. GHOULS ARE BEING HURT. THE ATTACKS ARE BECOMING MORE AND MORE BRUTAL. DISMEMBERMENT, FIRE, ATTACKS THAT EVEN THE UNDEAD CANNOT SURVIVE. WE MUST ACT NOW. YOUR DETECTIVE FRIEND CANNOT HELP US.
WE WILL GO INTO THE TUNNELS AND FIGHT FOR WHAT IS OURS! THE TIME IS NOW!! ARE YOU WITH US!?
YES!
YEAH!
WHOO!

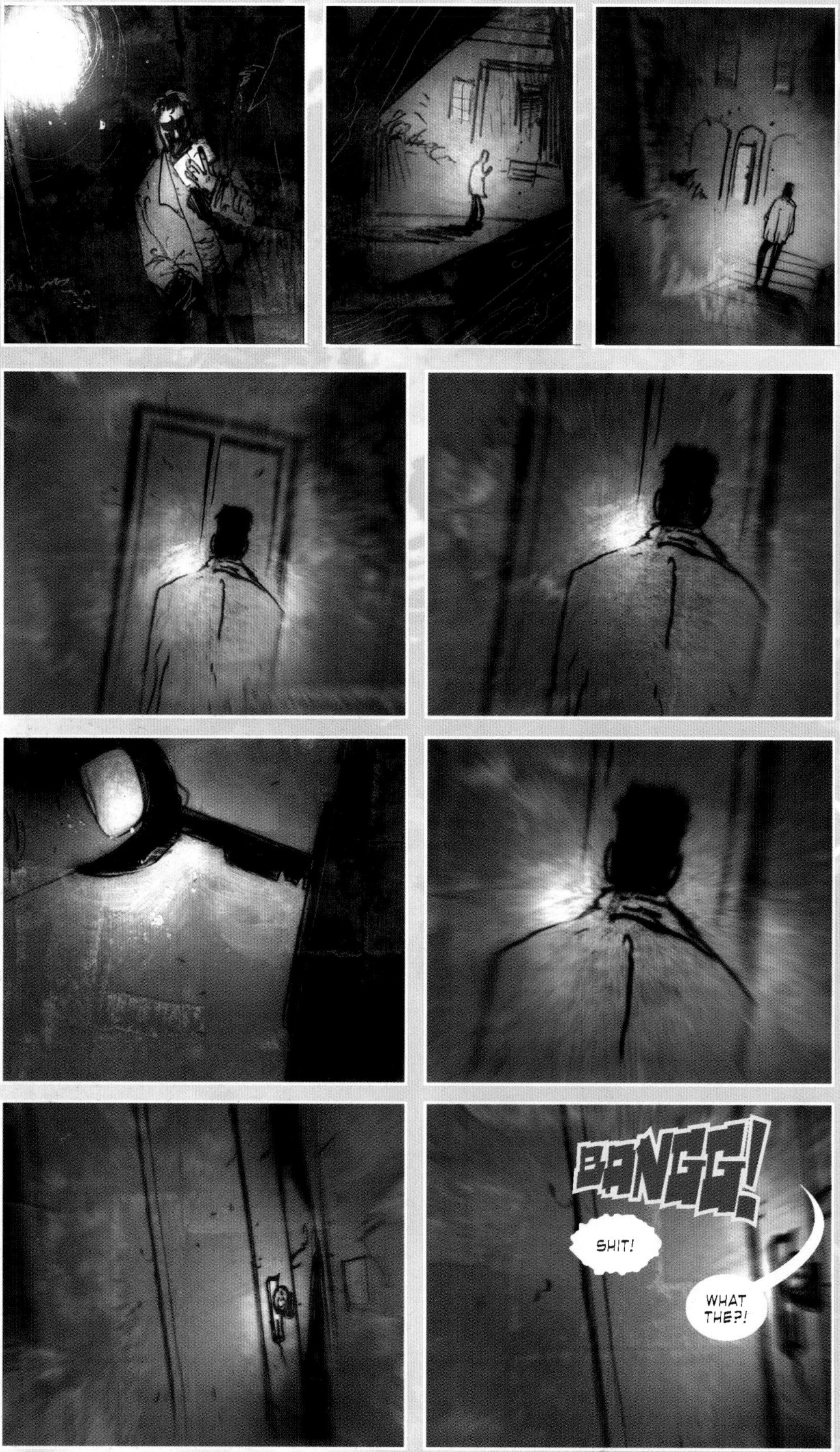
BANGG!
SHIT!
WHAT THE?!

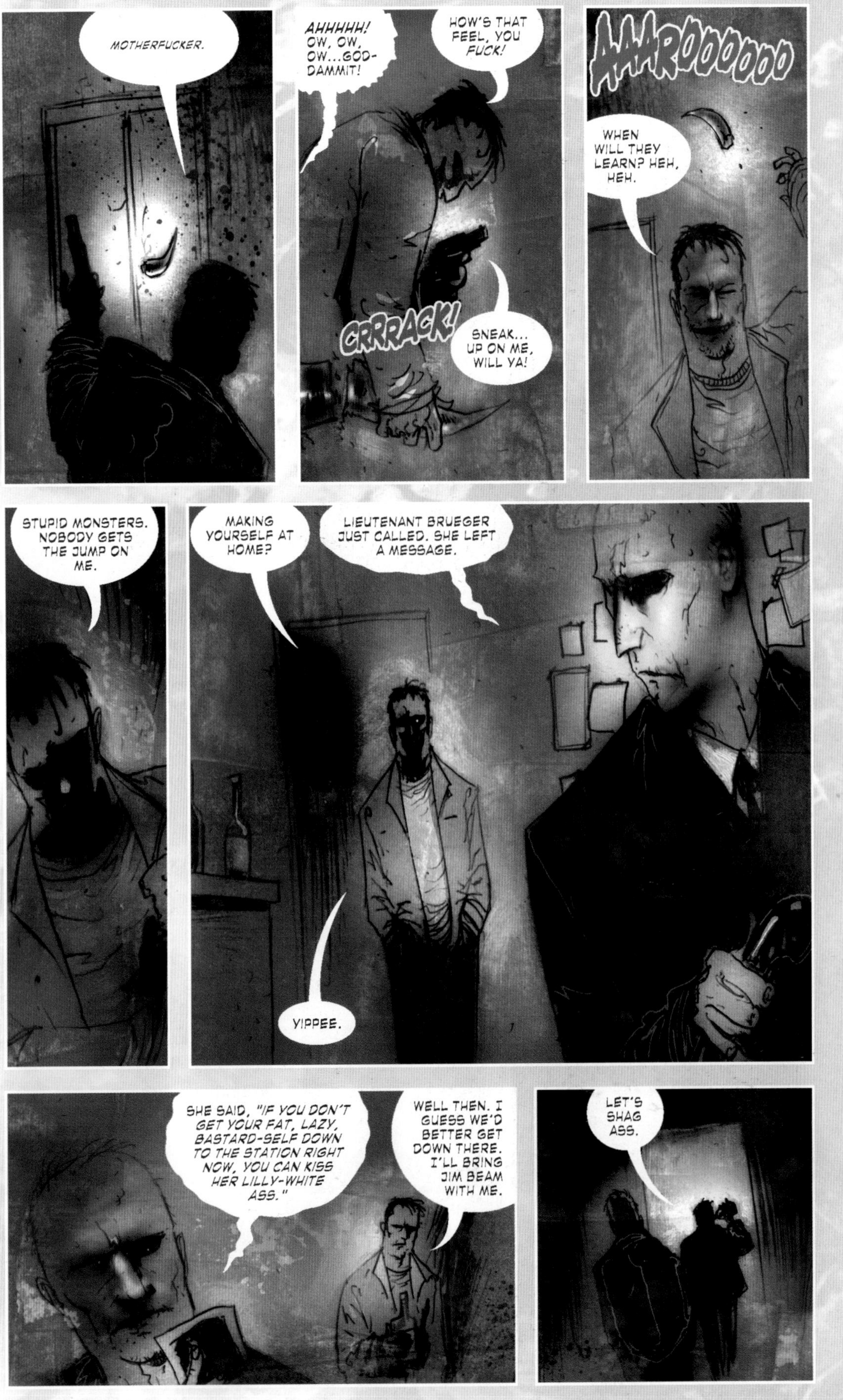

MOTHERFUCKER.
AHHHHH! OW, OW, OW...GOD-DAMMIT!
HOW'S THAT FEEL, YOU FUCK!
CRRRACK!
SNEAK... UP ON ME, WILL YA!
AAAROOOOOO
WHEN WILL THEY LEARN? HEH, HEH.
STUPID MONSTERS. NOBODY GETS THE JUMP ON ME.
MAKING YOURSELF AT HOME?
LIEUTENANT BRUEGER JUST CALLED. SHE LEFT A MESSAGE.
YIPPEE.
SHE SAID, "IF YOU DON'T GET YOUR FAT, LAZY, BASTARD-SELF DOWN TO THE STATION RIGHT NOW, YOU CAN KISS HER LILLY-WHITE ASS."
WELL THEN. I GUESS WE'D BETTER GET DOWN THERE. I'LL BRING JIM BEAM WITH ME.
LET'S SHAG ASS.

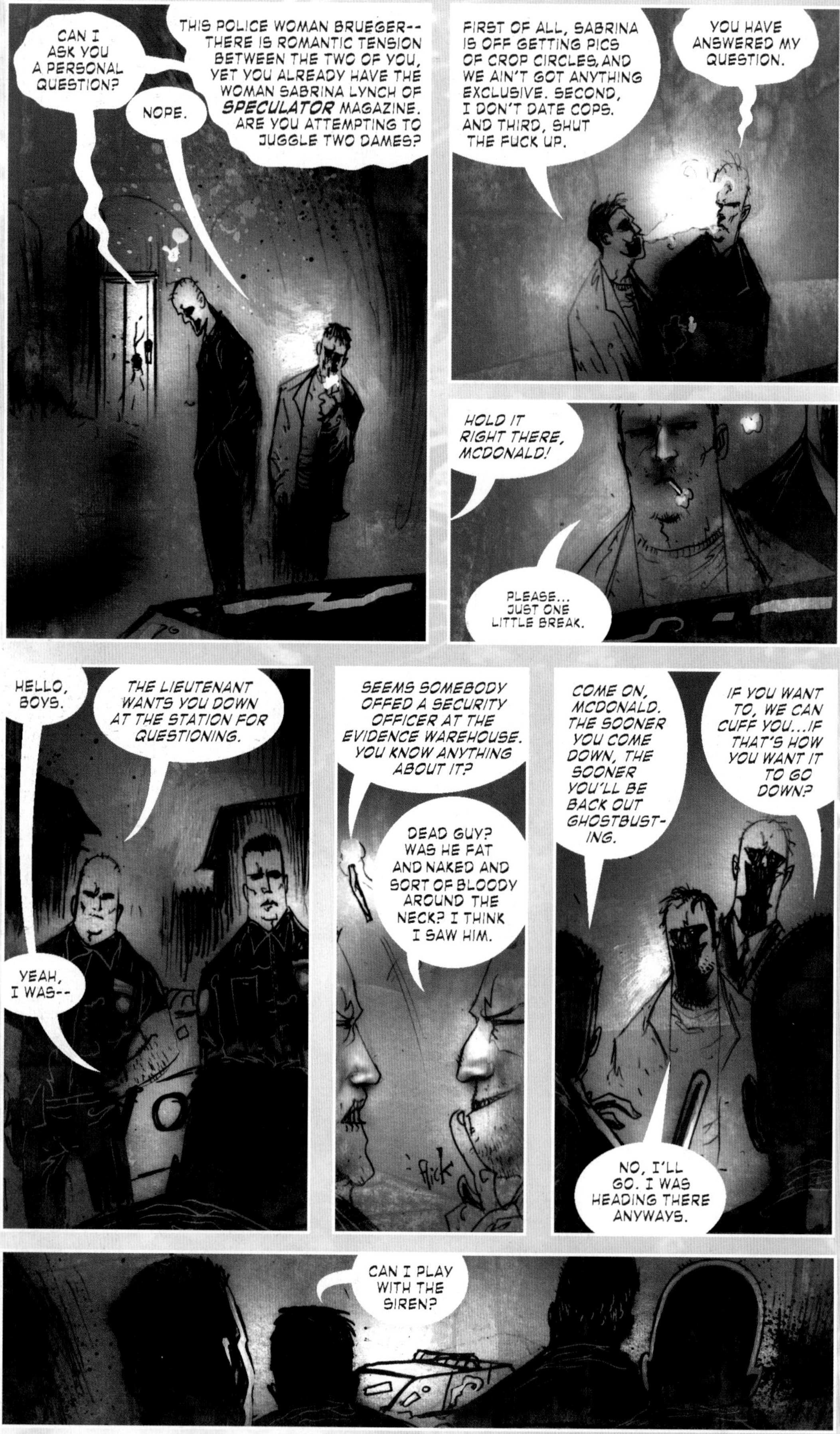

CAN I ASK YOU A PERSONAL QUESTION?
NOPE.
THIS POLICE WOMAN BRUEGER-- THERE IS ROMANTIC TENSION BETWEEN THE TWO OF YOU, YET YOU ALREADY HAVE THE WOMAN SABRINA LYNCH OF SPECULATOR MAGAZINE. ARE YOU ATTEMPTING TO JUGGLE TWO DAMES?
FIRST OF ALL, SABRINA IS OFF GETTING PICS OF CROP CIRCLES, AND WE AIN'T GOT ANYTHING EXCLUSIVE. SECOND, I DON'T DATE COPS. AND THIRD, SHUT THE FUCK UP.
YOU HAVE ANSWERED MY QUESTION.
HOLD IT RIGHT THERE, MCDONALD!
PLEASE... JUST ONE LITTLE BREAK.
HELLO, BOYS.
THE LIEUTENANT WANTS YOU DOWN AT THE STATION FOR QUESTIONING.
YEAH, I WAS--
SEEMS SOMEBODY OFFED A SECURITY OFFICER AT THE EVIDENCE WAREHOUSE. YOU KNOW ANYTHING ABOUT IT?
DEAD GUY? WAS HE FAT AND NAKED AND SORT OF BLOODY AROUND THE NECK? I THINK I SAW HIM.
COME ON, MCDONALD. THE SOONER YOU COME DOWN, THE SOONER YOU'LL BE BACK OUT GHOSTBUSTING.
IF YOU WANT TO, WE CAN CUFF YOU...IF THAT'S HOW YOU WANT IT TO GO DOWN?
NO, I'LL GO. I WAS HEADING THERE ANYWAYS.
CAN I PLAY WITH THE SIREN?

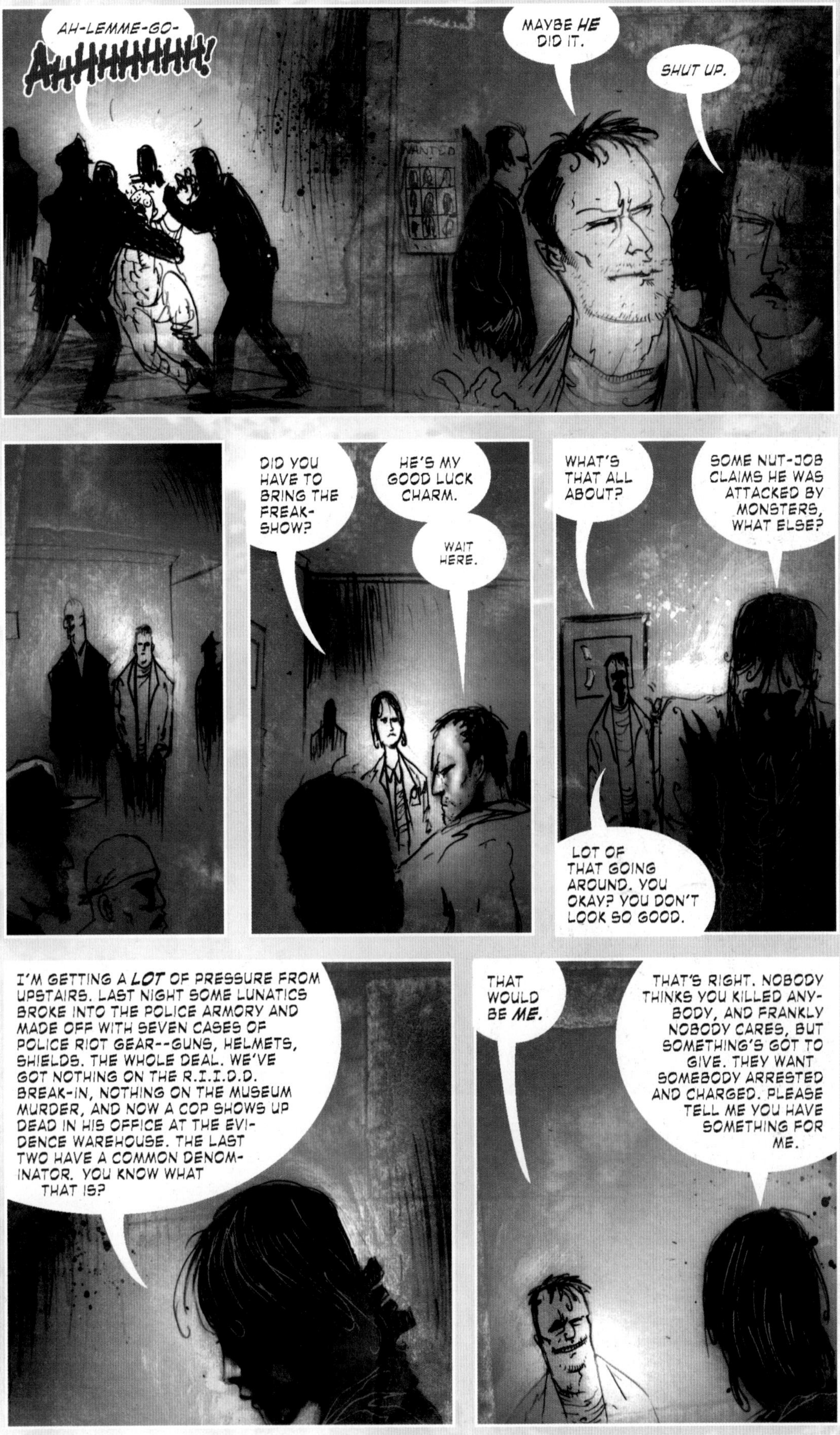
AH-LEMME-GO-
AHHHHHHHH!
MAYBE HE DID IT.
SHUT UP.
DID YOU HAVE TO BRING THE FREAK-SHOW?
HE'S MY GOOD LUCK CHARM.
WAIT HERE.
WHAT'S THAT ALL ABOUT?
SOME NUT-JOB CLAIMS HE WAS ATTACKED BY MONSTERS, WHAT ELSE?
LOT OF THAT GOING AROUND. YOU OKAY? YOU DON'T LOOK SO GOOD.
I'M GETTING A LOT OF PRESSURE FROM UPSTAIRS. LAST NIGHT SOME LUNATICS BROKE INTO THE POLICE ARMORY AND MADE OFF WITH SEVEN CASES OF POLICE RIOT GEAR--GUNS, HELMETS, SHIELDS. THE WHOLE DEAL. WE'VE GOT NOTHING ON THE R.I.I.D.D. BREAK-IN, NOTHING ON THE MUSEUM MURDER, AND NOW A COP SHOWS UP DEAD IN HIS OFFICE AT THE EVIDENCE WAREHOUSE. THE LAST TWO HAVE A COMMON DENOMINATOR. YOU KNOW WHAT THAT IS?
THAT WOULD BE ME.
THAT'S RIGHT. NOBODY THINKS YOU KILLED ANYBODY, AND FRANKLY NOBODY CARES, BUT SOMETHING'S GOT TO GIVE. THEY WANT SOMEBODY ARRESTED AND CHARGED. PLEASE TELL ME YOU HAVE SOMETHING FOR ME.

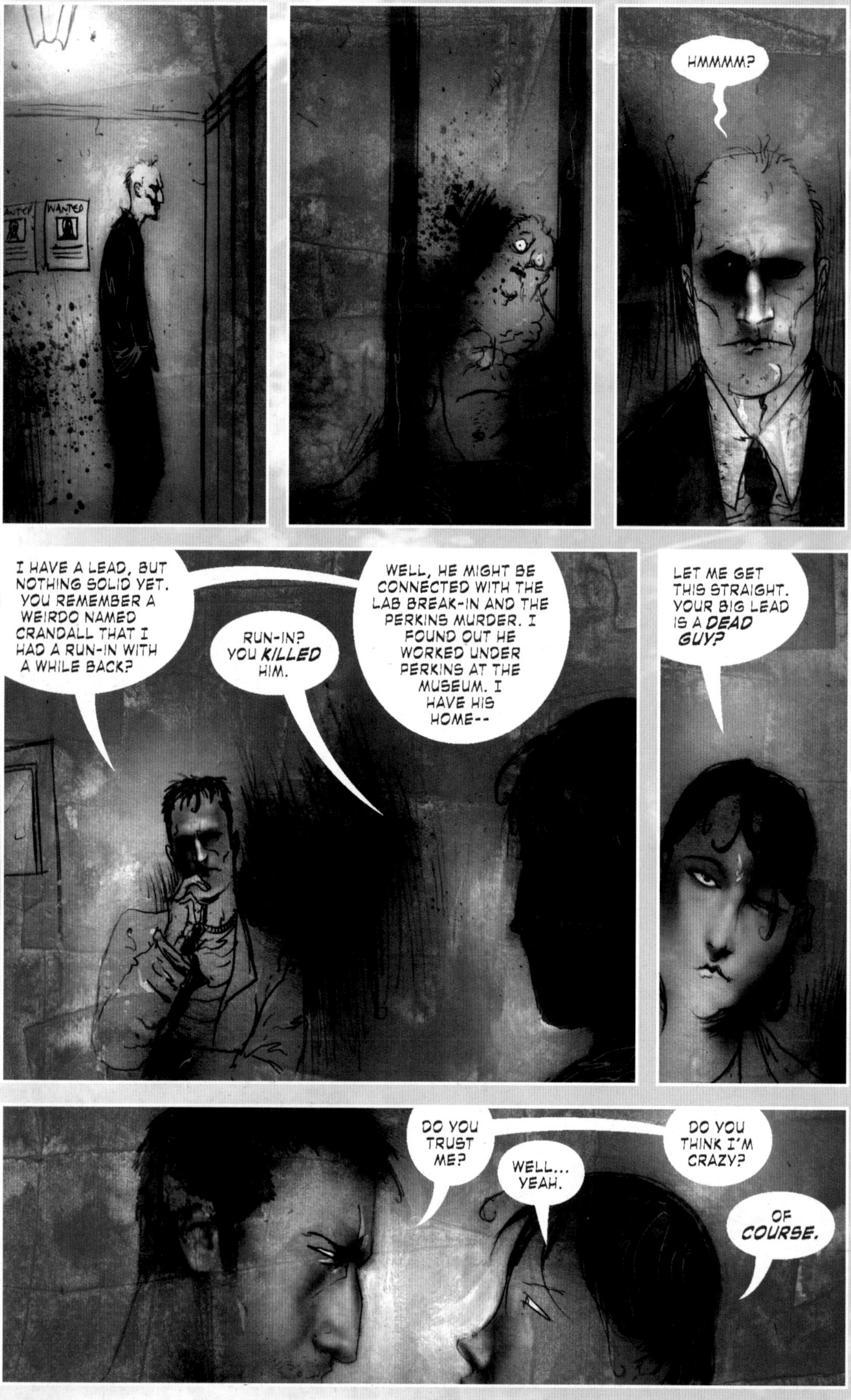

WANTED
WANTED
HMMMM?
I HAVE A LEAD, BUT NOTHING SOLID YET. YOU REMEMBER A WEIRDO NAMED CRANDALL THAT I HAD A RUN-IN WITH A WHILE BACK?
RUN-IN? YOU KILLED HIM.
WELL, HE MIGHT BE CONNECTED WITH THE LAB BREAK-IN AND THE PERKINS MURDER. I FOUND OUT HE WORKED UNDER PERKINS AT THE MUSEUM. I HAVE HIS HOME--
LET ME GET THIS STRAIGHT. YOUR BIG LEAD IS A DEAD GUY?
DO YOU TRUST ME?
WELL... YEAH.
DO YOU THINK I'M CRAZY?
OF COURSE.

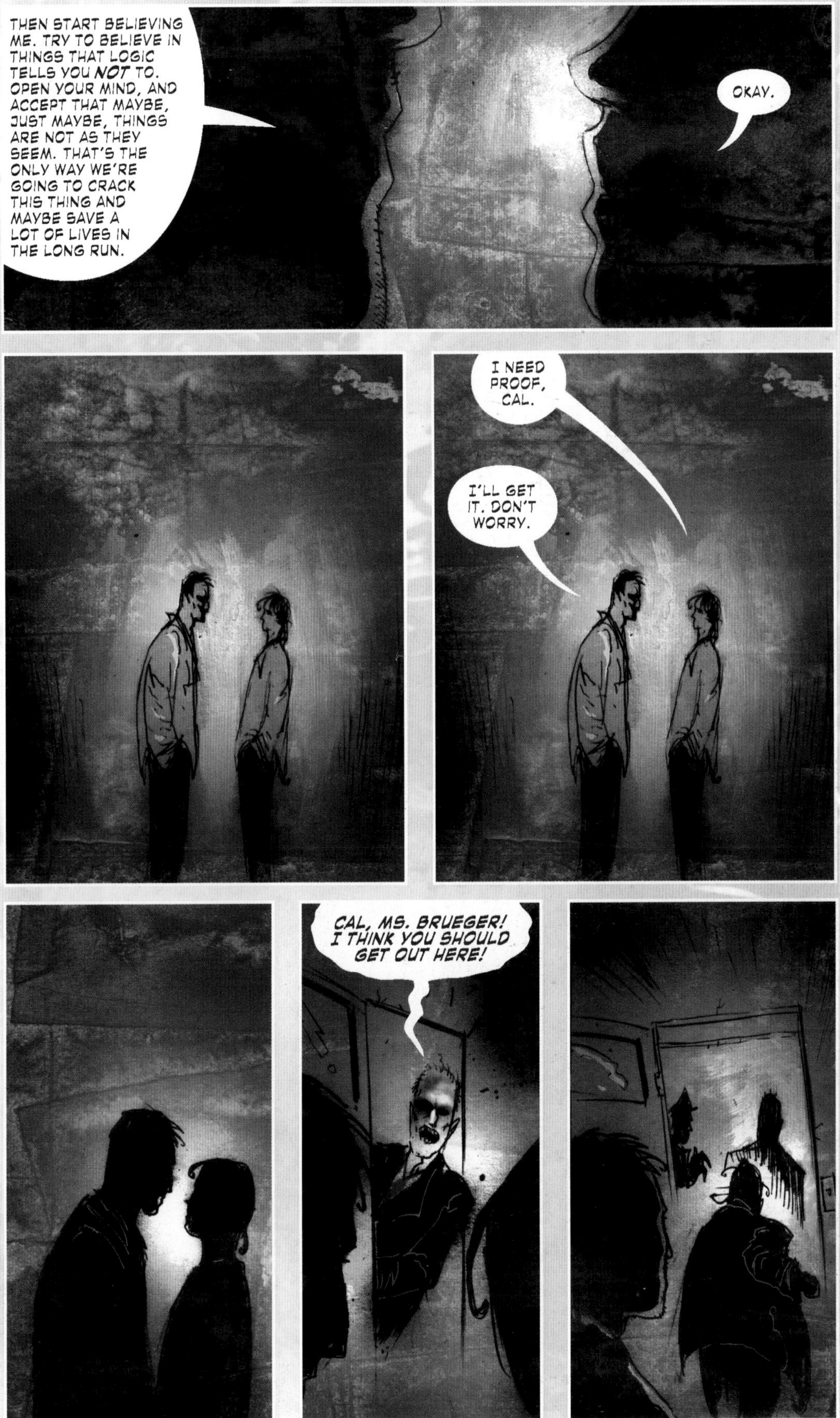
THEN START BELIEVING ME. TRY TO BELIEVE IN THINGS THAT LOGIC TELLS YOU *NOT* TO. OPEN YOUR MIND, AND ACCEPT THAT MAYBE, JUST MAYBE, THINGS ARE NOT AS THEY SEEM. THAT'S THE ONLY WAY WE'RE GOING TO CRACK THIS THING AND MAYBE SAVE A LOT OF LIVES IN THE LONG RUN.
OKAY.
I NEED PROOF, CAL.
I'LL GET IT. DON'T WORRY.
CAL, MS. BRUEGER! I THINK YOU SHOULD GET OUT HERE!

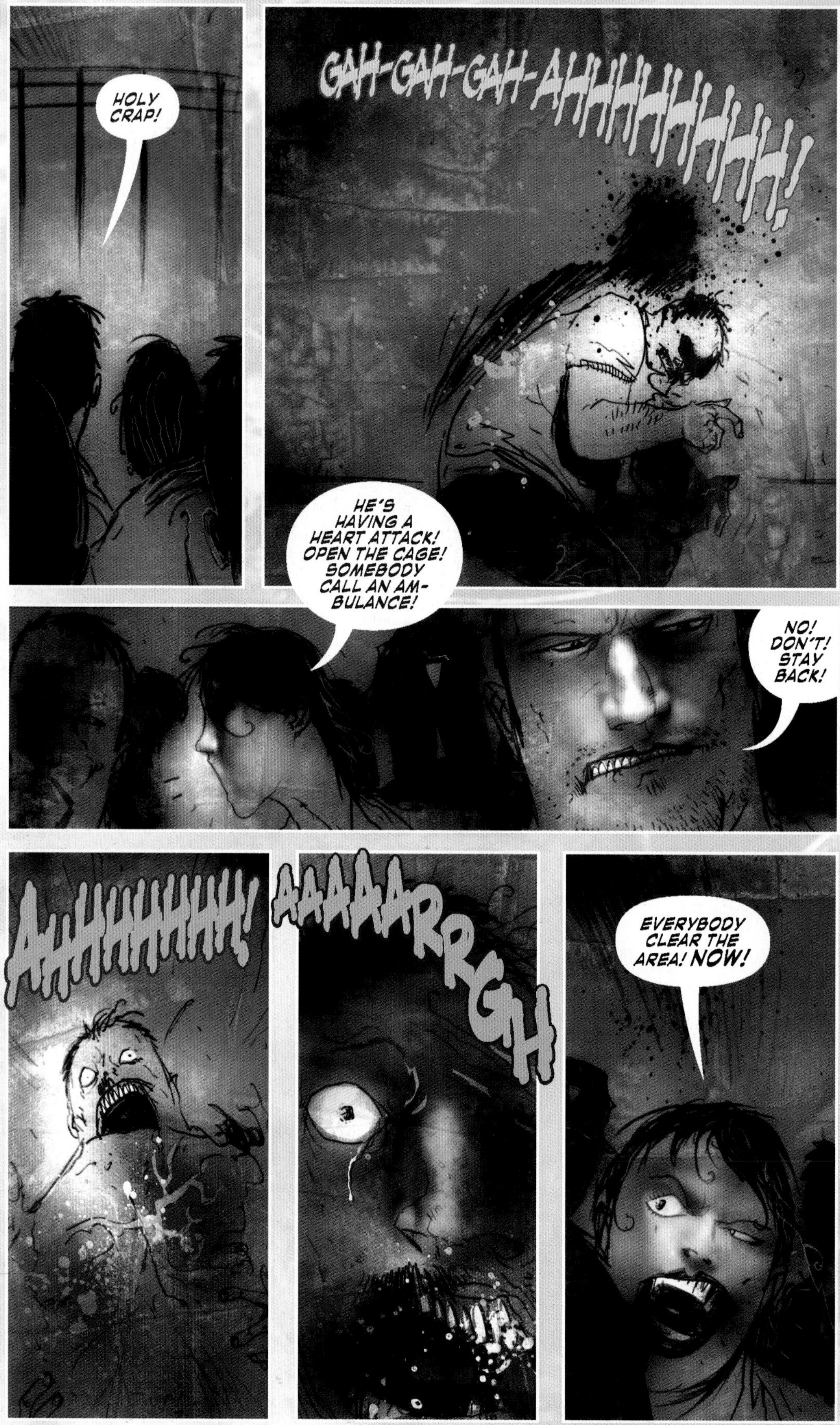
HOLY CRAP!
GAH-GAH-GAH-AHHHHHHHHH!
HE'S HAVING A HEART ATTACK! OPEN THE CAGE! SOMEBODY CALL AN AMBULANCE!
NO! DON'T! STAY BACK!
AHHHHHHH!
AAAAARRGH
EVERYBODY CLEAR THE AREA! NOW!

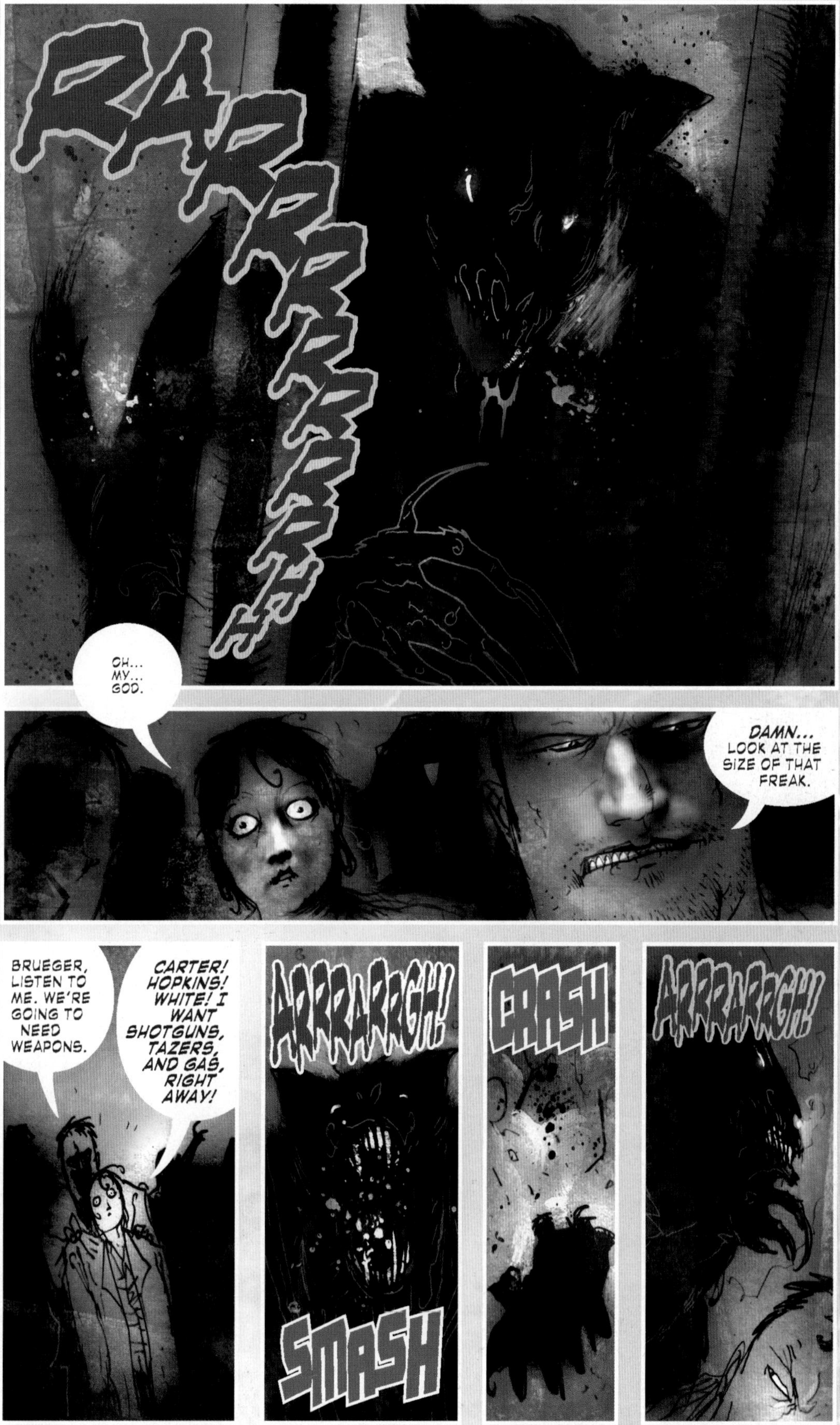
RARRRRRRRRRRRH!!
OH... MY... GOD.
DAMN... LOOK AT THE SIZE OF THAT FREAK.
BRUEGER, LISTEN TO ME. WE'RE GOING TO NEED WEAPONS.
CARTER! HOPKINS! WHITE! I WANT SHOTGUNS, TAZERS, AND GAS, RIGHT AWAY!
ARRRARRGH!
SMASH
CRASH
ARRRARRGH!

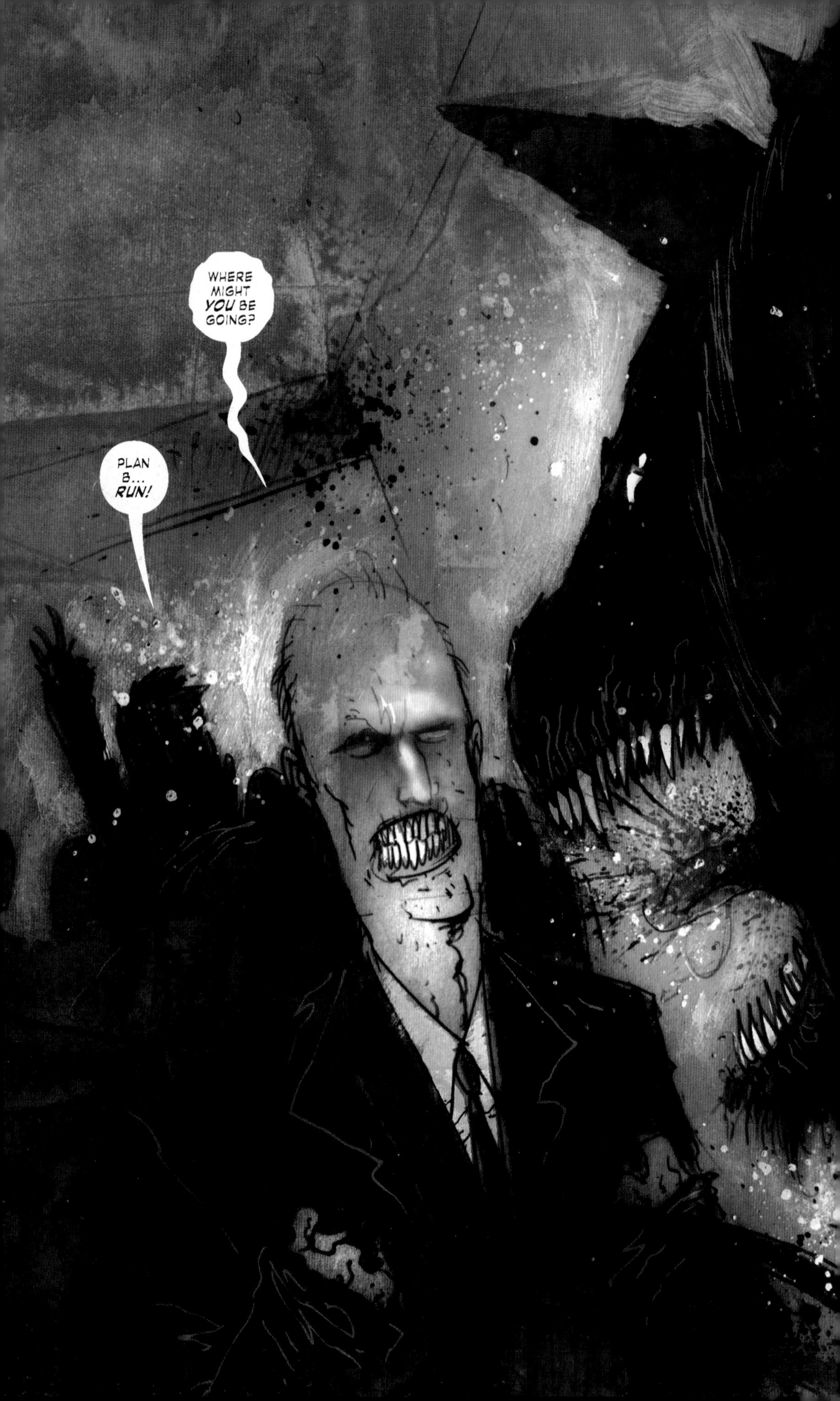
PLAN B... RUN!
WHERE MIGHT YOU BE GOING?

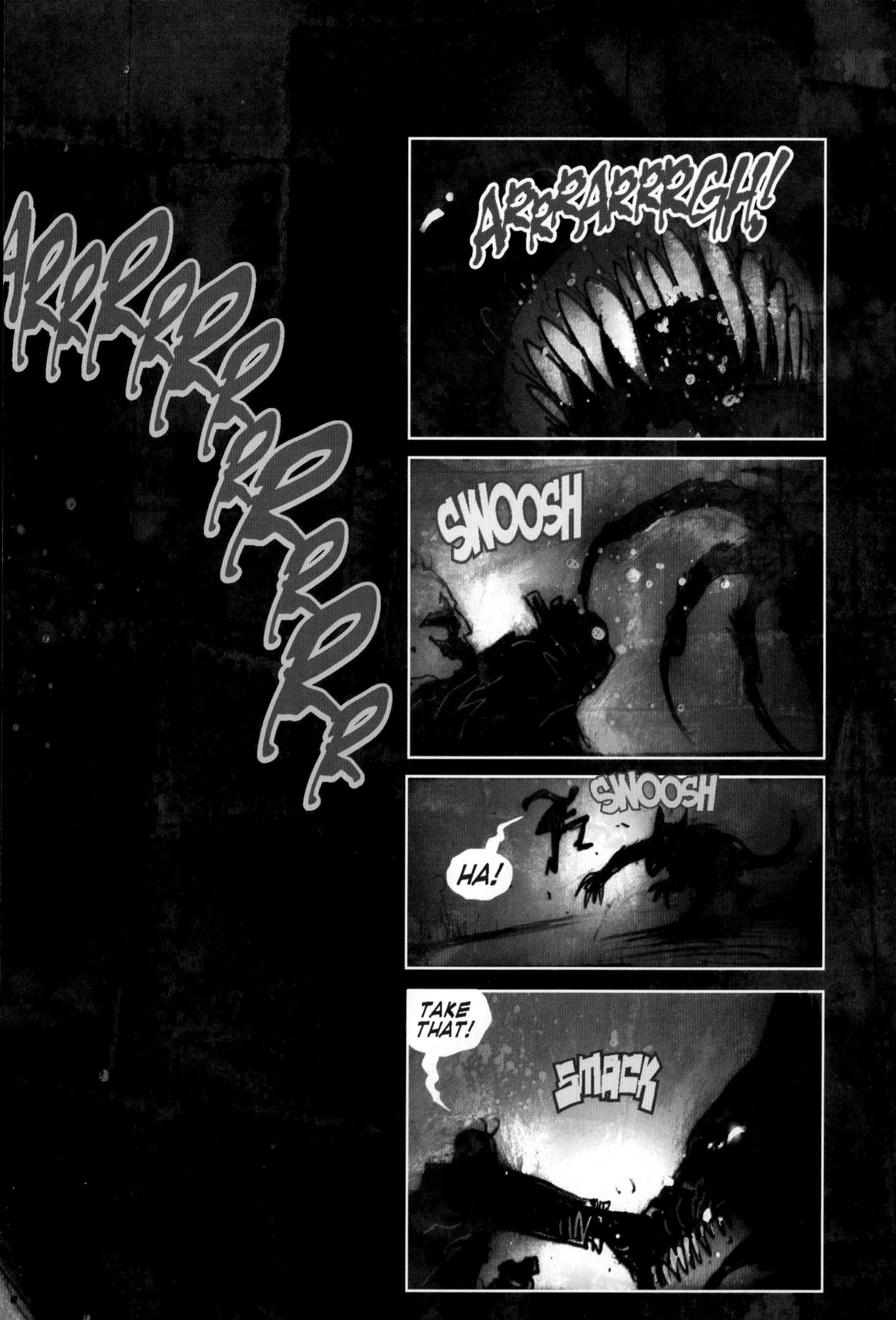
SWOOSH
SWOOSH
HA!
TAKE THAT!
SMACK

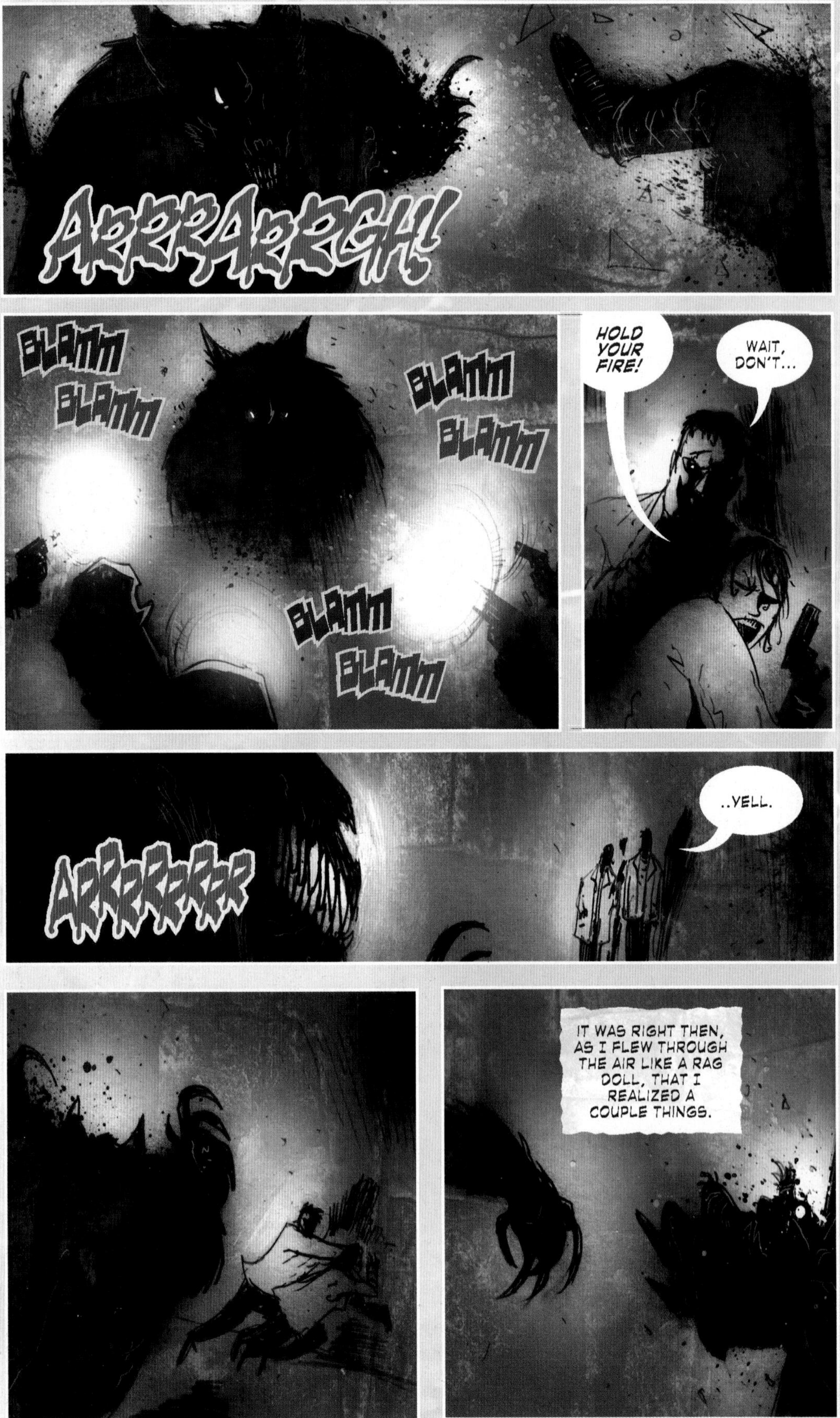
ARRRARRGH!
BLAMM
BLAMM
BLAMM
BLAMM
BLAMM
BLAMM
HOLD YOUR FIRE!
WAIT, DON'T...
ARRRRRRR
..YELL.
IT WAS RIGHT THEN, AS I FLEW THROUGH THE AIR LIKE A RAG DOLL, THAT I REALIZED A COUPLE THINGS.

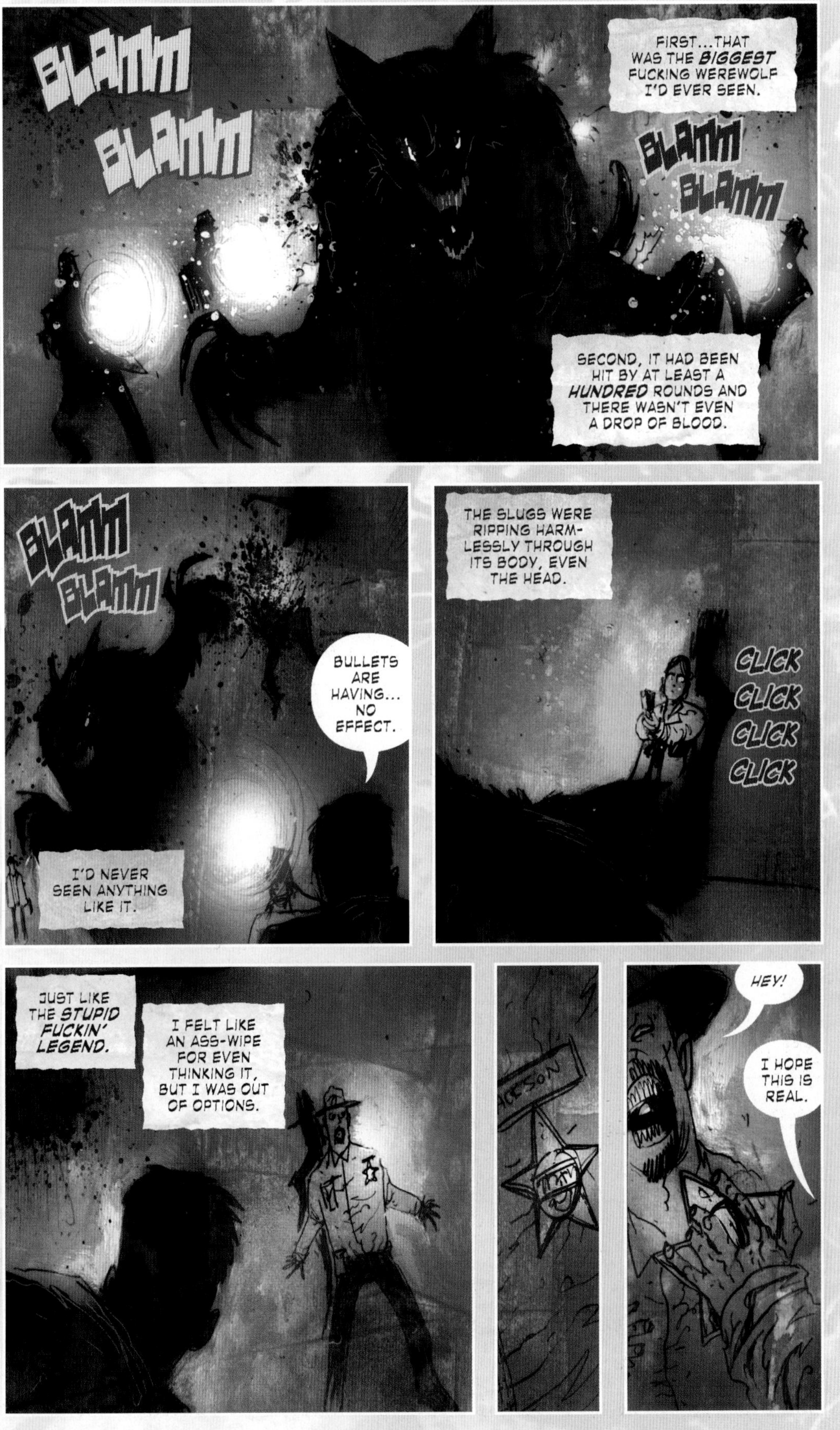
BLAMM BLAMM
FIRST...THAT WAS THE BIGGEST FUCKING WEREWOLF I'D EVER SEEN.
BLAMM BLAMM
SECOND, IT HAD BEEN HIT BY AT LEAST A HUNDRED ROUNDS AND THERE WASN'T EVEN A DROP OF BLOOD.
BLAMM BLAMM
BULLETS ARE HAVING... NO EFFECT.
I'D NEVER SEEN ANYTHING LIKE IT.
THE SLUGS WERE RIPPING HARM-LESSLY THROUGH ITS BODY, EVEN THE HEAD.
CLICK CLICK CLICK CLICK
JUST LIKE THE STUPID FUCKIN' LEGEND.
I FELT LIKE AN ASS-WIPE FOR EVEN THINKING IT, BUT I WAS OUT OF OPTIONS.
HEY!
I HOPE THIS IS REAL.

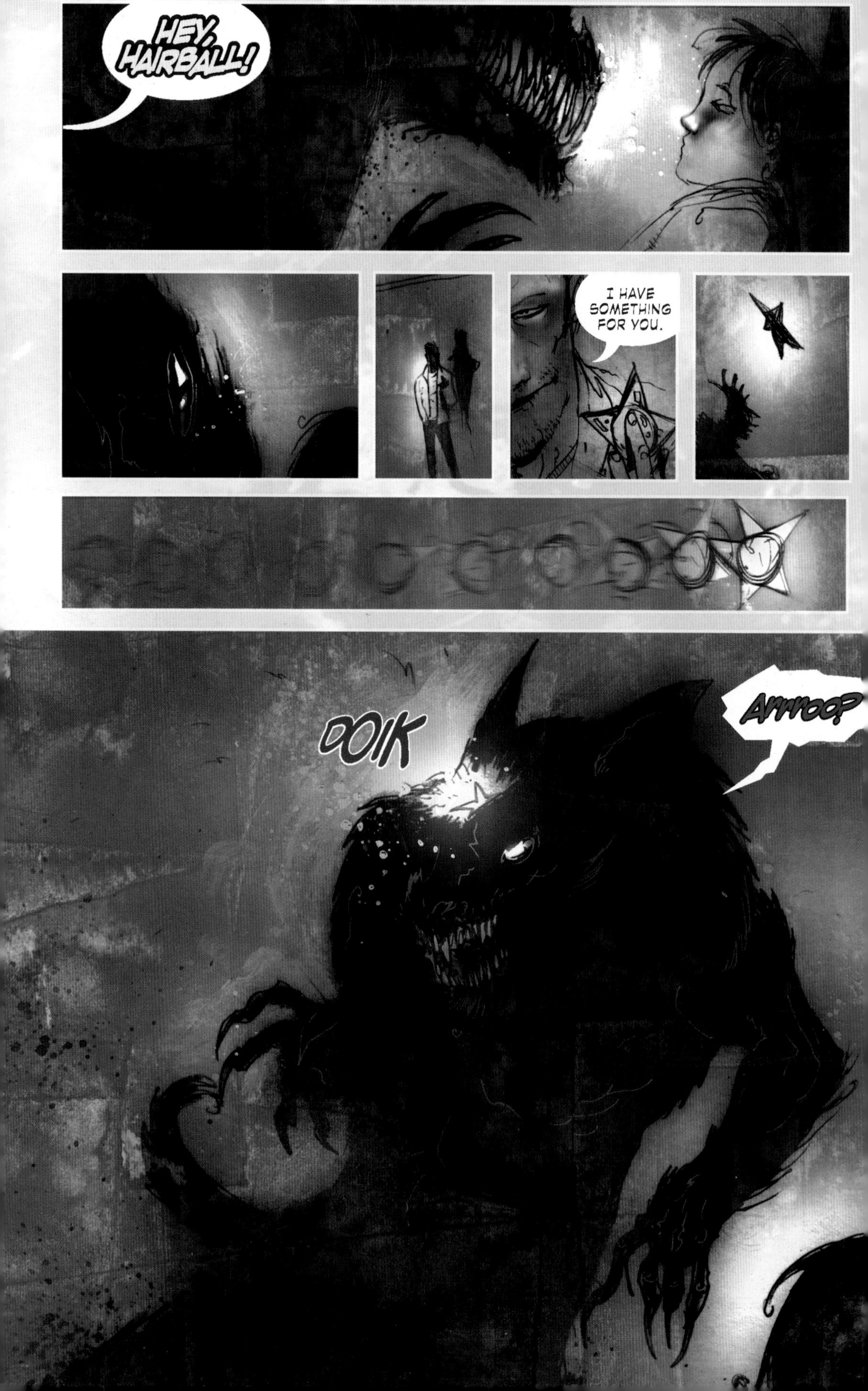
HEY, HAIRBALL!
I HAVE SOMETHING FOR YOU.
DOIK
Arrroo?

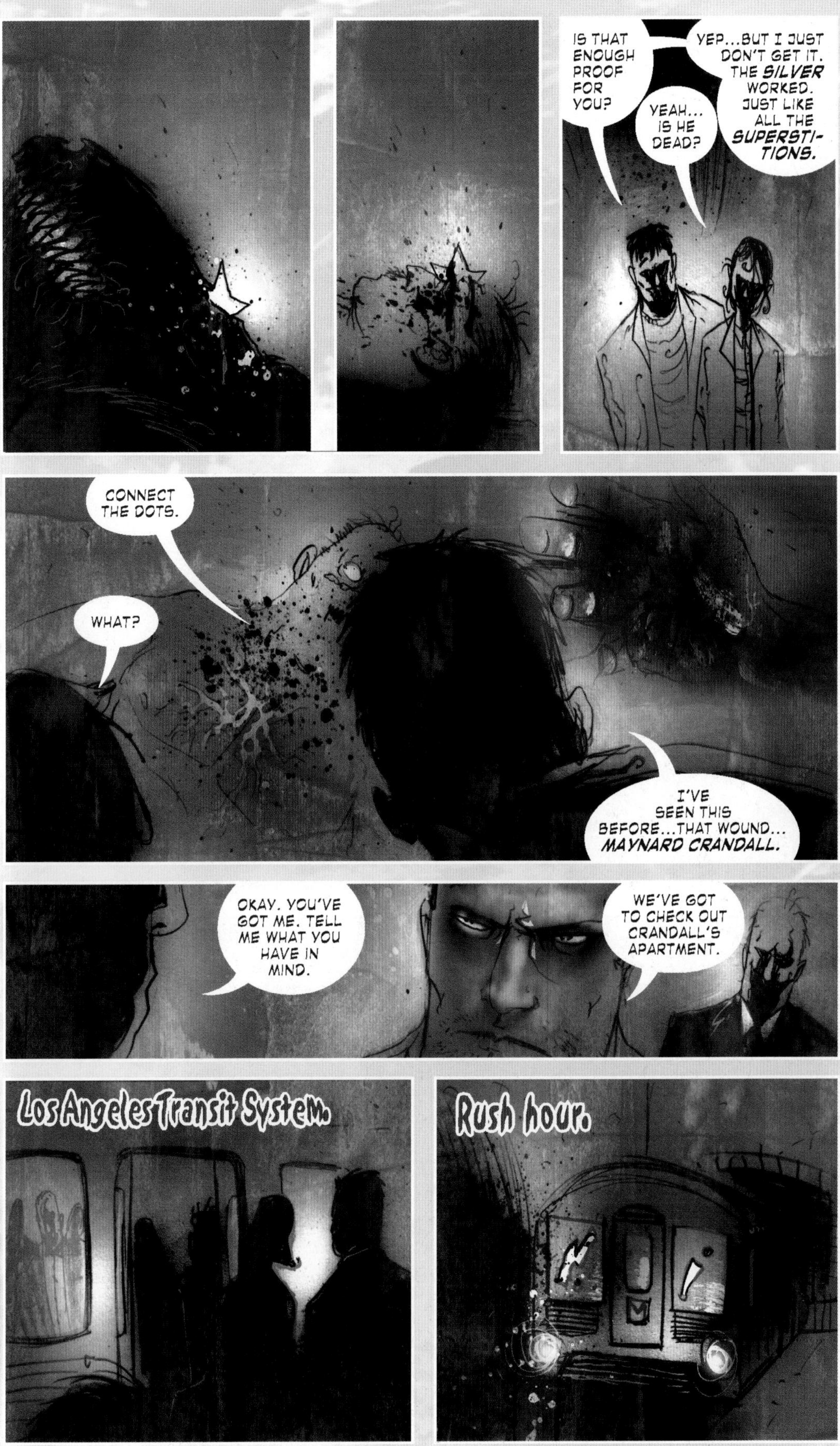
IS THAT ENOUGH PROOF FOR YOU?
YEP...BUT I JUST DON'T GET IT. THE SILVER WORKED. JUST LIKE ALL THE SUPERSTI-TIONS.
YEAH... IS HE DEAD?
CONNECT THE DOTS.
WHAT?
I'VE SEEN THIS BEFORE...THAT WOUND... MAYNARD CRANDALL.
OKAY. YOU'VE GOT ME. TELL ME WHAT YOU HAVE IN MIND.
WE'VE GOT TO CHECK OUT CRANDALL'S APARTMENT.
Los Angeles Transit System.
Rush hour.

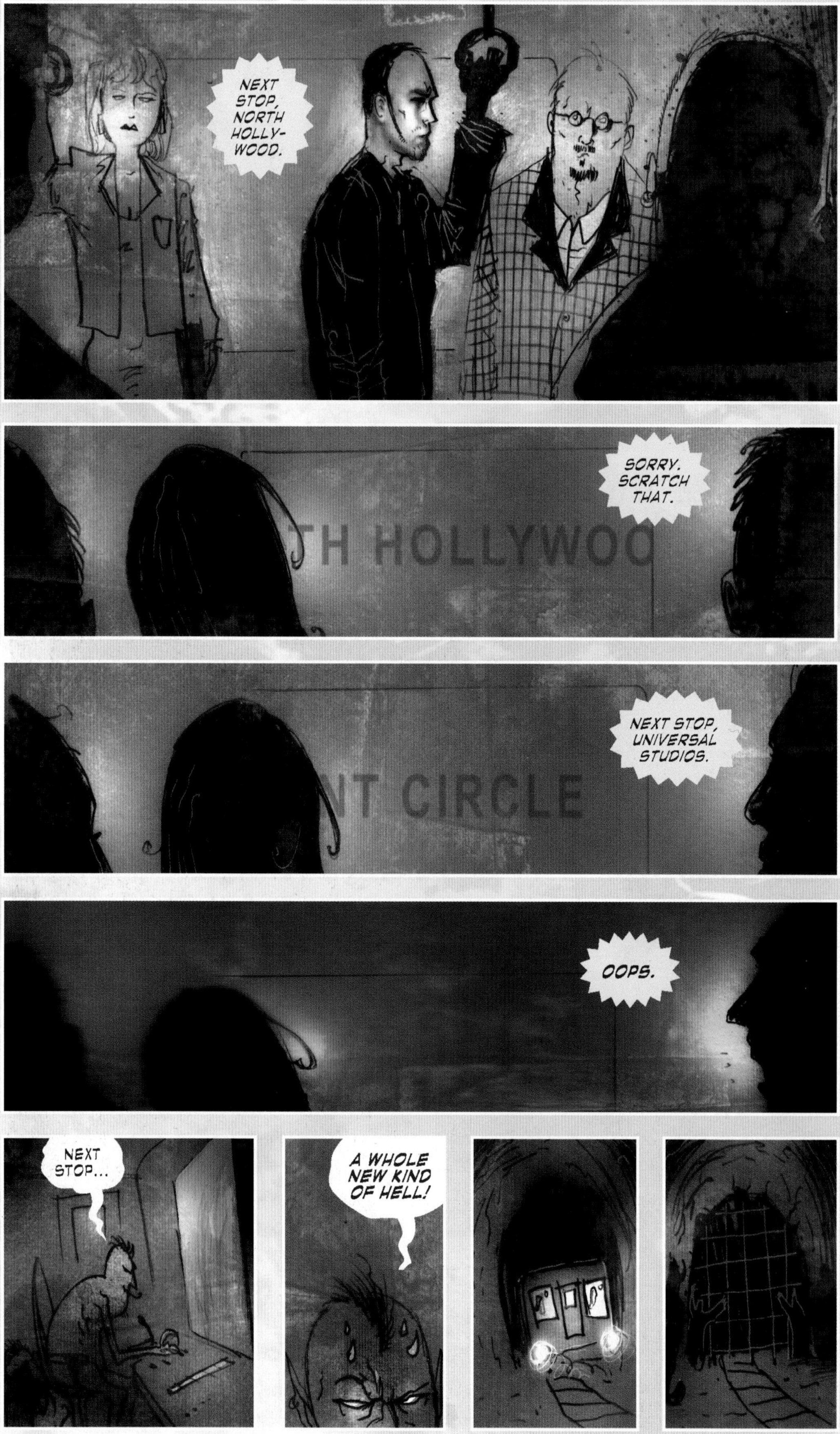
NEXT STOP, NORTH HOLLY-WOOD.
SORRY. SCRATCH THAT.
TH HOLLYWOO
NEXT STOP, UNIVERSAL STUDIOS.
NT CIRCLE
OOPS.
NEXT STOP...
A WHOLE NEW KIND OF HELL!

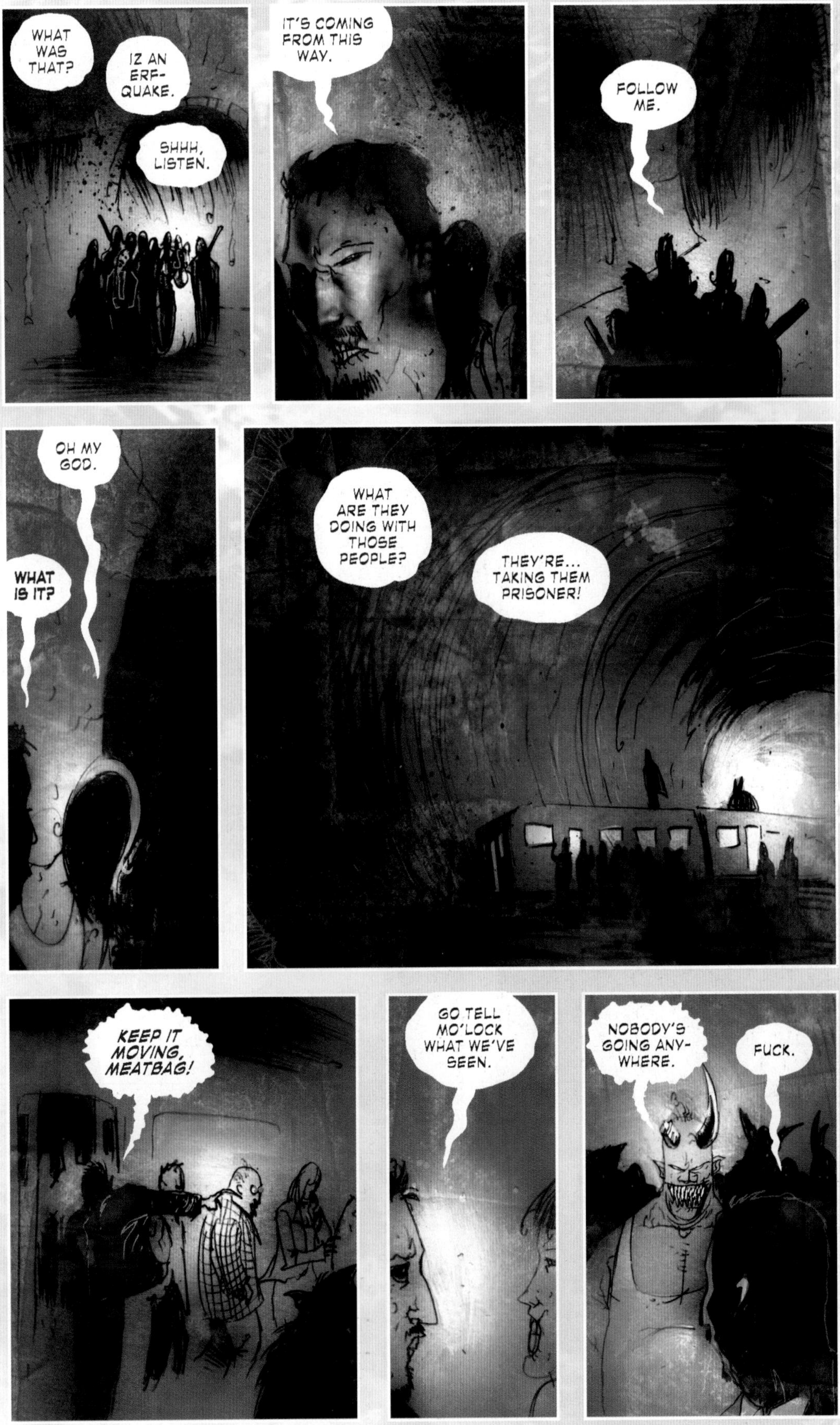

WHAT WAS THAT?
IZ AN ERF-QUAKE.
SHHH, LISTEN.
IT'S COMING FROM THIS WAY.
FOLLOW ME.
OH MY GOD.
WHAT IS IT?
WHAT ARE THEY DOING WITH THOSE PEOPLE?
THEY'RE... TAKING THEM PRISONER!
KEEP IT MOVING, MEATBAG!
GO TELL MO'LOCK WHAT WE'VE SEEN.
NOBODY'S GOING ANY-WHERE.
FUCK.

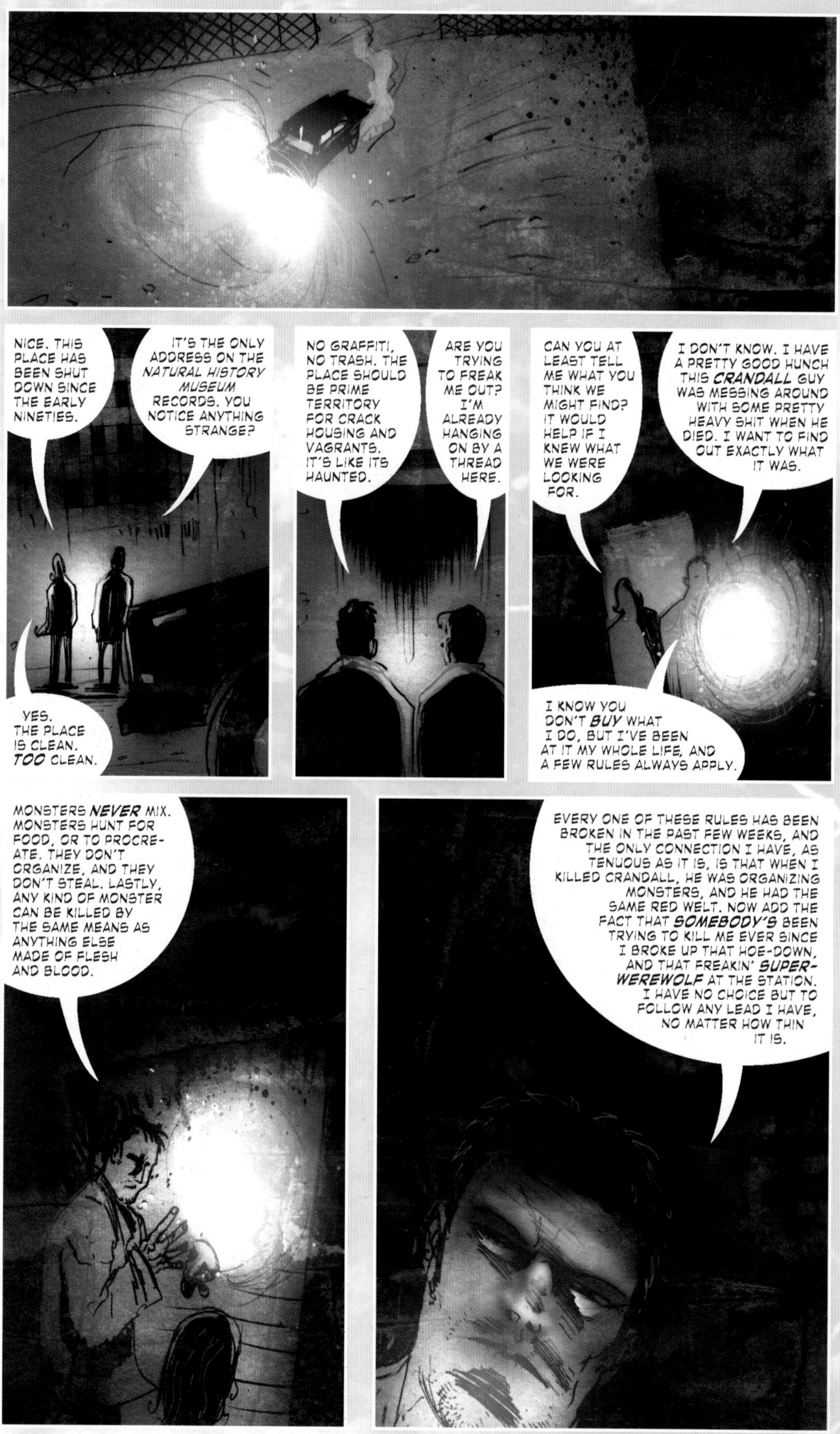

NICE. THIS PLACE HAS BEEN SHUT DOWN SINCE THE EARLY NINETIES.
IT'S THE ONLY ADDRESS ON THE *NATURAL HISTORY MUSEUM* RECORDS. YOU NOTICE ANYTHING STRANGE?
YES. THE PLACE IS CLEAN. ***TOO*** CLEAN.
NO GRAFFITI, NO TRASH. THE PLACE SHOULD BE PRIME TERRITORY FOR CRACK HOUSING AND VAGRANTS. IT'S LIKE ITS HAUNTED.
ARE YOU TRYING TO FREAK ME OUT? I'M ALREADY HANGING ON BY A THREAD HERE.
CAN YOU AT LEAST TELL ME WHAT YOU THINK WE MIGHT FIND? IT WOULD HELP IF I KNEW WHAT WE WERE LOOKING FOR.
I DON'T KNOW. I HAVE A PRETTY GOOD HUNCH THIS ***CRANDALL*** GUY WAS MESSING AROUND WITH SOME PRETTY HEAVY SHIT WHEN HE DIED. I WANT TO FIND OUT EXACTLY WHAT IT WAS.
I KNOW YOU DON'T ***BUY*** WHAT I DO, BUT I'VE BEEN AT IT MY WHOLE LIFE, AND A FEW RULES ALWAYS APPLY.
MONSTERS ***NEVER*** MIX. MONSTERS HUNT FOR FOOD, OR TO PROCREATE. THEY DON'T ORGANIZE, AND THEY DON'T STEAL. LASTLY, ANY KIND OF MONSTER CAN BE KILLED BY THE SAME MEANS AS ANYTHING ELSE MADE OF FLESH AND BLOOD.
EVERY ONE OF THESE RULES HAS BEEN BROKEN IN THE PAST FEW WEEKS, AND THE ONLY CONNECTION I HAVE, AS TENUOUS AS IT IS, IS THAT WHEN I KILLED CRANDALL, HE WAS ORGANIZING MONSTERS, AND HE HAD THE SAME RED WELT. NOW ADD THE FACT THAT ***SOMEBODY'S*** BEEN TRYING TO KILL ME EVER SINCE I BROKE UP THAT HOE-DOWN, AND THAT FREAKIN' ***SUPER-WEREWOLF*** AT THE STATION. I HAVE NO CHOICE BUT TO FOLLOW ANY LEAD I HAVE, NO MATTER HOW THIN IT IS.

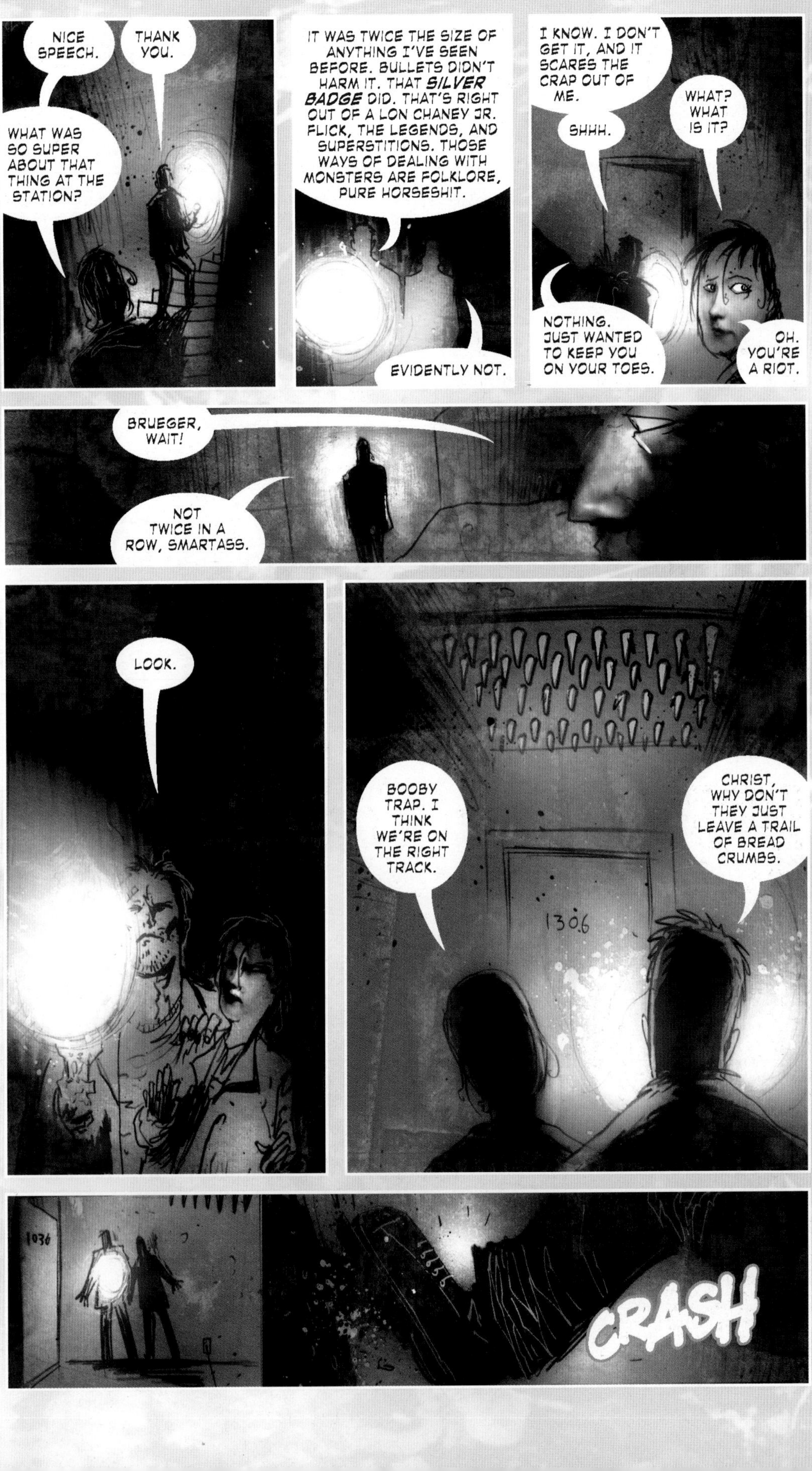
NICE SPEECH.
THANK YOU.
WHAT WAS SO SUPER ABOUT THAT THING AT THE STATION?
IT WAS TWICE THE SIZE OF ANYTHING I'VE SEEN BEFORE. BULLETS DIDN'T HARM IT. THAT SILVER BADGE DID. THAT'S RIGHT OUT OF A LON CHANEY JR. FLICK, THE LEGENDS, AND SUPERSTITIONS. THOSE WAYS OF DEALING WITH MONSTERS ARE FOLKLORE, PURE HORSESHIT.
EVIDENTLY NOT.
I KNOW. I DON'T GET IT, AND IT SCARES THE CRAP OUT OF ME.
SHHH.
WHAT? WHAT IS IT?
NOTHING. JUST WANTED TO KEEP YOU ON YOUR TOES.
OH. YOU'RE A RIOT.
BRUEGER, WAIT!
NOT TWICE IN A ROW, SMARTASS.
LOOK.
BOOBY TRAP. I THINK WE'RE ON THE RIGHT TRACK.
CHRIST, WHY DON'T THEY JUST LEAVE A TRAIL OF BREAD CRUMBS.
1306
1036
CRASH

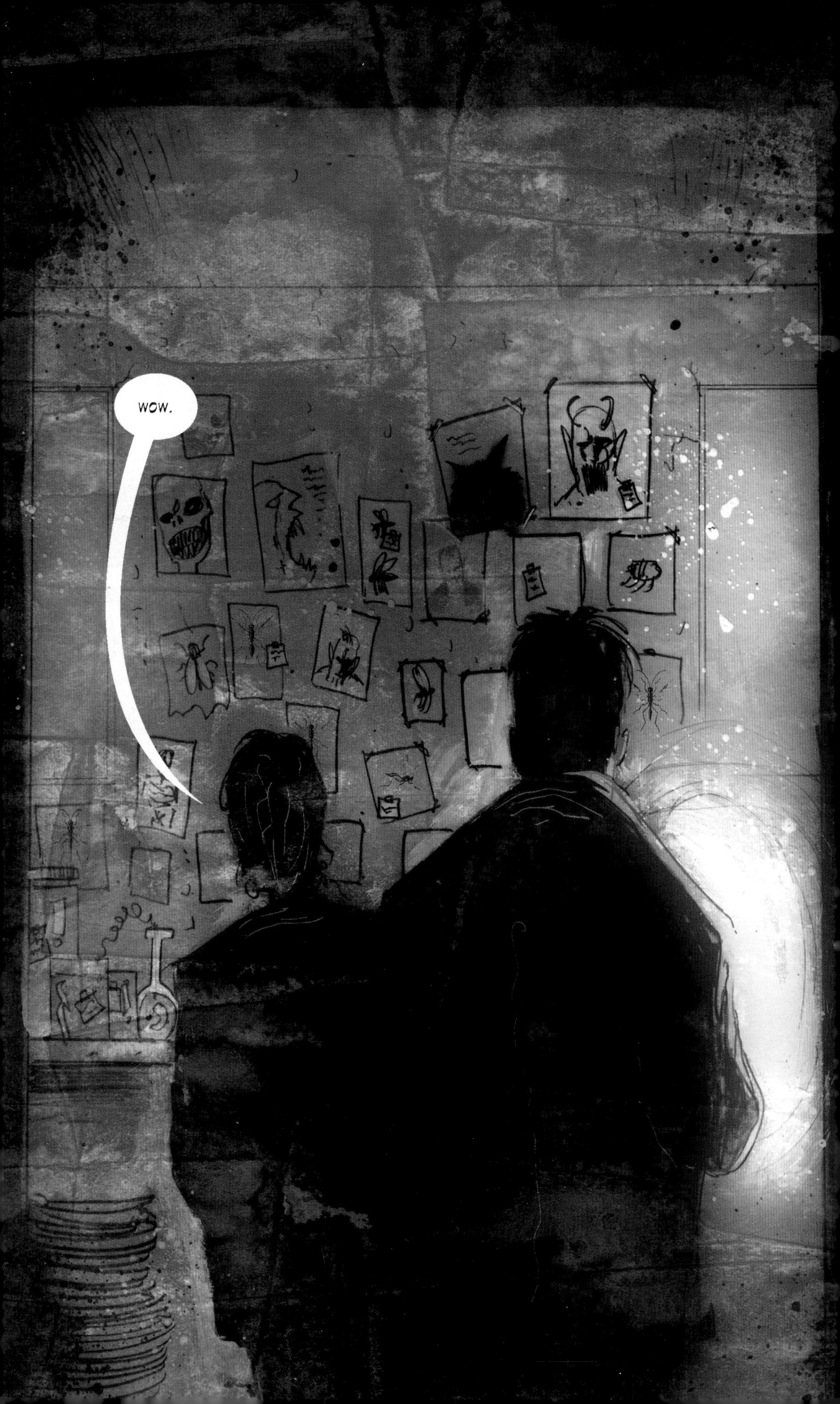
WOW.

CHAPTER FOUR
Bubonic Nights

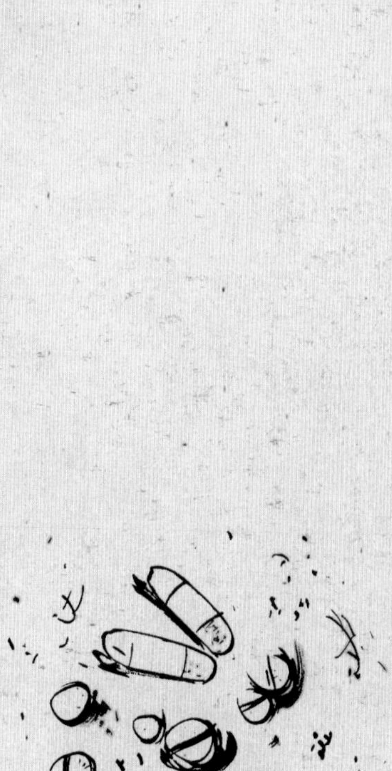

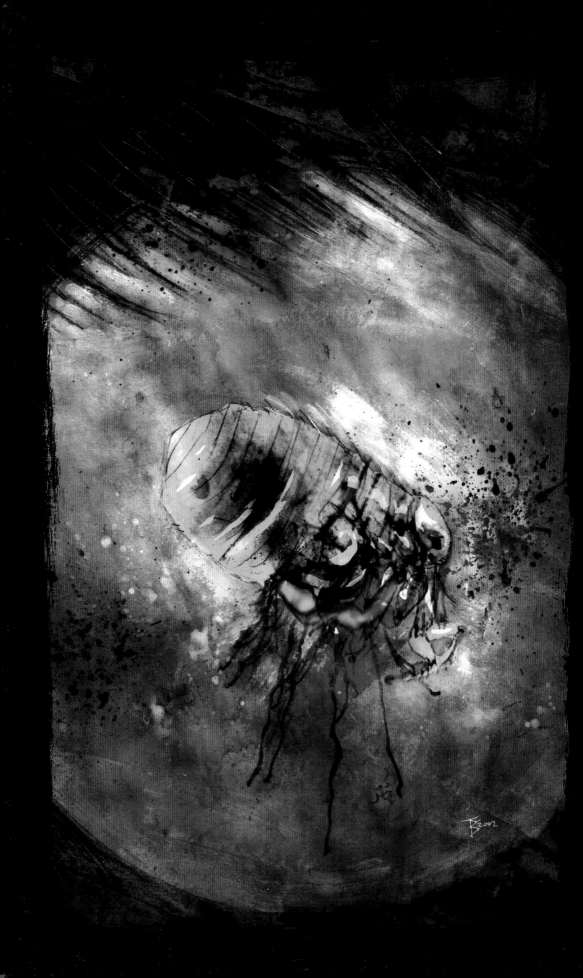

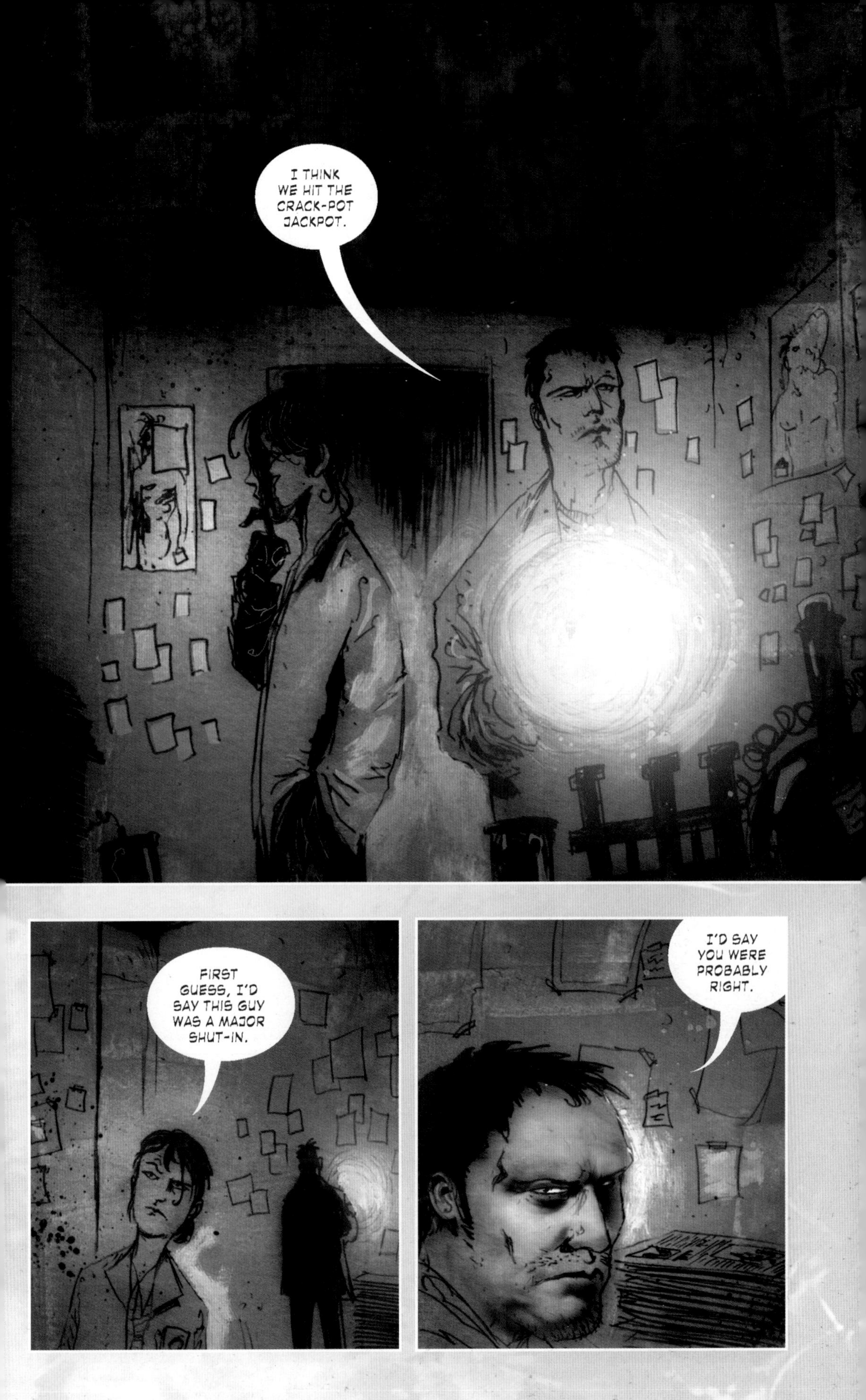
I THINK WE HIT THE CRACK-POT JACKPOT.
FIRST GUESS, I'D SAY THIS GUY WAS A MAJOR SHUT-IN.
I'D SAY YOU WERE PROBABLY RIGHT.

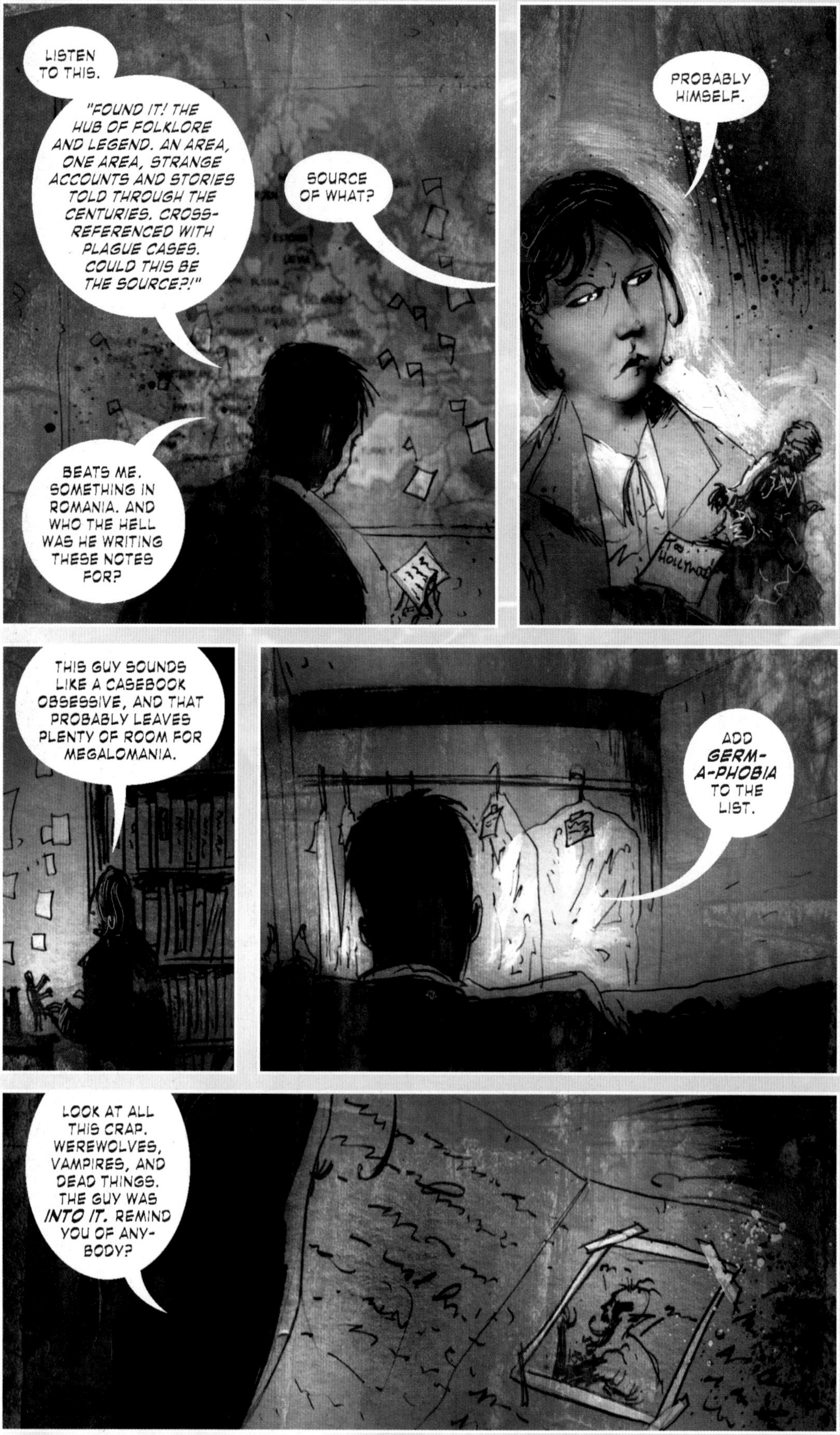
LISTEN TO THIS.
"FOUND IT! THE HUB OF FOLKLORE AND LEGEND. AN AREA, ONE AREA, STRANGE ACCOUNTS AND STORIES TOLD THROUGH THE CENTURIES. CROSS-REFERENCED WITH PLAGUE CASES. COULD THIS BE THE SOURCE?!"
SOURCE OF WHAT?
BEATS ME. SOMETHING IN ROMANIA. AND WHO THE HELL WAS HE WRITING THESE NOTES FOR?
PROBABLY HIMSELF.
HOLLYWOOD
THIS GUY SOUNDS LIKE A CASEBOOK OBSESSIVE, AND THAT PROBABLY LEAVES PLENTY OF ROOM FOR MEGALOMANIA.
ADD *GERM-A-PHOBIA* TO THE LIST.
LOOK AT ALL THIS CRAP. WEREWOLVES, VAMPIRES, AND DEAD THINGS. THE GUY WAS *INTO IT.* REMIND YOU OF ANY-BODY?

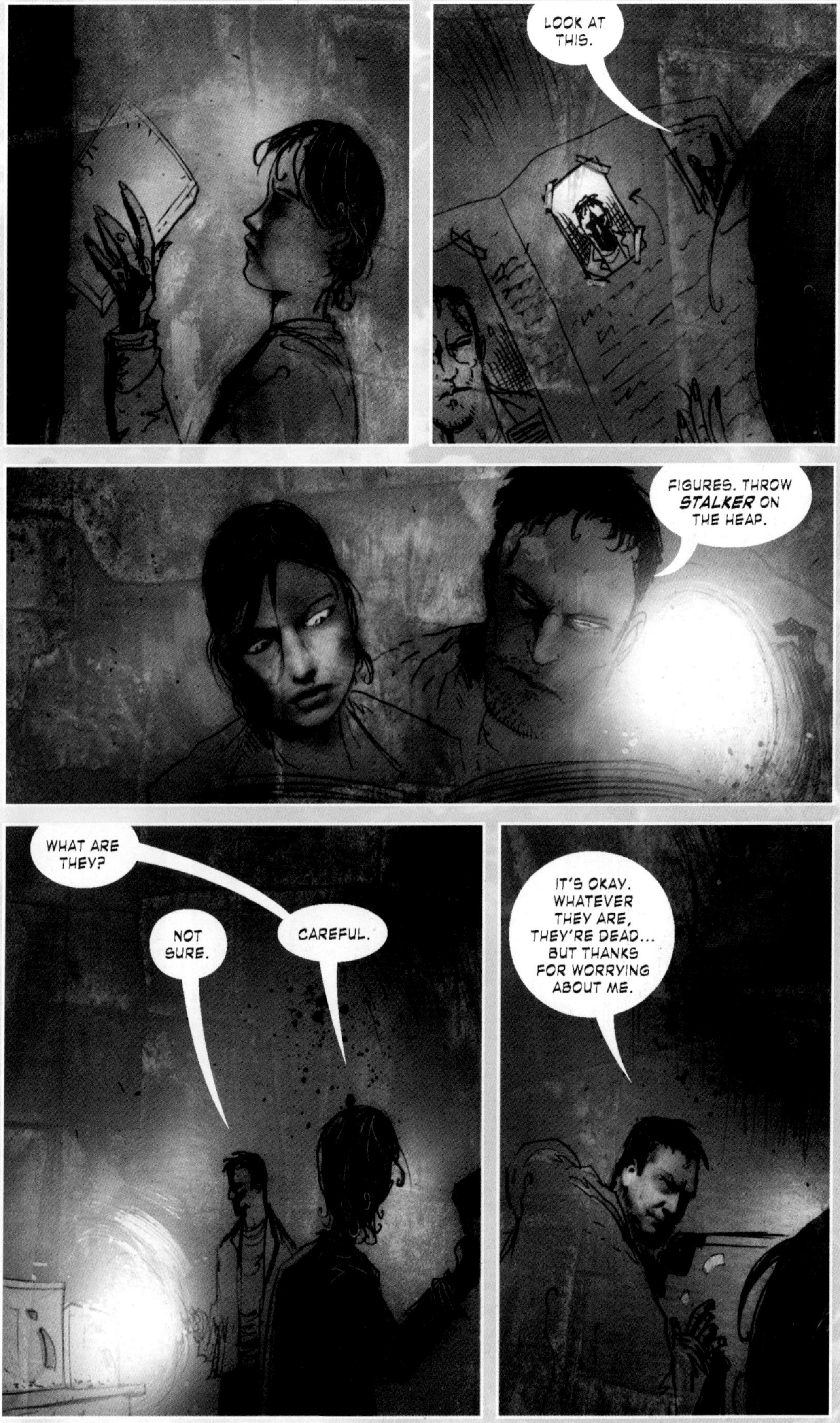
LOOK AT THIS.
FIGURES. THROW STALKER ON THE HEAP.
WHAT ARE THEY?
NOT SURE.
CAREFUL.
IT'S OKAY. WHATEVER THEY ARE, THEY'RE DEAD... BUT THANKS FOR WORRYING ABOUT ME.

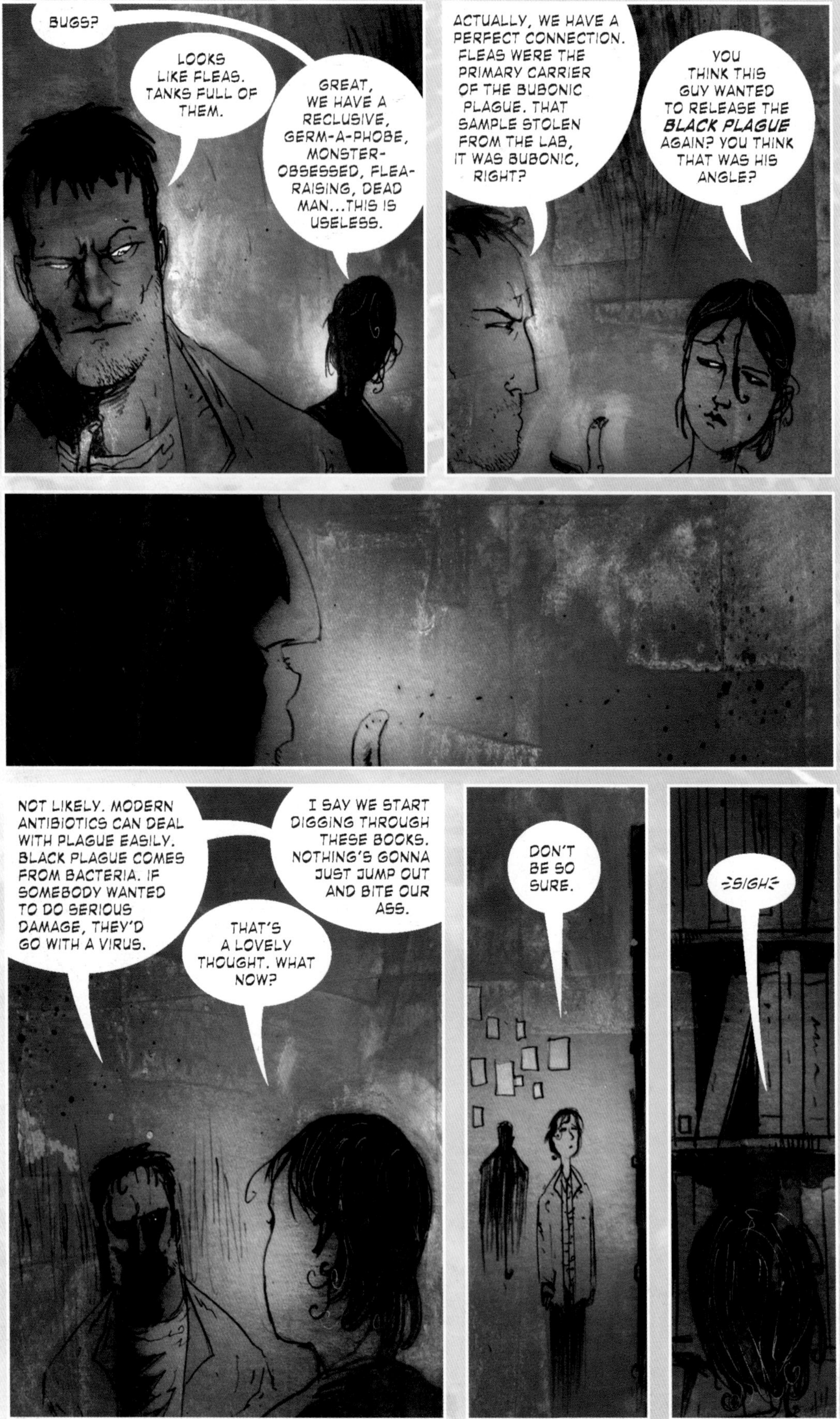

BUGS?
LOOKS LIKE FLEAS. TANKS FULL OF THEM.
GREAT, WE HAVE A RECLUSIVE, GERM-A-PHOBE, MONSTER-OBSESSED, FLEA-RAISING, DEAD MAN...THIS IS USELESS.
ACTUALLY, WE HAVE A PERFECT CONNECTION. FLEAS WERE THE PRIMARY CARRIER OF THE BUBONIC PLAGUE. THAT SAMPLE STOLEN FROM THE LAB, IT WAS BUBONIC, RIGHT?
YOU THINK THIS GUY WANTED TO RELEASE THE BLACK PLAGUE AGAIN? YOU THINK THAT WAS HIS ANGLE?
NOT LIKELY. MODERN ANTIBIOTICS CAN DEAL WITH PLAGUE EASILY. BLACK PLAGUE COMES FROM BACTERIA. IF SOMEBODY WANTED TO DO SERIOUS DAMAGE, THEY'D GO WITH A VIRUS.
I SAY WE START DIGGING THROUGH THESE BOOKS. NOTHING'S GONNA JUST JUMP OUT AND BITE OUR ASS.
THAT'S A LOVELY THOUGHT. WHAT NOW?
DON'T BE SO SURE.
SIGH

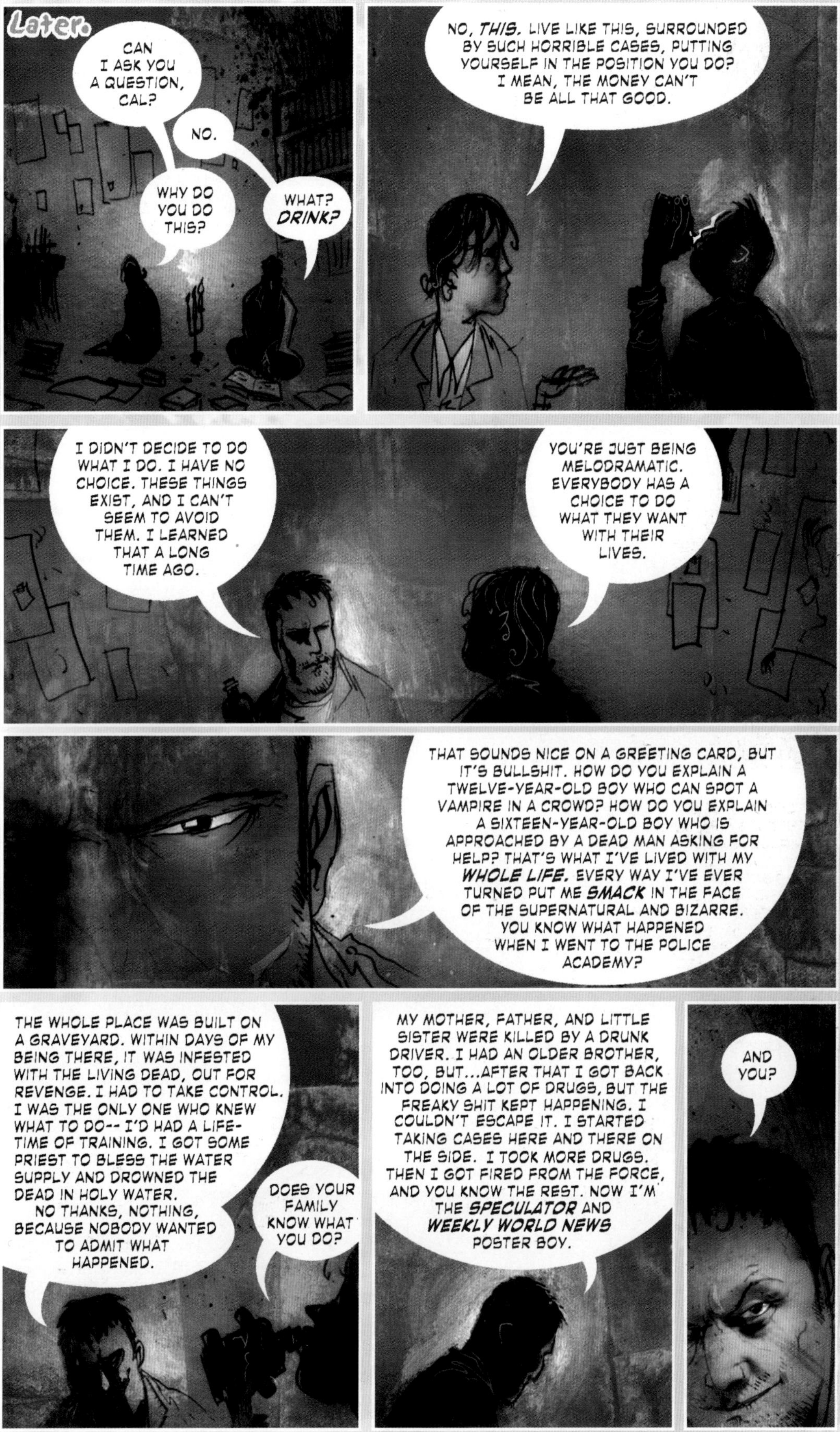
Later.
CAN I ASK YOU A QUESTION, CAL?
NO.
WHY DO YOU DO THIS?
WHAT? DRINK?
NO, THIS. LIVE LIKE THIS, SURROUNDED BY SUCH HORRIBLE CASES, PUTTING YOURSELF IN THE POSITION YOU DO? I MEAN, THE MONEY CAN'T BE ALL THAT GOOD.
I DIDN'T DECIDE TO DO WHAT I DO. I HAVE NO CHOICE. THESE THINGS EXIST, AND I CAN'T SEEM TO AVOID THEM. I LEARNED THAT A LONG TIME AGO.
YOU'RE JUST BEING MELODRAMATIC. EVERYBODY HAS A CHOICE TO DO WHAT THEY WANT WITH THEIR LIVES.
THAT SOUNDS NICE ON A GREETING CARD, BUT IT'S BULLSHIT. HOW DO YOU EXPLAIN A TWELVE-YEAR-OLD BOY WHO CAN SPOT A VAMPIRE IN A CROWD? HOW DO YOU EXPLAIN A SIXTEEN-YEAR-OLD BOY WHO IS APPROACHED BY A DEAD MAN ASKING FOR HELP? THAT'S WHAT I'VE LIVED WITH MY WHOLE LIFE. EVERY WAY I'VE EVER TURNED PUT ME SMACK IN THE FACE OF THE SUPERNATURAL AND BIZARRE. YOU KNOW WHAT HAPPENED WHEN I WENT TO THE POLICE ACADEMY?
THE WHOLE PLACE WAS BUILT ON A GRAVEYARD. WITHIN DAYS OF MY BEING THERE, IT WAS INFESTED WITH THE LIVING DEAD, OUT FOR REVENGE. I HAD TO TAKE CONTROL. I WAS THE ONLY ONE WHO KNEW WHAT TO DO-- I'D HAD A LIFE-TIME OF TRAINING. I GOT SOME PRIEST TO BLESS THE WATER SUPPLY AND DROWNED THE DEAD IN HOLY WATER. NO THANKS, NOTHING, BECAUSE NOBODY WANTED TO ADMIT WHAT HAPPENED.
DOES YOUR FAMILY KNOW WHAT YOU DO?
MY MOTHER, FATHER, AND LITTLE SISTER WERE KILLED BY A DRUNK DRIVER. I HAD AN OLDER BROTHER, TOO, BUT...AFTER THAT I GOT BACK INTO DOING A LOT OF DRUGS, BUT THE FREAKY SHIT KEPT HAPPENING. I COULDN'T ESCAPE IT. I STARTED TAKING CASES HERE AND THERE ON THE SIDE. I TOOK MORE DRUGS. THEN I GOT FIRED FROM THE FORCE, AND YOU KNOW THE REST. NOW I'M THE SPECULATOR AND WEEKLY WORLD NEWS POSTER BOY.
AND YOU?

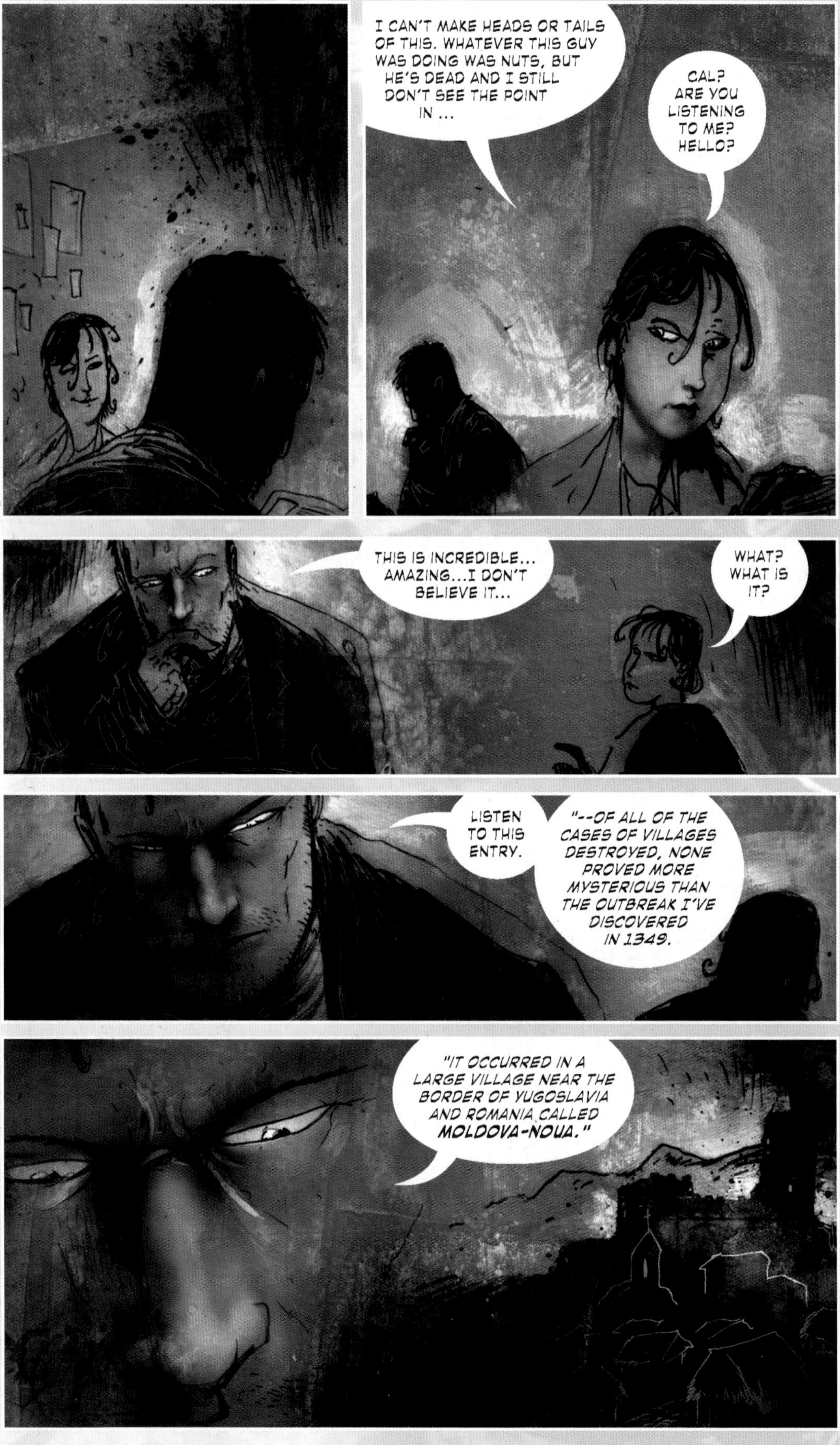
I CAN'T MAKE HEADS OR TAILS OF THIS. WHATEVER THIS GUY WAS DOING WAS NUTS, BUT HE'S DEAD AND I STILL DON'T SEE THE POINT IN ...
CAL? ARE YOU LISTENING TO ME? HELLO?
THIS IS INCREDIBLE... AMAZING...I DON'T BELIEVE IT...
WHAT? WHAT IS IT?
LISTEN TO THIS ENTRY.
"--OF ALL OF THE CASES OF VILLAGES DESTROYED, NONE PROVED MORE MYSTERIOUS THAN THE OUTBREAK I'VE DISCOVERED IN 1349.
"IT OCCURRED IN A LARGE VILLAGE NEAR THE BORDER OF YUGOSLAVIA AND ROMANIA CALLED **MOLDOVA-NOUA.**"

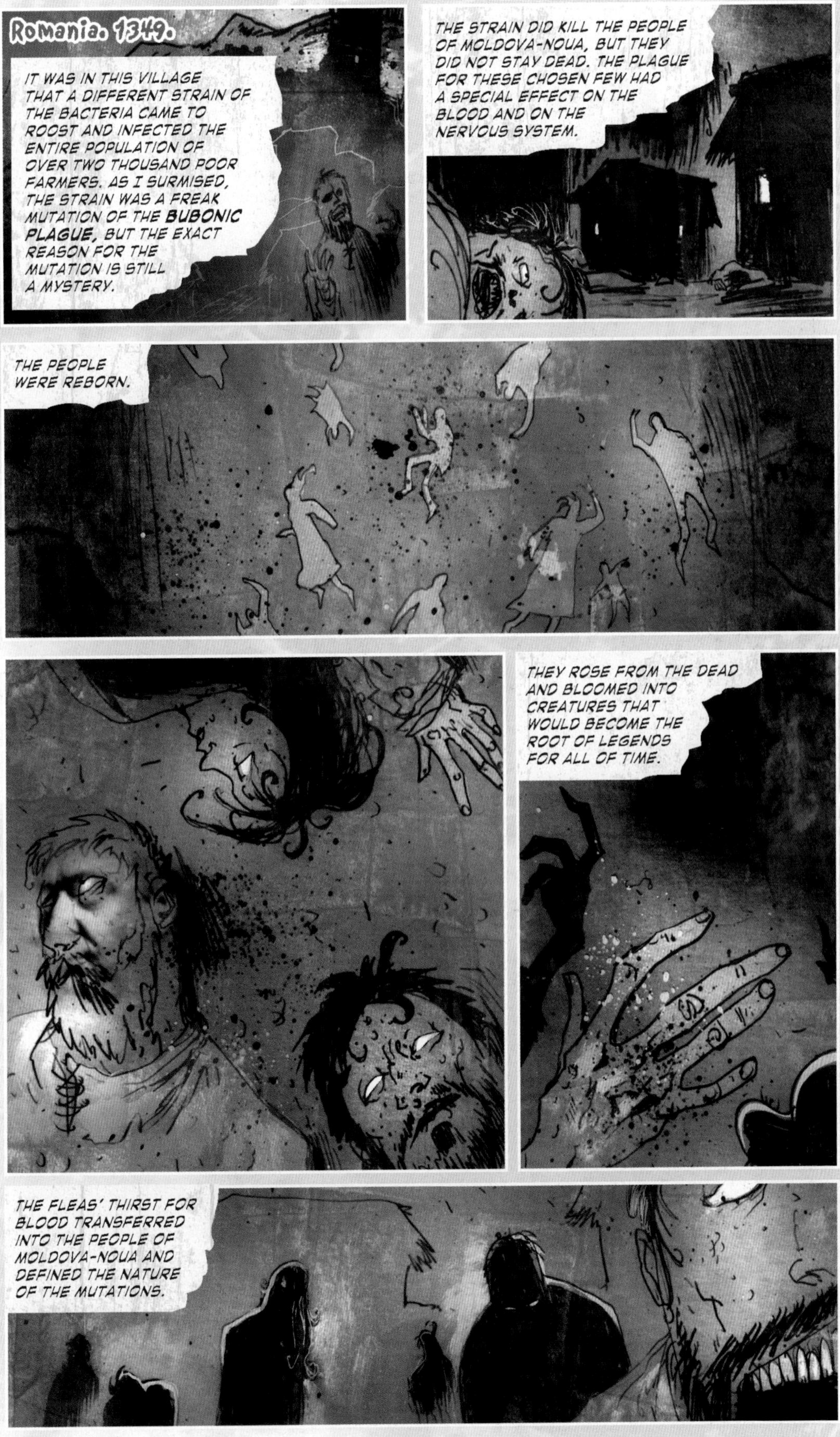
Romania. 1349.
IT WAS IN THIS VILLAGE THAT A DIFFERENT STRAIN OF THE BACTERIA CAME TO ROOST AND INFECTED THE ENTIRE POPULATION OF OVER TWO THOUSAND POOR FARMERS. AS I SURMISED, THE STRAIN WAS A FREAK MUTATION OF THE BUBONIC PLAGUE, BUT THE EXACT REASON FOR THE MUTATION IS STILL A MYSTERY.
THE STRAIN DID KILL THE PEOPLE OF MOLDOVA-NOUA, BUT THEY DID NOT STAY DEAD. THE PLAGUE FOR THESE CHOSEN FEW HAD A SPECIAL EFFECT ON THE BLOOD AND ON THE NERVOUS SYSTEM.
THE PEOPLE WERE REBORN.
THEY ROSE FROM THE DEAD AND BLOOMED INTO CREATURES THAT WOULD BECOME THE ROOT OF LEGENDS FOR ALL OF TIME.
THE FLEAS' THIRST FOR BLOOD TRANSFERRED INTO THE PEOPLE OF MOLDOVA-NOUA AND DEFINED THE NATURE OF THE MUTATIONS.

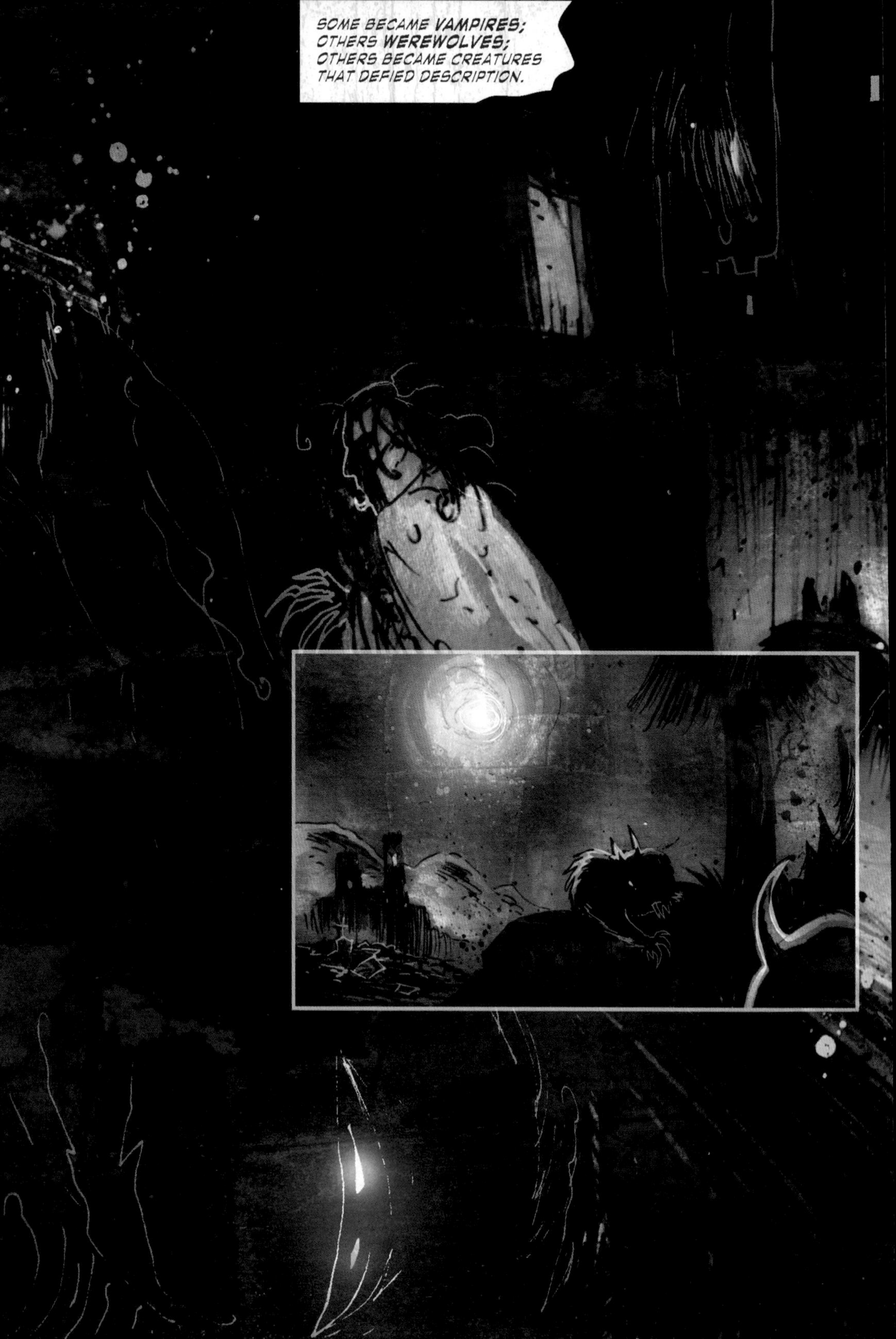
SOME BECAME **VAMPIRES**; OTHERS **WEREWOLVES**; OTHERS BECAME CREATURES THAT DEFIED DESCRIPTION.

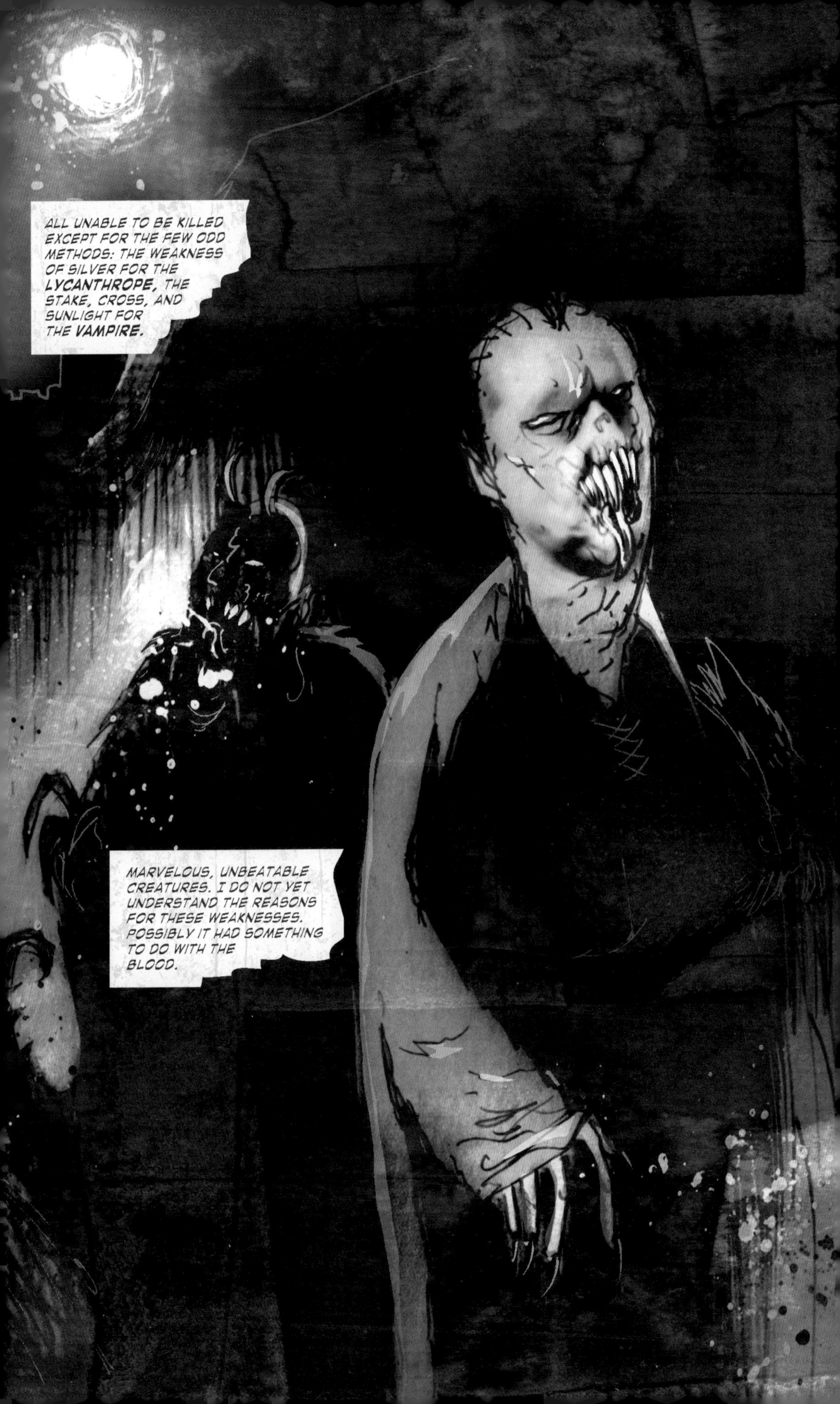
ALL UNABLE TO BE KILLED EXCEPT FOR THE FEW ODD METHODS: THE WEAKNESS OF SILVER FOR THE **LYCANTHROPE,** THE STAKE, CROSS, AND SUNLIGHT FOR THE **VAMPIRE.**
MARVELOUS, UNBEATABLE CREATURES. I DO NOT YET UNDERSTAND THE REASONS FOR THESE WEAKNESSES. POSSIBLY IT HAD SOMETHING TO DO WITH THE BLOOD.

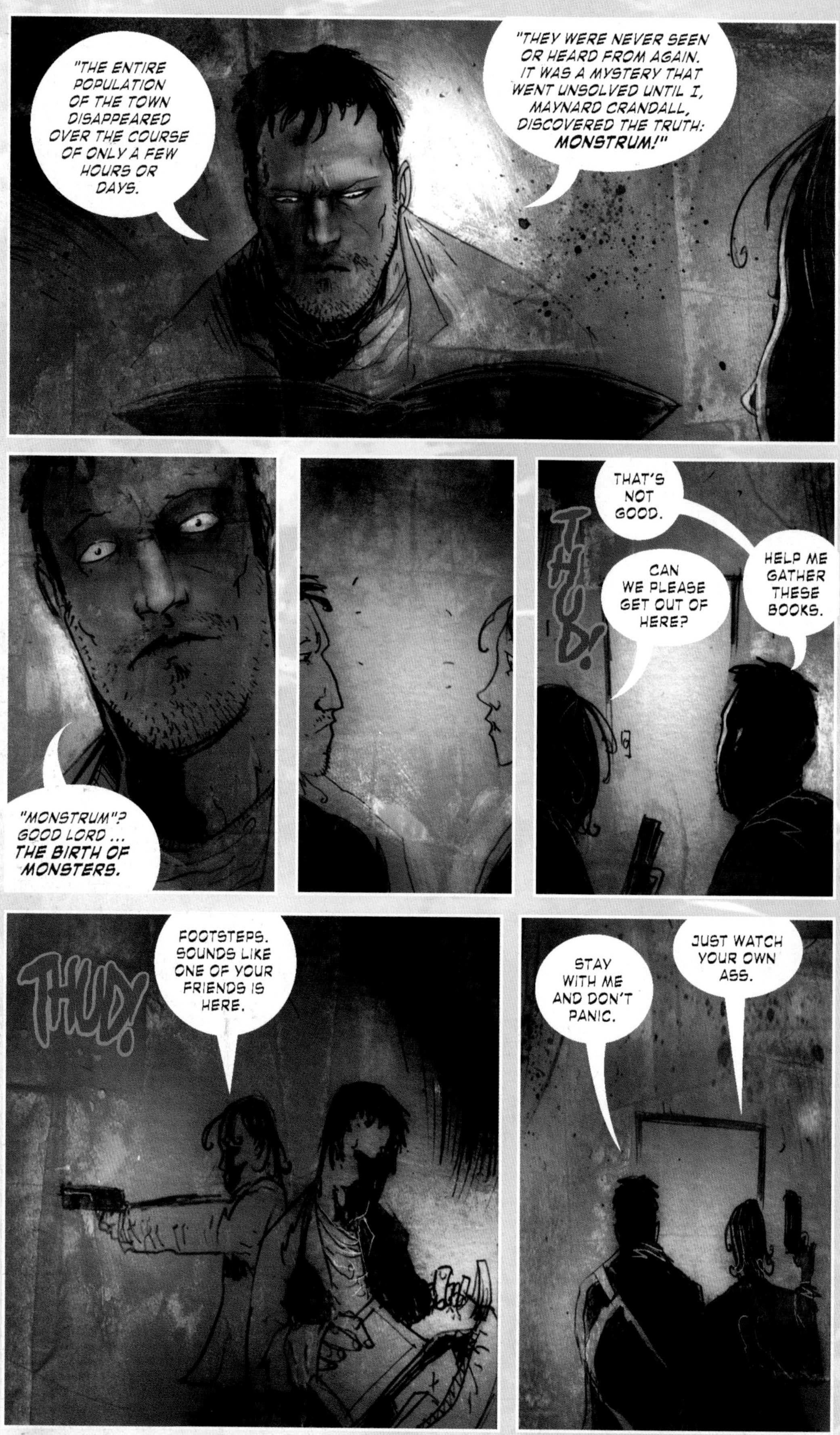
"THE ENTIRE POPULATION OF THE TOWN DISAPPEARED OVER THE COURSE OF ONLY A FEW HOURS OR DAYS.
"THEY WERE NEVER SEEN OR HEARD FROM AGAIN. IT WAS A MYSTERY THAT WENT UNSOLVED UNTIL I, MAYNARD CRANDALL, DISCOVERED THE TRUTH: MONSTRUM!"
"MONSTRUM"? GOOD LORD ... THE BIRTH OF MONSTERS.
THUD!
THAT'S NOT GOOD.
CAN WE PLEASE GET OUT OF HERE?
HELP ME GATHER THESE BOOKS.
THUD!
FOOTSTEPS. SOUNDS LIKE ONE OF YOUR FRIENDS IS HERE.
STAY WITH ME AND DON'T PANIC.
JUST WATCH YOUR OWN ASS.

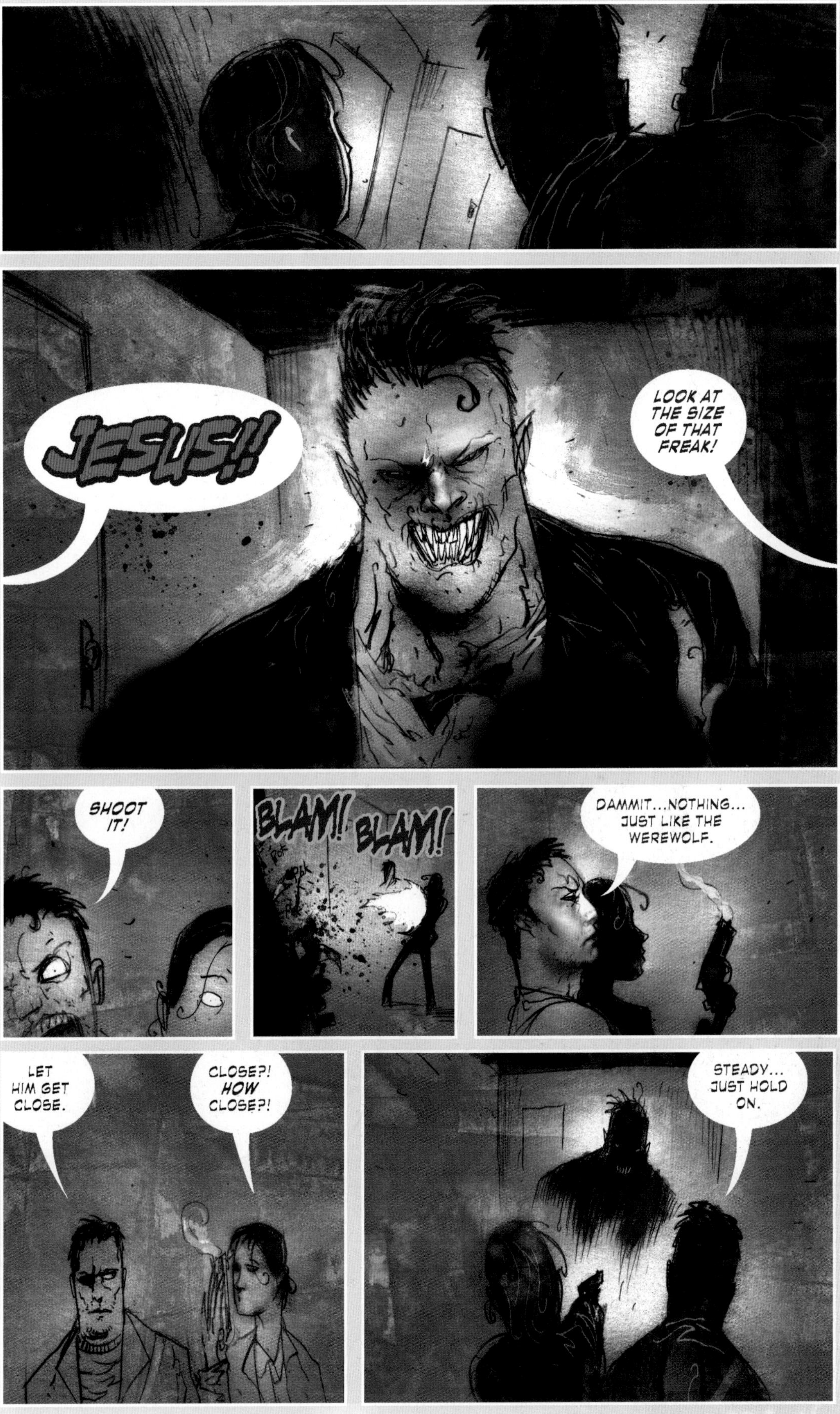
JESUS!!
LOOK AT THE SIZE OF THAT FREAK!
SHOOT IT!
BLAM! BLAM!
DAMMIT...NOTHING... JUST LIKE THE WEREWOLF.
LET HIM GET CLOSE.
CLOSE?! HOW CLOSE?!
STEADY... JUST HOLD ON.

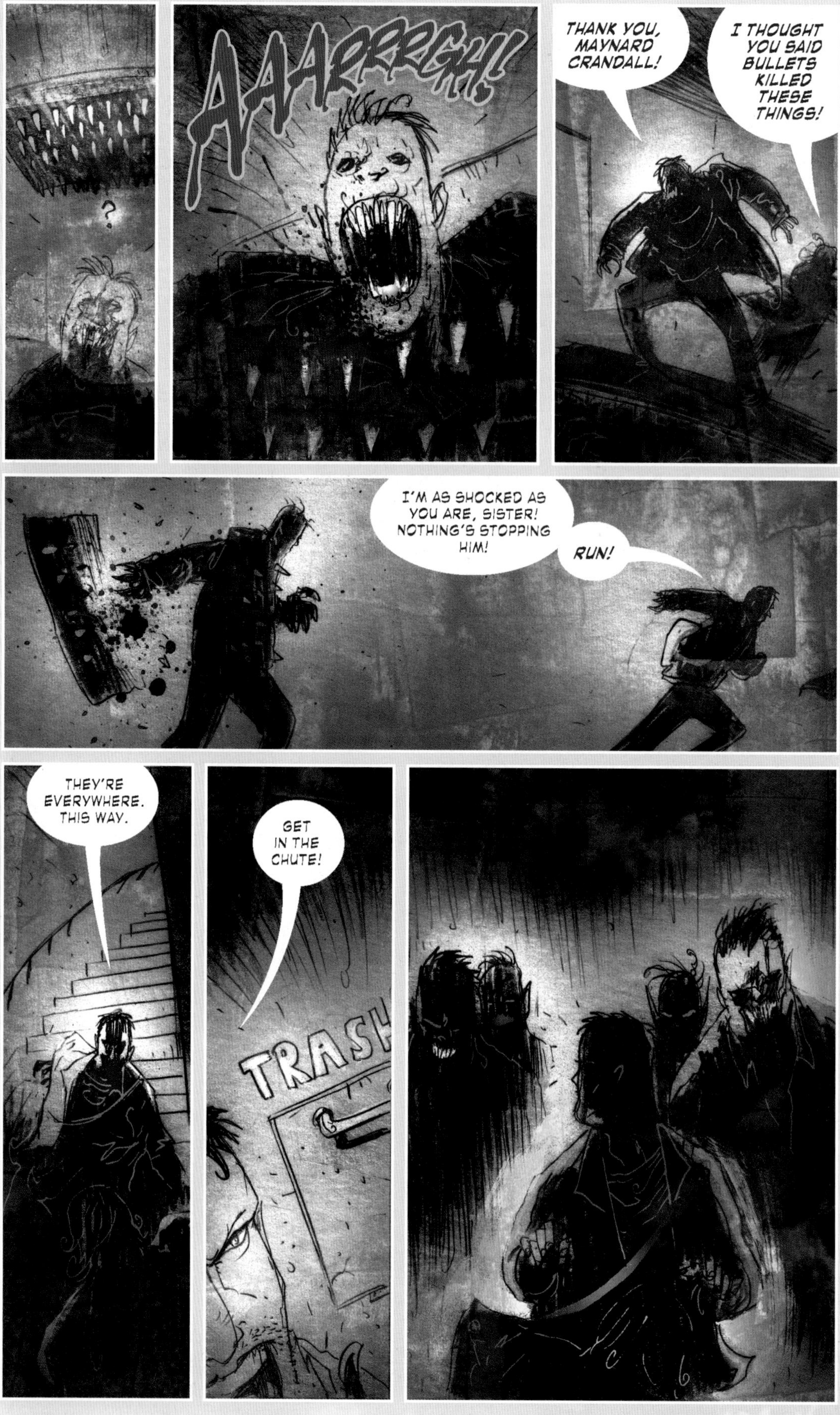
?
AAARRRGH!!
THANK YOU, MAYNARD CRANDALL!
I THOUGHT YOU SAID BULLETS KILLED THESE THINGS!
I'M AS SHOCKED AS YOU ARE, SISTER! NOTHING'S STOPPING HIM!
RUN!
THEY'RE EVERYWHERE. THIS WAY.
GET IN THE CHUTE!
TRASH

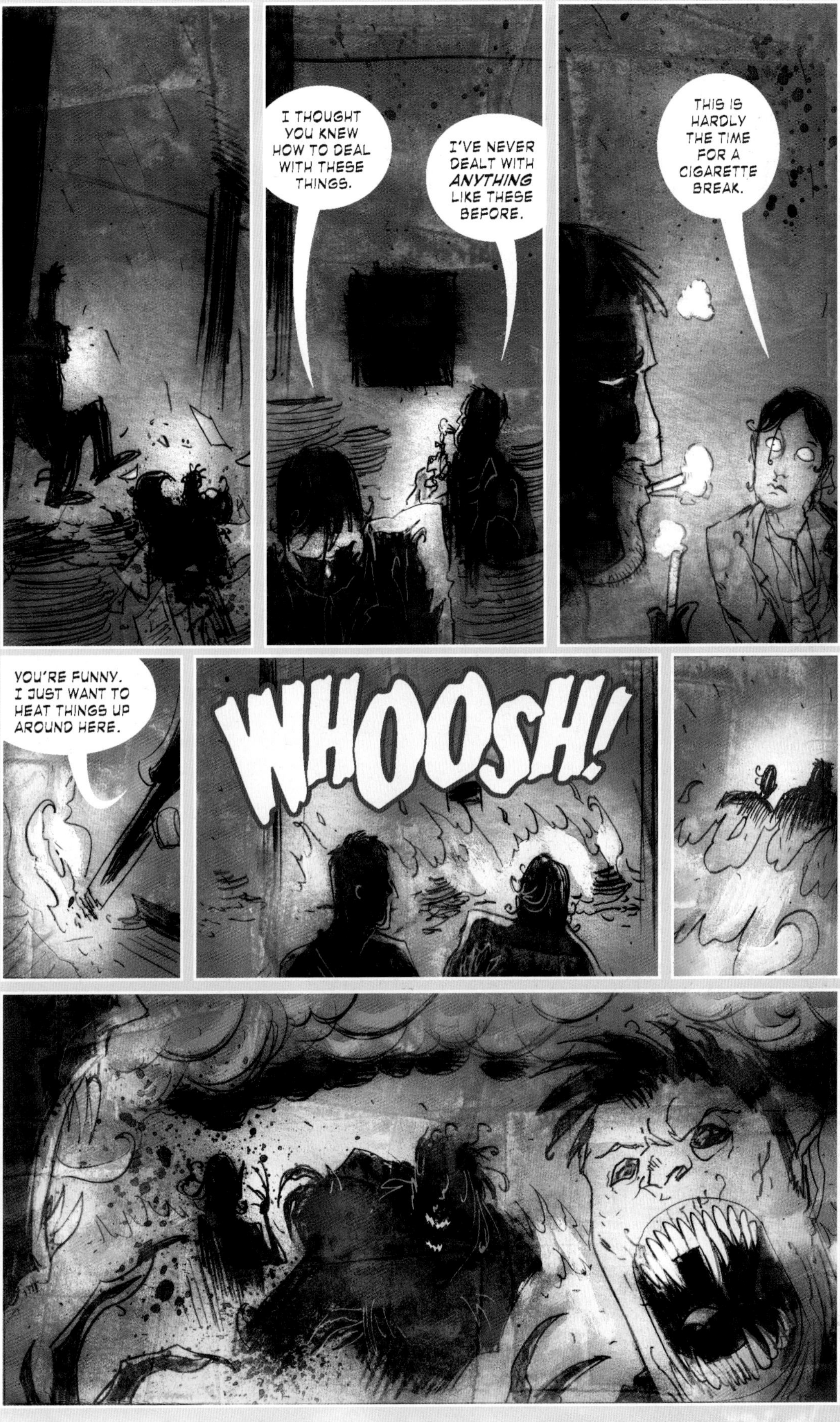
I THOUGHT YOU KNEW HOW TO DEAL WITH THESE THINGS.
I'VE NEVER DEALT WITH *ANYTHING* LIKE THESE BEFORE.
THIS IS HARDLY THE TIME FOR A CIGARETTE BREAK.
YOU'RE FUNNY. I JUST WANT TO HEAT THINGS UP AROUND HERE.
WHOOSH!

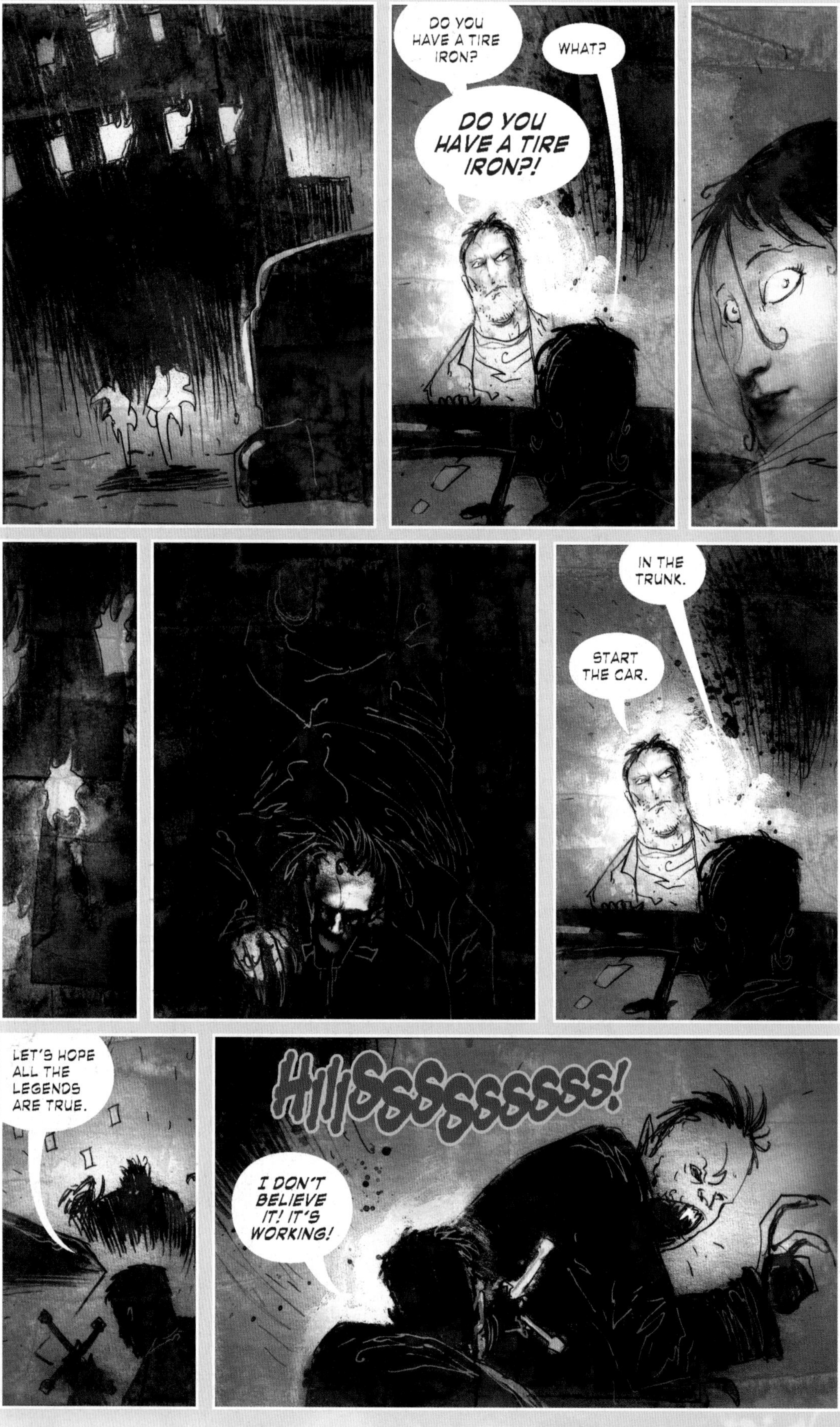

DO YOU HAVE A TIRE IRON?
WHAT?
DO YOU HAVE A TIRE IRON?!
IN THE TRUNK.
START THE CAR.
LET'S HOPE ALL THE LEGENDS ARE TRUE.
HHHSSSSSSSSS!
I DON'T BELIEVE IT! IT'S WORKING!

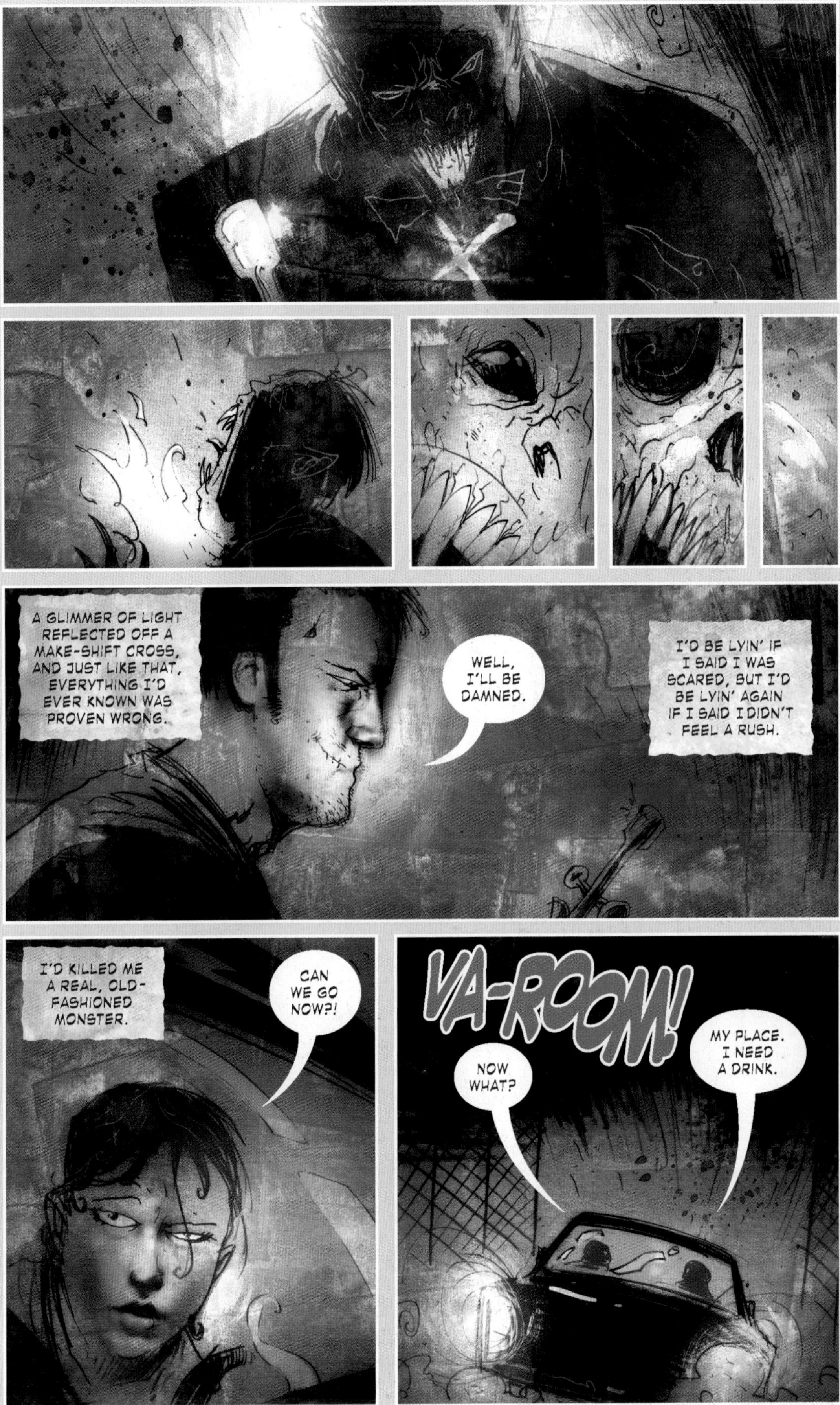
A GLIMMER OF LIGHT REFLECTED OFF A MAKE-SHIFT CROSS, AND JUST LIKE THAT, EVERYTHING I'D EVER KNOWN WAS PROVEN WRONG.
WELL, I'LL BE DAMNED.
I'D BE LYIN' IF I SAID I WAS SCARED, BUT I'D BE LYIN' AGAIN IF I SAID I DIDN'T FEEL A RUSH.
I'D KILLED ME A REAL, OLD-FASHIONED MONSTER.
CAN WE GO NOW?!
VA-ROOM!
NOW WHAT?
MY PLACE. I NEED A DRINK.

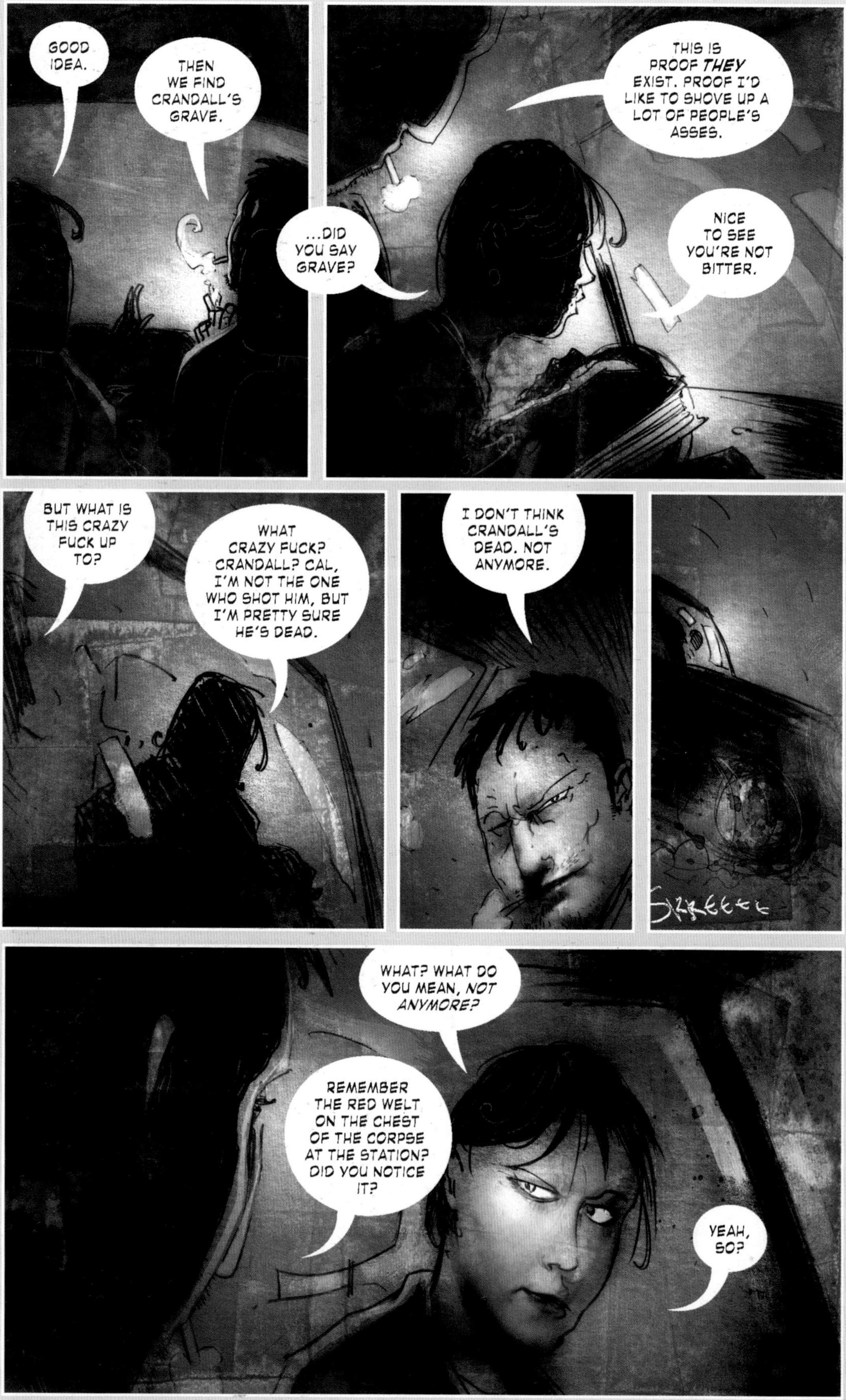
GOOD IDEA.
THEN WE FIND CRANDALL'S GRAVE.
THIS IS PROOF *THEY* EXIST. PROOF I'D LIKE TO SHOVE UP A LOT OF PEOPLE'S ASSES.
...DID YOU SAY GRAVE?
NICE TO SEE YOU'RE NOT BITTER.
BUT WHAT IS THIS CRAZY FUCK UP TO?
WHAT CRAZY FUCK? CRANDALL? CAL, I'M NOT THE ONE WHO SHOT HIM, BUT I'M PRETTY SURE HE'S DEAD.
I DON'T THINK CRANDALL'S DEAD. NOT ANYMORE.
SKREEEE
WHAT? WHAT DO YOU MEAN, *NOT ANYMORE?*
REMEMBER THE RED WELT ON THE CHEST OF THE CORPSE AT THE STATION? DID YOU NOTICE IT?
YEAH, SO?

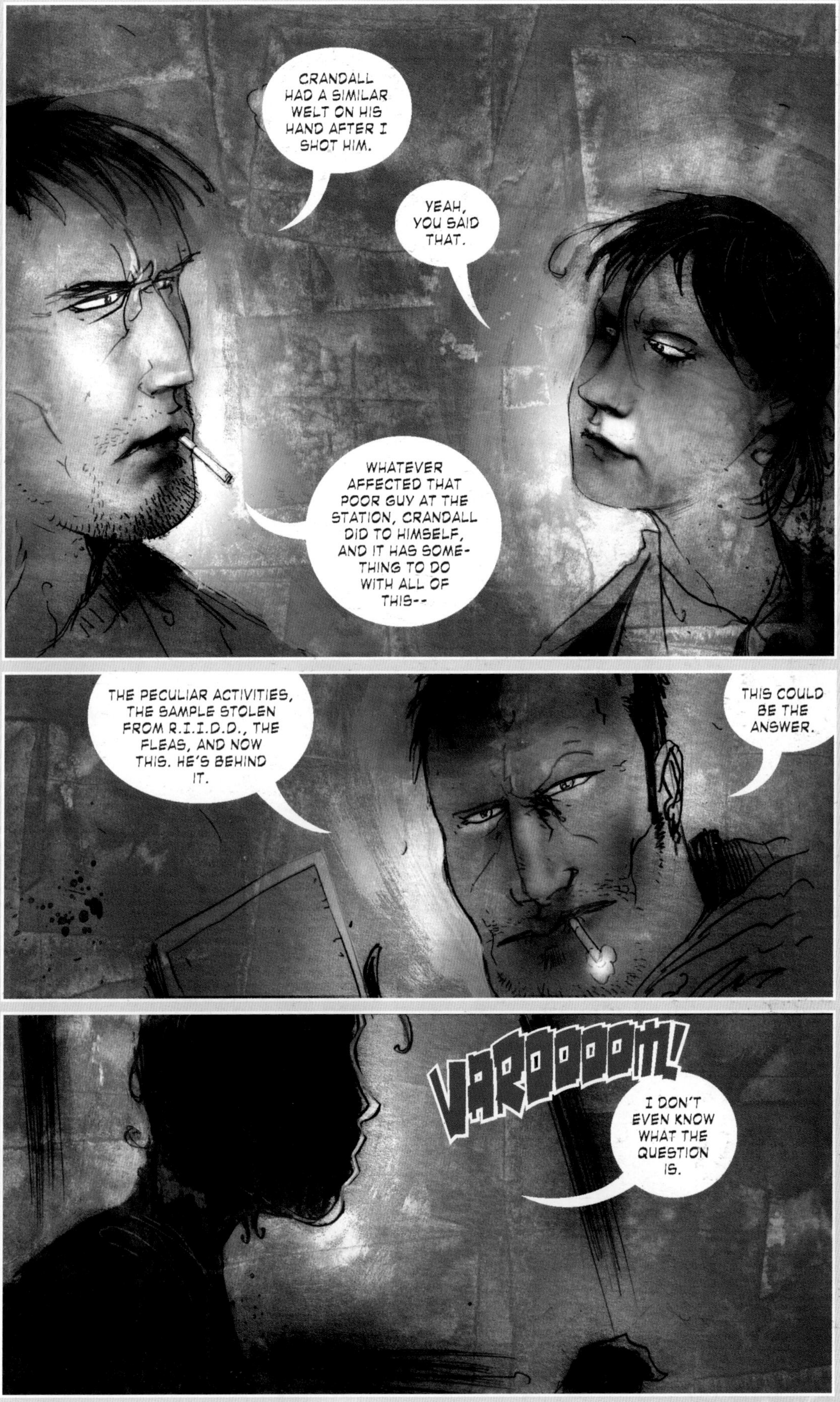
CRANDALL HAD A SIMILAR WELT ON HIS HAND AFTER I SHOT HIM.
YEAH, YOU SAID THAT.
WHATEVER AFFECTED THAT POOR GUY AT THE STATION, CRANDALL DID TO HIMSELF, AND IT HAS SOME-THING TO DO WITH ALL OF THIS--
THE PECULIAR ACTIVITIES, THE SAMPLE STOLEN FROM R.I.I.D.D., THE FLEAS, AND NOW THIS. HE'S BEHIND IT.
THIS COULD BE THE ANSWER.
VAROOOOOM!
I DON'T EVEN KNOW WHAT THE QUESTION IS.

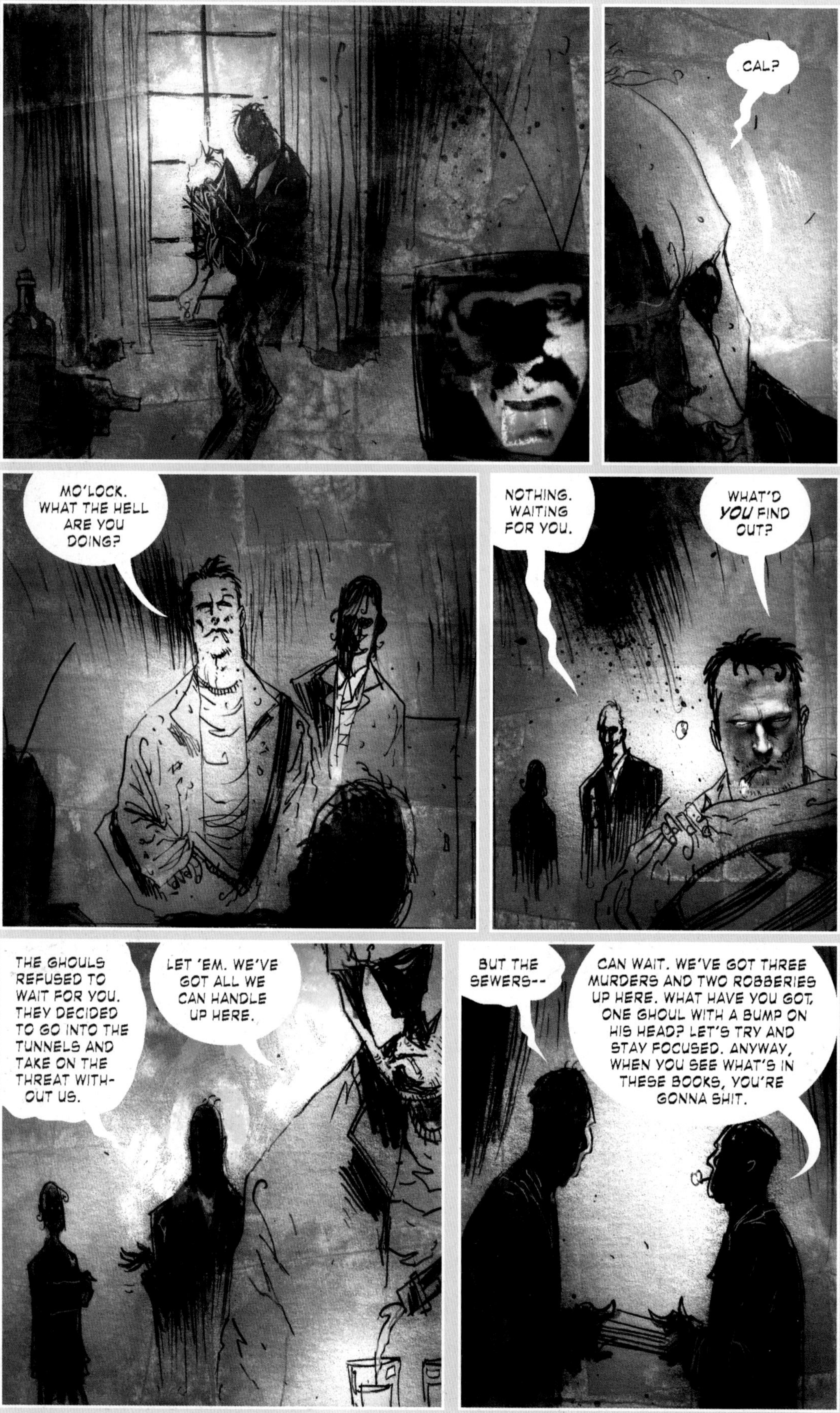
CAL?
MO'LOCK. WHAT THE HELL ARE YOU DOING?
NOTHING. WAITING FOR YOU.
WHAT'D *YOU* FIND OUT?
THE GHOULS REFUSED TO WAIT FOR YOU. THEY DECIDED TO GO INTO THE TUNNELS AND TAKE ON THE THREAT WITH- OUT US.
LET 'EM. WE'VE GOT ALL WE CAN HANDLE UP HERE.
BUT THE SEWERS--
CAN WAIT. WE'VE GOT THREE MURDERS AND TWO ROBBERIES UP HERE. WHAT HAVE YOU GOT, ONE GHOUL WITH A BUMP ON HIS HEAD? LET'S TRY AND STAY FOCUSED. ANYWAY, WHEN YOU SEE WHAT'S IN THESE BOOKS, YOU'RE GONNA SHIT.

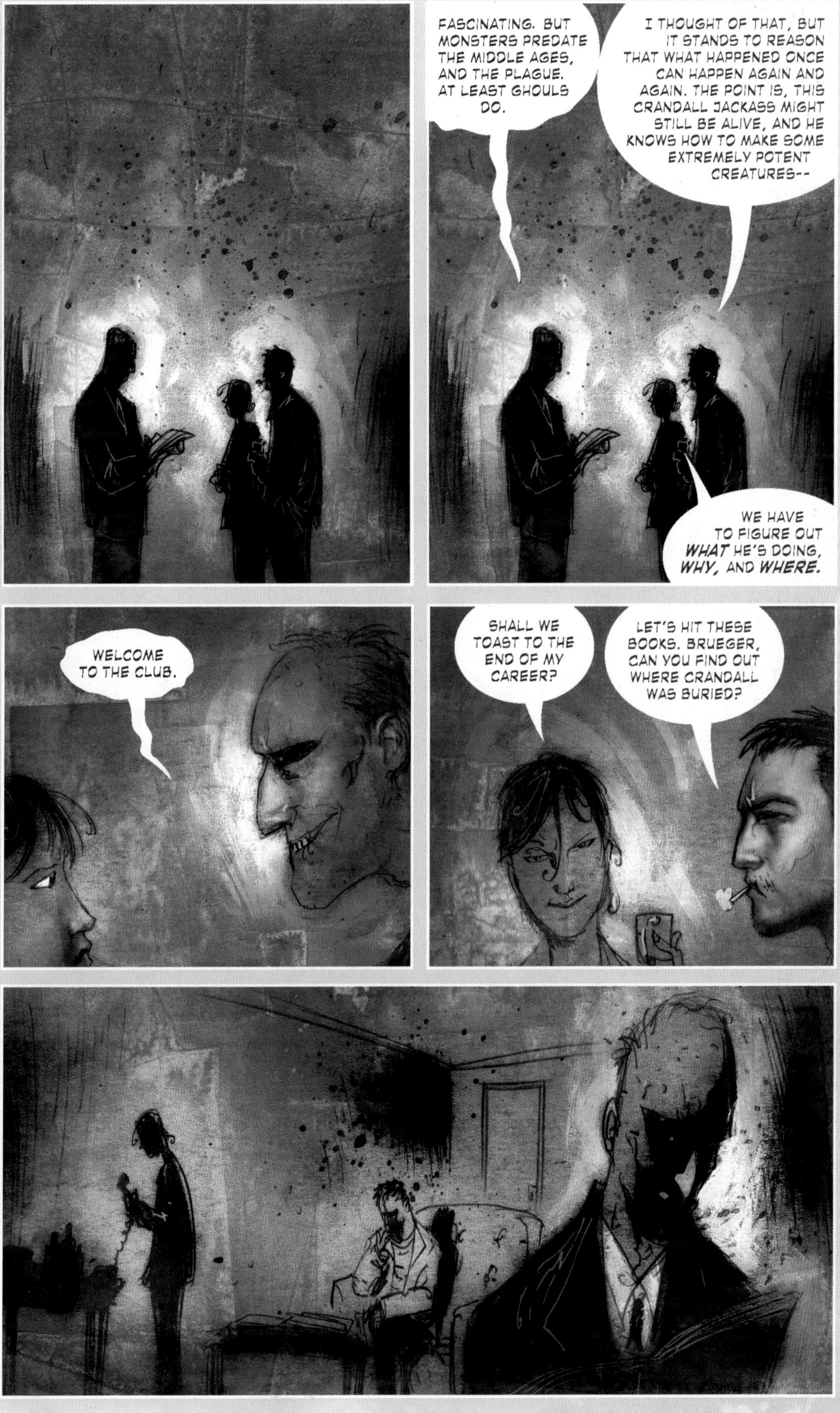
FASCINATING. BUT MONSTERS PREDATE THE MIDDLE AGES, AND THE PLAGUE. AT LEAST GHOULS DO.
I THOUGHT OF THAT, BUT IT STANDS TO REASON THAT WHAT HAPPENED ONCE CAN HAPPEN AGAIN AND AGAIN. THE POINT IS, THIS CRANDALL JACKASS MIGHT STILL BE ALIVE, AND HE KNOWS HOW TO MAKE SOME EXTREMELY POTENT CREATURES--
WE HAVE TO FIGURE OUT *WHAT* HE'S DOING, *WHY,* AND *WHERE.*
WELCOME TO THE CLUB.
SHALL WE TOAST TO THE END OF MY CAREER?
LET'S HIT THESE BOOKS. BRUEGER, CAN YOU FIND OUT WHERE CRANDALL WAS BURIED?

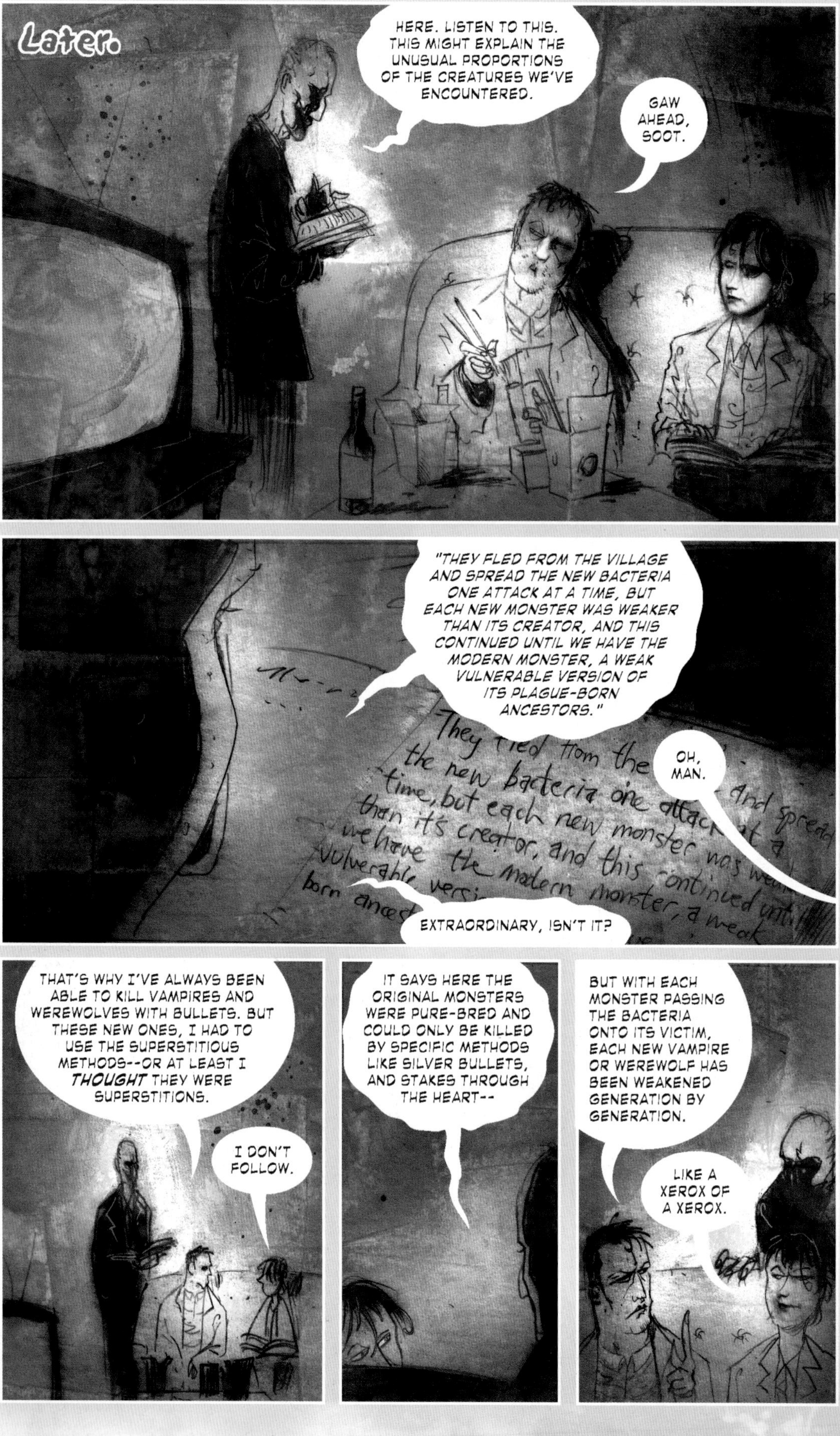
Later.
HERE. LISTEN TO THIS. THIS MIGHT EXPLAIN THE UNUSUAL PROPORTIONS OF THE CREATURES WE'VE ENCOUNTERED.
GAW AHEAD, SOOT.
"THEY FLED FROM THE VILLAGE AND SPREAD THE NEW BACTERIA ONE ATTACK AT A TIME, BUT EACH NEW MONSTER WAS WEAKER THAN ITS CREATOR, AND THIS CONTINUED UNTIL WE HAVE THE MODERN MONSTER, A WEAK VULNERABLE VERSION OF ITS PLAGUE-BORN ANCESTORS."
OH, MAN.
EXTRAORDINARY, ISN'T IT?
THAT'S WHY I'VE ALWAYS BEEN ABLE TO KILL VAMPIRES AND WEREWOLVES WITH BULLETS. BUT THESE NEW ONES, I HAD TO USE THE SUPERSTITIOUS METHODS--OR AT LEAST I *THOUGHT* THEY WERE SUPERSTITIONS.
I DON'T FOLLOW.
IT SAYS HERE THE ORIGINAL MONSTERS WERE PURE-BRED AND COULD ONLY BE KILLED BY SPECIFIC METHODS LIKE SILVER BULLETS, AND STAKES THROUGH THE HEART--
BUT WITH EACH MONSTER PASSING THE BACTERIA ONTO ITS VICTIM, EACH NEW VAMPIRE OR WEREWOLF HAS BEEN WEAKENED GENERATION BY GENERATION.
LIKE A XEROX OF A XEROX.

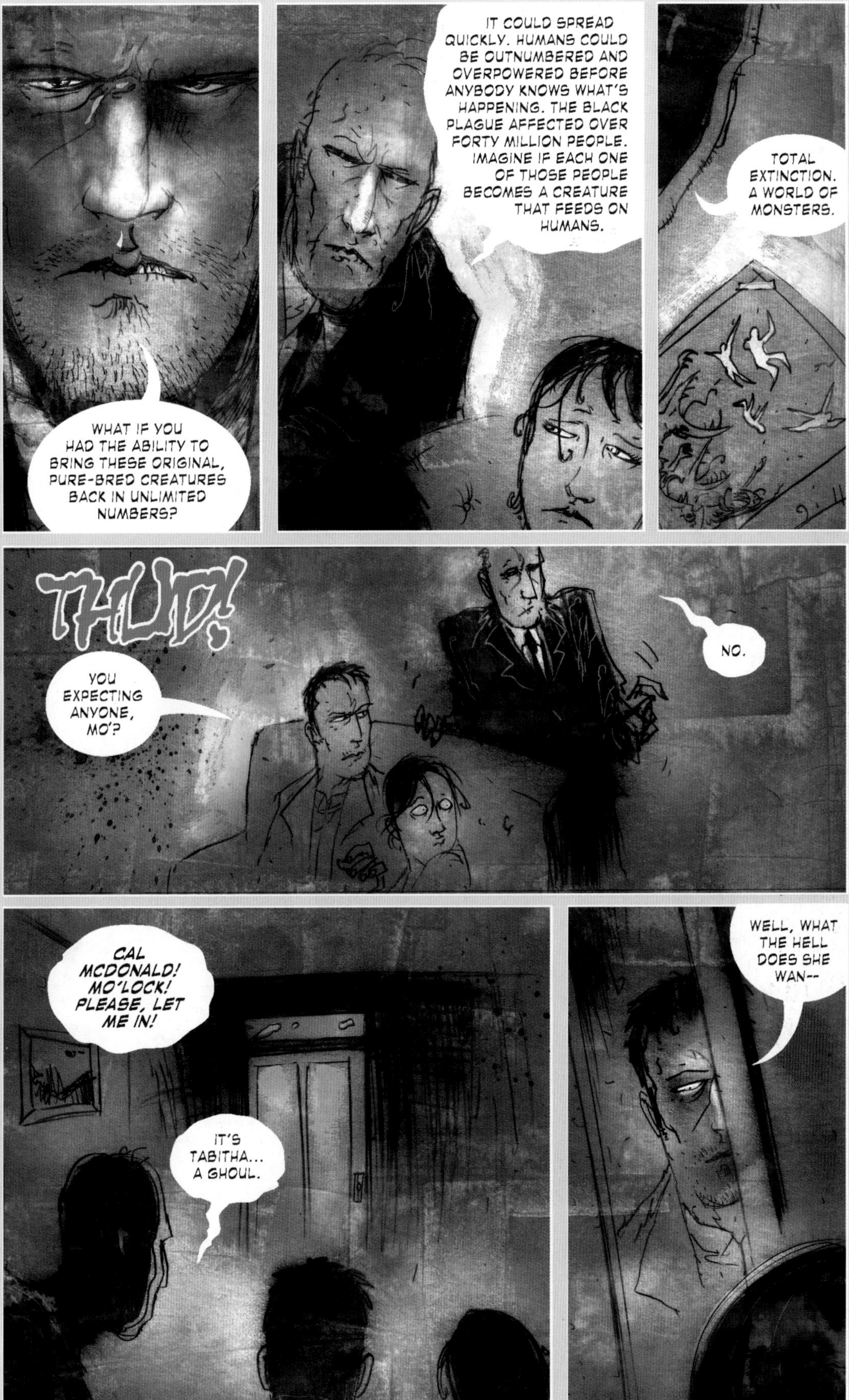

WHAT IF YOU HAD THE ABILITY TO BRING THESE ORIGINAL, PURE-BRED CREATURES BACK IN UNLIMITED NUMBERS?
IT COULD SPREAD QUICKLY. HUMANS COULD BE OUTNUMBERED AND OVERPOWERED BEFORE ANYBODY KNOWS WHAT'S HAPPENING. THE BLACK PLAGUE AFFECTED OVER FORTY MILLION PEOPLE. IMAGINE IF EACH ONE OF THOSE PEOPLE BECOMES A CREATURE THAT FEEDS ON HUMANS.
TOTAL EXTINCTION. A WORLD OF MONSTERS.
THUD!
YOU EXPECTING ANYONE, MO'?
NO.
CAL MCDONALD! MO'LOCK! PLEASE, LET ME IN!
IT'S TABITHA... A GHOUL.
WELL, WHAT THE HELL DOES SHE WAN--

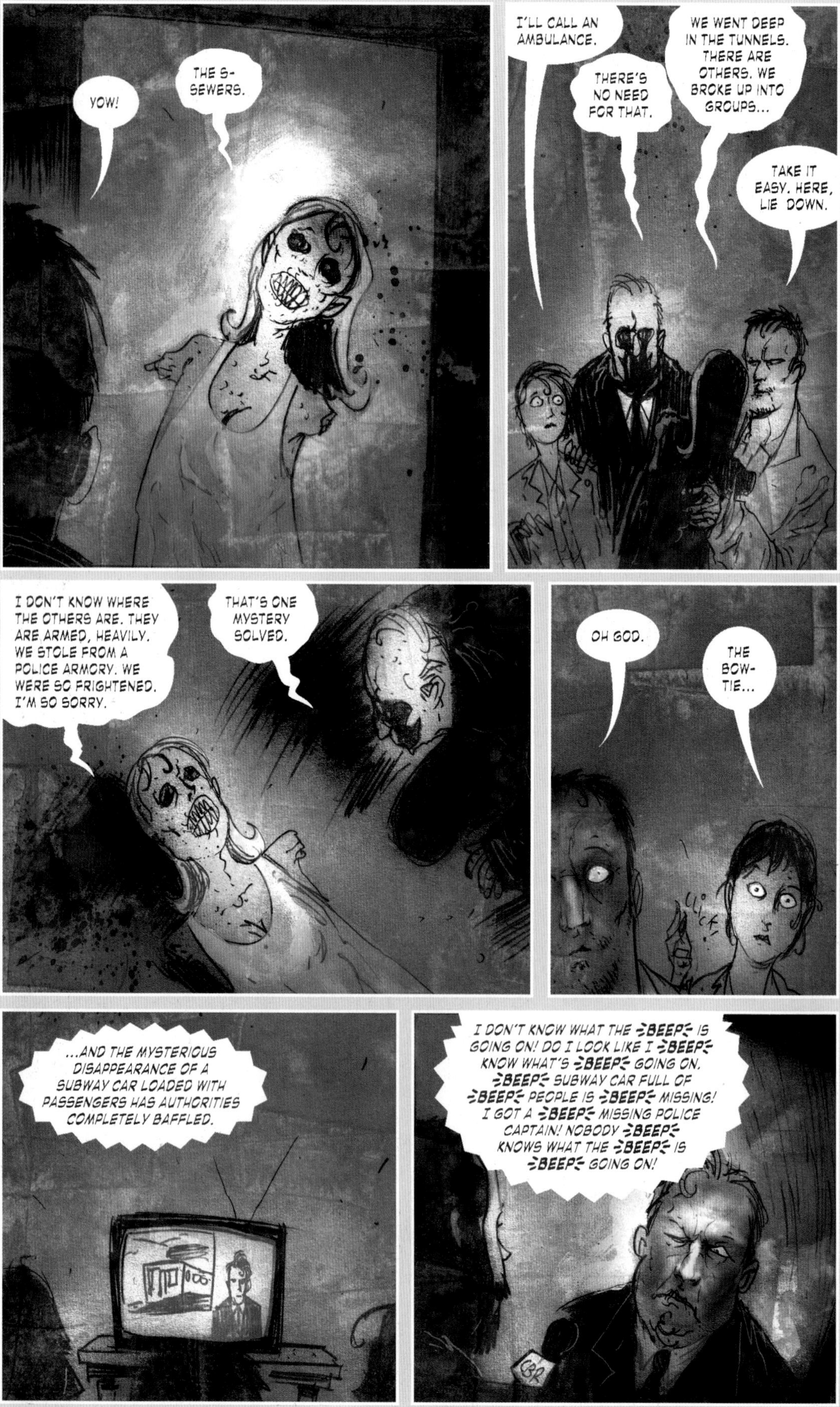
YOW!
THE S-SEWERS.
I'LL CALL AN AMBULANCE.
THERE'S NO NEED FOR THAT.
WE WENT DEEP IN THE TUNNELS. THERE ARE OTHERS. WE BROKE UP INTO GROUPS...
TAKE IT EASY. HERE, LIE DOWN.
I DON'T KNOW WHERE THE OTHERS ARE. THEY ARE ARMED, HEAVILY. WE STOLE FROM A POLICE ARMORY. WE WERE SO FRIGHTENED. I'M SO SORRY.
THAT'S ONE MYSTERY SOLVED.
OH GOD.
THE BOW-TIE...
CLICK!
...AND THE MYSTERIOUS DISAPPEARANCE OF A SUBWAY CAR LOADED WITH PASSENGERS HAS AUTHORITIES COMPLETELY BAFFLED.
I DON'T KNOW WHAT THE BEEP IS GOING ON! DO I LOOK LIKE I BEEP KNOW WHAT'S BEEP GOING ON. BEEP SUBWAY CAR FULL OF BEEP PEOPLE IS BEEP MISSING! I GOT A BEEP MISSING POLICE CAPTAIN! NOBODY BEEP KNOWS WHAT THE BEEP IS BEEP GOING ON!
CBR

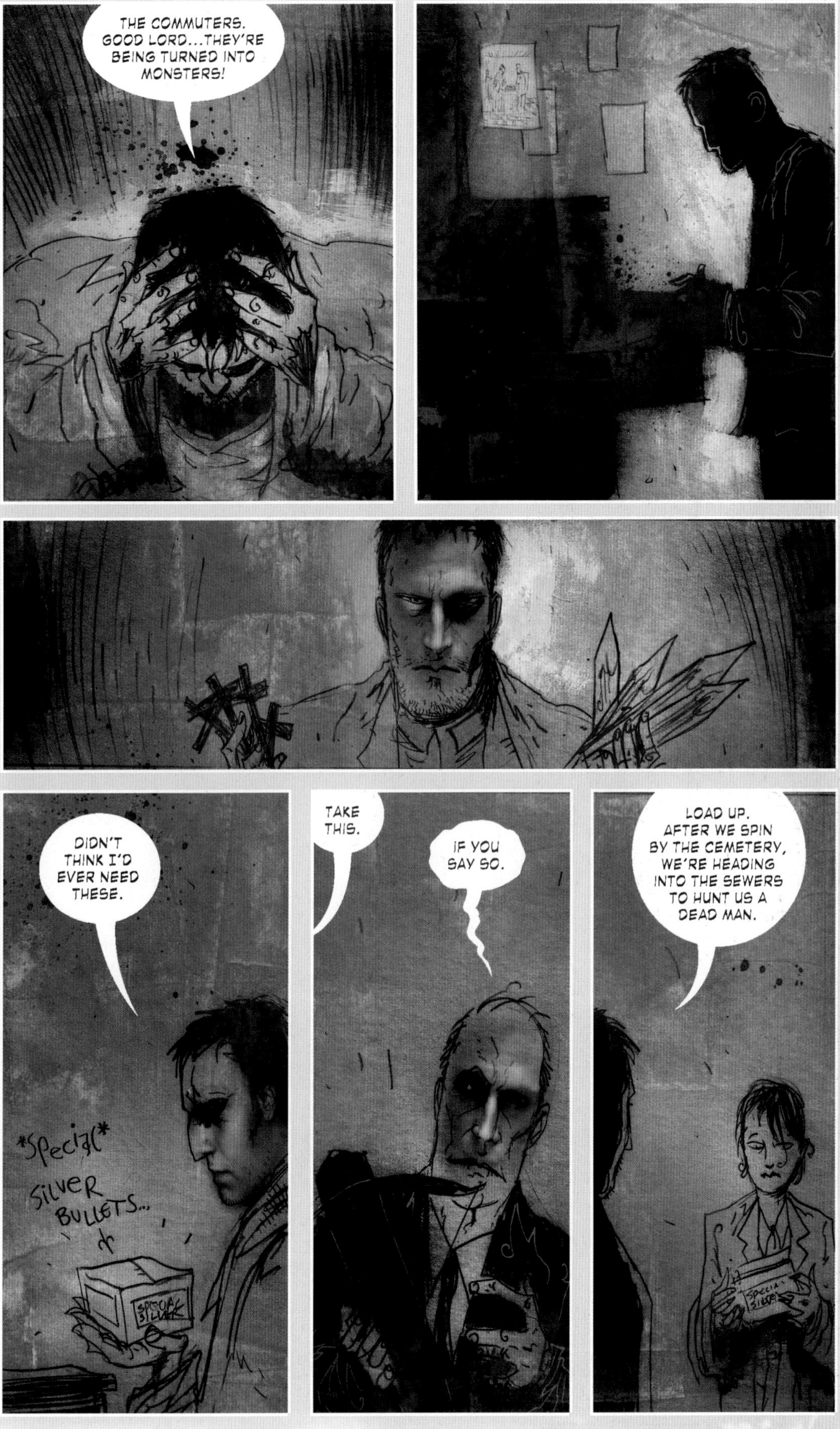
THE COMMUTERS. GOOD LORD...THEY'RE BEING TURNED INTO MONSTERS!
DIDN'T THINK I'D EVER NEED THESE.
Special SILVER BULLETS...
TAKE THIS.
IF YOU SAY SO.
LOAD UP. AFTER WE SPIN BY THE CEMETERY, WE'RE HEADING INTO THE SEWERS TO HUNT US A DEAD MAN.

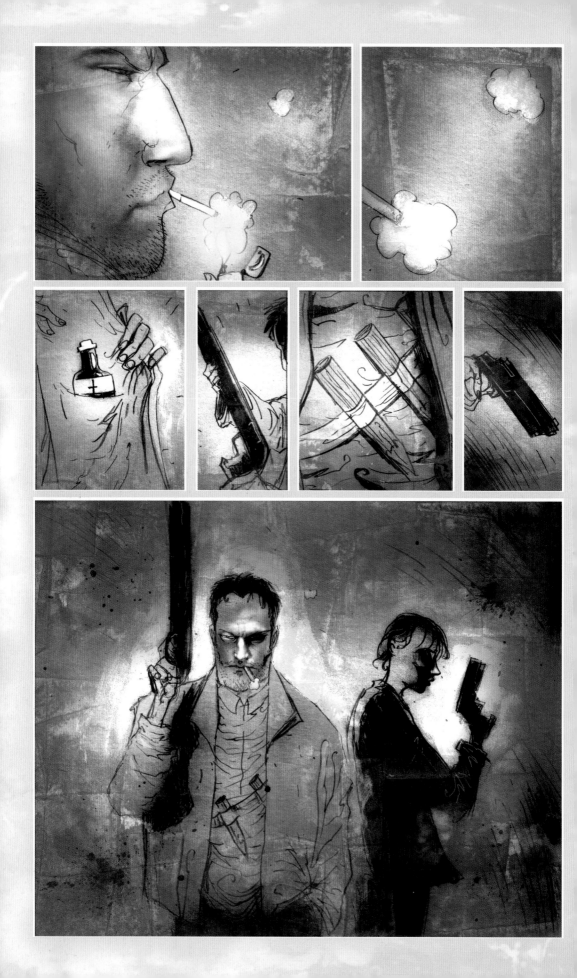

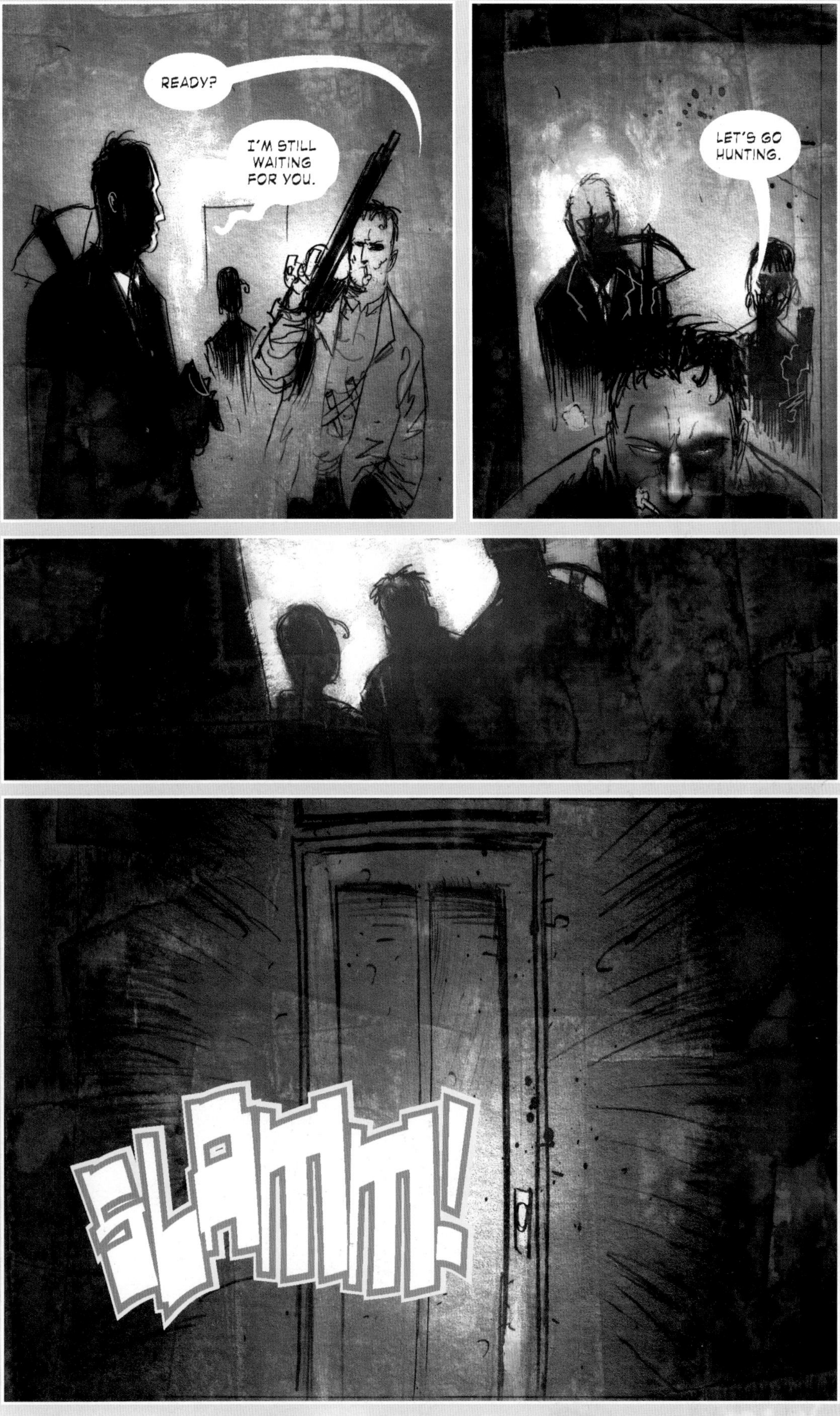
READY?
I'M STILL WAITING FOR YOU.
LET'S GO HUNTING.
SLAMM!

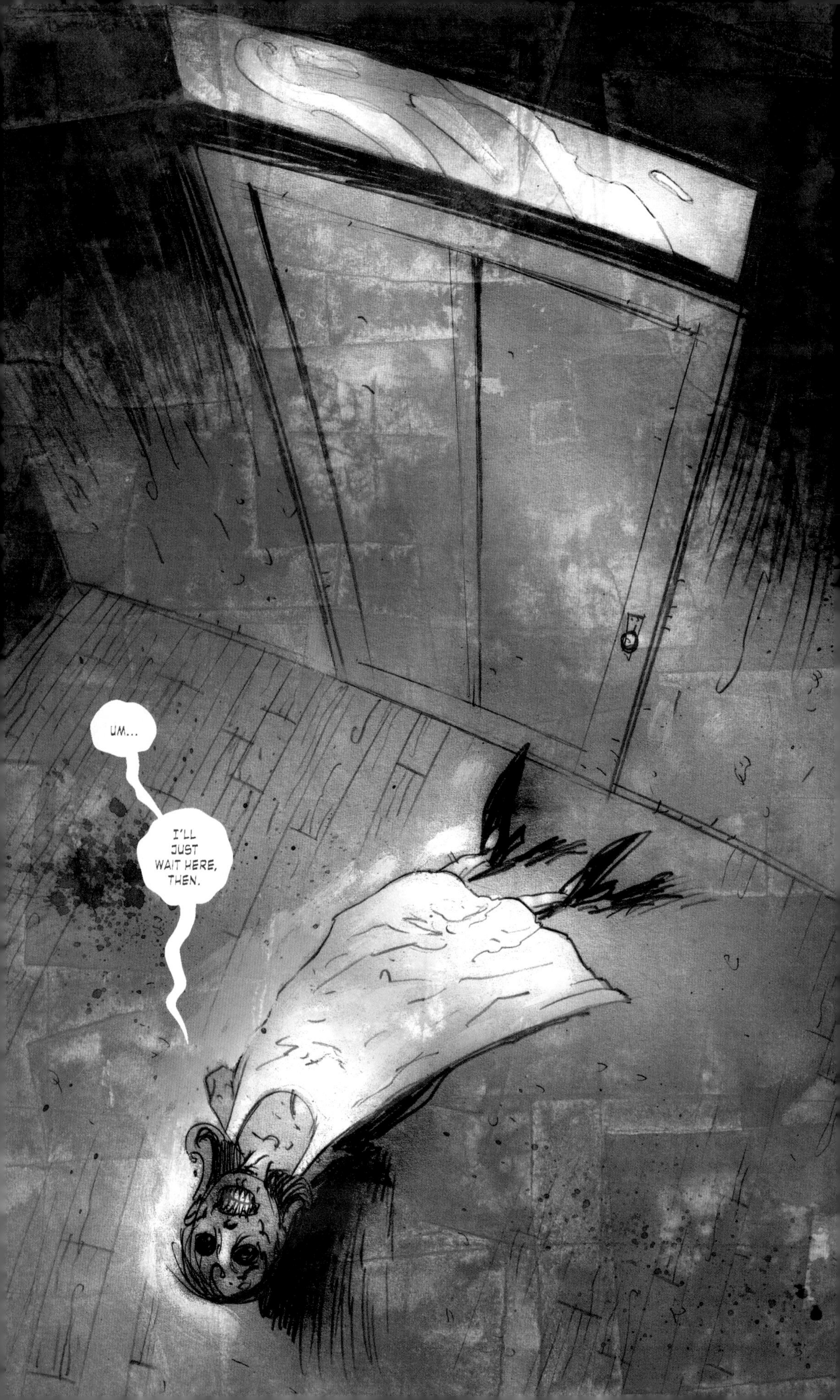
UM...
I'LL JUST WAIT HERE, THEN.

CHAPTER FIVE
American Freakshow

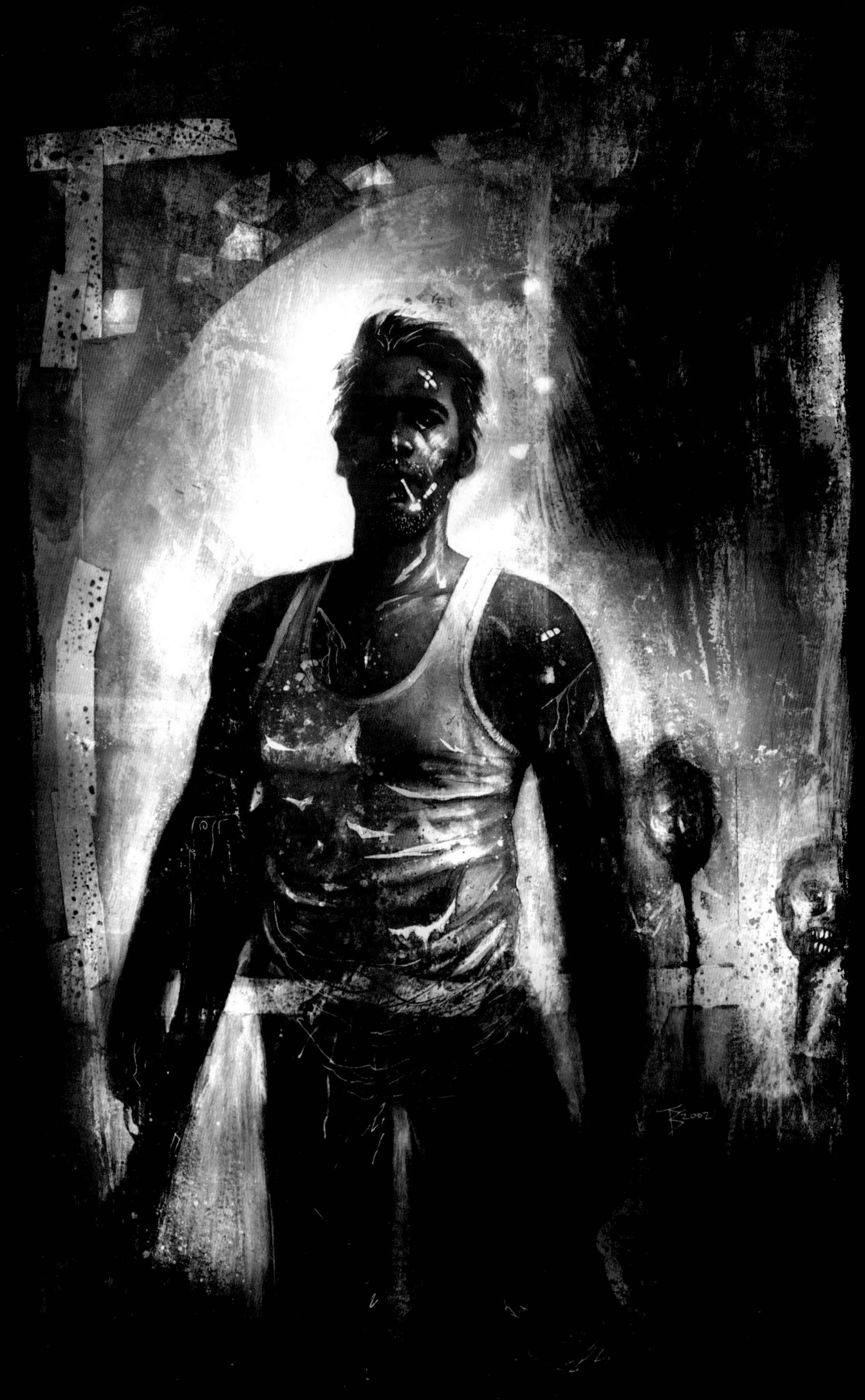

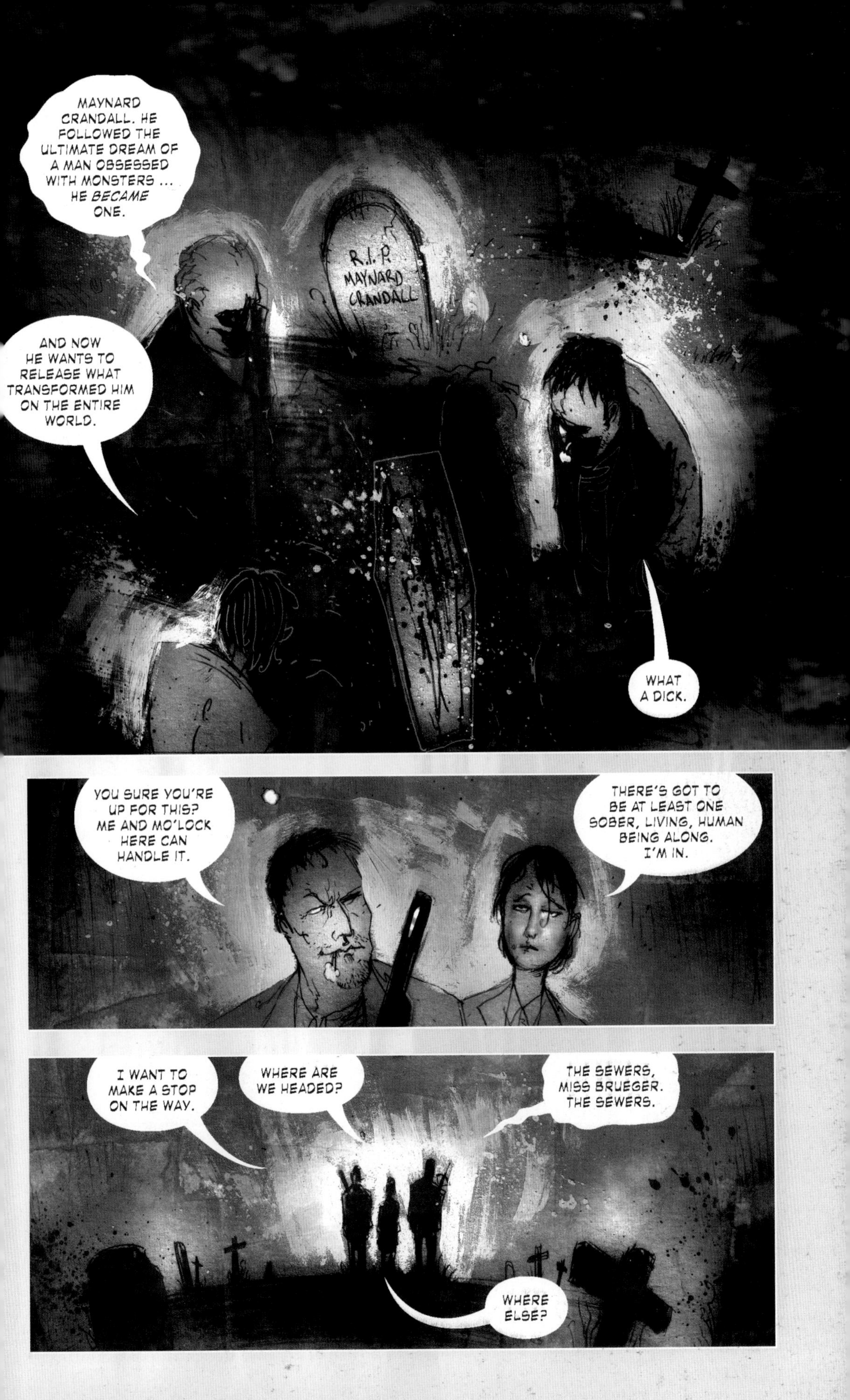
MAYNARD CRANDALL. HE FOLLOWED THE ULTIMATE DREAM OF A MAN OBSESSED WITH MONSTERS ... HE *BECAME* ONE.
R.I.P. MAYNARD CRANDALL
AND NOW HE WANTS TO RELEASE WHAT TRANSFORMED HIM ON THE ENTIRE WORLD.
WHAT A DICK.
YOU SURE YOU'RE UP FOR THIS? ME AND MO'LOCK HERE CAN HANDLE IT.
THERE'S GOT TO BE AT LEAST ONE SOBER, LIVING, HUMAN BEING ALONG. I'M IN.
I WANT TO MAKE A STOP ON THE WAY.
WHERE ARE WE HEADED?
THE SEWERS, MISS BRUEGER. THE SEWERS.
WHERE ELSE?

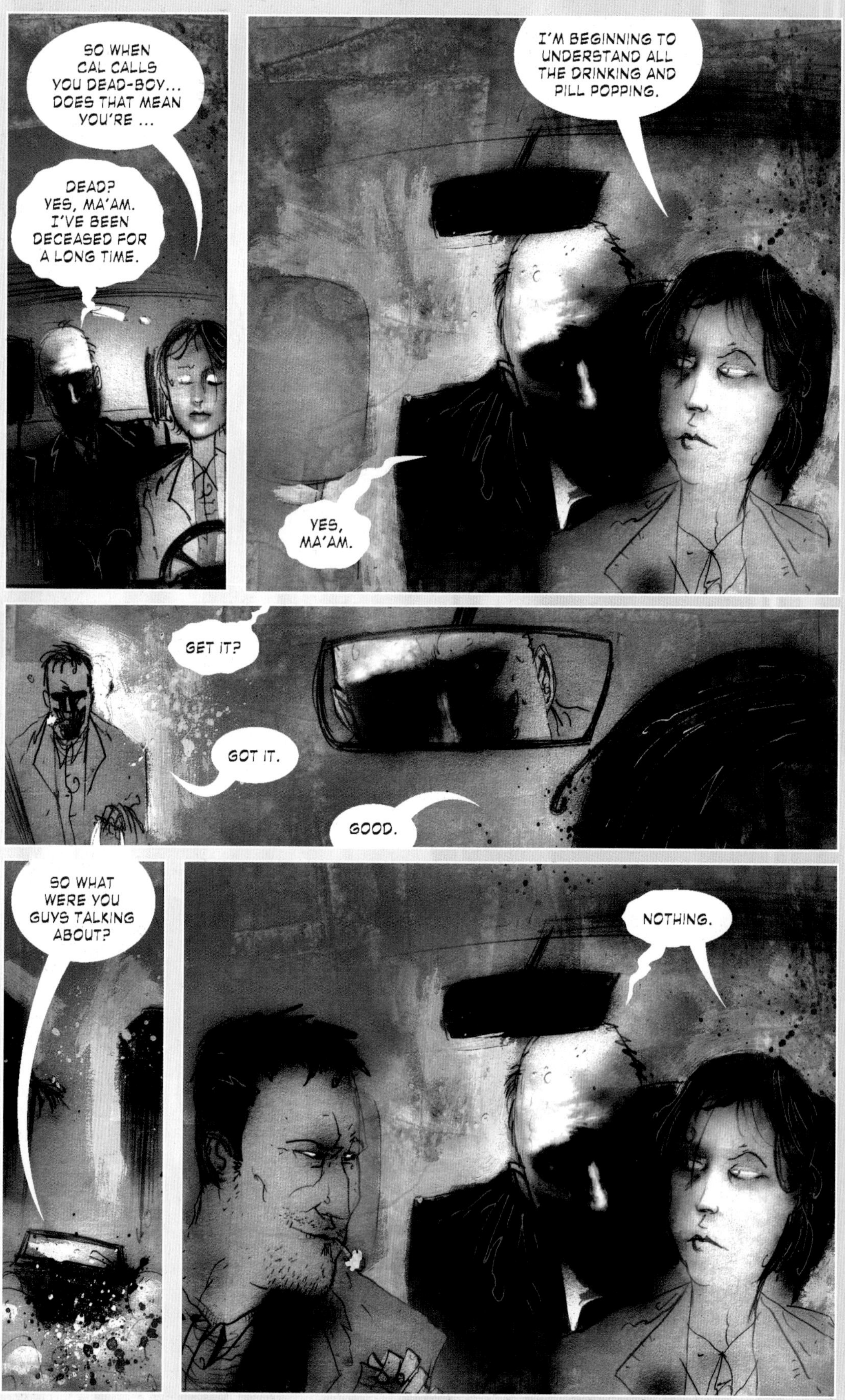
SO WHEN CAL CALLS YOU DEAD-BOY... DOES THAT MEAN YOU'RE ...
DEAD? YES, MA'AM. I'VE BEEN DECEASED FOR A LONG TIME.
I'M BEGINNING TO UNDERSTAND ALL THE DRINKING AND PILL POPPING.
YES, MA'AM.
GET IT?
GOT IT.
GOOD.
SO WHAT WERE YOU GUYS TALKING ABOUT?
NOTHING.

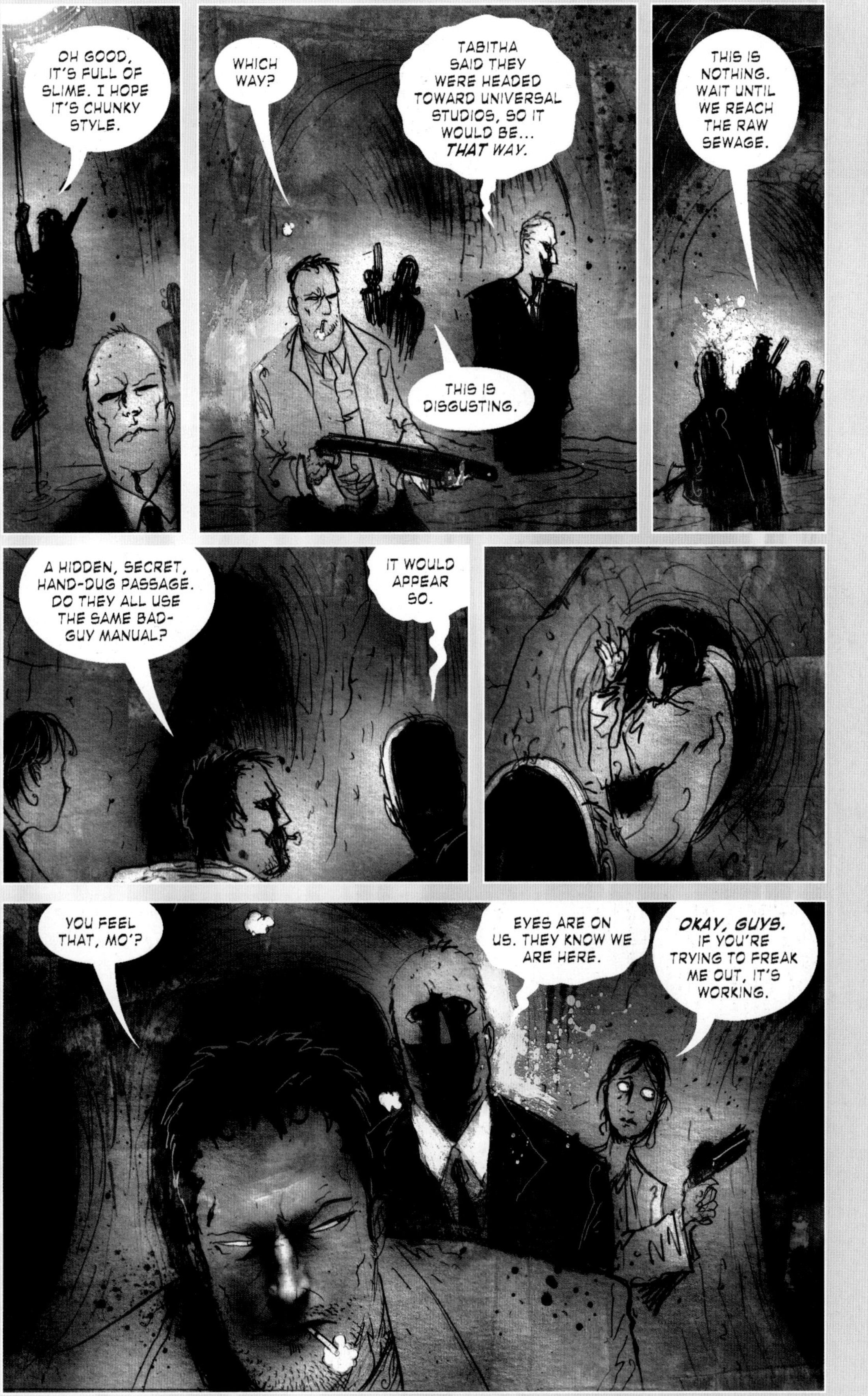
OH GOOD, IT'S FULL OF SLIME. I HOPE IT'S CHUNKY STYLE.
WHICH WAY?
TABITHA SAID THEY WERE HEADED TOWARD UNIVERSAL STUDIOS, SO IT WOULD BE... *THAT* WAY.
THIS IS DISGUSTING.
THIS IS NOTHING. WAIT UNTIL WE REACH THE RAW SEWAGE.
A HIDDEN, SECRET, HAND-DUG PASSAGE. DO THEY ALL USE THE SAME BAD-GUY MANUAL?
IT WOULD APPEAR SO.
YOU FEEL THAT, MO'?
EYES ARE ON US. THEY KNOW WE ARE HERE.
OKAY, GUYS. IF YOU'RE TRYING TO FREAK ME OUT, IT'S WORKING.

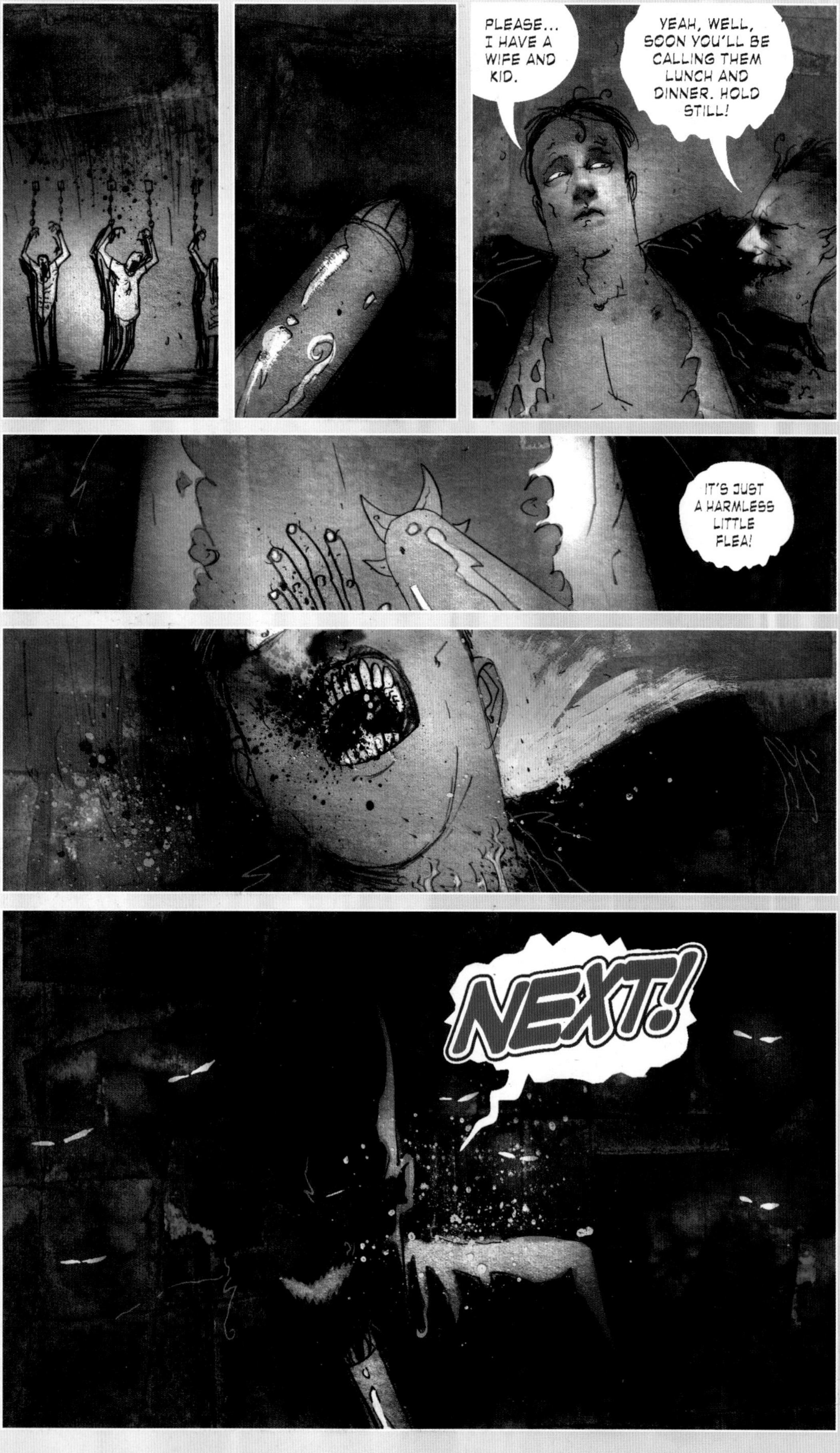
PLEASE... I HAVE A WIFE AND KID.
YEAH, WELL, SOON YOU'LL BE CALLING THEM LUNCH AND DINNER. HOLD STILL!
IT'S JUST A HARMLESS LITTLE FLEA!
NEXT!

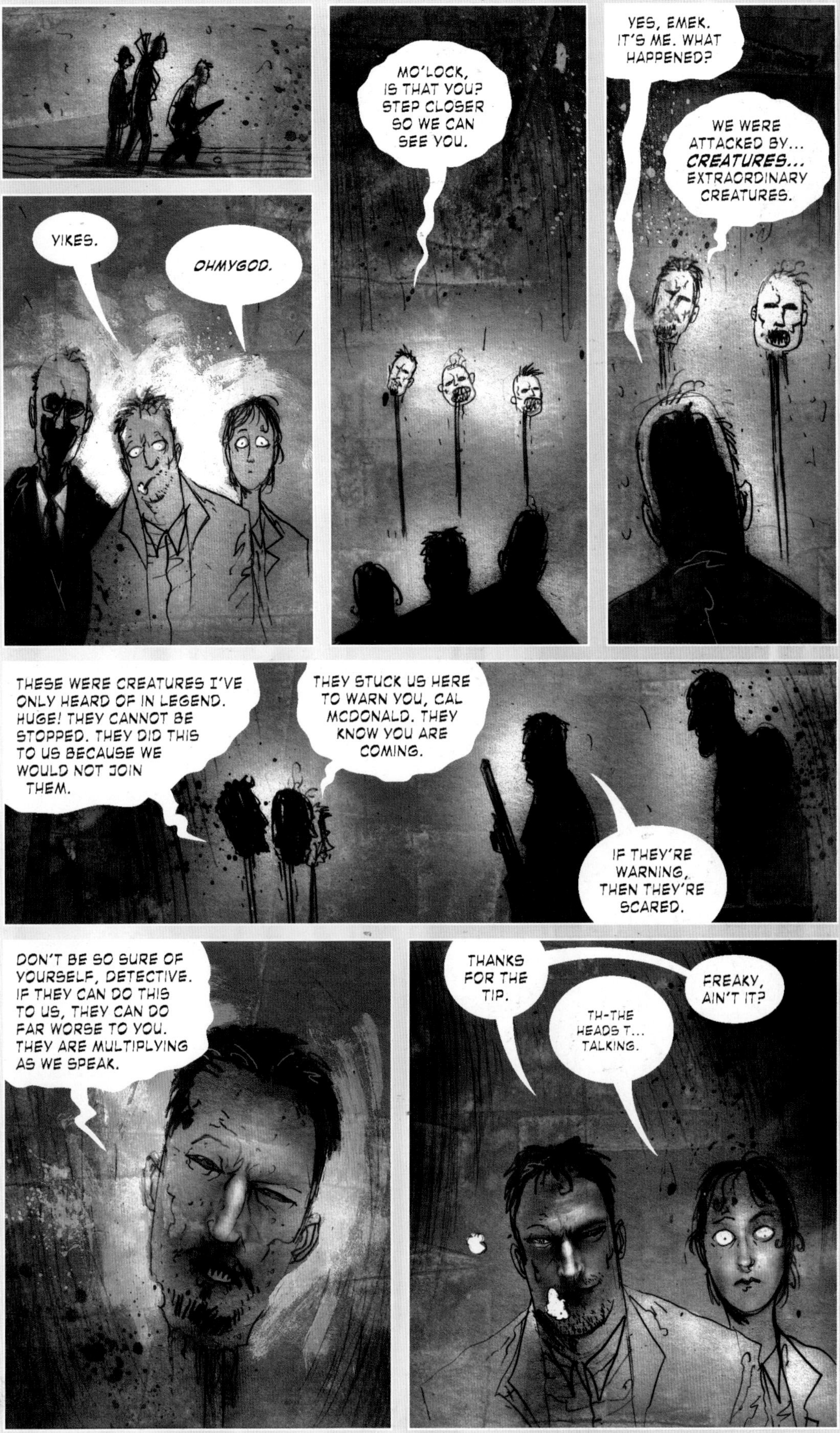

YIKES.
OHMYGOD.
MO'LOCK, IS THAT YOU? STEP CLOSER SO WE CAN SEE YOU.
YES, EMEK. IT'S ME. WHAT HAPPENED?
WE WERE ATTACKED BY... CREATURES... EXTRAORDINARY CREATURES.
THESE WERE CREATURES I'VE ONLY HEARD OF IN LEGEND. HUGE! THEY CANNOT BE STOPPED. THEY DID THIS TO US BECAUSE WE WOULD NOT JOIN THEM.
THEY STUCK US HERE TO WARN YOU, CAL MCDONALD. THEY KNOW YOU ARE COMING.
IF THEY'RE WARNING, THEN THEY'RE SCARED.
DON'T BE SO SURE OF YOURSELF, DETECTIVE. IF THEY CAN DO THIS TO US, THEY CAN DO FAR WORSE TO YOU. THEY ARE MULTIPLYING AS WE SPEAK.
THANKS FOR THE TIP.
FREAKY, AIN'T IT?
TH-THE HEADS T... TALKING.

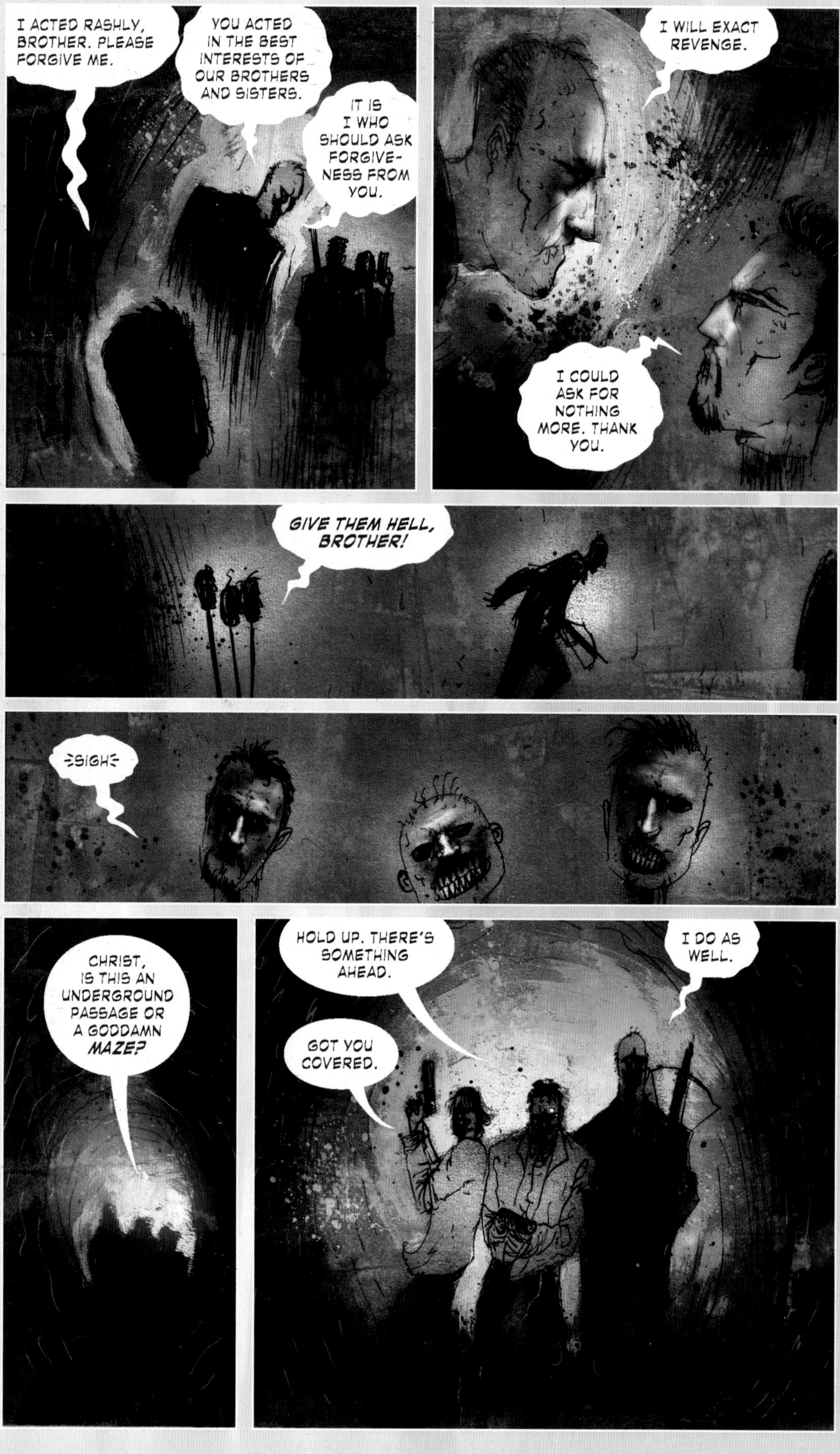
I ACTED RASHLY, BROTHER. PLEASE FORGIVE ME.
YOU ACTED IN THE BEST INTERESTS OF OUR BROTHERS AND SISTERS.
IT IS I WHO SHOULD ASK FORGIVE-NESS FROM YOU.
I WILL EXACT REVENGE.
I COULD ASK FOR NOTHING MORE. THANK YOU.
GIVE THEM HELL, BROTHER!
=SIGH=
CHRIST, IS THIS AN UNDERGROUND PASSAGE OR A GODDAMN MAZE?
HOLD UP. THERE'S SOMETHING AHEAD.
I DO AS WELL.
GOT YOU COVERED.

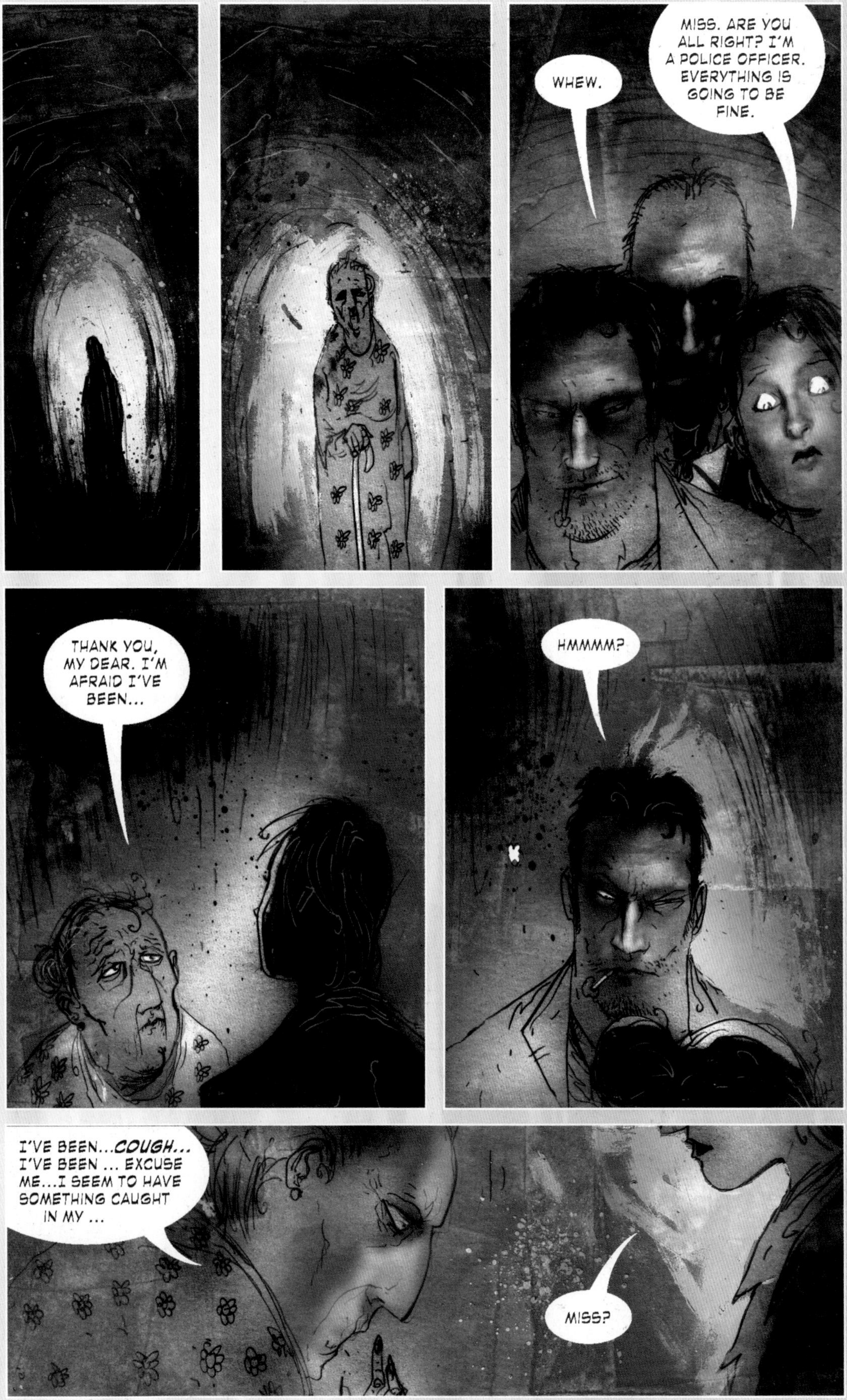
WHEW.
MISS. ARE YOU ALL RIGHT? I'M A POLICE OFFICER. EVERYTHING IS GOING TO BE FINE.
THANK YOU, MY DEAR. I'M AFRAID I'VE BEEN...
HMMMM?
I'VE BEEN...*COUGH*... I'VE BEEN ... EXCUSE ME...I SEEM TO HAVE SOMETHING CAUGHT IN MY ...
MISS?

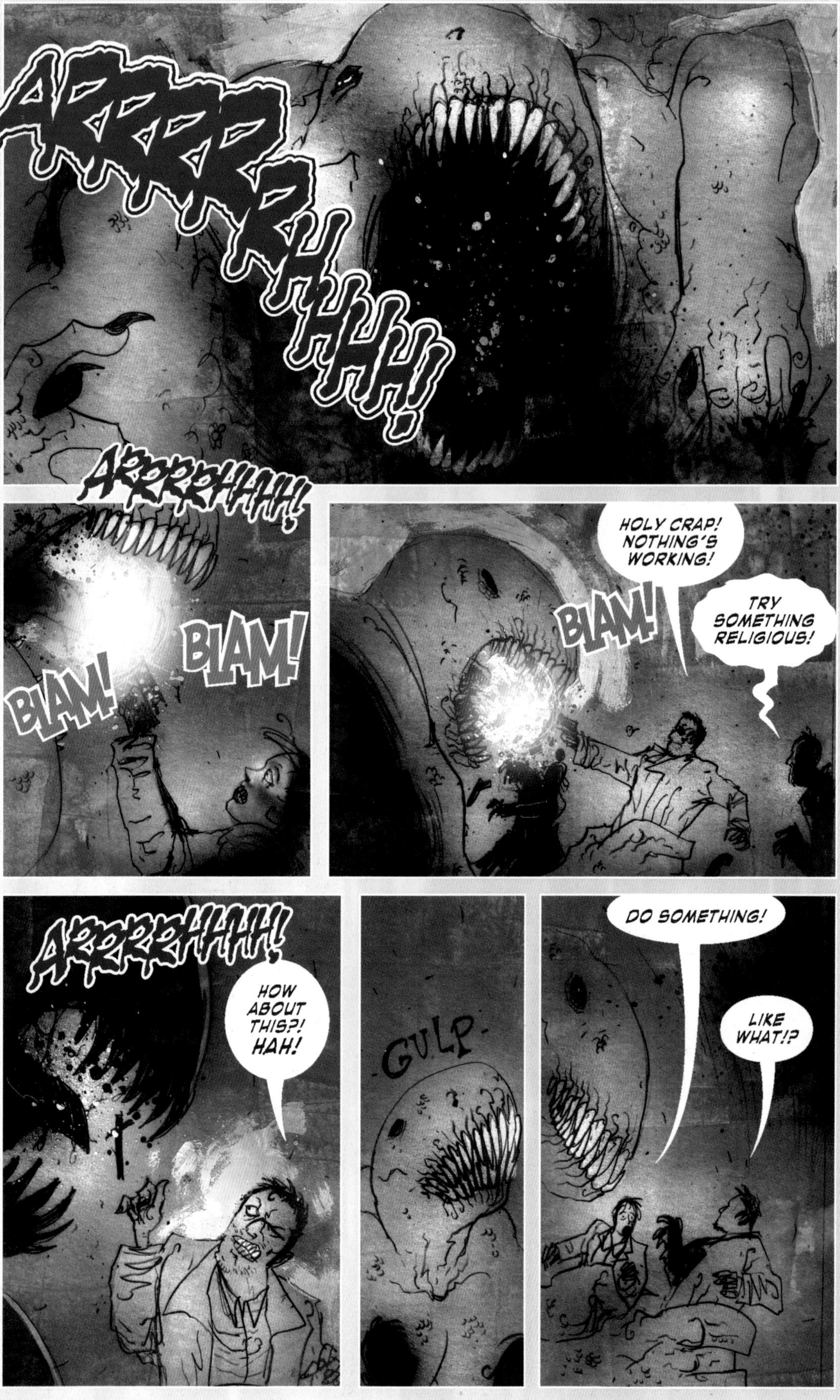

ARRRRRHHHH!
ARRRRHHHH!
BLAM!
BLAM!
BLAM!
HOLY CRAP! NOTHING'S WORKING!
TRY SOMETHING RELIGIOUS!
ARRRRHHHH!
HOW ABOUT THIS?! HAH!
GULP
DO SOMETHING!
LIKE WHAT!?

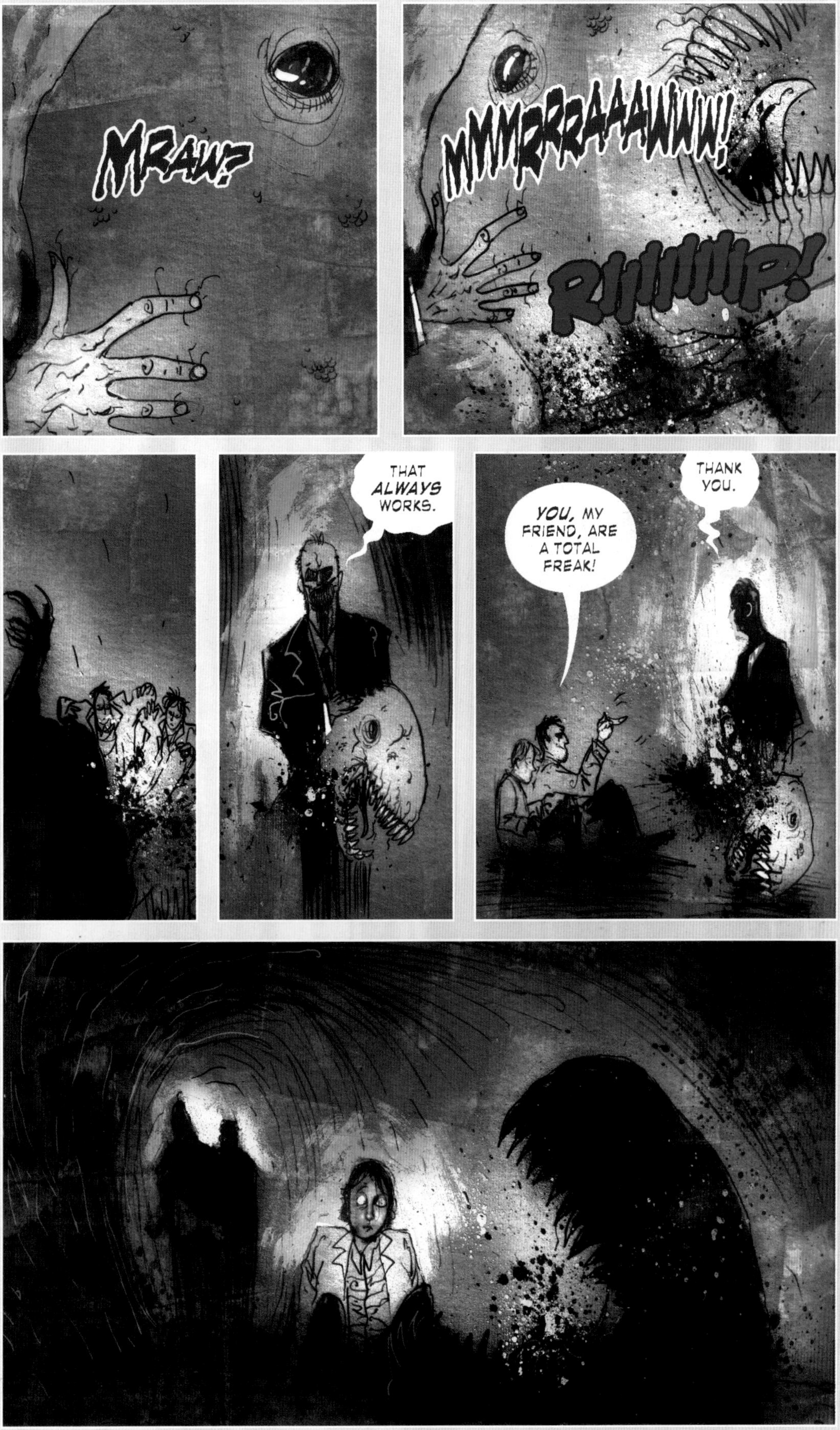
MRAW?
MMMRRRAAAWWW!
RIIIIIIIP!
THAT ALWAYS WORKS.
THANK YOU.
YOU, MY FRIEND, ARE A TOTAL FREAK!

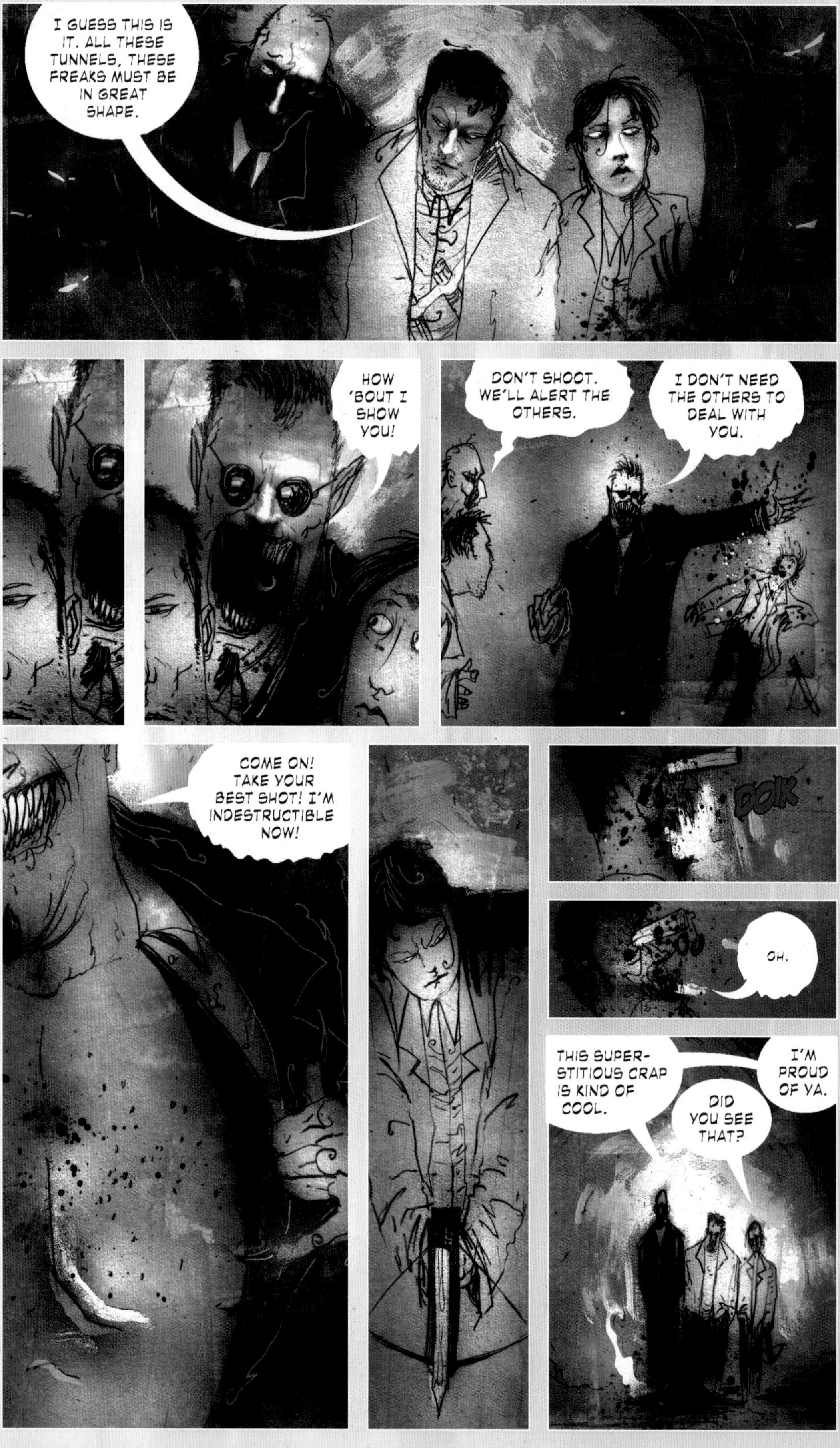
I GUESS THIS IS IT. ALL THESE TUNNELS, THESE FREAKS MUST BE IN GREAT SHAPE.
HOW 'BOUT I SHOW YOU!
DON'T SHOOT. WE'LL ALERT THE OTHERS.
I DON'T NEED THE OTHERS TO DEAL WITH YOU.
COME ON! TAKE YOUR BEST SHOT! I'M INDESTRUCTIBLE NOW!
DOIK
OH.
THIS SUPER-STITIOUS CRAP IS KIND OF COOL.
I'M PROUD OF YA.
DID YOU SEE THAT?

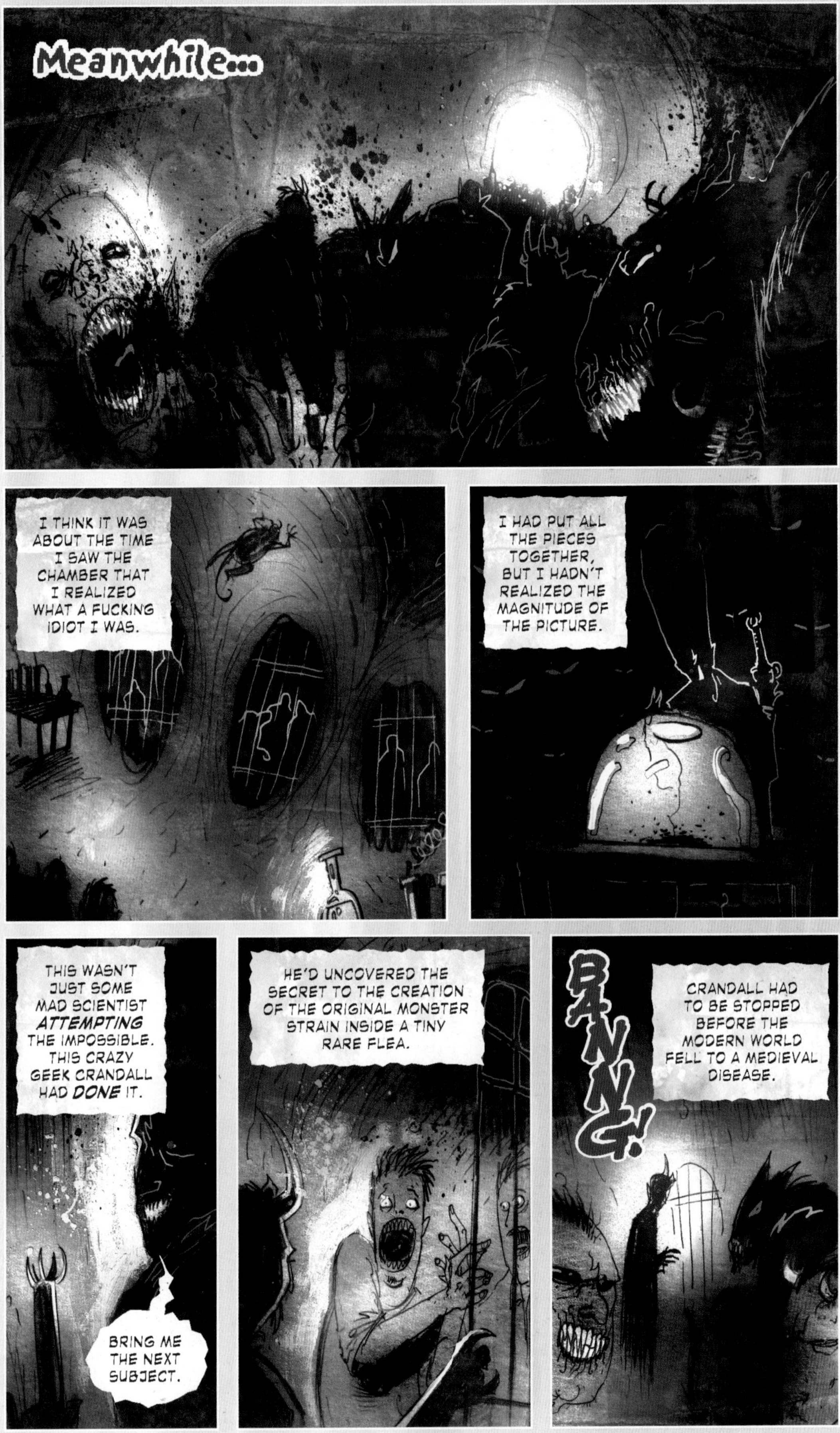
Meanwhile...
I THINK IT WAS ABOUT THE TIME I SAW THE CHAMBER THAT I REALIZED WHAT A FUCKING IDIOT I WAS.
I HAD PUT ALL THE PIECES TOGETHER, BUT I HADN'T REALIZED THE MAGNITUDE OF THE PICTURE.
THIS WASN'T JUST SOME MAD SCIENTIST *ATTEMPTING* THE IMPOSSIBLE. THIS CRAZY GEEK CRANDALL HAD *DONE* IT.
BRING ME THE NEXT SUBJECT.
HE'D UNCOVERED THE SECRET TO THE CREATION OF THE ORIGINAL MONSTER STRAIN INSIDE A TINY RARE FLEA.
BANNG!
CRANDALL HAD TO BE STOPPED BEFORE THE MODERN WORLD FELL TO A MEDIEVAL DISEASE.

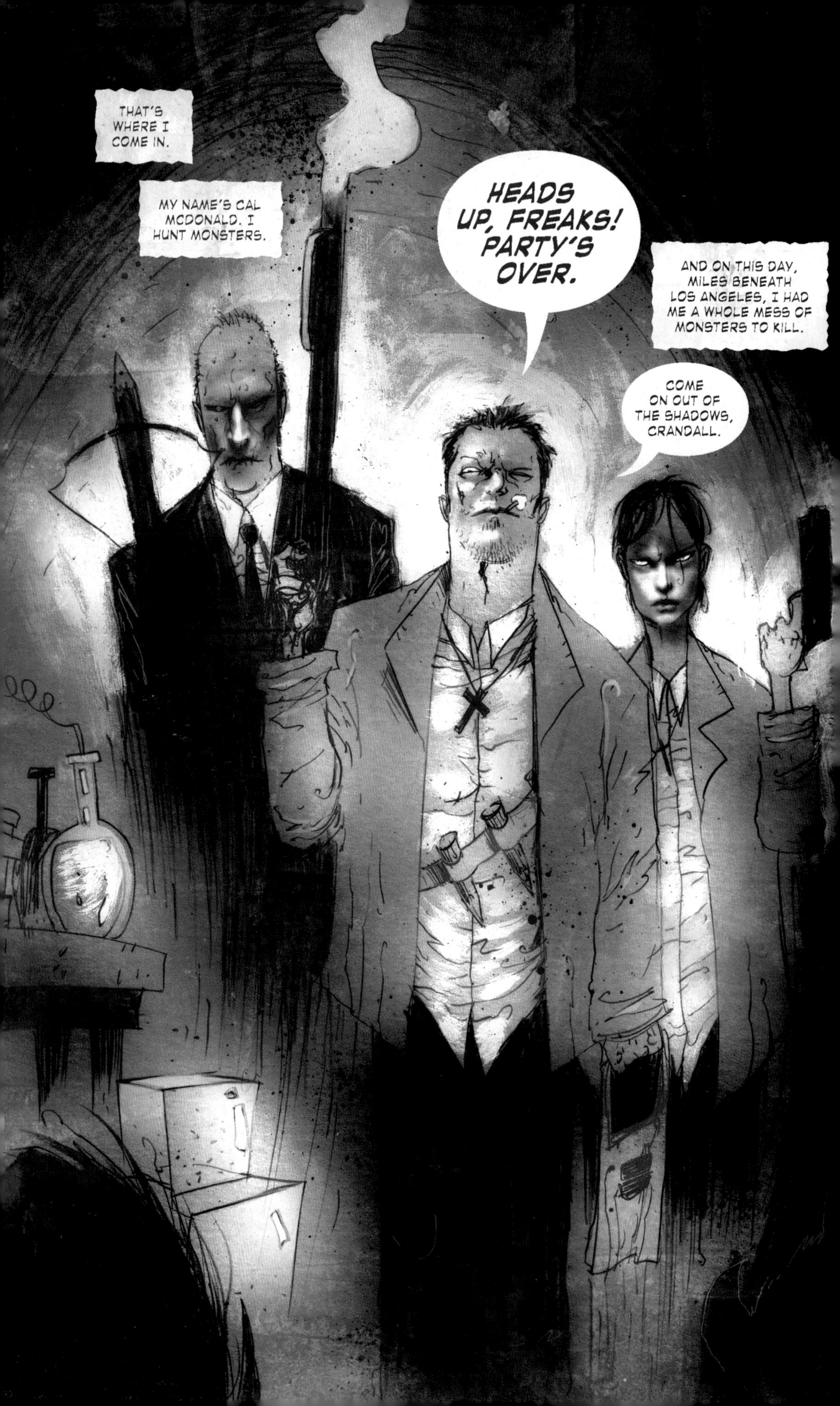
THAT'S WHERE I COME IN.
MY NAME'S CAL MCDONALD. I HUNT MONSTERS.
HEADS UP, FREAKS! PARTY'S OVER.
AND ON THIS DAY, MILES BENEATH LOS ANGELES, I HAD ME A WHOLE MESS OF MONSTERS TO KILL.
COME ON OUT OF THE SHADOWS, CRANDALL.

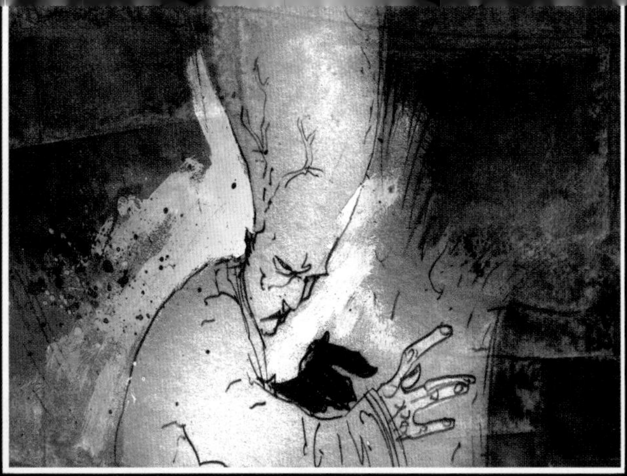

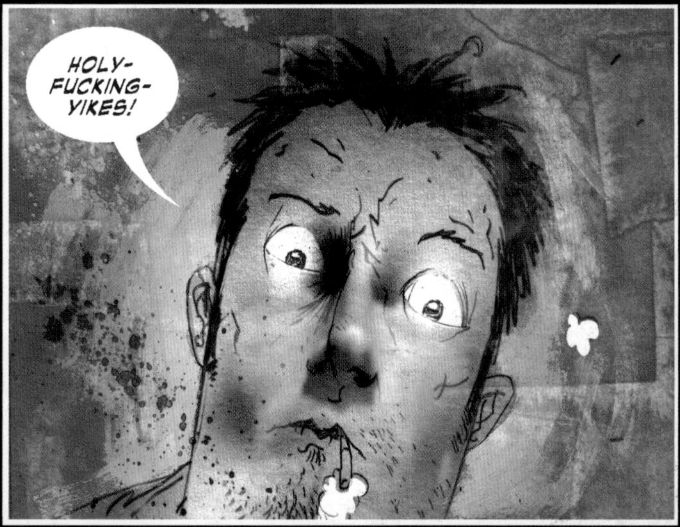
HOLY-FUCKING-YIKES!

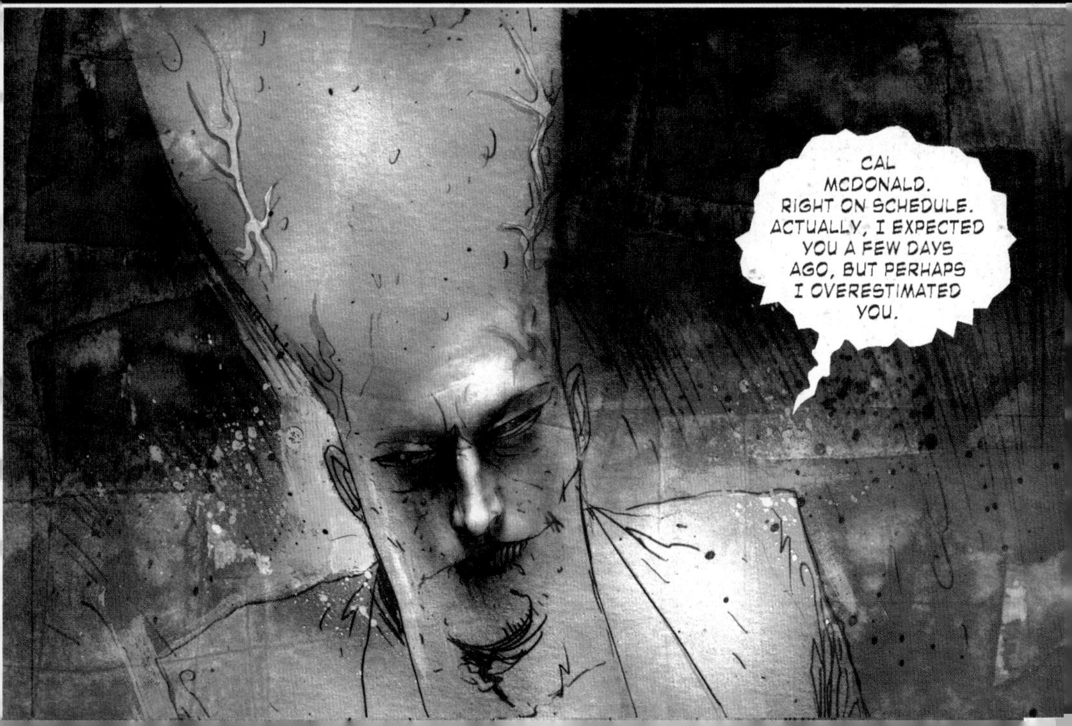
CAL MCDONALD. RIGHT ON SCHEDULE. ACTUALLY, I EXPECTED YOU A FEW DAYS AGO, BUT PERHAPS I OVERESTIMATED YOU.

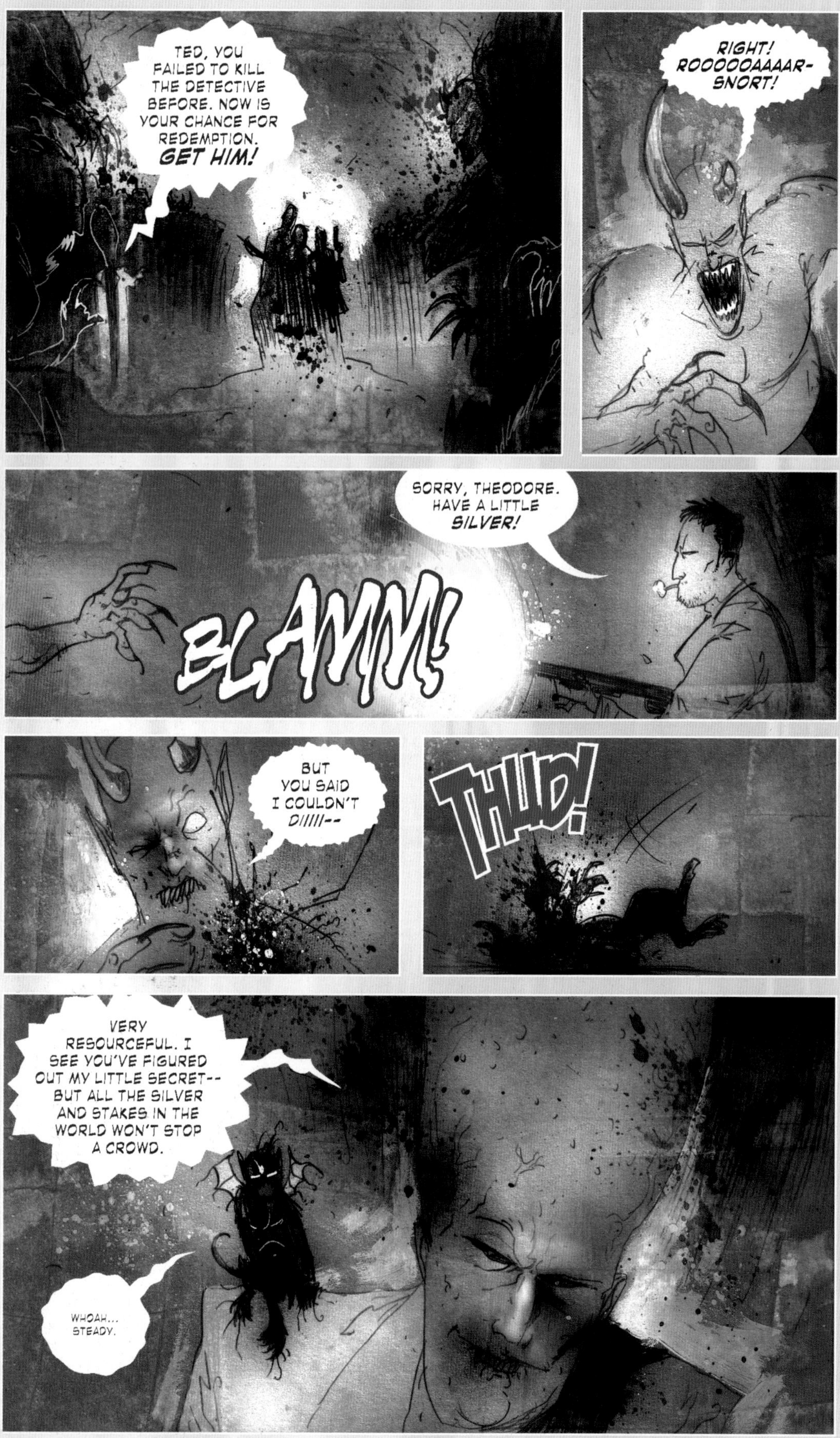

TED, YOU FAILED TO KILL THE DETECTIVE BEFORE. NOW IS YOUR CHANCE FOR REDEMPTION. GET HIM!
RIGHT! ROOOOOAAAAR-SNORT!
SORRY, THEODORE. HAVE A LITTLE SILVER!
BLAMM!
BUT YOU SAID I COULDN'T DIIIII--
THUD!
VERY RESOURCEFUL. I SEE YOU'VE FIGURED OUT MY LITTLE SECRET--BUT ALL THE SILVER AND STAKES IN THE WORLD WON'T STOP A CROWD.
WHOAH... STEADY.

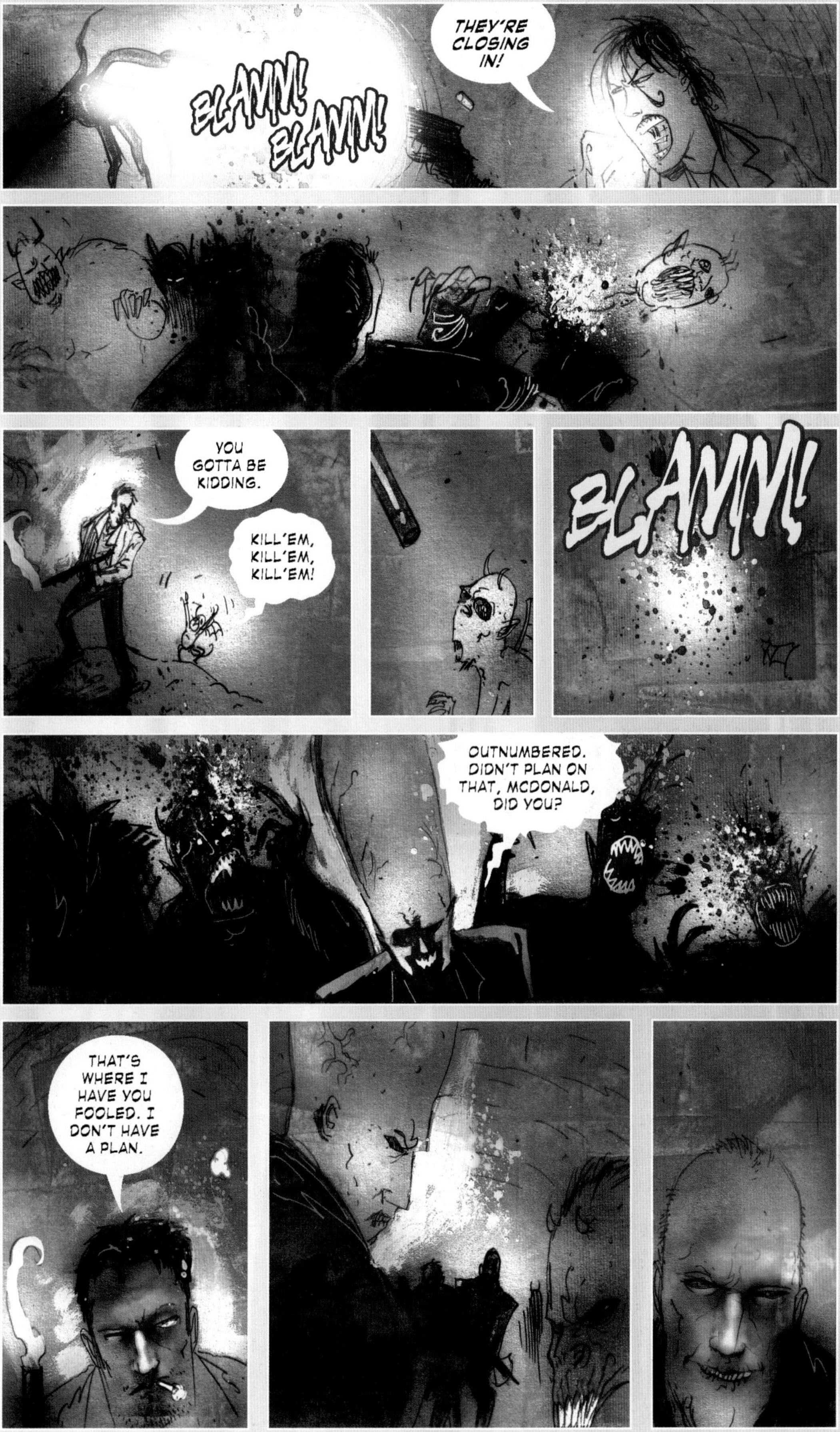
BLAMM! BLAMM!
THEY'RE CLOSING IN!
YOU GOTTA BE KIDDING.
KILL'EM, KILL'EM, KILL'EM!
BLAMM!
OUTNUMBERED. DIDN'T PLAN ON THAT, MCDONALD, DID YOU?
THAT'S WHERE I HAVE YOU FOOLED. I DON'T HAVE A PLAN.

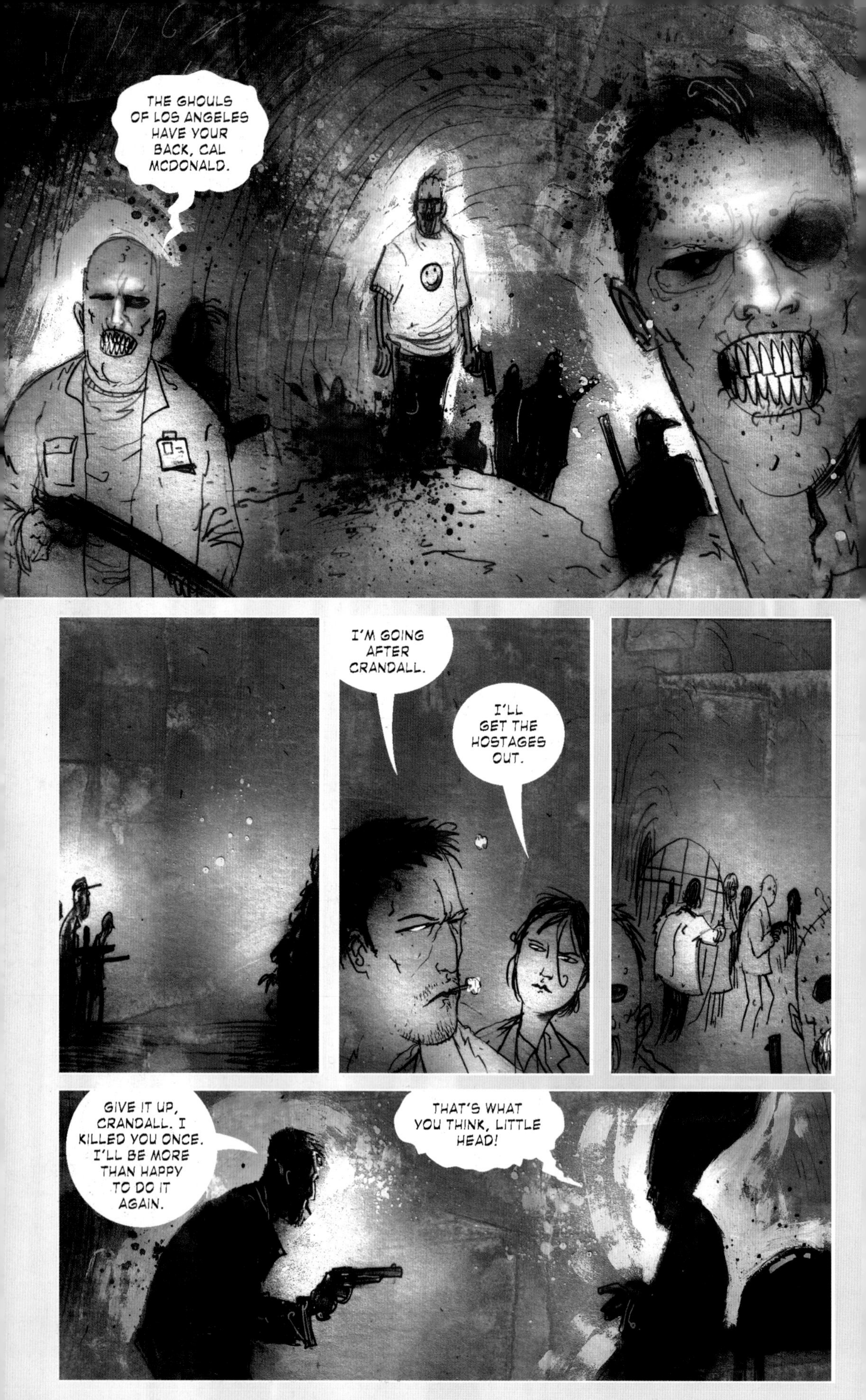
THE GHOULS OF LOS ANGELES HAVE YOUR BACK, CAL MCDONALD.
I'M GOING AFTER CRANDALL.
I'LL GET THE HOSTAGES OUT.
GIVE IT UP, CRANDALL. I KILLED YOU ONCE. I'LL BE MORE THAN HAPPY TO DO IT AGAIN.
THAT'S WHAT YOU THINK, LITTLE HEAD!

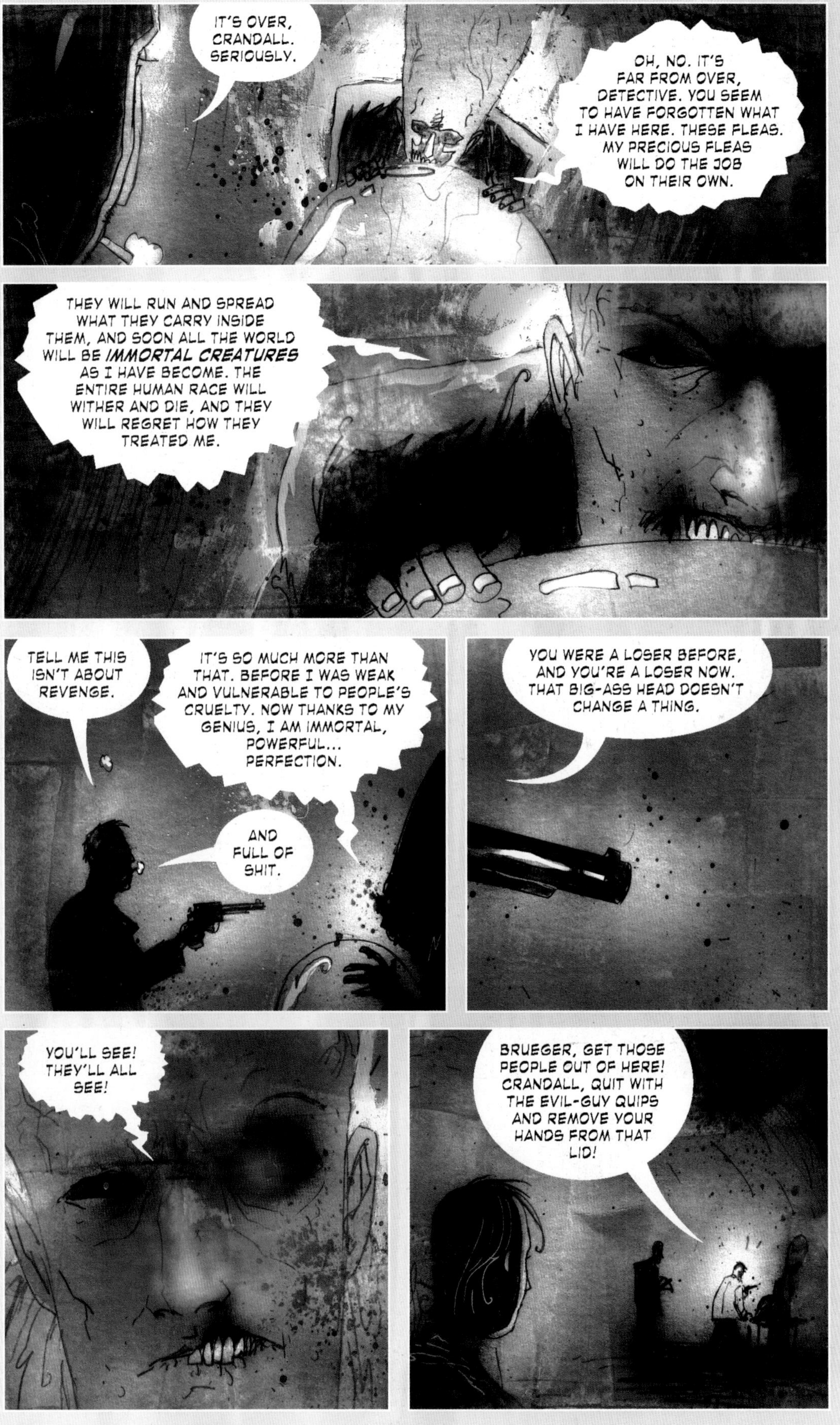
IT'S OVER, CRANDALL. SERIOUSLY.
OH, NO. IT'S FAR FROM OVER, DETECTIVE. YOU SEEM TO HAVE FORGOTTEN WHAT I HAVE HERE. THESE FLEAS. MY PRECIOUS FLEAS WILL DO THE JOB ON THEIR OWN.
THEY WILL RUN AND SPREAD WHAT THEY CARRY INSIDE THEM, AND SOON ALL THE WORLD WILL BE *IMMORTAL CREATURES* AS I HAVE BECOME. THE ENTIRE HUMAN RACE WILL WITHER AND DIE, AND THEY WILL REGRET HOW THEY TREATED ME.
TELL ME THIS ISN'T ABOUT REVENGE.
IT'S SO MUCH MORE THAN THAT. BEFORE I WAS WEAK AND VULNERABLE TO PEOPLE'S CRUELTY. NOW THANKS TO MY GENIUS, I AM IMMORTAL, POWERFUL... PERFECTION.
AND FULL OF SHIT.
YOU WERE A LOSER BEFORE, AND YOU'RE A LOSER NOW. THAT BIG-ASS HEAD DOESN'T CHANGE A THING.
YOU'LL SEE! THEY'LL ALL SEE!
BRUEGER, GET THOSE PEOPLE OUT OF HERE! CRANDALL, QUIT WITH THE EVIL-GUY QUIPS AND REMOVE YOUR HANDS FROM THAT LID!

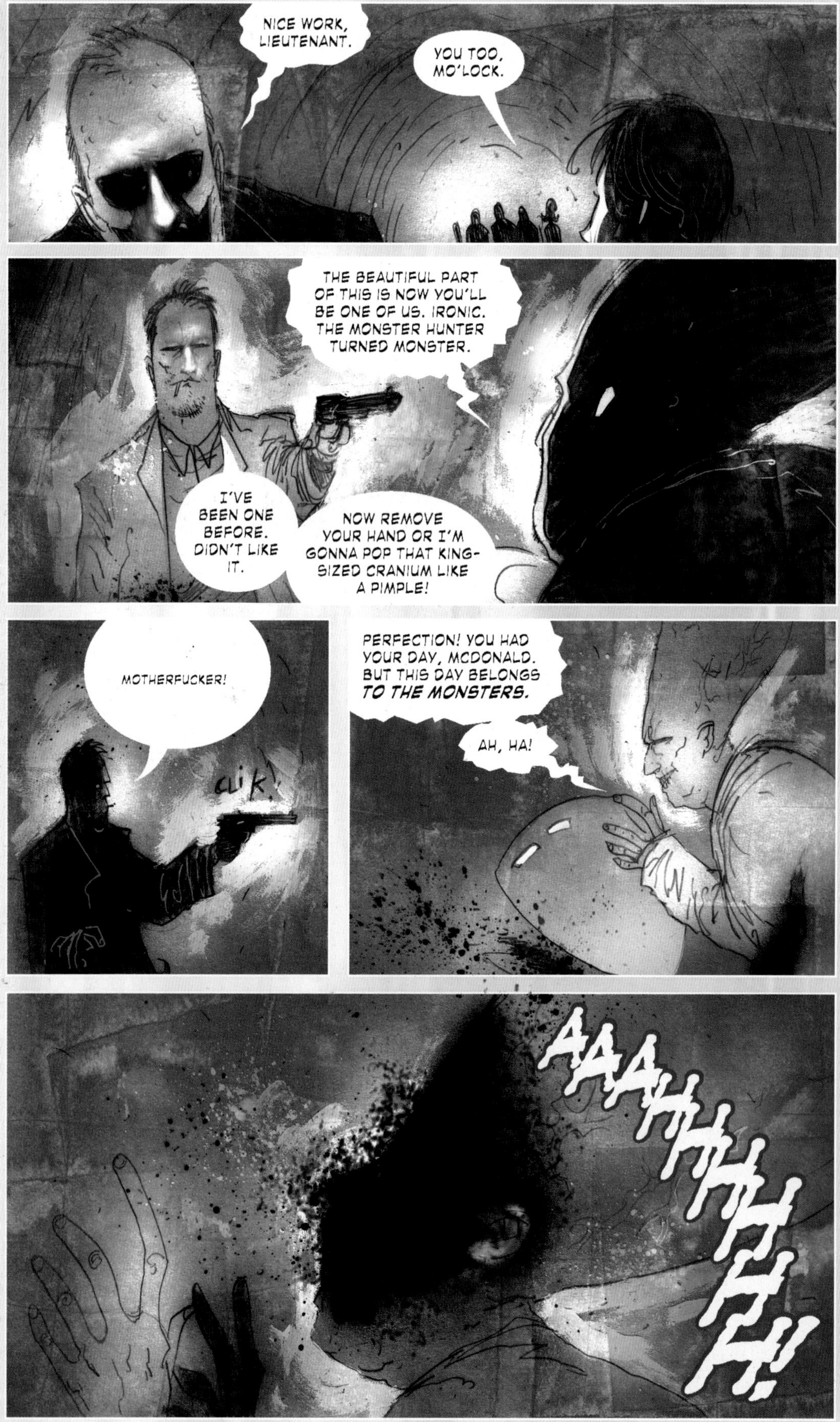
NICE WORK, LIEUTENANT.
YOU TOO, MO'LOCK.
THE BEAUTIFUL PART OF THIS IS NOW YOU'LL BE ONE OF US. IRONIC. THE MONSTER HUNTER TURNED MONSTER.
I'VE BEEN ONE BEFORE. DIDN'T LIKE IT.
NOW REMOVE YOUR HAND OR I'M GONNA POP THAT KING-SIZED CRANIUM LIKE A PIMPLE!
MOTHERFUCKER!
CLIK!
PERFECTION! YOU HAD YOUR DAY, MCDONALD. BUT THIS DAY BELONGS *TO THE MONSTERS.*
AH, HA!
AAAHHHHHHH!

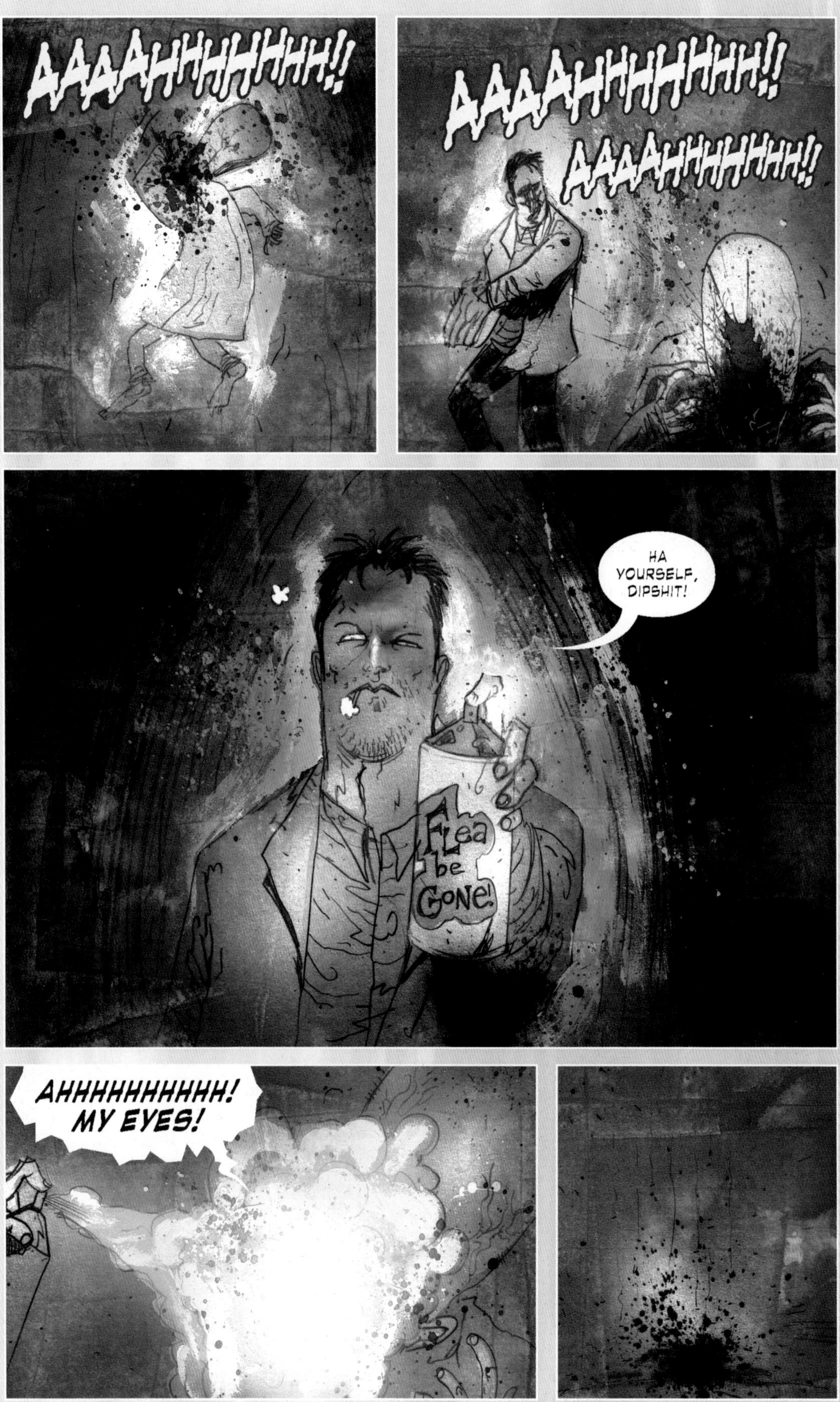
AAAAHHHHHHH!!
AAAAHHHHHHH!!
AAAAHHHHHHH!!
HA YOURSELF, DIPSHIT!
Flea be Gone!
AHHHHHHHHHH! MY EYES!

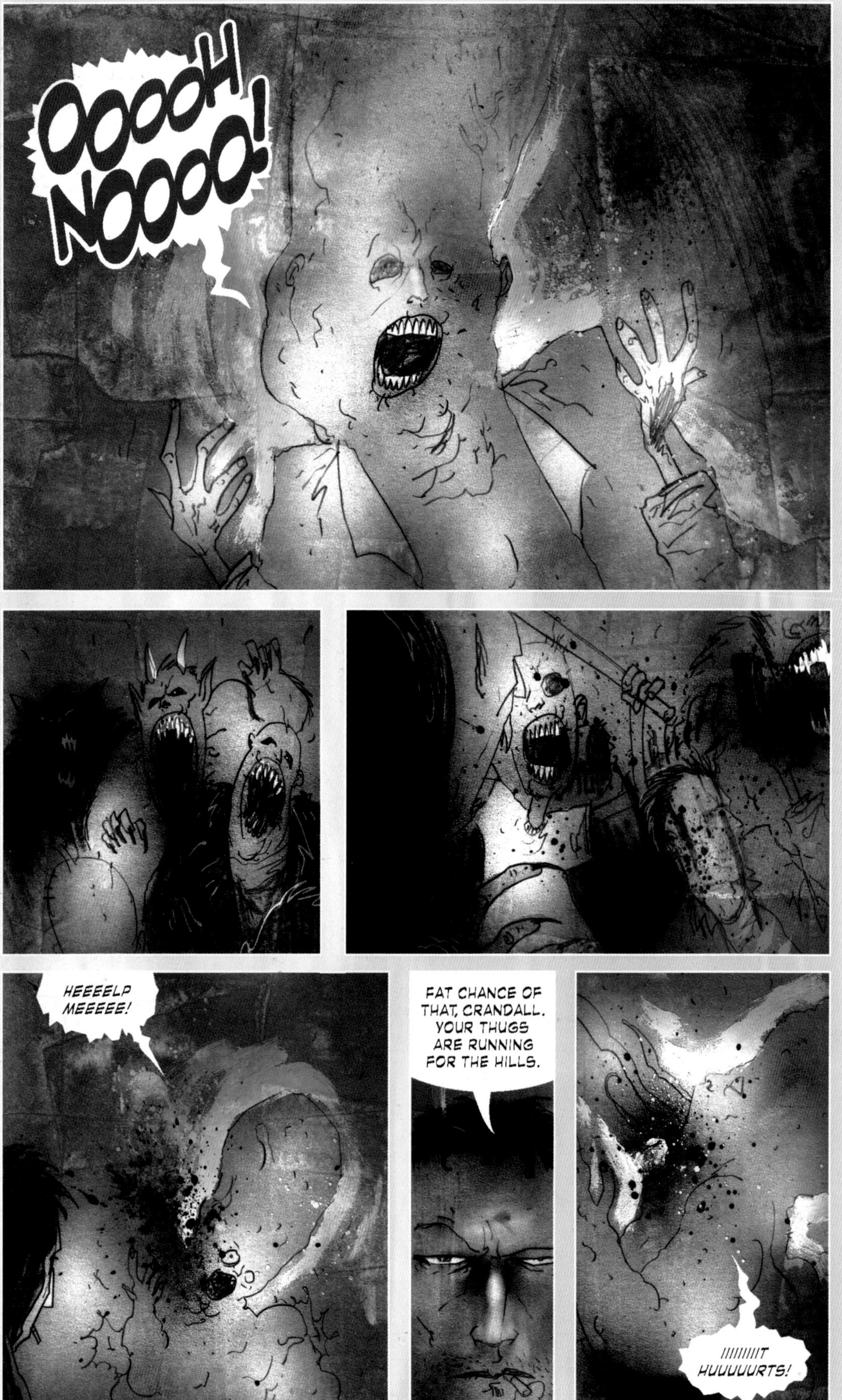
OOOOH NOOOO!
HEEEELP MEEEEE!
FAT CHANCE OF THAT, CRANDALL. YOUR THUGS ARE RUNNING FOR THE HILLS.
IIIIIIIIIT HUUUUURTS!

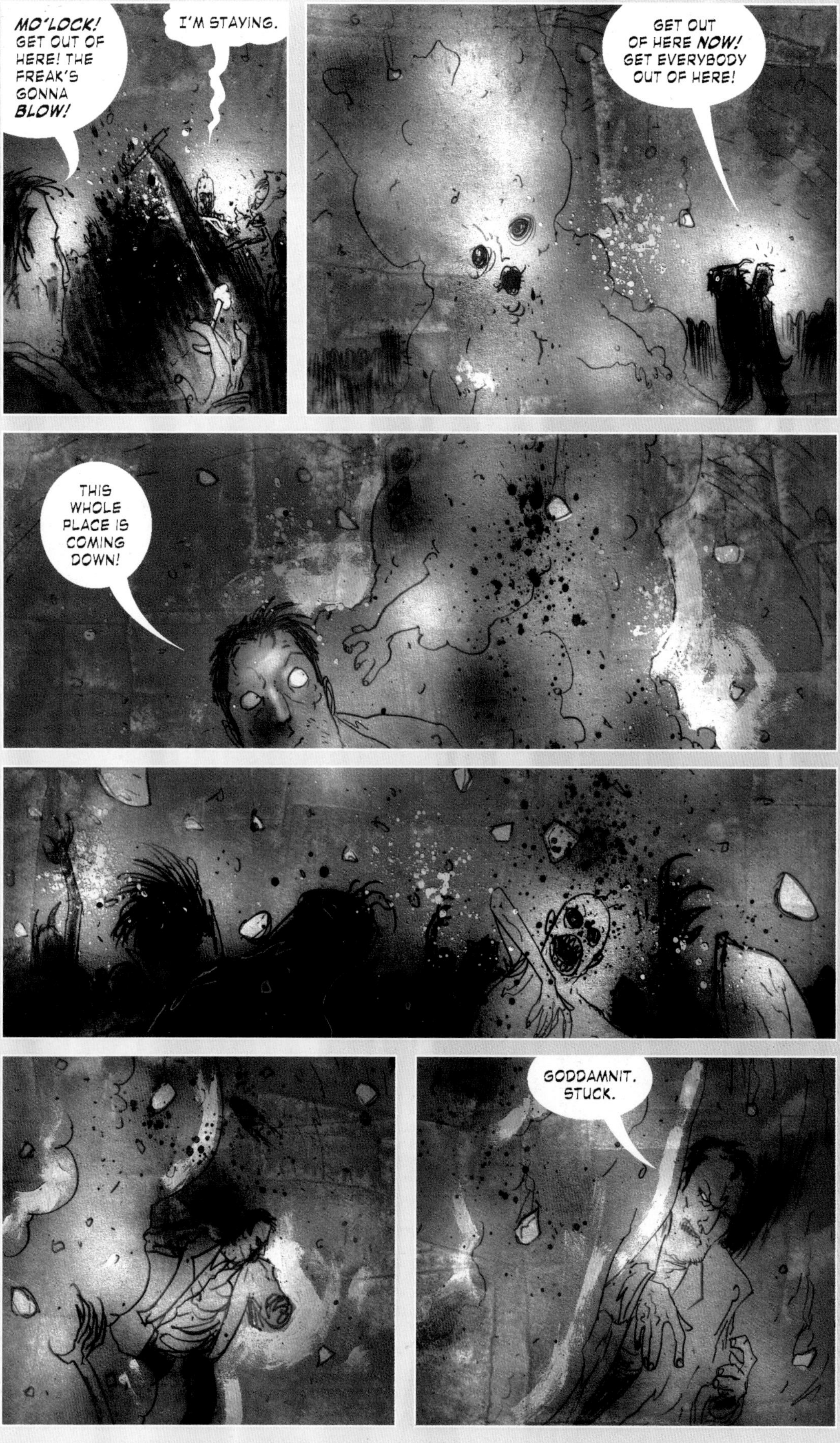
MO'LOCK! GET OUT OF HERE! THE FREAK'S GONNA BLOW!
I'M STAYING.
GET OUT OF HERE NOW! GET EVERYBODY OUT OF HERE!
THIS WHOLE PLACE IS COMING DOWN!
GODDAMNIT. STUCK.

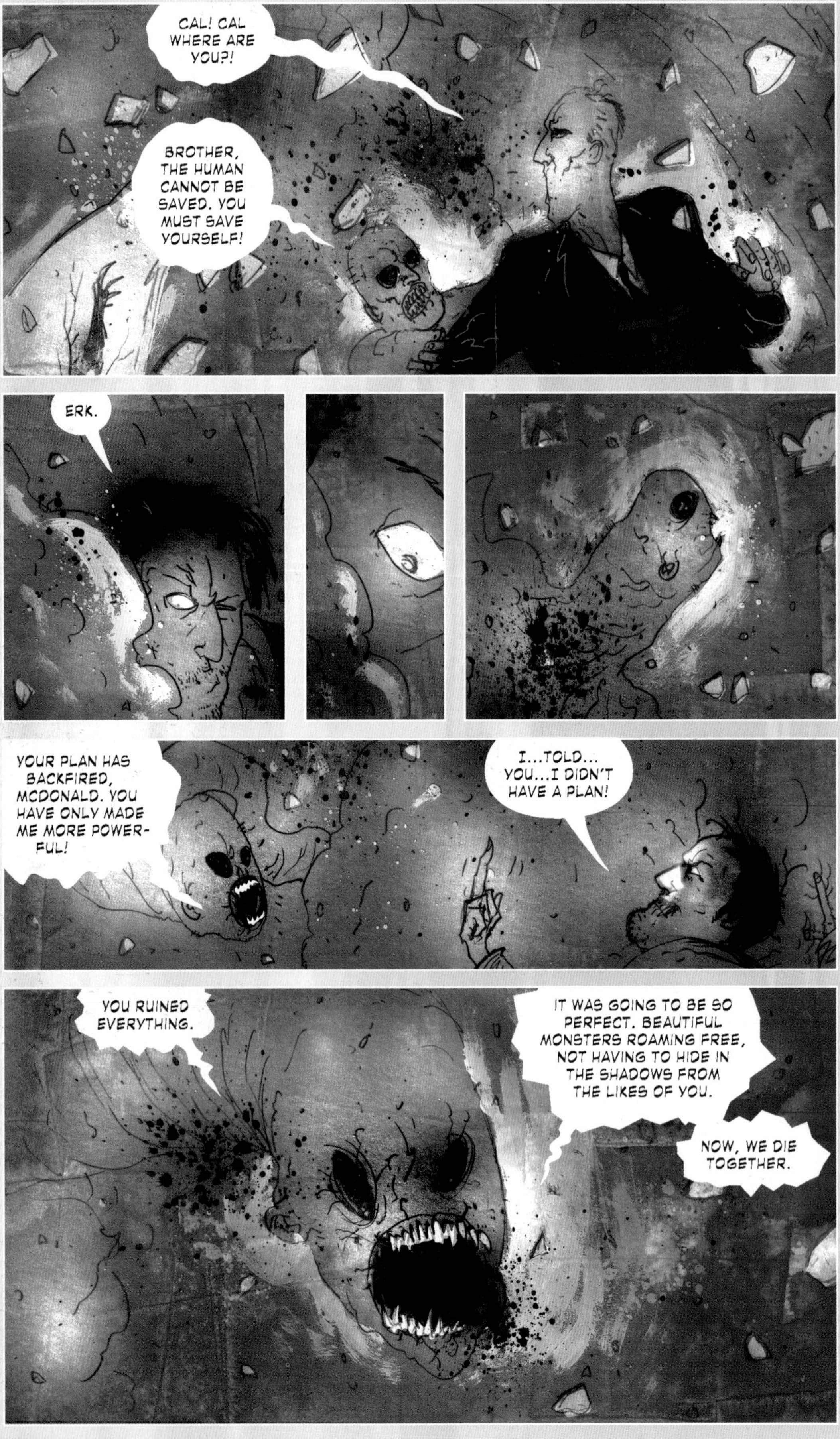
CAL! CAL WHERE ARE YOU?!
BROTHER, THE HUMAN CANNOT BE SAVED. YOU MUST SAVE YOURSELF!
ERK.
YOUR PLAN HAS BACKFIRED, MCDONALD. YOU HAVE ONLY MADE ME MORE POWER-FUL!
I...TOLD... YOU...I DIDN'T HAVE A PLAN!
YOU RUINED EVERYTHING.
IT WAS GOING TO BE SO PERFECT. BEAUTIFUL MONSTERS ROAMING FREE, NOT HAVING TO HIDE IN THE SHADOWS FROM THE LIKES OF YOU.
NOW, WE DIE TOGETHER.

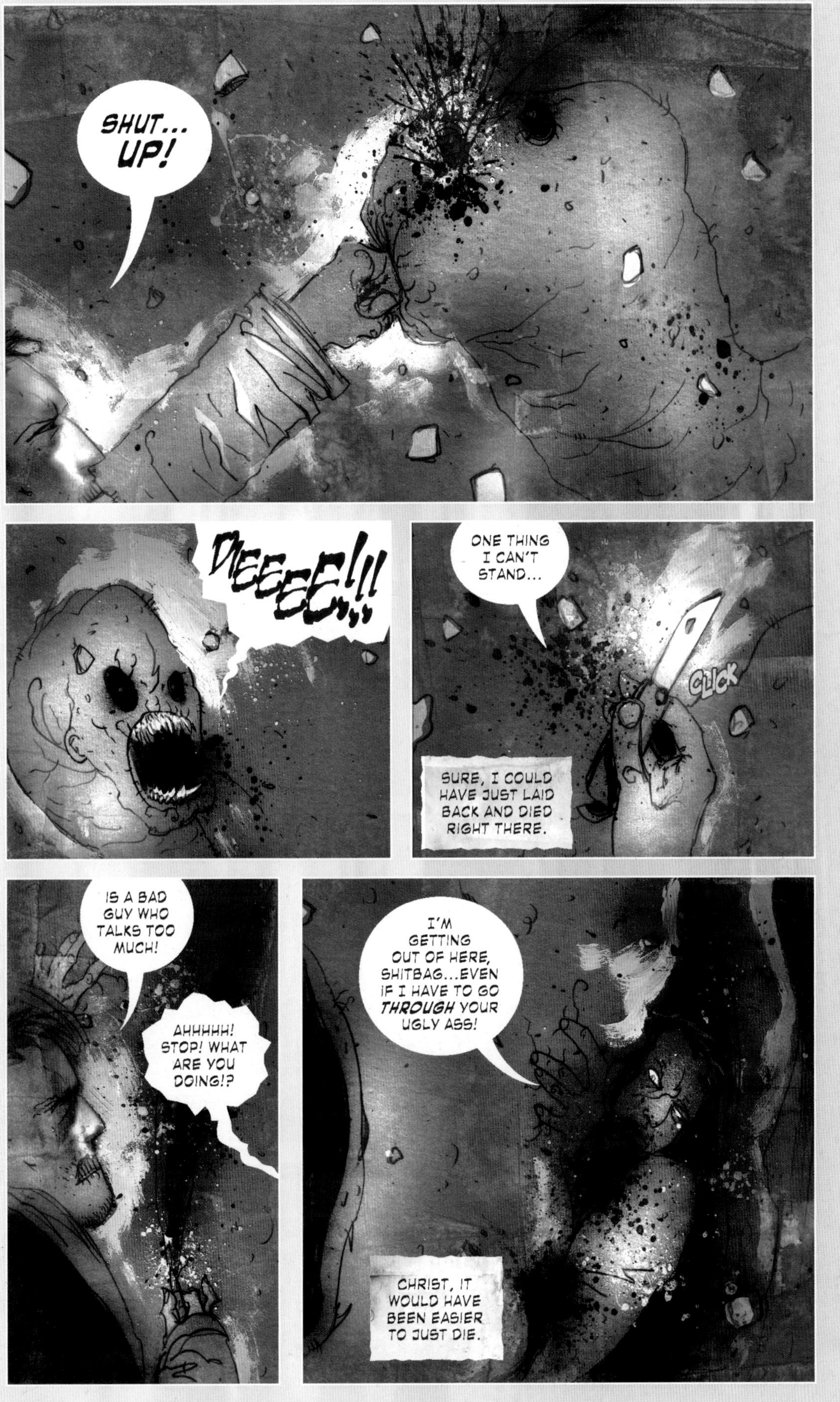
SHUT... UP!
DIEEEEE!!!
ONE THING I CAN'T STAND...
CLICK
SURE, I COULD HAVE JUST LAID BACK AND DIED RIGHT THERE.
IS A BAD GUY WHO TALKS TOO MUCH!
AHHHHH! STOP! WHAT ARE YOU DOING!?
I'M GETTING OUT OF HERE, SHITBAG...EVEN IF I HAVE TO GO *THROUGH* YOUR UGLY ASS!
CHRIST, IT WOULD HAVE BEEN EASIER TO JUST DIE.

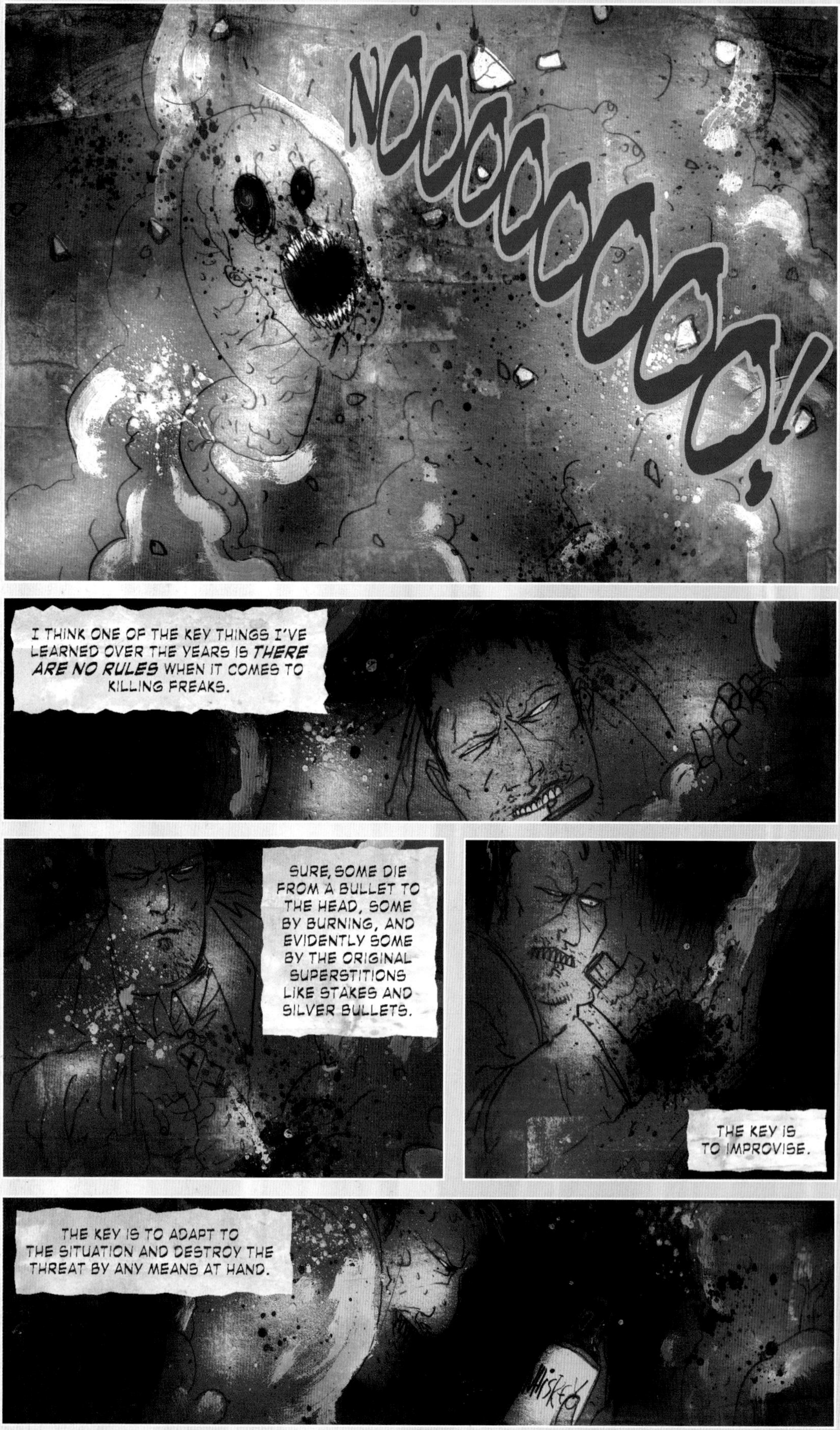
NOOOOOOOOOO!
I THINK ONE OF THE KEY THINGS I'VE LEARNED OVER THE YEARS IS *THERE ARE NO RULES* WHEN IT COMES TO KILLING FREAKS.
SURE, SOME DIE FROM A BULLET TO THE HEAD, SOME BY BURNING, AND EVIDENTLY SOME BY THE ORIGINAL SUPERSTITIONS LIKE STAKES AND SILVER BULLETS.
THE KEY IS TO IMPROVISE.
THE KEY IS TO ADAPT TO THE SITUATION AND DESTROY THE THREAT BY ANY MEANS AT HAND.
WHISKEY

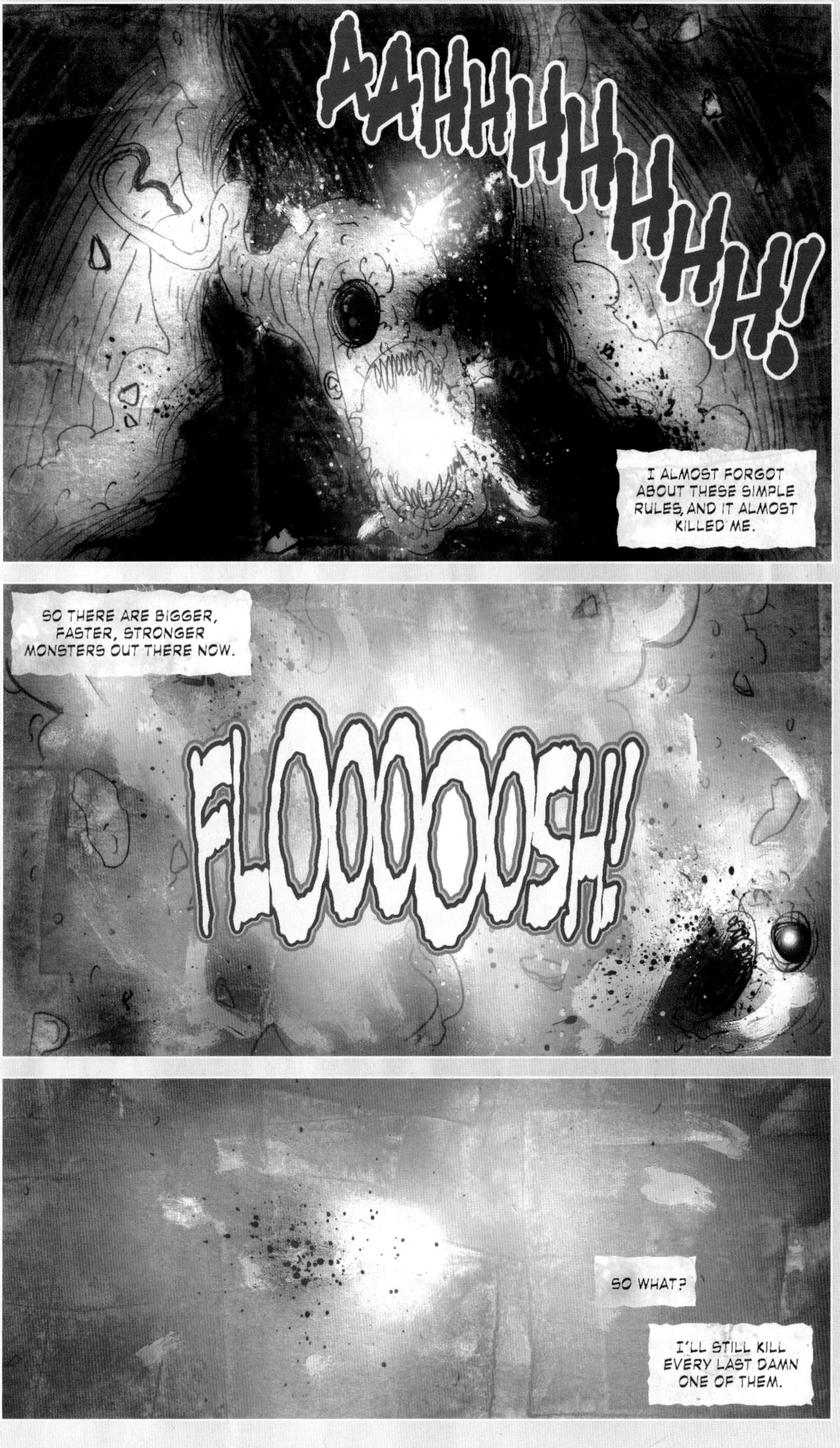
AAHHHHHHHH!
I ALMOST FORGOT ABOUT THESE SIMPLE RULES, AND IT ALMOST KILLED ME.
SO THERE ARE BIGGER, FASTER, STRONGER MONSTERS OUT THERE NOW.
FLOOOOOSH!
SO WHAT?
I'LL STILL KILL EVERY LAST DAMN ONE OF THEM.

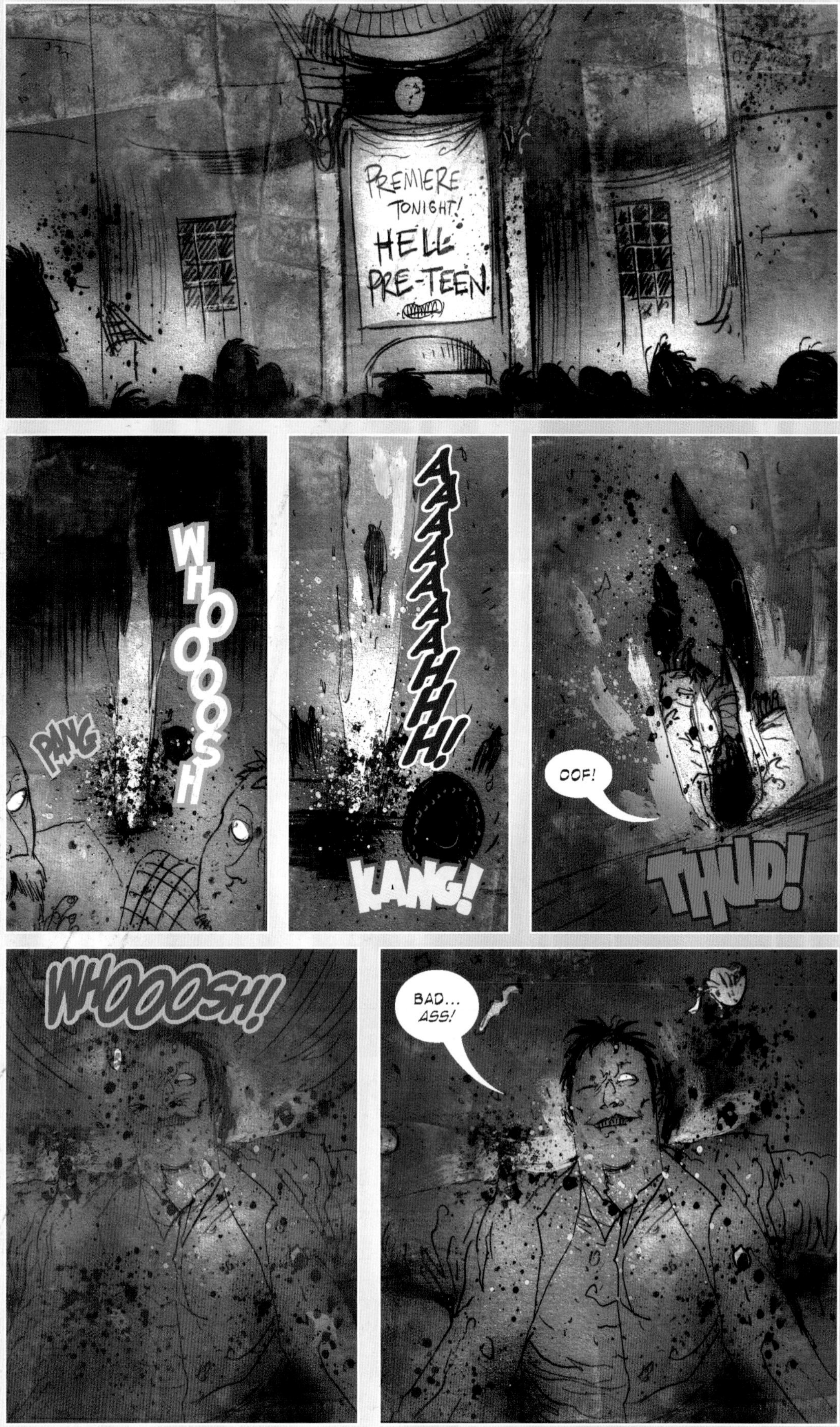
PREMIERE TONIGHT!
HELL PRE-TEEN
WHOOOOOSH
PANG
AAAAAAAHHHH!
KANG!
OOF!
THUD!
WHOOOSH!
BAD... ASS!

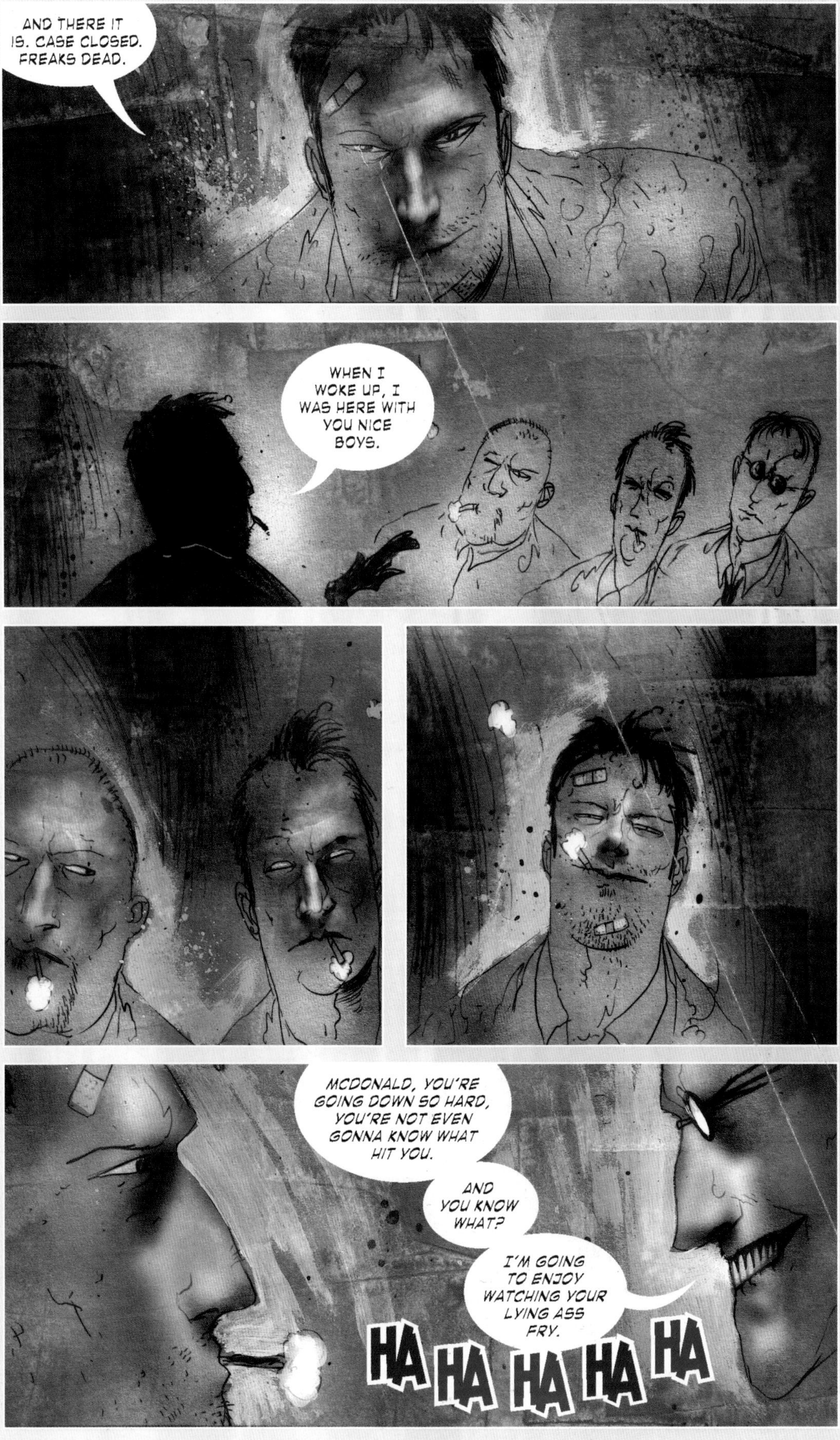
AND THERE IT IS. CASE CLOSED. FREAKS DEAD.
WHEN I WOKE UP, I WAS HERE WITH YOU NICE BOYS.
MCDONALD, YOU'RE GOING DOWN SO HARD, YOU'RE NOT EVEN GONNA KNOW WHAT HIT YOU.
AND YOU KNOW WHAT?
I'M GOING TO ENJOY WATCHING YOUR LYING ASS FRY.
HA HA HA HA HA HA

WHAT'S GOING ON IN HERE?

THIS MAN ISN'T A SUSPECT. WHAT KIND OF BULLSHIT PRECINCT ARE YOU RUNNING HERE? RELEASE HIM NOW, AND I WANT FULL REPORTS--COMPLETE WITH APOLOGIES--ON MY DESK BY MORNING.

BUT WE THOUGHT--

SHUT UP WHILE YOU STILL HAVE A BADGE, SERGEANT.

MR. MCDONALD... MEET ME OUTSIDE WHEN YOU'RE THROUGH HERE.

THANKS FOR THE TIME, BOYS. IT'S BEEN A PLEASURE, AS USUAL.

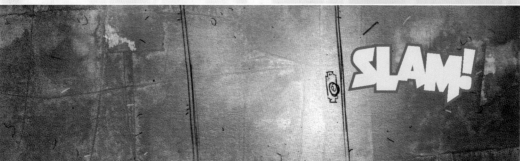

SLAM!

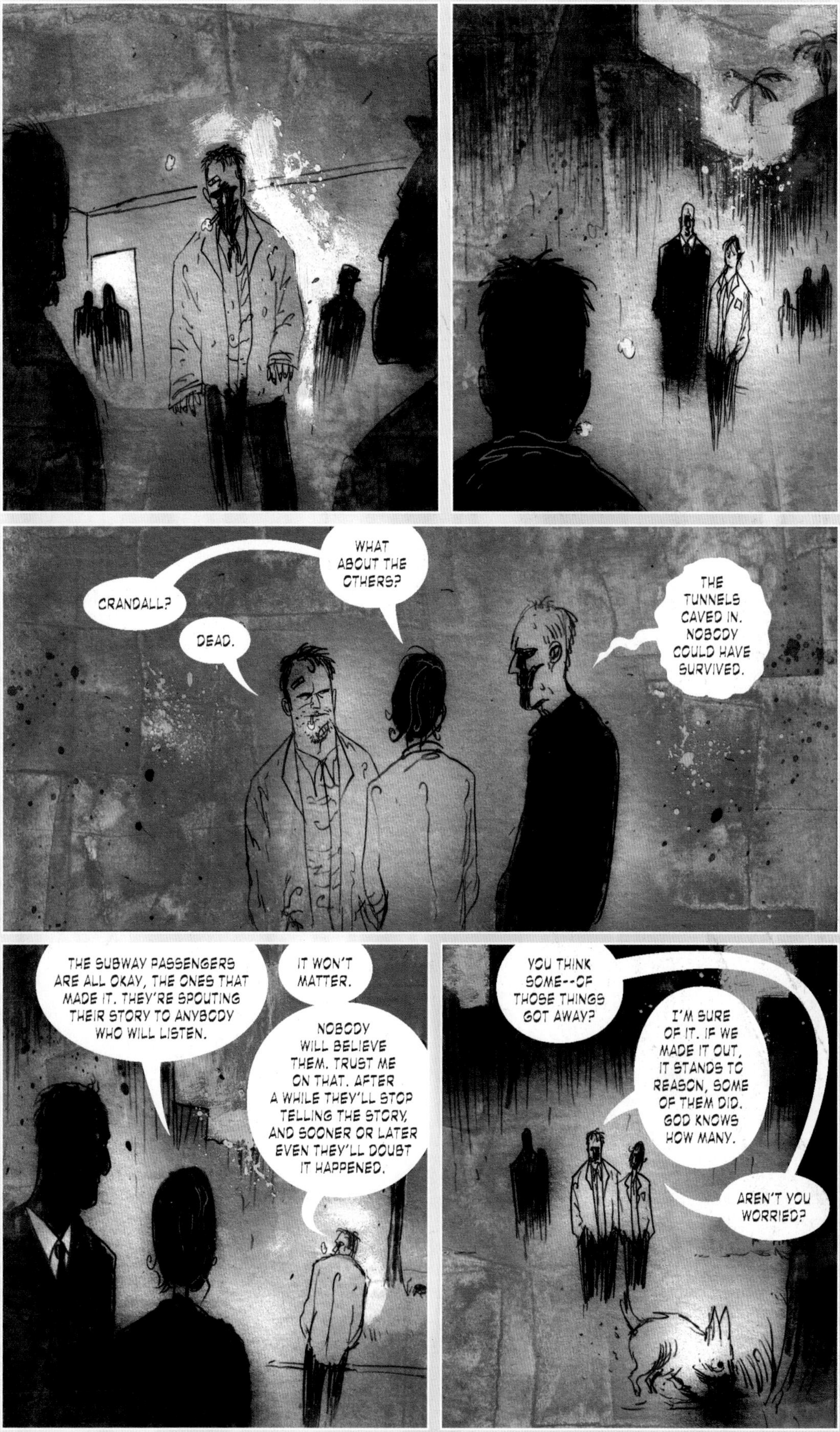

CRANDALL?
DEAD.
WHAT ABOUT THE OTHERS?
THE TUNNELS CAVED IN. NOBODY COULD HAVE SURVIVED.
THE SUBWAY PASSENGERS ARE ALL OKAY, THE ONES THAT MADE IT. THEY'RE SPOUTING THEIR STORY TO ANYBODY WHO WILL LISTEN.
IT WON'T MATTER.
NOBODY WILL BELIEVE THEM. TRUST ME ON THAT. AFTER A WHILE THEY'LL STOP TELLING THE STORY, AND SOONER OR LATER EVEN THEY'LL DOUBT IT HAPPENED.
YOU THINK SOME--OF THOSE THINGS GOT AWAY?
I'M SURE OF IT. IF WE MADE IT OUT, IT STANDS TO REASON, SOME OF THEM DID. GOD KNOWS HOW MANY.
AREN'T YOU WORRIED?

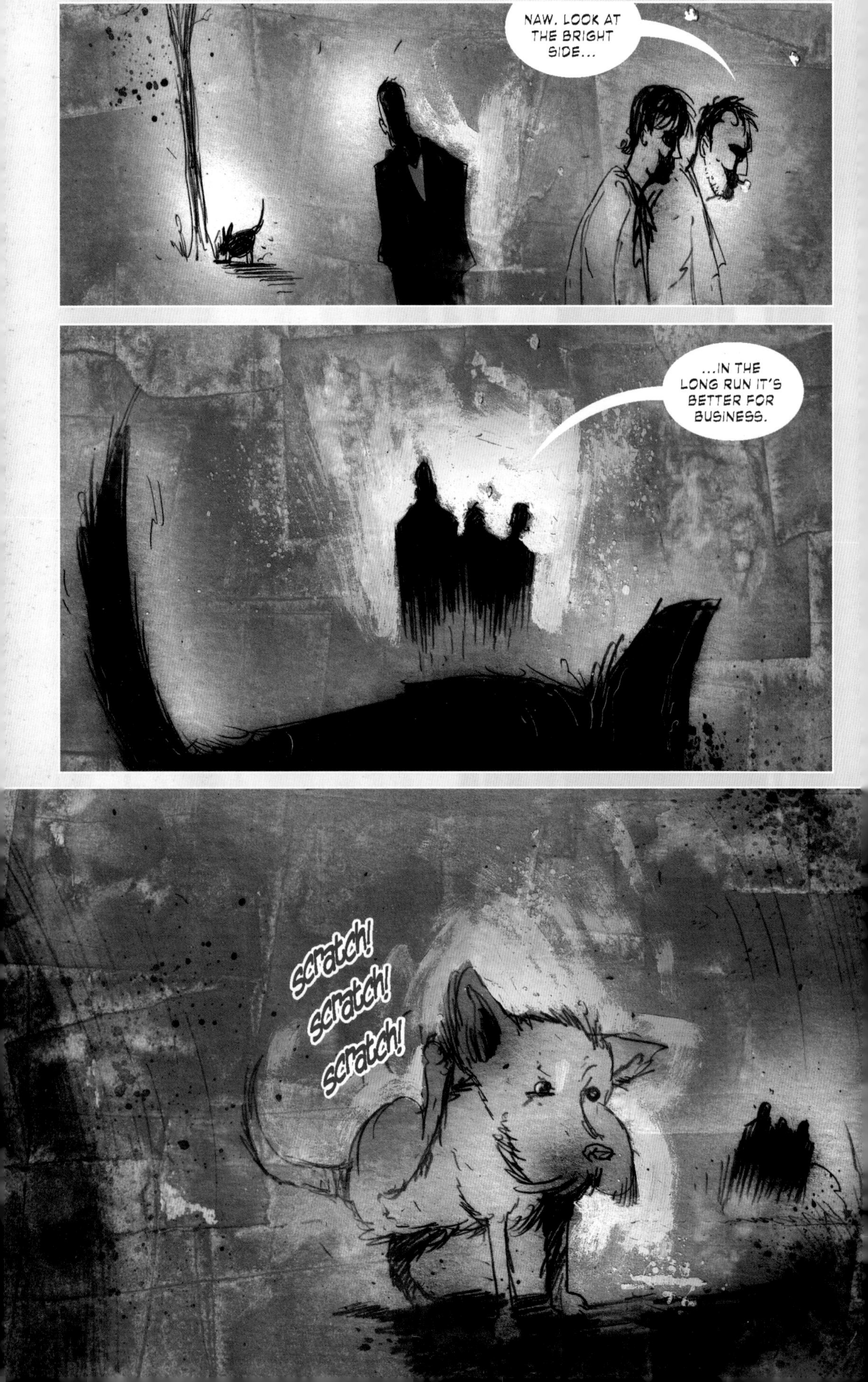
NAW. LOOK AT THE BRIGHT SIDE...
...IN THE LONG RUN IT'S BETTER FOR BUSINESS.
scratch! scratch! scratch!

MR. HORRORPANTS

Steve Niles

I'd like to start by saying I suck ass at these types of things. You know, the writing about yourself and your character. I can talk it, but when it comes down to writing my thoughts and opinions I always feel like an ass. I think that's my deepest, darkest secret ... I don't read into my stuff. It is what it is. I'll leave the in-depth analysis to the eggheads and creators who like to talk about themselves.

Now, let's talk about me and this wreck of a human being Cal McDonald.

(You see that? In less than one breath I completely contradicted myself. What a jerk!)

Cal McDonald and I have something in common and it's not what most people think. Granted, I can be grouchy and some of my best friends are damn close to being the living dead, but where Cal and I have the most common ground are *monsters*.

We've both had them in our lives since childhood.

For Cal it was a nightmarish realization that there were monsters in the world, strange creatures of every imaginable shape and size waiting in the shadows to take a bite out of you ...

... or me.

That was the first reaction I had toward monsters and horror. They scared the living shit out of me. Not Cal. He stood up to the first freak he ever encountered.

Me? Not so much.

When I was eight or nine I vividly remember being fascinated with horror movies, comics, books, toys ... *during the day*. Night time was another story. There's no gentle way to put this ... I was scared out of my mind. It got so bad that my mother forbade me to watch *Creature Feature* ever again! I didn't listen. I couldn't stop. I was like a little seven-year-old junkie unable to kick a habit. I tried, but as soon as I heard that theme and the announcement of what ghoulish treat they had in store for me, I had to watch. I had to wait and see the monster! This went on for a long time ... I'd watch, and then at night I'd be traumatized.

It didn't help that I had an imagination that could not be controlled. I would sit under the covers with a flashlight and imagine every sort of scenario I could, each one more horrific than the last. Each one more real. I would imagine the monsters I saw in the movies systematically killing my family while I lay in bed, saving me for last! I imagined pods growing in my dad's tomato garden duplicating us as we slept. There was no stopping me from watching horror, and at night there was no stopping the sheer terror my tiny little brain mustered for me.

Then, one day, it just stopped. Just like that. I was no longer afraid. I went from shuddering teeth-rattler to wide-eyed consumer of everything horror in the blink of an eye.

It was such an about-face that my parents didn't buy it at first. They thought I was bluffing. They thought it was Day-boy not looking out for Night-boy, but I proved them wrong. I began devouring horror like my life depended on it. I bought every *Creepy*, *Eerie*, and *Famous Monster* magazine I could get my hands on. I watched Creature Feature religiously, and, to prove to them I was all better, I slept like a baby. Horror and I had come to terms.

I wasn't what you'd call "the popular kid" at school. I wasn't a total freak, but I was just enough of a freak to stand apart. I was the kid who had complete runs of comics and an encyclopedic knowledge of horror movies. I think part of this was that I related to certain monsters, too.

Monsters like the Creature from the Black Lagoon and King Kong saved me. These freaks weren't all bad, were they? The Creature was just defending his home, and King Kong was taken from his home. Of course they're going to run amok. Of course they're going to rampage. That's what monsters do.

So, at a young age my fear turned to love, and here we are today. I love horror, mystery, and, most of all, monsters! I love 'em!

Cal McDonald? Not so much.

I started writing Cal as a completely straight detective/noir character. In my late teens I became obsessed with writers like Chandler and Hammett, so I set out to create my own hard-boiled gumshoe. I wrote two or three stories and a short novella. They all sucked. They lacked conviction and enthusiasm. They were a drag.

Then one day I'm writing a new Cal story, and, just for kicks, I chuck in a werewolf ... and then a ghoul, and all of a sudden things started taking shape. This character just sort of poured out ... and so did the stories. Cal McDonald, monster-hunting, fuck-up detective was born, and he's been with me ever since. It's been a long, sometimes frustrating trip, but Cal and I finally found a home. Shit, we found a few homes!

It's almost surreal. In the course of a year Cal has come a long way from having two rather uneventful publishing appearances. The first was a self-published short comic *Bighead* back in the 1980s, and the other was the four-part story "Hairball" which ran in *Dark Horse Presents* ... but evil forces set in to scramble the last pages of the episode, and Cal and I fell into the black hole of the unemployed writer and detective for *years* to follow.

Throughout the — we'll call them "The Lean Years" — I kept Cal alive in stories and even one novel, but nobody wanted to hear these strange stories of an ex-junkie who fights giant heads and whose best friend is a ghoul. It's not hard to understand. I'd hear myself pitching Cal McDonald stories at times and I thought it sounded stupid.

Monster-hunting detective with a drug problem ... please.

But I kept writing the stories because I loved them and I had a handful of friends (Mark! Geoff!) who would always read and enjoy them, so that kept me going. During those years I clerked my ass off. I was a bookstore clerk, a video-store clerk, and a comic-store clerk. I clerked like no clerk has clerked before.

Then a breakthrough occurred. My old friend Ted Adams started his own publishing company, IDW Publishing, and he asked if I had any stuff lying around in my drawers. Boy, did I ever! Before Ted could say avalanche I sent him a box full of pitches, comic scripts, short stories, and my first Cal McDonald novel. They loved everything and started by publishing *30 Days of Night* (another story, for another trade) and the Cal McDonald novel, *Savage Membrane*.

Both were huge successes. So much so that Mike Richardson (DH's big boss) offered to publish Cal McDonald comics, and *Criminal Macabre* was born.

It's been a long, scary road, but Cal and I are still here, and, who knows, maybe we'll be around tomorrow.

Whatever the case, I hope you enjoy Cal's adventures as much as I do. And parents, if you have a little son or daughter who seems to have odd tastes, nurture it. Sometimes it pays to be the weird kid.

Steve Niles
Los Angeles
November 29, 2003

A Letter from B.S.

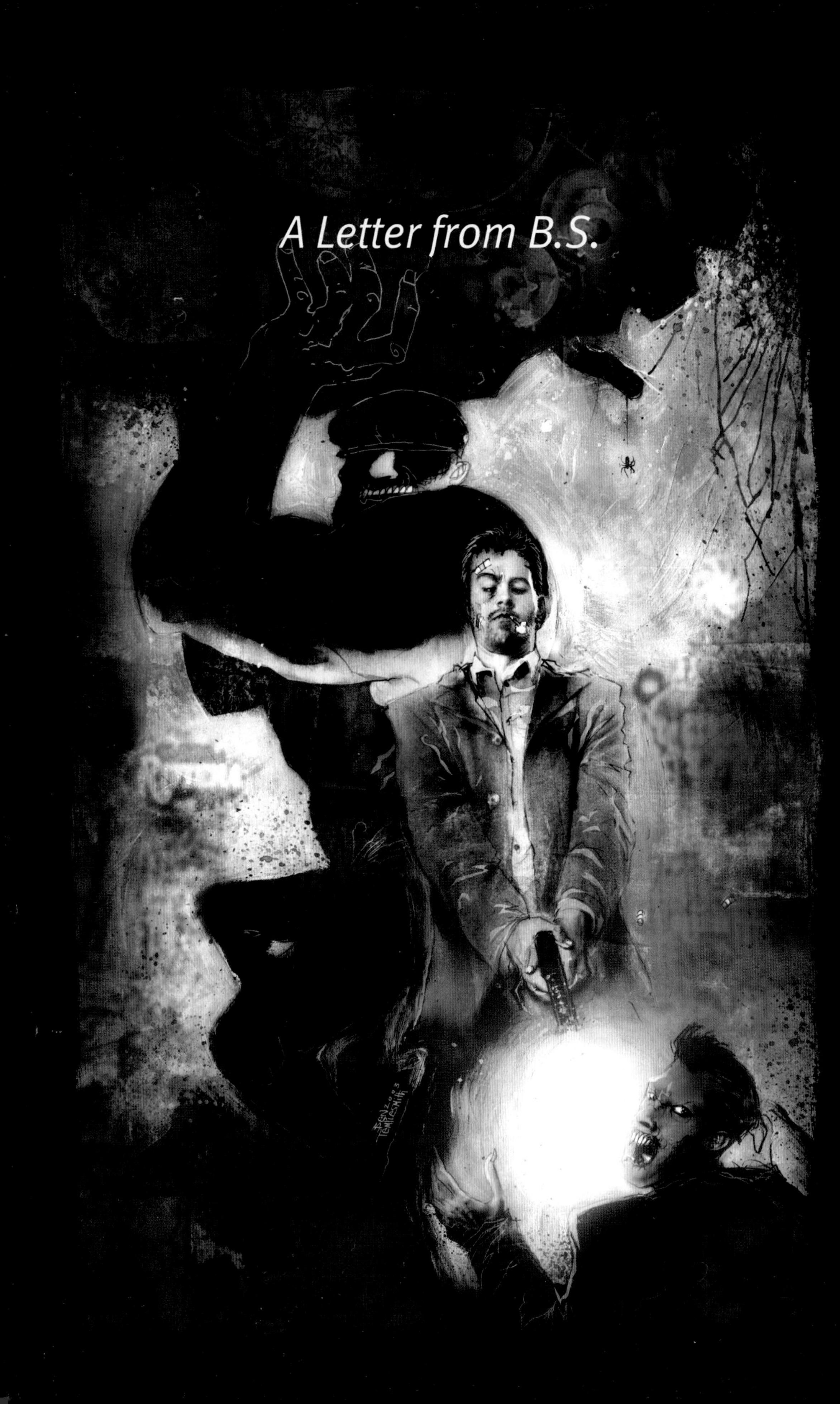

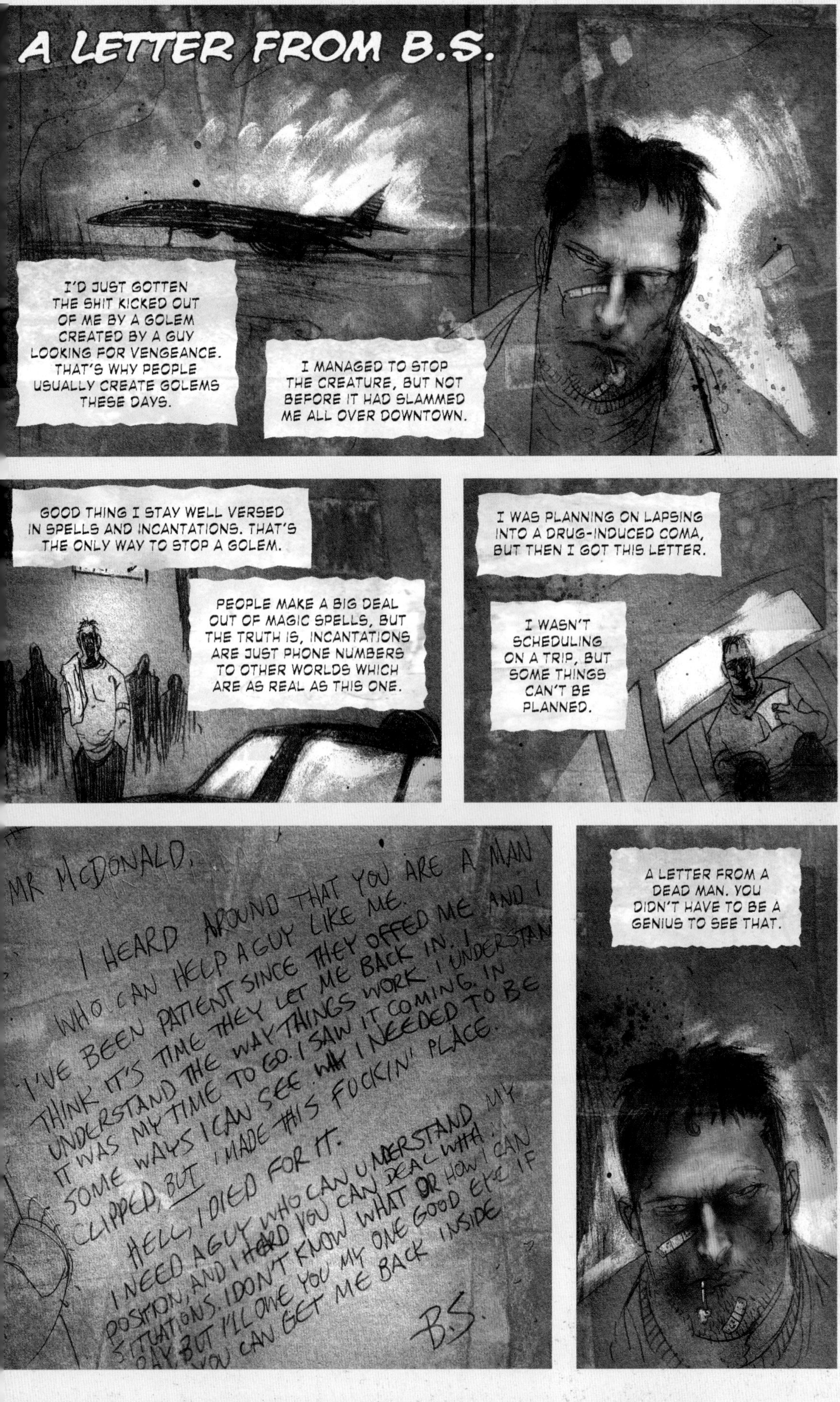
A LETTER FROM B.S.
I'D JUST GOTTEN THE SHIT KICKED OUT OF ME BY A GOLEM CREATED BY A GUY LOOKING FOR VENGEANCE. THAT'S WHY PEOPLE USUALLY CREATE GOLEMS THESE DAYS.
I MANAGED TO STOP THE CREATURE, BUT NOT BEFORE IT HAD SLAMMED ME ALL OVER DOWNTOWN.
GOOD THING I STAY WELL VERSED IN SPELLS AND INCANTATIONS. THAT'S THE ONLY WAY TO STOP A GOLEM.
PEOPLE MAKE A BIG DEAL OUT OF MAGIC SPELLS, BUT THE TRUTH IS, INCANTATIONS ARE JUST PHONE NUMBERS TO OTHER WORLDS WHICH ARE AS REAL AS THIS ONE.
I WAS PLANNING ON LAPSING INTO A DRUG-INDUCED COMA, BUT THEN I GOT THIS LETTER.
I WASN'T SCHEDULING ON A TRIP, BUT SOME THINGS CAN'T BE PLANNED.
MR MCDONALD,
I HEARD AROUND THAT YOU ARE A MAN WHO CAN HELP A GUY LIKE ME.
I'VE BEEN PATIENT SINCE THEY OFFED ME AND I THINK IT'S TIME THEY LET ME BACK IN. I UNDERSTAND THE WAY THINGS WORK. I UNDERSTAN IT WAS MY TIME TO GO. I SAW IT COMING. IN SOME WAYS I CAN SEE I NEEDED TO BE CLIPPED, BUT I MADE THIS FUCKIN' PLACE.
HELL, I DIED FOR IT.
I NEED A GUY WHO CAN UNDERSTAND MY POSITION, AND I HEARD YOU CAN DEAL WITH SITUATIONS. I DON'T KNOW WHAT OR HOW I CAN PAY, BUT I'LL OWE YOU MY ONE GOOD EYE IF YOU CAN GET ME BACK INSIDE.
B.S.
A LETTER FROM A DEAD MAN. YOU DIDN'T HAVE TO BE A GENIUS TO SEE THAT.

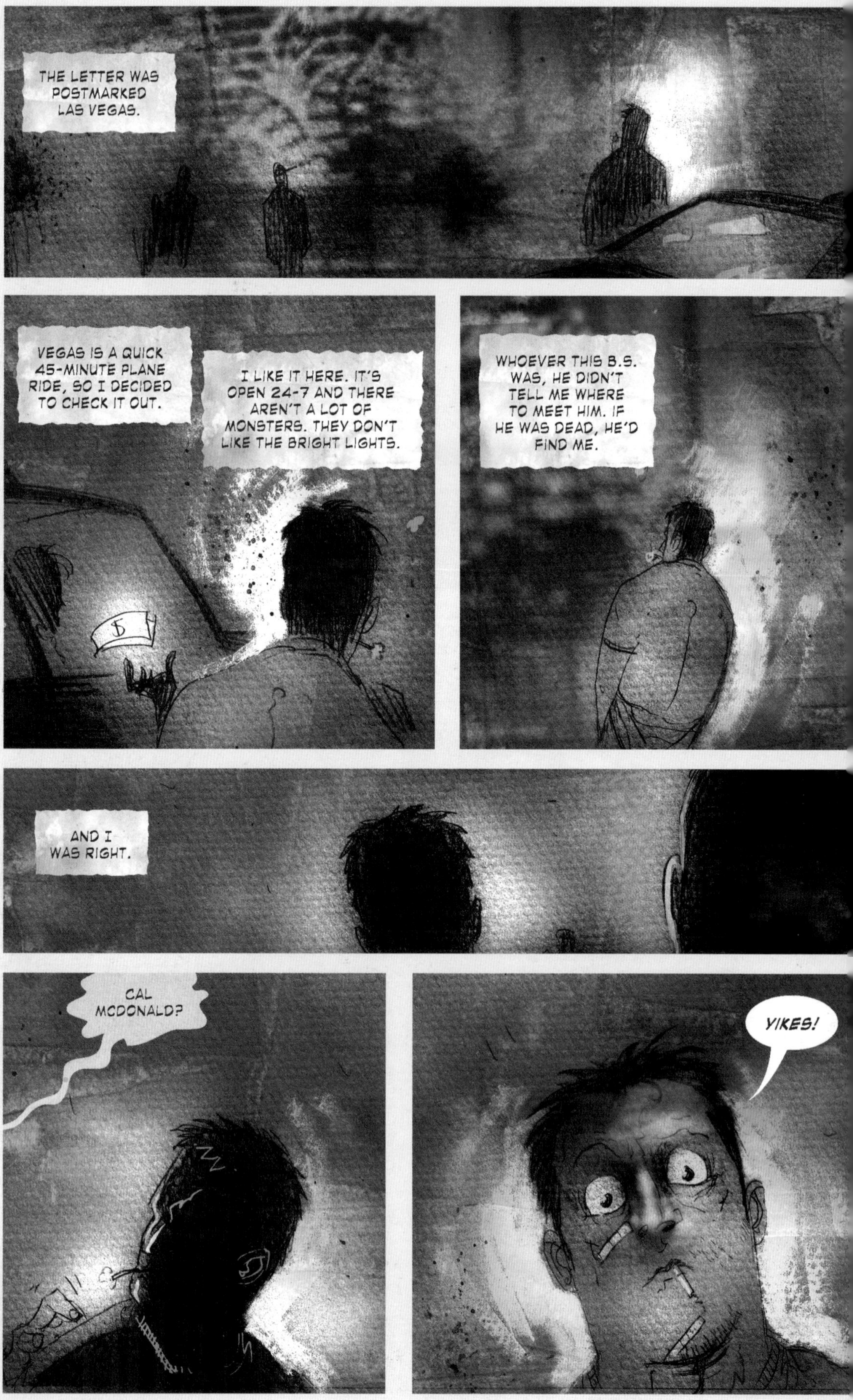

THE LETTER WAS POSTMARKED LAS VEGAS.
VEGAS IS A QUICK 45-MINUTE PLANE RIDE, SO I DECIDED TO CHECK IT OUT.
I LIKE IT HERE. IT'S OPEN 24-7 AND THERE AREN'T A LOT OF MONSTERS. THEY DON'T LIKE THE BRIGHT LIGHTS.
WHOEVER THIS B.S. WAS, HE DIDN'T TELL ME WHERE TO MEET HIM. IF HE WAS DEAD, HE'D FIND ME.
AND I WAS RIGHT.
CAL MCDONALD?
YIKES!

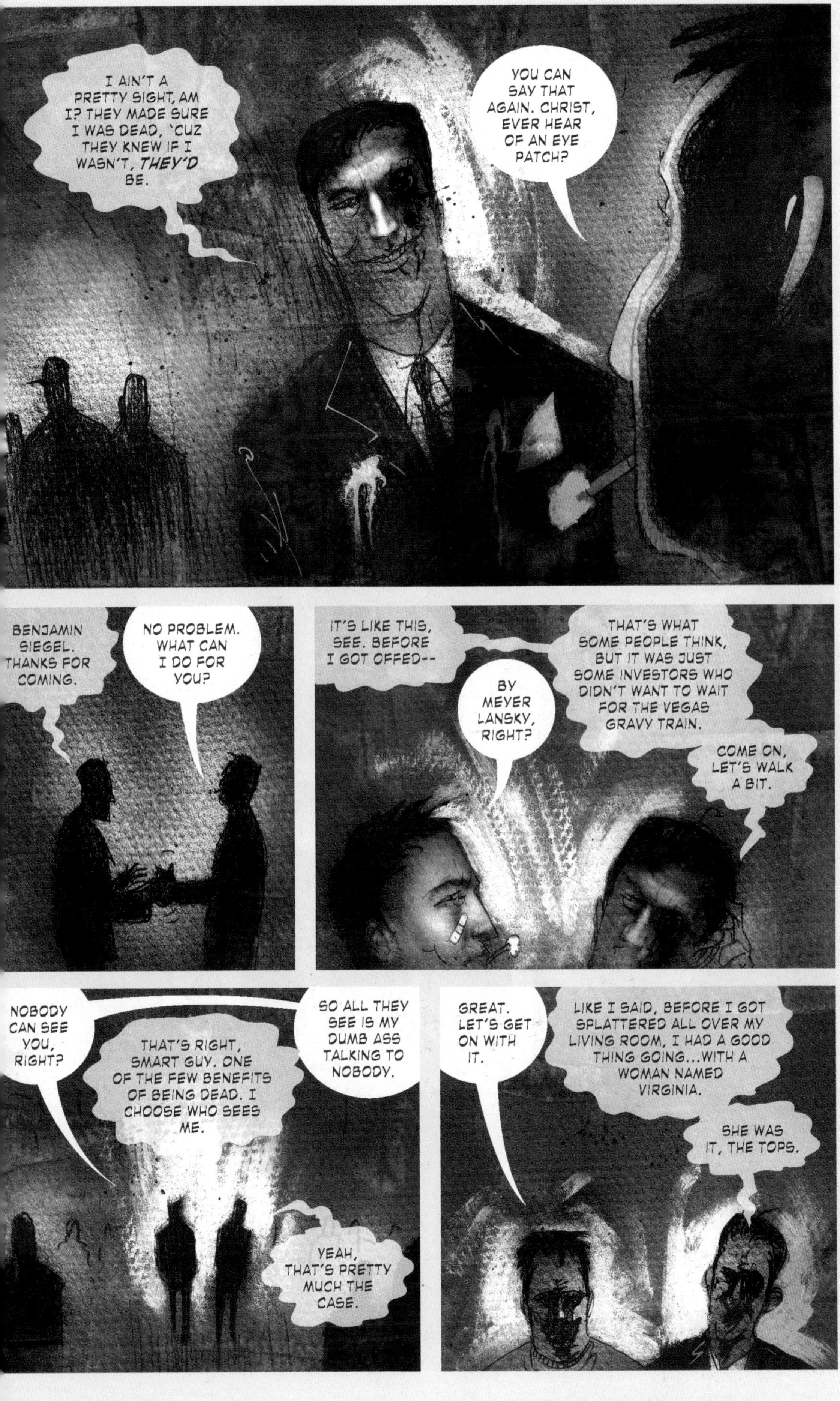
I AIN'T A PRETTY SIGHT, AM I? THEY MADE SURE I WAS DEAD, 'CUZ THEY KNEW IF I WASN'T, *THEY'D* BE.
YOU CAN SAY THAT AGAIN. CHRIST, EVER HEAR OF AN EYE PATCH?
BENJAMIN SIEGEL. THANKS FOR COMING.
NO PROBLEM. WHAT CAN I DO FOR YOU?
IT'S LIKE THIS, SEE. BEFORE I GOT OFFED--
BY MEYER LANSKY, RIGHT?
THAT'S WHAT SOME PEOPLE THINK, BUT IT WAS JUST SOME INVESTORS WHO DIDN'T WANT TO WAIT FOR THE VEGAS GRAVY TRAIN.
COME ON, LET'S WALK A BIT.
NOBODY CAN SEE YOU, RIGHT?
THAT'S RIGHT, SMART GUY. ONE OF THE FEW BENEFITS OF BEING DEAD. I CHOOSE WHO SEES ME.
SO ALL THEY SEE IS MY DUMB ASS TALKING TO NOBODY.
YEAH, THAT'S PRETTY MUCH THE CASE.
GREAT. LET'S GET ON WITH IT.
LIKE I SAID, BEFORE I GOT SPLATTERED ALL OVER MY LIVING ROOM, I HAD A GOOD THING GOING...WITH A WOMAN NAMED VIRGINIA.
SHE WAS IT, THE TOPS.

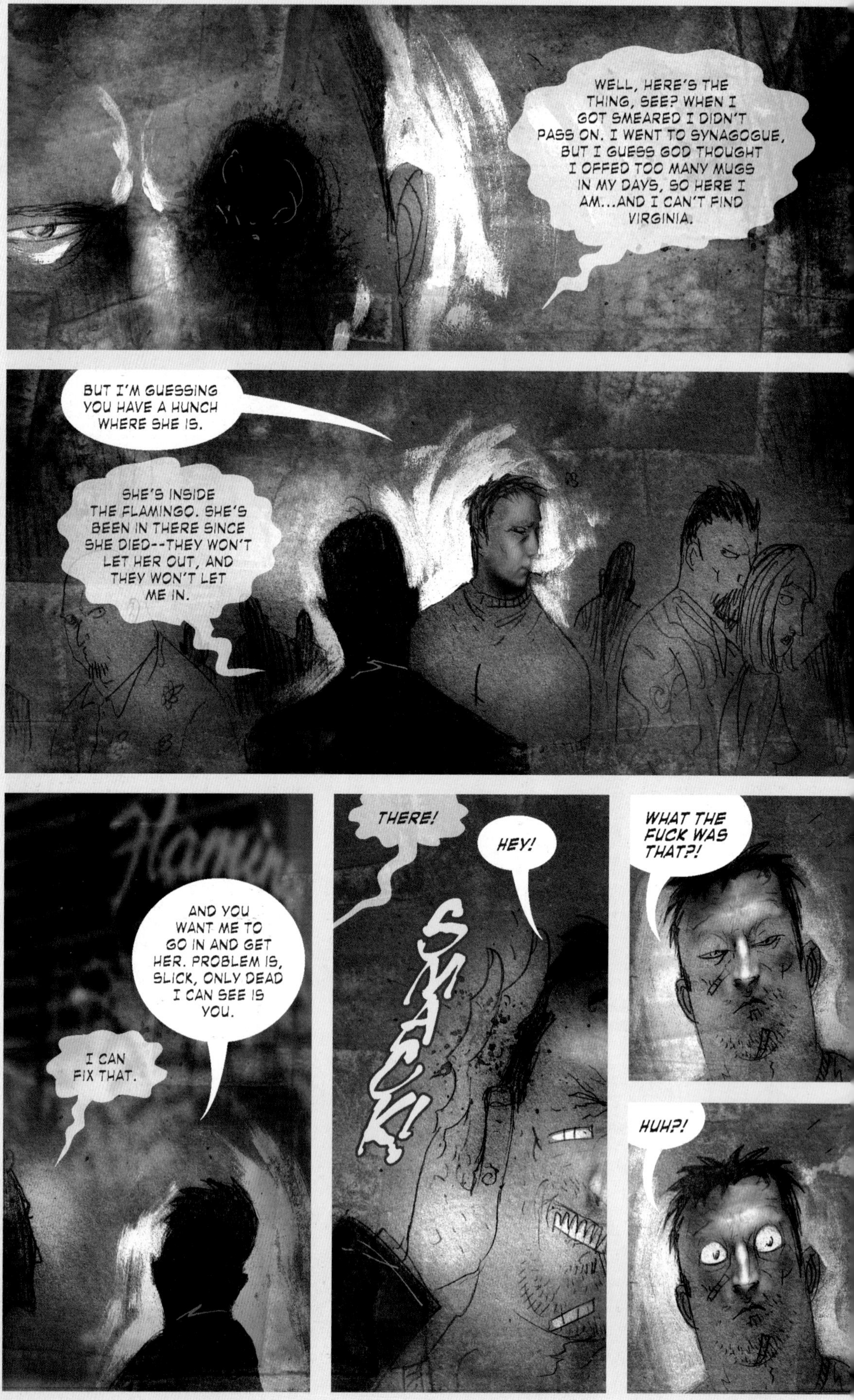
WELL, HERE'S THE THING, SEE? WHEN I GOT SMEARED I DIDN'T PASS ON. I WENT TO SYNAGOGUE, BUT I GUESS GOD THOUGHT I OFFED TOO MANY MUGS IN MY DAYS, SO HERE I AM...AND I CAN'T FIND VIRGINIA.
BUT I'M GUESSING YOU HAVE A HUNCH WHERE SHE IS.
SHE'S INSIDE THE FLAMINGO. SHE'S BEEN IN THERE SINCE SHE DIED--THEY WON'T LET HER OUT, AND THEY WON'T LET ME IN.
AND YOU WANT ME TO GO IN AND GET HER. PROBLEM IS, SLICK, ONLY DEAD I CAN SEE IS YOU.
I CAN FIX THAT.
THERE!
HEY!
SMACK!
WHAT THE FUCK WAS THAT?!
HUH?!

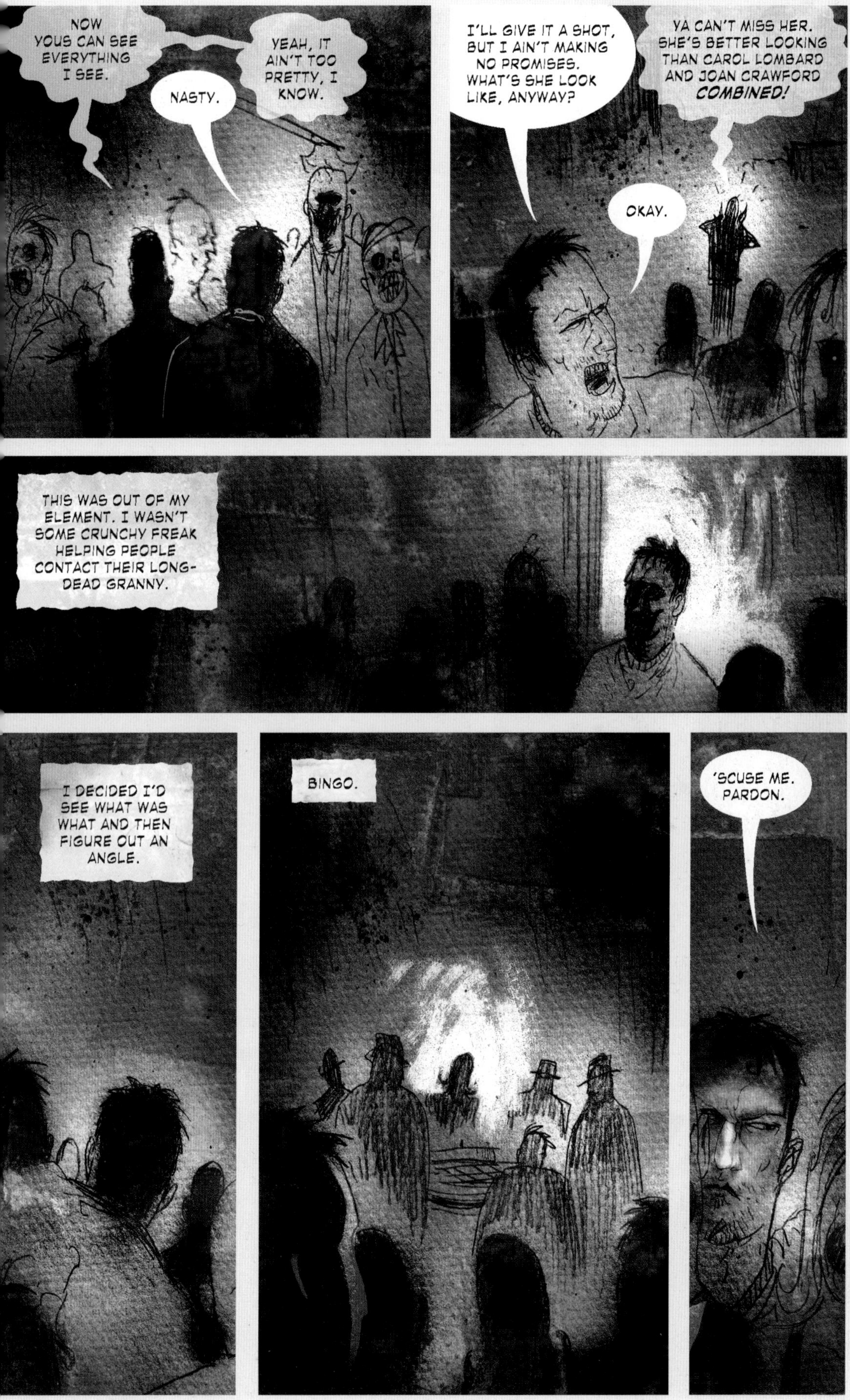
NOW YOUS CAN SEE EVERYTHING I SEE.
NASTY.
YEAH, IT AIN'T TOO PRETTY, I KNOW.
I'LL GIVE IT A SHOT, BUT I AIN'T MAKING NO PROMISES. WHAT'S SHE LOOK LIKE, ANYWAY?
YA CAN'T MISS HER. SHE'S BETTER LOOKING THAN CAROL LOMBARD AND JOAN CRAWFORD *COMBINED!*
OKAY.
THIS WAS OUT OF MY ELEMENT. I WASN'T SOME CRUNCHY FREAK HELPING PEOPLE CONTACT THEIR LONG-DEAD GRANNY.
I DECIDED I'D SEE WHAT WAS WHAT AND THEN FIGURE OUT AN ANGLE.
BINGO.
'SCUSE ME. PARDON.

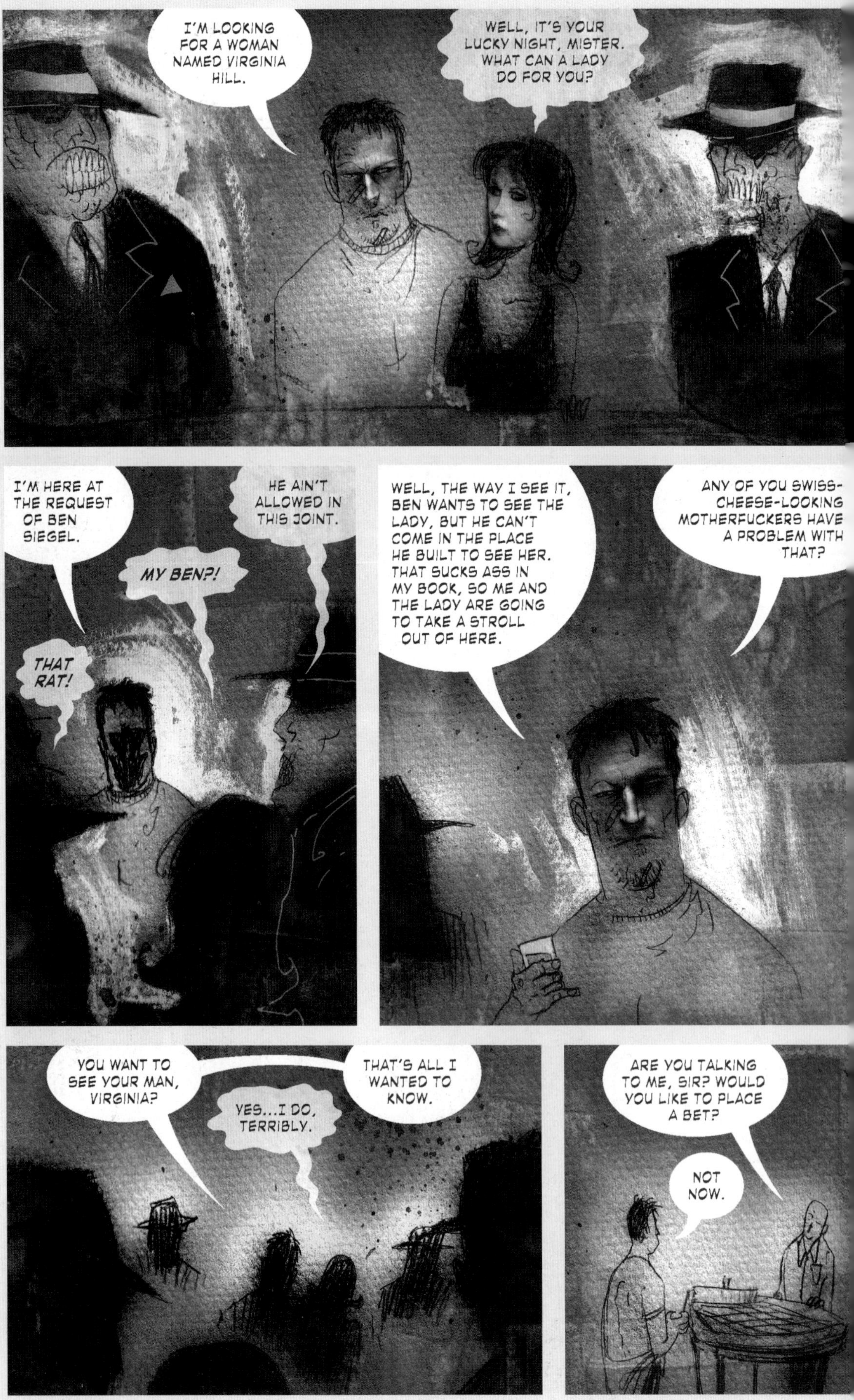
I'M LOOKING FOR A WOMAN NAMED VIRGINIA HILL.
WELL, IT'S YOUR LUCKY NIGHT, MISTER. WHAT CAN A LADY DO FOR YOU?
I'M HERE AT THE REQUEST OF BEN SIEGEL.
HE AIN'T ALLOWED IN THIS JOINT.
MY BEN?!
THAT RAT!
WELL, THE WAY I SEE IT, BEN WANTS TO SEE THE LADY, BUT HE CAN'T COME IN THE PLACE HE BUILT TO SEE HER. THAT SUCKS ASS IN MY BOOK, SO ME AND THE LADY ARE GOING TO TAKE A STROLL OUT OF HERE.
ANY OF YOU SWISS-CHEESE-LOOKING MOTHERFUCKERS HAVE A PROBLEM WITH THAT?
YOU WANT TO SEE YOUR MAN, VIRGINIA?
YES...I DO, TERRIBLY.
THAT'S ALL I WANTED TO KNOW.
ARE YOU TALKING TO ME, SIR? WOULD YOU LIKE TO PLACE A BET?
NOT NOW.

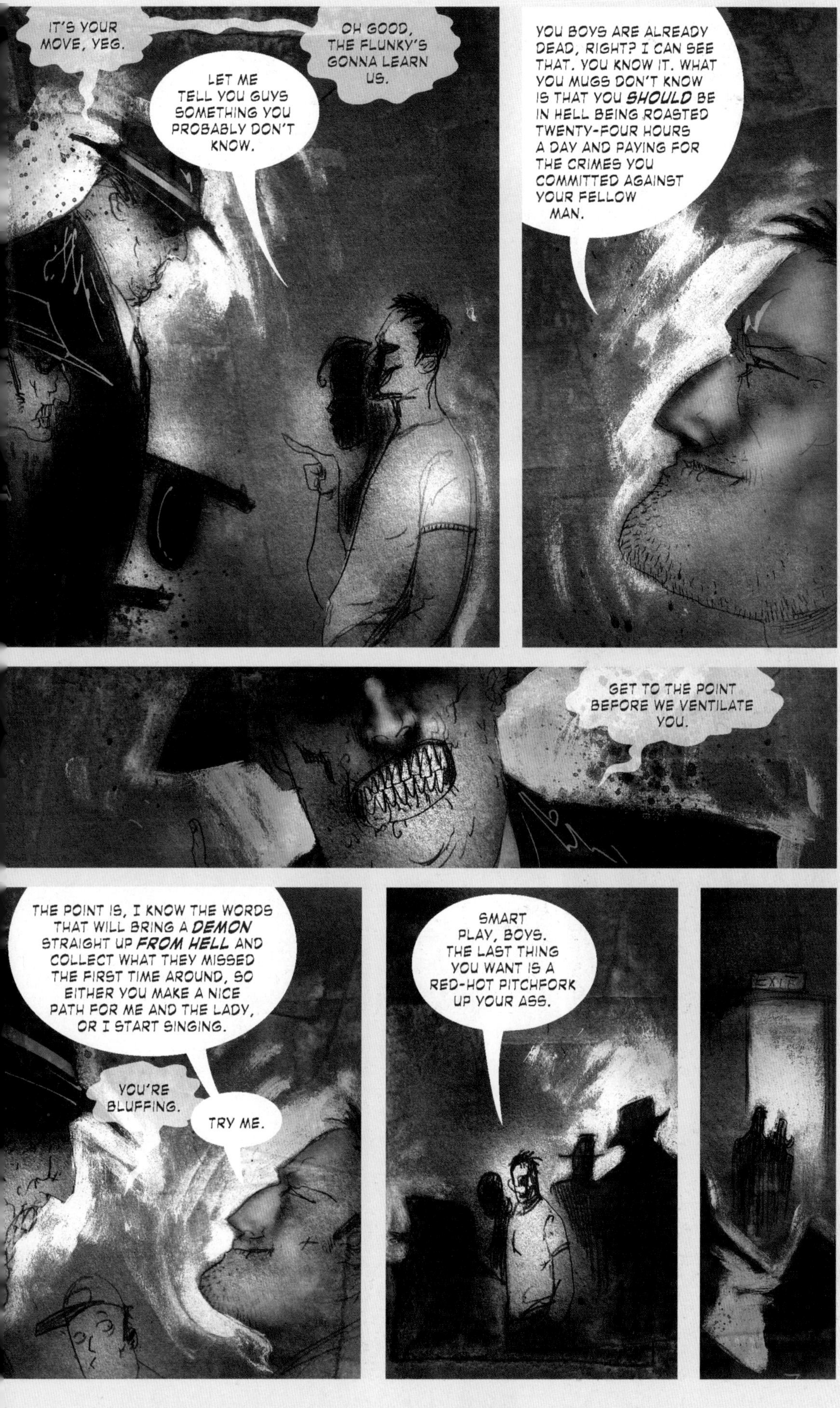
IT'S YOUR MOVE, YEG.
OH GOOD, THE FLUNKY'S GONNA LEARN US.
LET ME TELL YOU GUYS SOMETHING YOU PROBABLY DON'T KNOW.
YOU BOYS ARE ALREADY DEAD, RIGHT? I CAN SEE THAT. YOU KNOW IT. WHAT YOU MUGS DON'T KNOW IS THAT YOU *SHOULD* BE IN HELL BEING ROASTED TWENTY-FOUR HOURS A DAY AND PAYING FOR THE CRIMES YOU COMMITTED AGAINST YOUR FELLOW MAN.
GET TO THE POINT BEFORE WE VENTILATE YOU.
THE POINT IS, I KNOW THE WORDS THAT WILL BRING A *DEMON* STRAIGHT UP *FROM HELL* AND COLLECT WHAT THEY MISSED THE FIRST TIME AROUND, SO EITHER YOU MAKE A NICE PATH FOR ME AND THE LADY, OR I START SINGING.
YOU'RE BLUFFING.
TRY ME.
SMART PLAY, BOYS. THE LAST THING YOU WANT IS A RED-HOT PITCHFORK UP YOUR ASS.
EXIT

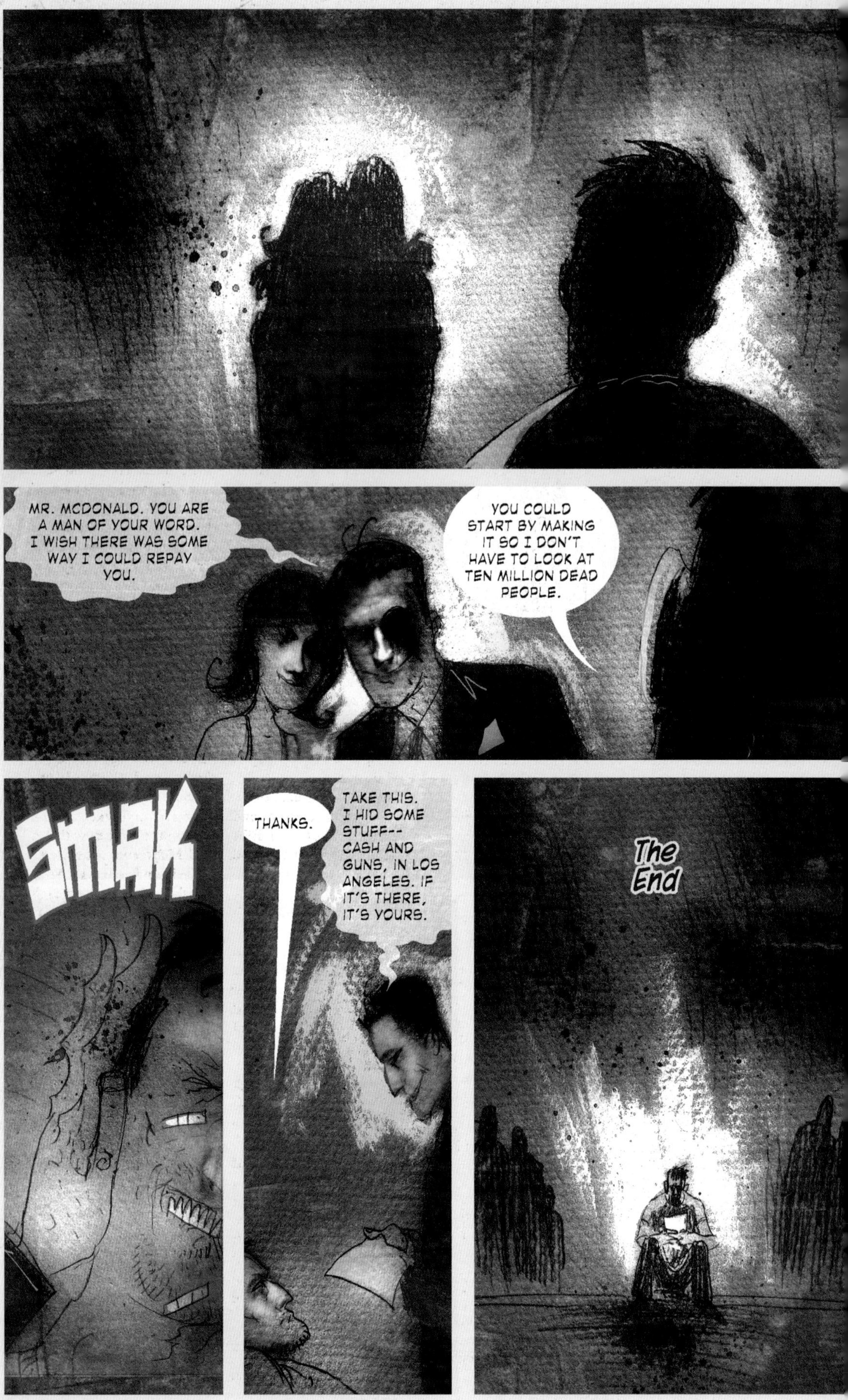
MR. MCDONALD. YOU ARE A MAN OF YOUR WORD. I WISH THERE WAS SOME WAY I COULD REPAY YOU.
YOU COULD START BY MAKING IT SO I DON'T HAVE TO LOOK AT TEN MILLION DEAD PEOPLE.
SMAK
THANKS.
TAKE THIS. I HID SOME STUFF-- CASH AND GUNS, IN LOS ANGELES. IF IT'S THERE, IT'S YOURS.
The End

the Speculator

HE REALLY BLEW HIS TOP!
Comic-book editor's head explodes **Page 18**

MONSTER MASH IN MASSACHUSETTS!
Wannabe warlock incites demonic debacle in Ipswich **Page 22**

LAPD INVESTIGATES CRIMES AT SCIENTIFIC INSTITUTIONS

By Sabrina Lynch

Detectives with the Los Angeles Police Department are investigating apparent break-ins and two bizarre murders at prestigious local scientific institutions. While official statements from an LAPD spokesman claim that there's no physical evidence directly linking the events at the facilities, eyewitness accounts from unnamed sources at the scene of each crime suggest differently.

Early Sunday morning, police were dispatched to the Rockwell Institute of Infectious and Deadly Diseases after a security guard on duty there called 911 to report a break-in. Officers on the scene would not discuss details of the robbery or the guard's phone call, but a Rockwell official who declined to give his name said that a container housing a rare strain of Bubonic plague was the only item unaccounted for.

A transcript of the guard's call obtained by *The Speculator* reveals some additional startling information. The male guard who placed the call is shown to babble incoherently for most of the duration of the call, but among his intelligible statements are the phrases "…big and hairy, with teeth…lots of teeth," and "it was a werewolf. I know it sounds crazy, but it was a werewolf."

Rockwell spokesman Mark Dryer would not release the guard's name but did say that the man has been employed at the Institute since 1994 and is highly regarded within the company.

Monday evening, police responded to security alarms sounding within the Natural History Museum of Los Angeles. Again, details of what was found on the scene were not made available to the press,

Artist's rendering of L.A. private dick Cal McDonald

DATSUN TRAN

but a deputy of the Los Angeles County Medical Examiner's office released information stating that the bodies of two apparent homicide victims were found on the premises. A third person, who was not identified as either a victim or as one of the alleged assailants, was taken to an area hospital.

The identity and condition of that person has not been confirmed by the LAPD, but sources close to the investigation say that detectives involved in the case will be "keeping an eye" on the individual, who is reported to be a "disheveled white male in his mid-30s." *The Speculator*'s speculation specialists suggest the patient in question is none other than infamous L.A. private dick Cal McDonald, whose name should be familiar to our loyal readers.

This morning, an unidentified employee of Torrance Memorial Hospital told this reporter that the patient from the museum attack was overheard describing a "balls-out fight with a werewolf, and a gunfight with an ugly-ass vampire" in his deposition to an L.A. County Detective.

The Speculator remains on the case.

THE GREAT GRAY MATTER FLOOD OF '95 REVISITED

By David Cercone

The Speculator travels back through time for another look at one of the most mysterious—and disgusting—events in recent history!

It's been more than seven years since Washington, D.C. resident Meghan Adkins awoke one morning to take her daily jog along the Potomac River and encountered the most disturbing scene she might ever imagine.

"It was everywhere," Adkins said, still shaking her head in disbelief at the memory. "As far as I could see, upstream and down, floating on top of the water, and just…glooping over everything. I'd never seen anything like it, and I hope I never do again."

The "it" in question is human brain matter, and according to official EPA estimates more than 12,000 tons of the grayish-pink goo were chemically and physically removed from the U.S. capital's largest water source.

The floating mass appeared suddenly, with no warning, and with no apparent source, and within a matter of hours, it blanketed a six-mile stretch of the Potomac River. Small islands, water-borne landmarks, docked vessels, and even sea-birds who call the Potomac home were covered in the murky mess.

The bizarre barrage of brains could be seen as near as Mount Vernon and as far away as the Chesapeake Bay. Travelers flying into Virginia's Ronald Reagan International Airport at the time even reported seeing the massive expanse from the air.

Virginia resident and master crab-trapper Alec "Crabbo" MacKaye recalled finding an entire human brain inside one of his crab traps. "We thought a bunch of fraternity kids from the school dumped pink Jell-O in the water as a stunt of some kind, but when I got my first look at the mess in my trap, I knew there was something even more wrong than frat-boy pranks afoot."

Now, more than five years after this mind-bending discovery, and despite public and government pressure, no explanation of the bizarre flood has ever been given by the Washington, D.C. officials who oversaw the investigation.

Jefferson Blake was an active-duty officer with the D.C. Metro Police at the time of the brain fiasco, and to this day, the now-retired cop can't positively confirm how the mess originated.

"We're pretty sure at this point that we were dealing with some sort of medical dumping," said Blake, speaking by phone from his rural Virginia home. "The problem all along has been figuring out where that much brain tissue could come from. I mean, we couldn't find a medical institution anywhere in the world that would admit to ever storing or using such a bulk of human brain matter, much less dumping it illegally in the Potomac."

Blake added, "This one may remain a mystery."

THANK-YOUS

Cal would like to thank nobody — fucking crowders!

Steve would like to thank: Ted Adams and everybody at IDW, Rob Zombie, Jon Levin, Gretchen Bruggeman Rush, Mike Richardson, Stephanie Palmer, Barry Levine, my family, my friends and, most of all, Nikki, for reminding me that monsters can be cute and funny as hell, too!

Ben would like to thank: Caffeine, for all the company on those long nights. Four A.M. is a bitch to get through, trust me. Additional thanks to Scott and Mike, for making the whole thing tick. And to Steve for, quite simply, doing his thing and letting me play with his baby (Cal, that is!).

CREATOR BIOS

photo by Rochelle Heagh Phister

Steve Niles — Steve Niles began his career in comics by founding the publishing house Arcane Comix. Through Arcane, he published, edited, and adapted comics and anthologies for Eclipse Comics, and adapted to comics works by such luminaries as Clive Barker, Harlan Ellison, and Richard Matheson — all the while developing and drafting stories from his own prolific imagination.

In 2002, Niles wrote a screenplay called *30 Days of Night*, which he developed into a comic-book miniseries with artist Ben Templesmith. *30 Days of Night* quickly jumped from the comics underground to become one of the most acclaimed and commercially successful comic titles of the year. *30 Days of Night* is now in development as a major motion picture, with *Spider-Man*'s Sam Raimi directing.

Niles continues to write comics, novels, and screenplays from his home in Los Angeles, where he lives with his wife, Nikki, and their three black cats.

Ben Templesmith — Contrary to popular mythology on the comic-book convention circuit, Ben Templesmith was not raised by dingoes and he doesn't drink *that* much tequila. There is a lot about Ben that we don't know, and only a few things that we do: Ben was born in Perth, Australia in 1978. He earned a B.A. in graphic design, majored in illustration, and has made quite the reputation for himself as the go-to-guy for dark, spooky illustrations in various industries, including comics, movies, books, and games. He likes sumo wrestling and cats, and he employs phrases such as "arsing about" to describe what he does with his time. If you can't find him in Australia or in San Diego, California, it's highly likely he's on a plane somewhere in the sky between those locales.

a cal mcdonald mystery
CRIMINAL MACABRE
steve NILES
ben TEMPLESMITH

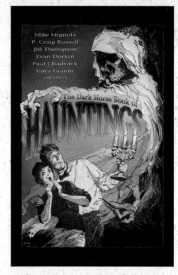

CRIMINAL MACABRE
A Cal McDonald Mystery
By Steve Niles and Ben Templesmith

The creative team behind *30 Days of Night* launch a new series of occult detective stories featuring the monstrously hard-boiled Cal McDonald, a pill-popping alcoholic, and the only line of defense between Los Angeles and a growing horde of zombies, vampires, and werewolves. The best-selling comics series is collected in this massive graphic novel.

Soft cover, 170 pages, Full color
$17.95, ISBN: 1-56971-935-7

Mike Mignola
P. Craig Russell
Jill Thompson
Evan Dorkin
Paul Chadwick
Gary Gianni
and others
The Dark Horse Book of
HAUNTINGS

THE DARK HORSE BOOK OF HAUNTINGS HC
Featuring Mike Mignola, P. Craig Russell, Paul Chadwick, Evan Dorkin, Jill Thompson, and others. Cover by Gary Gianni

Mike Mignola's Hellboy investigates a haunted house and discovers his own unexpected connection to the spirits within. P. Craig Russell and Mike Richardson tell the story of a child who vanishes into an abandoned house, and Paul Chadwick and Randy Stradley team up for a creepy short about a haunted suit. Jill Thompson and Evan Dorkin recount the legend of a haunted doghouse.

Hard cover, 96 pages, Full color
$14.95, ISBN: 1-56971-958-6

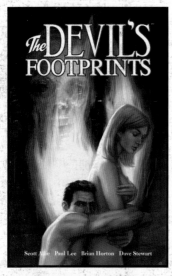

The DEVIL'S FOOTPRINTS
Scott Allie Paul Lee Brian Horton Dave Stewart

THE DEVIL'S FOOTPRINTS
By Scott Allie, Paul Lee, Brian Horton, and Dave Stewart

Brandon Waite investigates his dead father's study of witchcraft. But his desire to protect loved ones forces him to cover up his own tentative steps into the black arts, leading him to mix deception with demon conjuration, and isolating himself in a terrible world where his soul hangs in the balance.

Soft cover, 144 pages, Full color
$14.95, ISBN: 1-56971-933-0

the BLACKBURNE COVENANT
fabian NICIEZA
stefano RAFFAELE

THE BLACKBURNE COVENANT
By Fabian Nicieza and Stefano Raffaele

Someone is following novelist Richard Kaine. Someone interested in finding out how Richard came up with his best-selling first novel; because unbeknownst to Richard, his fantasy novel was non-fiction. Could Richard have written about an event that had been meticulously eradicated from human history? Who are the Blackburne Covenant? Why are they willing to kill Richard Kaine in order to keep him quiet?

Soft cover, 104 pages, Full color
$11.95, ISBN: 1-56971-889-X

AVAILABLE AT YOUR LOCAL COMICS SHOP OR BOOKSTORE

To find a comics shop in your area, call 1-888-266-4226

For more information or to order direct visit darkhorse.com or call 1-800-862-0052 • Mon.-Sat. 9 A.M. to 5 P.M. Pacific Time

***Prices and availability subject to change without notice**

DARK HORSE COMICS drawing on your nightmares
darkhorse.com

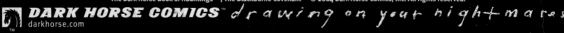